FOOD FINDS

To our husbands, Bruce Adams and Scott Kirkpatrick, for their patience.

Thanks also to the efforts of researchers Linda Evans, Barb Folkerts, and Angela Renkoski, who helped out in the crunch, and Nora Kirkpatrick, for her computer skills.

CONTENTS

INTRODUCTION

At times it feels as if our national culinary landscape has devolved to an unholy trinity: pizza, tacos, and hamburgers. Pessimists survey the American menu and moan that it lacks individuality. The complaint is that you can eat the same predictably (bad) food from Maine to California.

We have a different map of America. It wanders from farmsteads to bakeries to small factories and smokehouses, stopping at the thousands of American food makers creating unique products. Most of these products—barbecue sauces, cheeses, candy bars, smoked fish, preserves, and more—have been made for decades and have legions of loyal followers. They operate simply, below the radar screen of national ad campaigns and costly grocery store promotions.

This book is a roadmap to many of our country's superlative foods. Happily, the Internet, 800 numbers, and efficient shipping allow the armchair traveler to acquire them easily. Of course, personal visits are the most engaging way to see their interesting factories and the sometimes quirky production methods.

There's the vintage candy factory in downtown Boise, where the Idaho Spud is made. That's America's only candy bar shaped like a potato. The factory, with its leather belts, wooden pulleys, and oversized copper kettles, is a look back at another century.

At Ekone Oyster Company in Washington's Willapa Bay, you can watch oyster farmer Nick Jambor and his employees raising mollusks from seed to harvest to market, growing oysters on lines staked along acres of tide flats. They then brine and smoke the plump oysters, and will sell them to you at their cannery's door.

Appleton, Wisconsin, is the home to one of the country's few farmstead cheesemakers, where the cheese is made from the milk of the farm's own cows. At the Mossholder farm, aged, raw milk cheese has been made in the farmstead's basement for more than seventy years. Customers are greeted with a sign: "Ring doorbell for cheese."

We delight in these hardworking food purveyors and rejoice in their success.

We're thrilled that not even a devastating fire could keep Schwartz chocolate-covered marshmallows out of production for long in New Hyde Park, New York.

We are pleased to report that the Shaharazad Bakery, a tiny storefront operation in its fortieth year in San Francisco, still thrives by selling fragile, thin-as-paper filo dough that is hand-stretched in its back room.

And we are proud that Kehr's Kandy Kitchen remains in an improving downtown neighborhood of Milwaukee, even after the retirement of eighty-two-year-old identical twin sisters who hand-dipped its chocolates.

We too are identical twin sisters, and we've been concerning ourselves with small, special food companies for nearly two decades. We have yet to lose our capacity to be amazed at the hard work, artistry, and low prices that flourish in this extraordinary group. We expected the abundant examples of highly educated professionals who have left established careers to produce cheese, small-batch potato chips, or salsas. It is the updated version of the American Dream. Forget writing the Great American Novel. Bring on the biscotti.

What continues to surprise us are the numbers of small, high-quality food producers who have been in business for decades, quietly turning out topnotch foods. These firms do not hire public relations agents, take out booths at national gourmet shows, or hit the talk-show circuit. Many, thankfully, never change their labels, giving eaters a visual history of American food graphics from the turn of the century on. C. Howard's mints from upstate New York probably were in your grandmother's purse. The Fralinger's Art Deco macaroon box is so out of date it has become fashionable again, as has the tiny box for Bell's Poultry Seasoning, with its blue Technicolor turkey, circa 1867.

We were happy to find many vintage companies, such as the White Lily Flour from Knoxville, (since the 1850s), Taylor's Mexican Chili (since 1904) in Carlinville, Illinois, and Moxie Soda Pop, our nation's oldest carbonated drink, which is the spark for a town festival every summer in Lisbon Falls, Maine.

We tend to include products that have been made for at least twenty years, simply owing to high mortality in the food business. Some of these superlative food makers are unknown outside their immediate city or state. Indeed, some have been a part of the social fabric of an area for so long that its residents don't realize how unusual they are. In Denver, for example, we were surprised that there is so little fuss over Hammond's Candy, a shop whose range of homemade items and candy-making skill have few equals in the nation.

Many of these companies, having made it through the years when Americans craved Spam and Velveeta, are assured of a bright future. But many others are endangered because they so often depend on one or two key people. When there is no family member or employee willing to keep the tradition alive, these special foods are lost. We profiled several companies whose elderly owners are uncertain about the future of their businesses.

It is with great sadness that we report the demise of some of our favorites from the first book. Lasser's Soda Pop in Chicago, which had been run by the Lasser family for nearly one hundred years, is no more. The bottling plant, located in a gentrifying neighborhood near DePaul University, is now a condominium, the only clue to its flavorful history being a small display of Lasser bottles in one window. Another sweet memory is Avignone Fréres Algaras, a black-and-white-striped candy named after the bizarre hair coloring of an obscure Mexican diplomat.

Schimpff's Confectioners, in Jeffersonville, Indiana, possibly this country's oldest candy shop still run by the founding family, closed after the death of owner Catherine Schimpff. With it went the store's unequaled square cinnamon red hots, which had been made since 1876. We also hated to see North Lubec sardines in eastern Maine; Castle Farms cottage cheese from Emmitsburg, Maryland; Mineral Point (Wisconsin) Bakery's Cornish pasty; and Pixiana Tomato Juice, from Swayzee, Indiana, go by the wayside.

We were sorry to learn that Ute Kohn is no longer smoking fish and lobster in Thomaston, Maine, and were pained to get the news that Baune's Minnesota farmstead cheese was no longer in business. The monks at the Abbey of the Holy Trinity in Huntsville, Utah, no longer sell creamed honey, and that Sun Ripe Tomatoes from central Florida, a welcome mid-winter treat for those in cold climates, is no more.

There have, however, been some happy resurrections. C.C. Brown's golden mocha and hot fudge sauces were served on Hollywood Boulevard for decades, only to vanish when its soda fountain closed. The Internet revived them. Patrons no longer can sit at a vintage wooden booth and spoon the sauce over ice cream, but the taste is the same when you order for home consumption. The web is now the only place to buy Widow's Mite Vinegar, an unusual salad dressing that has been resurrected from culinary oblivion at least three times since the 1940s. It's illuminating to see where products are made, but we'd rather have a web presence than no presence.

There also have been some fortunate transitions. Lucy Ortelecan, Cleveland's premier strudel maker, has retired, but her recipes and methods live on, thanks to a talented baker who has taken over her business and is continuing to turn out labor-intensive Hungarian pastries.

At Ruef's Meat Market in New Glarus, Wisconsin, home of one-of-a-kind smoked sausages and hams, Willy and Annette Ruef sold the business to their son, Bill, about a year ago. Bill had been working there since high school, nearly twenty years, and his parents still help out part time. The transition was so smooth, says Bill, that many customers don't realize yet that his parents are no longer the owners!

Government regulations, however, pose another threat to some of these small entrepreneurs. Small meatpackers, for example, rarely can afford to pay the inspector's salary and make the design modifications required for federal licensing, thus allowing them to send their products across state lines. So legions of eaters in other states are denied the efforts of small sausage makers. It took the intervention of U.S. senators and representatives to get the USDA to back off from requiring a bakery in Fairmount, West Virginia, famed for its pepperoni rolls, to conform to health regulations required for meat-processing plants.

Linden Beverage Company of Virginia, maker of the incomparable Alpenglow sparkling cider, was nearly closed by federal and state inspectors, in a raid that was ridiculed on the pages of the *Wall Street Journal.* The Lacy family has persevered, and now continues in the apple business, as it has for the past hundred years.

What can be done to assure that these culinary landmarks remain? First, they need the continued support of the public—locally and those who order long distance. State and local tourism and agriculture agencies have done much more in recent years to highlight small food producers in their midst, but much more could be done. Rarely, if ever, do tourist brochures list food makers who welcome visitors. These settings often make a personal visit infinitely more rewarding than ordering by mail. Drier's Meat Market in Three Oaks, Michigan, is in a clapboard-front building that has housed a meat market since 1875. Virginia Diner Peanuts are cooked next to a bustling 165-seat diner in Wakefield. At idyllic Kozlowski Farms north of San Francisco, travelers can see fruit grown, harvested, and turned into preserves in one charming stop. Thousands of visitors brave the flour to tour the Rossi Pasta Company in Marietta, Ohio. (Fashion tip: Don't wear dark clothes.)

There is a National Register of Historic Places in this country. While it has not been successful in saving all architecturally significant buildings from demolition, it has saved some and given pause to communities about the value of structures in their midst. The country should consider a National Register of Culinary Landmarks that would use similar legislation to protect the buildings, methods, and ingredients of America's treasured food resources.

Going beyond the obvious trends of jalapeño and Cajun overload, it does seem that this country is beginning to recapture some of its vast culinary heritage. In their thoughtful book, *The Taste of America,* John and Karen Hess made a compelling case that our contemporary diet pales in comparison to the diversity of colonial days. In the past years, we've seen a growing number of enterprises built around long-forgotten foods: mayhaw berries in Georgia; lingonberries in Washington State; America's only tea plantation in Charleston, South Carolina; wild game from Texas; American chestnuts from Washington State; wild thimbleberries and hickory nuts from northern Michigan; and so on. Several mail-order and Internet companies have sprung up to connect eaters with the foods from their childhood or with favorites they encountered while traveling.

Immigrants have helped make us more global and varied in our eating. A watershed may have been passed when Samadi Sweets, a chain of bakeries in the Middle East, opened in northern Virginia. Authentic finds like Portuguese sweet muffins, Indian curries, Ethiopian pancake mix, and ethnic spices can be yours from American suppliers. Bill Penzey, the co-owner of a Wisconsin-based spice company, has as his mission an international version of *Food Finds.* He travels the globe searching for top-quality spice farmers and sells their best to his far-flung customers.

Alternatives to highly salted, fat-laden supermarket foods exist everywhere, and many a small company has found success by emphasizing wholesome qualities. Walnut Acres in Pennsylvania is a one-stop cornucopia of everything from healthy soups to honest mayonnaise. Smokehouse, Inc. in Massachusetts has superb low-fat and nonnitrite cured meats. A host of spice purveyors offer excellent no-salt seasonings.

Healthy foods are emerging from their plain brown wrappers and are as likely to be sent as gifts as chocolate truffles. Virginia's Shawnee Springs Canning Company's hand-peeled no-sugar peach halves, a graphic rebuke to prevalent canned fruits, can be ordered in a gift basket, as can a selection of whole-grain mixes from Fiddler's Green in Maine.

Packaging has taken a quantum leap forward in recent years. Highly perishable goods are sent reliably in Styrofoam coolers with the contents chilled by plastic ice packets or dry ice. Competition in the overnight-delivery industry has lowered prices and made the service commonplace. Cheesecake, pastrami, fresh bagels, even ice cream can be sent with top-notch results. Ever skeptical, we ordered dainty frozen fruits from Connecticut's St. Clair Ice Cream Fruit Company in the heat of midsummer, and they arrived with nary a berry melted. Breakable bottles come cushioned in bubble pack and nestled in those irritating—but effective—foam peanuts. Coffees and spices come in heavy coated bags with reclosable tops. Smoked fish is kept moist in shrink wrap.

Ordering from companies closely identified with their particular region allows you to experience another part of the country vicariously. Order a flashy King Cake from New Orleans at Mardi Gras time. Open a box from Ducktrap River Smoked Fish in Maine and find a small balsam sprig tucked inside. Unwrap a birch basket filled with wild fruit products from Michigan's American Spoon Foods and be transported via sight, smell, and taste.

Even though many small firms have embraced state-of-the-art packaging, websites, fax, toll-free order numbers, and overnight delivery, don't jump to the conclusion that cold-blooded efficiency rules. Many firms remain charmingly obsolete in their pricing policies and customer relations. We are amazed, in updating our 1990 book, at the number of companies that have kept price increases to a modest 2 to 5 percent. This is the antithesis of bottom-line myopia, a side of business different from the merger mania presented as the American standard in this new century. In our admittedly distorted world of small food companies, items are often sent and billed later, loyal customers order regularly for decades, ingredient lists never change, and owners regularly answer their own phones.

There was no attempt to balance the book by geographical region or food type. There's no getting around the fact that certain states are richer in small food companies than others. California, awash in fresh produce and entrepreneurs, is loaded with good examples. So are Wisconsin, Massachusetts, and Vermont. Also, there is no denying that America has a sweet tooth of gigantic proportions. The vintage foods that have endured over the years are disproportionately in the candy, cake, and cookie lines. This book reflects that disparity.

Prices listed are not engraved in stone. Products are added, sizes change, shipping costs rise regularly enough to make keeping current an impossibility. The information here is accurate as of mid-2000. Remember that telephone area codes change frequently. A dead number doesn't always mean a company is out of business.

Many companies accept credit cards and we have noted those that do. If an entry states "no credit cards," personal checks are almost always accepted.

Over the years we've been flattered by the number of travelers who use our book as a travel guide, sometimes getting the food producers to autograph their book entry, making *Food Finds* a passport record of America's farms, mills, monasteries, and factories where unique food is made. We are heartened by the entrepreneurial spirit, talent, and insistence on quality that make these foods special. We think they represent the best of America.

BEVERAGES

ALPENGLOW SPARKLING CIDER

Despite America's enchantment with apples and apple cider, sparkling ciders have not been commonly bottled. The few that are often are too sweet. But when the Lacy family of Linden, Virginia, decided to add carbonation to the juice from Red Delicious and Winesaps, it did it right. No additional sugar is added, or preservatives, and the blend of apples (three Red Delicious to each Winesap) produces a taste that's on the light side, with no cloying aftertaste. The carbonation is sufficient for Alpenglow to double as a nonalcoholic champagne, as numerous brides and grooms happily have discovered.

The family began the business using apples from its own orchard, which was begun in 1900. Now, it purchases apples from other local growers, but still does its own bottling. It sells its beverages at its family-run retail store, The Apple House, that also is noted for homemade apple butter doughnuts, country hams, and quilts.

There are four flavors of cider. A mulled sparkling cider, a blend of cider and mulling spices, is often referred to as "apple pie in a bottle." There's a scuppernong cider made with wild muscadine grapes; a classic blush made with varietal apples, red grapes, and muscadine; and sparkling apple juice.

The company recently added two new labels featuring the historic artwork of artist Mort Kunstler. The labels are "Lee at Fredericksburg" and "The Angle," that depicts a battle at Gettysburg.

The beverages are distributed throughout Virginia and in selected stores nationwide. If you can't find them, they can be sent via UPS. A gift pack of four 750 ml (25.4-ounce) bottles that includes one of each of the four flavors is $22 plus shipping, through The Apple House. Full cases of a dozen 25.4-ounce bottles can be shipped for $25 a case, plus shipping costs. Split cases containing 24 bottles of 6.3-ounce ciders also are available for $23 plus shipping.

The beverages with the art labels also can be shipped. They cost $50 a case, or $25 for a four-bottle pack. Shipping costs are added to both prices.

ORDERING ADDRESS
The Linden Beverage Company
The Apple House
4675 John Marshall Highway
Linden, VA 22642
540/636-6329
800/462-1867
FAX: 540/636-4470
www.nvim.com/applehouse/
Credit cards accepted

VISITS: Linden is in northwestern Virginia, about 90 minutes from Washington, D.C. From the city, take Route 66 west. Take exit 13 (marked "Linden" and "Skyline Drive"), and turn left at the bottom of the ramp. Turn right at the stoplight onto John Marshall Highway. The Apple House will be on your right about half a block down, beside the Mobil gas station.
Every day, 8 a.m.–5 p.m.

AMERICAN CLASSIC TEA

Unlike some wines and most haircuts, tea does not improve with age. All teas sold in America, with one exception, are imported, and some celebrate their first birthday before reaching the consumer's shopping cart. The inevitable result, says professional tea taster Bill Hall, is a loss of smoothness and a heavier, less delicate tea. Fresh tea, on the other hand, does not have a bitter aftertaste.

The one native to America, now being grown on Wadmalaw Island, South Carolina, is a light, sweet orange pekoe tea that moves from the field to the grocery shelf in less than a month. If you take sugar in your tea you'll find yourself using less with American Classic.

Tea is harvested about every two weeks during the growing season, from early May through the end of October, which makes tasting each batch critical. "With wine or coffee, grapes or beans are harvested once and you have a certain quality for the year," explained Hall. 'With tea, it can change every fifteen to eighteen days, depending on the amount of rain, if it's too hot, too cold, or whatever. That's why the tasting part of tea is much more involved."

American Classic is a blended black, completely fermented tea. The other major types of tea—green tea and oolong tea—surprisingly enough come from the same plant. The difference is in the amount of fermentation. (*Fermentation* is a deceiving word because it implies the use of yeast. No yeast is used. Rather, the withered tea leaves are simply exposed to the air, or oxi-

dized, for various lengths of time.)

Fleming and Hall use only liquid propane gas to dry the tea, which they feel is a plus. Many foreign countries use fuel oil, whose fumes can affect the tea's flavor.

Tea consumption is increasing in this country, although it is still a shadow of what is consumed in England. We drink 12–14 ounces per capita here, versus 8 pounds per person there. However, that 12–14 ounces adds up to more than 190 million pounds of imported tea leaves. Charleston Tea Plantation is counting on patriotic Americans who appreciate fresh, smooth tea to help an upstart company chip away at those imports.

The plantation has a Gazebo Gift Shop open weekdays to the public. After watching a video on tea production, visitors can sample iced tea, Charleston benne wafers, and tea jellies, and walk to the tea fields. It also will mail-order its products to those who can't visit. A box of 20 tea bags is $2.50, and a box of 70 bags is $3.50. There is a $3.50 shipping charge for orders up to $25, so it makes sense to add some of the company's unique jellies: tea jelly, orange jelly, raspberry jelly, or mint jelly. A 4.5-ounce glass jar is $2.50. For details, request the company's free catalog.

ORDERING ADDRESS
Charleston Tea Plantation
6617 Maybank Highway
Wadmalaw Island, SC 29487
843/559-0383
800/443-5987
FAX 843/559-3049
e-mail: chastea@awod.com

Credit cards accepted

VISITS: From Charleston on Highway 17, take either Main Road or Folly Road (Highway 171) to Maybank Highway (Highway 700). Follow Maybank Highway almost to Rockville. The plantation is located 2 miles before Rockville on the left side of the highway.

The gift shop is open weekdays and no appointments are necessary. Private tours are available for groups of 10 to 45 at a cost of $5 per person. Arrangements for these must be made in advance.

Monday–Friday, 10 A.M.–3 P.M.

BEST FRIENDS COCOA

There are days when we push a grocery cart up and down the aisles and can't find anything to put in it. Too much sodium in those frozen fish sticks. Palm oil in those crackers. Aspartame in that vanilla pudding.

There may be a glut of high-quality specialty foods, but there are opportunities aplenty for small entrepreneurs to improve upon supermarket fare. Consider cocoa mix. This is one food category that has absolutely stymied us at the supermarket. It would be great to make cocoa quickly, on demand, we think as we stand there scanning the labels of Swiss Miss and the like. But the ingredient list sounds so unhealthy that we never can bring ourselves to drop it in the cart.

Naomi Storm and Karen Levine, who happened to be best friends, developed Best Friends Cocoa in 1988. "Cocoa is cozy solace, as is a good friend," maintains Naomi. Best Friends Cocoa needs only the addition of hot water, so cocoa can be made in a flash in a microwave. It has no preservatives or artificial flavors, and is certified kosher. The ingredients are simply nonfat dry milk, sugar, Dutch-process cocoa, corn syrup solids, cream, corn flour, spices, and natural flavorings. It is low in cholesterol (5 mg per serving) and low in sodium. One cup provides 110 calories, but only 1.5 mg of fat. Statistics aside, the taste is very good. Best Friends comes in 11 flavors, including the traditional not-too-sweet variety and a cinnamon spice version. Kid-friendly flavors are Marshmallow Cloud, Mighty Malt, and Verry Cherry. Most can be stirred into coffee for a quick flavor enhancer, taken on camping trips, enjoyed as an after-school treat, or served as an after-dinner drink with

a bit of liqueur added. The mixes are even good cold, as iced cocoas or iced mochas.

Naomi bought out her partner several years ago, and expanded the company beyond her Newton, Massachusetts, home to a commercial space. She has several part-time employees, but she still mixes cocoa, adds flavors, and cuts ribbons for packages. "That's the nature of a cottage industry," she says.

The company logo is two steaming cocoa mugs. It appears on its 8-ounce bags ($5.75) and its single-serving "muglets" ($1.50), and a rectangular sampler tin ($9.75) of the four most popular flavors: Traditional Chocolate, Raspberry Truffle, Mocha, and Vanilla Velvet. Shipping and handling costs are added to these prices.

"Share Good Times with Best Friends" is the mission of the company. We think Best Friends Cocoa mix is just the gift for your best friend.

ORDERING ADDRESS
Best Friend Cocoa
P.O. Box 610157
Newton, MA 02461
781/329-8800
FAX: 781/329-8800
No credit cards

BLENHEIM GINGER ALE

Hamer, South Carolina, is the home of one of our nation's smallest commercial bottling companies. In an old-fashioned-looking glass bottle and made with spring water, Blenheim is a one-of-a-kind drink. This Jamaican ginger concoction will sear itself into your memory. Its unofficial motto, "We burn ya," is no idle threat.

What this drink needs is a warning label: "CAUTION: This Ginger Ale Bites." In all seriousness, do let the soda breathe for a minute before serving, particularly to children, because the good doctor from Bennetsville, South Carolina, who developed the ale in 1903 must have specialized in clearing sinuses. The doctor, C. R. May, devised the drink after encouraging his patients to drink local mineral-rich well water for stomach ailments. He added Jamaican ginger to make the drink more palatable, and a business was born.

The fumes from either variety of ale (the mislabeled "mild" Extra Pale and "hot" Old Number Three) invariably make first-timers choke and gasp. But by cautiously sipping this ginger ale you'll be left with the sweet aftertaste so favored in southern drinks. Mild is supposed to be calmer than Old Number Three, but we say it's a toss-up. The high sulphur content of the well water in Blenheim is responsible for some of the bite.

The Blenheim operations are now in a small bottling plant behind Porky's Truck Stop at South of the Border, that monument to kitsch on the border between North and South Carolina. Charles Thomas, the talented plant manager, came to Blenheim after 11 years in quality control for Coke. The original Blenheim plant was located on wetlands, so it couldn't be expanded when the Schafer family, which bought the firm in 1993, decided to increase production.

But the Blenheim spring water is used still, with two stainless steel tanker trucks making the 30-minute drive to Blenheim several times a week. The company now bottles the water as well, along with a wonderful strawberry soda. There's also a very good orange soda, grape soda, and ginger beer produced here. Old-fashioned 12-ounce glass bottles are the only containers used for the ginger ale, however the sodas currently are in plastic bottles because so many customers take them to the beach.

"Quality and consistency of product has always been something that is a unique selling point, even more than marketing and packaging," said Thomas. "Whether you like our product or not, you know the taste, the experience, and the legacy will always be the same."

Because of the company's size and the loyalty of its customers, who are more than willing to pay the handling charges, Blenheim will ship its ginger ale. The minimum is a case of 24 bottles, at a bargain $16, plus shipping. (The shipping to East Coast addresses, for example, is $11.47). Please note on your check whether you want mild (Extra Pale) or hot (Old Number Three) or a mixed case. You may buy the beverages at the plant or at the pantries and shops on the grounds of South of the Border.

ORDERING ADDRESS
Blenheim Bottling Company
P.O. Box 452
North Highway 301
Hamer, SC 29547
843/774-03222
800/270-9344
Credit cards accepted

VISITS: The plant is 6 miles south of Dillon, South Carolina. From I-95, take exit 1 at South of the Border. Watch for the black and orange Blenheim Bottlers sign behind the Porky's Truck Stop.
Monday–Friday, 9 a.m. –5 p.m.

CHEERWINE

When every other town had its own bottling plant, America had hundreds of local soda pops, all with colorful names like Misty Morning and Spruce Tonic. When the bottlers sold out to larger firms, these one of-a-kind drinks disappeared, except in a few isolated areas. Thank goodness the foothills of North Carolina were among them, and Cheerwine still is bottled in the town of Salisbury.

A mint cola was the specialty of the Piedmont-Cheerwine Bottling Company when it opened for business in 1913. Its owner, merchant L. D. Peeler, then began trying other flavors and developed Cheerwine in 1917. "He was experimenting with ways to sweeten the product and developed a totally unique soft drink," said Mark Ritchie, Peeler's great-grandson. "He liked what he came up with and named it Cheerwine."

MintCola was bottled until the 1930s. During the Great Depression, the company was forced to limit production to one flavor, and it chose its best seller, Cheerwine. The name, taken from the soda's burgundy color, has caused the company trouble in the alcohol-sensitive South. "There are some places [where] we have trouble . . . because people will think kids are drinking alcohol," said Ritchie.

The drink is an unusual cola with a hint of wild cherry. It is highly carbonated and pops, rather than foams, when poured over ice. Peeler's son, Clifford, age 96, is the company's president and has kept the recipe faithful to its origins. The firm distributes the drink in 14 eastern states. In the Carolinas, it has inspired local Cheerwine punches and hand-cranked Cheerwine ice cream. The recipe for the best-known Cheerwine punch is simple: 2 parts Cheerwine and 1 part unsweetened pineapple juice.

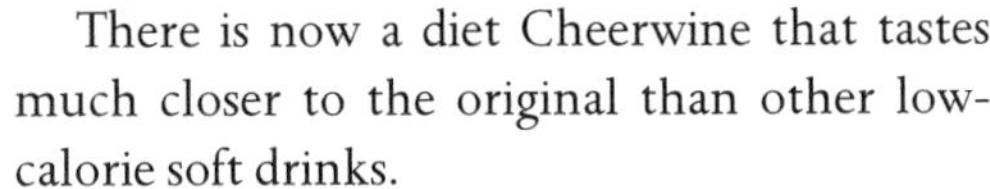

There is now a diet Cheerwine that tastes much closer to the original than other low-calorie soft drinks.

Owing to the many requests of homesick Carolinians, the bottler will ship cans of the soda. It also can be purchased at the main plant. One case (24 cans,) is $10.70, plus shipping.

ORDERING ADDRESS

Carolina Beverage Corp.
1413 Jake Alexander Boulevard
P.O. Box 697
Salisbury, NC 28245-0697
704/637-5881
FAX: 704/633-7491
www.cheerwine.com
No credit cards

CHEREFRESH

To know all about Cherefresh, "The Original Refreshing Cherry Juice," all you have to do is read the label. "The Pure Juice of Tart Red Cherries. Wholesome Refreshing . Natural Color. Natural Flavor. Natural Strength. No Dilution. Unsweetened. The Cherefresh process converts the natural goodness of luscious Sturgeon Bay red cherries into a pure, crystal clear, natural cherry juice. Refresh with Cherefresh. At Meal Time and Between Time. Packed in Enamel Lined Cans. Serve Chilled." A cup of the cherry juice is high in iron (15 percent of the RDA) and vitamin C.

Cherefresh has been made by Krier Foods for decades, and the label looks like it hasn't changed much over the years. Made from tart red cherries grown in picturesque Door County, Wisconsin, it is a pleasant alternative to apple juice. There are so few unsweetened or undiluted juices commonly available that it is a mystery why Cherefresh isn't more widely known.

Krier Foods says it makes no claims for the medicinal value of Cherefresh. However, the unsolicited letters it receives from customers aren't so shy. "It helped to tone down my arthritis," stated one. "My wife and I have been drinking this cherry juice so that we won't get the gout back again," went another. A group in Texas ordered several cases "for relief from joint pain."

Small children may find the taste too tart, but mixing it with apple juice makes it palatable to them. Cherefresh can be used to make a number of original punches and desserts—ask for the free recipe booklet.

The company will ship a case of twelve 46-ounce cans for $26.50, plus UPS charges. Be forewarned: the case is heavy, and shipping charges may approach the cost of the juice.

ORDERING ADDRESS
Krier Foods, Inc.
4555 West Schroeder Drive
Suite 190
Brown Deer, WI 53223
414/355 5400
FAX: 414/355-5577
No credit cards

MANHATTAN PURE ESPRESSO COFFEE SODA

There's a widespread suspicion that New Yorkers, with their high food prices, get the best of everything our nation's farm basket has to offer. We've often peered at the scrawny chickens and fatty pork in our Midwestern grocery coolers and surmised that our neighboring packers found it more profitable to ship the good stuff to those extravagant New Yorkers. While our logic may not be convincing in the meat department, we know that New Yorkers have the coffee soda market all sewn up for themselves with Passaro's Pure Espresso Coffee Soda.

The espresso boom may have started in this country at the end of the twentieth century, but this product has been made since the nineteenth century—since 1895, to be exact.

On its vintage yellow and red label and bottle caps, this 105-year-old soda proclaims itself "The World's Most Delicious Coffee Soda." You'll get no argument here; opening one of its 10-ounce glass bottles is like pouring yourself a fountain-made coffee phosphate. The firm, which is owned by Louis and Aurora Passaro, still uses coffee , ground from beans, as its base. No instant crystals allowed! It is very lightly carbonated, leaving you with a strong coffee flavor that's slightly effervescent.

It is available in all five boroughs of New York City, and in several eastern states. The company has entered the world of e-commerce, and is making its products available to the rest of the country via its website. There, you can view the full range of the company's excellent offerings: True Vanilla Bean Cream Soda, True Fruit Orange Soda and Cherry Soda (made from real fruit concentrate and natural flavors), True Root Sarsaparilla Soda, and Gassosa, a lemon-lime soda. The coffee soda is the original flavor and comes in regular or sugar-free versions.

ORDERING ADDRESS
Manhattan Special Bottling Corp.
342 Manhattan Avenue
Brooklyn, NY 11211
718/388-4144
FAX: 718/384-0244
www.manhattanspecial.com

MOXIE SODA POP

Isn't it wonderful that America still has Moxie, our oldest carbonated soft drink? This one-of-a-kind drink, first concocted as a nerve medicine in 1884 by Dr. Augustus Thompson in Union, Maine, still is available in bright-orange cans in selected outlets throughout the Eastern Seaboard.

The soda is based on the root of the yellow gentian plant, which is supposed to calm frayed nerves. The drink does have a slightly bitter aftertaste, but as its vintage ads say, it's "never sticky sweet." It is a sharp, feisty drink, which was the inspiration for the slang term "moxie."

The best place to taste Moxie is undoubtedly the Lisbon Falls, Maine, store of Frank Anicetti II, the nation's foremost Moxie memorabilia collector. He even makes Moxie ice cream at his corner store, the Kennebec Fruit Company, which has tin ceilings and a soda fountain, and sells one of the three (count 'em, three) books written on the soft drink. *The Moxie Mystique,* written by Frank N. Potter and published in 1982, is available by mail from Kennebec Fruit for $10.95 postpaid. Potter's later effort, *The Book of Moxie,* and *The Moxie Encyclopedia* by Q. David Bowers, published in 1984, are unfortunately out of print.

On the cover of his orange Moxie brochure, Anicetti writes: "Show your Moxie. Read about it. Wear it. Drink it." He isn't kidding about wearing it. He sells Moxie T-shirts , sweatshirts, hats, knitted hats, scarves, aprons, mittens, and tote bags.

It was the publication of *The Moxie Mystique* that led to the first Moxie party in Lisbon Falls, an event that has grown to the largest annual celebration in town. Held the second Saturday of July, the event attracts more than 25,000 thirsty people. It is the model of civic ecumenicalism: the chamber of commerce sponsors the festival and runs the Miss Moxie Pageant; the Masons handle the pancake breakfast; the Fire Department is the beneficiary of the auction; the Optimists Club organizes a Bicycle Rodeo; the spaghetti supper is held at the American Legion hall; the Shriners and the Boy Scouts participate in the parade, and so on.

Moxie headquarters is now in Atlanta, Georgia, at the Monarch Bottling Company. The drink is not shipped from there, but Anicetti will send a case of twenty-four 12-ounce cans for $17, plus UPS shipping costs. He estimates that he ships 150 to 200 cases annually to Moxie drinkers nationwide.

ORDERING ADDRESS
Kennebec Fruit Company
2 Main Street
Lisbon Falls, ME 04252
207/353 8173
No credit cards, money order only

VISITS: Lisbon Falls is in southeast Maine, south of Lewiston. The Kennebec Fruit Company, also known as The Moxie Store, is an archetypal soda fountain and corner store, located at the corner of Main Street and Route 196.
Every day, 8:30 A.M.–8 P.M.

PEET'S COFFEE

Coffee is hot in America, and magazine articles and books have been written about the hundreds of companies offering coffee beans for sale. These writings don't hold our interest because for us one company will suffice. Peet's Coffee & Tea, a San Francisco Bay area institution since the mid-1960s, cares passionately about coffee and doesn't stray from its mission. There are no gimmicky flavored beans, no "gourmet" items made elsewhere and given a Peet's label, no blends with silly names.

Although there has been a resurgence of serious coffee roasters in recent years, Peet's stands out for three reasons. First, its deep roasting style is rarely found in North America or northern Europe. As Peet's chairman, Jerry Baldwin, explains: "In some parts of southern Europe, dark roasting is mistakenly used in an attempt to mask the flavor of inferior coffees. In our case, we enhance the flavors of excellent coffees by developing them to this degree. Roasting dark is not the point. Developing flavor through appropriate application of heat is the technique that others only imitate. Furthermore, it has become a Peet's trademark."

Peet's second unique feature is its absolute mania about freshness. It buys its own green beans and does all of its own roasting by hand, as any serious coffee company must. All of its coffees are sold within seven days of roasting. In the interim, the beans are stored in bins that are closed at night. The company uses expensive, heavy, brown coated paper bags, lined with polypropylene, that reduce deterioration from oxygen and moisture. This contrasts with less expensive bags, even cellophane, used by other coffee sellers.

Peet's beans are so fresh and aromatic that their perfume lingers on the outside of the securely closed cardboard boxes used for mail orders. (The smell

drives UPS drivers crazy. When we have a Peet's order, they complain good-naturedly about being tantalized all day by the aroma of delicious coffee.)

Peet's third feature is its informed and committed employees. Jerry Baldwin, who says "there is no topic more fun to talk about than coffee," was taught to roast by owner Alfred Peet in the early 1970s. Jim Reynolds, vice president and general manager, started his career as a coffee roaster in 1973 and has been a full-time coffee buyer since 1977. "Few specialty coffee companies even have a full-time coffee buyer," notes Baldwin. "Fewer still have anyone with Jim's experience."

Alfred Peet, whose lifelong attachment to coffee and tea began at age 10 when he cleaned out his father's roaster in a town in northern Netherlands, stayed with the company for a while as a consultant when Baldwin purchased it in 1979. Although he has no formal relationship with the company now, "he continues to drop in from time to time to talk coffee and tea with Jim," reports Baldwin.

The store's employees participate in an intensive training program that includes a tasting group every month, so they can offer intelligent advice to customers. Peet's retail stores are located in neighborhoods, as opposed to shopping malls, and thereby make an important contribution to the community. At each store there is a coffee bar where patrons can buy a freshly brewed cup of coffee. Varieties change often during the day. These are true coffeehouses, with the emphasis on coffee, not pastries or poetry reading. Morning newspapers are discussed, customers take their conversations outside on nice days, and a sense of community prevails. Jane Jacobs, who wrote *The Death and Life of Great American Cities,* would approve.

Peet's rarely has advertised. (Its busiest store, the original Berkeley location at Walnut and Vine, to this day has no sign outside.) Word-of-mouth and transplanted Californians have built up a large mail-order business in every state of the union and overseas. Peet's has a good website, and its online presence has further extended its reach around the world.

Its most popular coffees are the French Roast, House Blend, Major Dickason's Blend (named after a Vine Street regular, not a military figure), and Italian Roast. "The fact that our blends are more popular than single-origin coffees is indicative of the experience and coffee sophistication of our customers," said Baldwin. "Generally, people start with single-origin coffees and, as they gain experience, migrate to the complexity of blends."

Peet's offers 12 single-origin coffees, from South America, Africa, and the Pacific islands, and 12 blends. The mail-order brochure and website show whether the coffee is light medium, or full-bodied. Eight decaffeinated coffees are also offered. Prices average about $11 a pound. The coffee can be ordered as whole beans or ground for espresso, drip, or Melitta coffee makers.

A staggering 28 varieties of tea can be ordered, allowing you the luxury of asking visitors to afternoon tea that all-impressive question, "China or India?"

Green teas, semifermented teas, and 8 blends round out the inventory. Prices are mostly in the $5 to $7 per quarter-pound range, but two special varieties cost more than $11. Shipping and handling averages $4 per order.

In 1978, we were lucky to live close enough to walk to Peet's Menlo Park store. Since then, despite five changes of address in three states, we have never bought any other coffee but Peet's. We particularly favor Sulawesi-Kalossie, a full-bodied coffee from Indonesia. A simple glance at Peet's glossy, dark, moist-looking beans next to the light, dried-out versions of others will convert you before you've brewed a cup.

ORDERING ADDRESS
Peet's Coffee & Tea
P.O. Box 12509
Berkeley, CA 94712-9901
800/999-2132
www.peets.com
e-mail: mailorder@peets.com
Credit cards accepted

VISITS: There are 55 Peet's stores nationwide. Many are in the San Francisco Bay Area, but Peet's also has a presence in Los Angeles, Chicago, Portland, and Boston.

VERNORS GINGER ALE

Having been raised near Cleveland, across Lake Erie from Detroit, home of Vernors Ginger Ale, we have a standard for ginger ale that is very different from the pale, flat soft drink that most of America consumes.

Outside of its home base of Michigan, Ohio, and New York, Vernors is available only in selected markets, including Florida, Phoenix, Chicago, Dallas, and Washington, D.C. As a result, fans have had to bring it home in suitcases during visits to the mid-Atlantic area. Vernors loyalists, like the fans of other soda pops, even cook with their beloved potion, using it to baste hams and turkeys. When we were children and had a cold, our grandmother used to serve Vernors to us warm, in mugs.

It's an exceptionally crisp drink, with lots of ginger supplying a sharp, heavily carbonated kick. Dark amber, the drink is made from an extract that's aged for four years in wooden barrels, a technique devised by James Vernor, a Detroit druggist, in 1866.

Actually, the aging was unintentional, due entirely to James Vernor's service in the Civil War. When Vernor was called to fight in 1862, he left his mixture of ginger, vanilla, and flavorings in an oak cask in his pharmacy. When he returned four years later, he found that his drink had been "deliciously transformed" and had a zippy, gingery flavor like nothing he had ever tasted.

Vernor first sold his formulated compound to customers of his store's fountain on Woodward Avenue in Detroit. His son developed the business by selling the extract to others that bottled the ginger ale, an arrangement that continues today. However, the concentrate still is made in only one place: St. Louis, Missouri. All the ginger ale is aged for six months in oak barrels prior to bottling.

Despite many requests from fans anxious to buy the product outside its normal distribution areas, its parent firm, Dr Pepper/7Up Inc., does not fill mail orders. But there is good news in Dr Pepper/7Up Inc.'s efforts to increase the reach of Vernors, as well as the much-loved lemon-lime drink Squirt, which the company also owns.

For those who can't wait for their grocery store to get the word about Vernors, travelers to Michigan and Ohio may buy the drink almost everywhere. It is sold in 12-ounce bottles, 6-packs, 1-liter, and 2-liter sizes. There also is a diet version. If you are unsure if Vernors or Squirt is sold in your area, call or write the company to locate the nearest distributor.

FOR INFORMATION ON DISTRIBUTORS
Dr Pepper/7Up, Inc.
Consumer Affairs
P.O. Box 869077
Plano, TX 75086-9077
800/696-5891

BREADS & CRACKERS

BALDWIN HILL BAKERY'S ORGANIC SOURDOUGH BREAD

Hy Lerner managed to achieve what many high-quality food manufacturers only dream of: control of the ingredients from the ground up. Lerner, a Boston physician who researched the relationship between diet and heart disease, put his longtime commitment to unadulterated foods into practice in 1975. To learn the art of baking healthful and delicious bread, Lerner traveled to Belgium to study with a baker named Omer Gevaert, who had revived the use of fermented wheat for producing hearty country breads. "The process is akin to wine making in that organic wheat is crushed and fermented to form the sourdough starter," Lerner said.

The starter, known in Flemish as *desem,* includes enzymes that make a bread easy to digest. Although yeast develops in any sourdough culture, no commercial yeast is added to desem bread, which makes it palatable even to those on yeast-free diets.

Desem breads have long rising times—as much as six times longer than yeast breads. Making them is an art, and attention must be paid to the vagaries of weather and humidity, oven temperature, wheat quality, and dough consistency.

To create his unusual breads, Lerner lovingly reproduced a Belgian country bakery on a 20-acre farm in the Massachusetts countryside, building a wood-fired oven that can hold up to 2,000 loaves. The water comes from a 500-foot artesian well and the sea salt is imported from a French supplier. All ingredients, including raisins and sesame seeds, are organically grown.

Spring wheat flour is supplied by the Little Bear Trading Company, in Winona, Minnesota, a company that contracts with more than one hundred organic wheat growers and certifies their methods are organic. As it is needed, the wheat is stone-ground at a mill two miles away. Flour for the French bread comes from Natural Way Mills, an organic grower in Middle River, Minnesota.

The bread has become a great success throughout the New England area, first in health food stores, then in standard grocery outlets. In 1999, Lerner sold the business to the Vermont Bread Company, but operations have remained much the same, with Lerner staying on as a consultant and his son, Adam, remaining as manager.

Currently, 14 bread varieties are offered. Whole-grain choices include Whole Wheat, Sesame Wheat, Salt-free Whole Wheat, 100 Percent Whole Spelt (an ancient member of the wheat family), Raisin Spelt, Rye (a mixture of whole rye, whole wheat, and caraway seeds), Raisin Cinnamon, and Rice (whole wheat with cooked brown rice added). Lighter varieties, in which the coarser bran is removed from the whole wheat flour but the germ is retained, include Sourdough French, Golden Sesame, Golden Light Rye (Jewish sour rye style), and Good Seeds Bread, which is whole wheat and rye flour, honey, whole-grain berries, brown rice, sunflower, sesame, and flax seeds. The two newest varieties are Sprouted Wheat and Honey and Oatmeal and Honey.

All the breads are made with the same starter, which imparts a slightly yeasty taste to the bread. But the sourdough taste is unlike the strong, nearly tart flavor commonly associated with that variety. Even in the raisin bread, which contains an astonishing 5 ounces of raisins in each 2-pound loaf, the wheat is the real star.

The raisin bread, with its dark brown crust, includes a hint of cinnamon. Compare this substantial, fragrant loaf to a raisin bread in which the weight of the fruit causes it to drop from the bread slices! The sesame wheat loaf is another favorite, with the crushed whole wheat fighting the sesame seeds for space.

The loaves are dense but not leaden, and stay fresher than other non-preserved breads. All the breads have no preservatives or refined sugars, and are certified kosher. They freeze extremely well.

All the breads come in a large size (22 to 28 ounces), and whole wheat, sesame wheat, and rye come in 1-pound small loaves as well. Large loaves range from $2.50 to $3; small loaves are $1.50. Rolls are $1.75 to $1.95. Rolls are available, 6 to a package, in French, sesame, spelt, good seeds, raisin spelt, and raisin varieties.

Sourdough bread crumbs are also available, in 12-ounce bags. Shipping and handling costs are added to these prices, and are described in the bakery's mail-order form. Send a check first, or the order will be sent COD for an added cost of $5 for the UPS collection fee.

Orders need to be received by noon Friday, Eastern time, for shipment the following week. Breads are usually shipped Mondays and Tuesdays only.

ORDERING ADDRESS
Baldwin Hill Bakery
15 Baldwin Hill Road
Phillipston, MA 01331
978/249-4691
800/749-2808
FAX: 978/249-0020
www.baldwinhill.com
e-mail: mail@baldwinhill.com
No credit cards

VISITS: Call ahead to schedule tours. From Boston, take Route 2 to the Phillipston exit, at Four Corners. Turn onto Route 2A. Drive west for 3 miles and watch for the Baldwin Hill sign. Turn right into the bakery.

RETAIL BAKERY HOURS: *Monday–Thursday, 8 A.M.–5 P.M.*

BOUDIN BAKERY SOURDOUGH FRENCH BREAD

San Francisco sourdough bread is the epitome of local food. Transplanted elsewhere, it simply does not work. The city's moderate year-round temperatures are said to be critical to the bread, as well as to the dry salami made there, and eating either makes us homesick for San Francisco. We challenge anyone to resist a warm round of sourdough served with unsalted butter. Uncounted fine meals in San Francisco have been willingly spoiled by a surfeit of sourdough and butter beforehand, we can attest.

Sourdough, which is fermented dough that rises without yeast, came to San Francisco during the Gold Rush. Sourdough was so common in mining camps that prospectors themselves were called "sourdoughs." It was altered by European bakers who immigrated to the city, including one Isadore Boudin, (pronounced "Bo-deen"), a Frenchman who had worked in Mexico before starting a bakery downtown in 1849. He used a sourdough starter to make crusty French bread, and created a San Francisco original. Today, Boudin bakers use starter that is a direct descendent of the mother dough created by Isadore Boudin.

More than 3.5 million loaves of sourdough bread are turned out at various bakeries each week in the Bay Area, and there are sharp differences of opinion on which bakery produces the best loaf. We stick with Boudin, "the Plymouth Rock of sourdough French," as the *San Francisco Chronicle* titled it on its 150th birthday in 1999. It produces hand-shaped loaves that are properly sour and chewy. In addition, we are partial to its striking logo, with shocks of wheat and furled ribbons. Designed by artist Primo Angeli, it has won graphics awards and is in the collection of the Smithsonian Institution.

The company now is owned by a Chicago firm, but is locally managed in San Francisco. Over the years, it has developed a well-thought-out system for shipping fresh bread throughout the country. It sends bread the day it is baked, and it arrives within two days. Currently, bread is shipped on Tuesdays. The mail-order catalog has a wealth of choices, from 1-pound long loaves, round loaves, half-pound baguettes, 7-inch sandwich rolls, and 8-ounce round Luigi rolls, which are perfect for hollowing out and using as bread or chili bowls. There is also sourdough bread flavored with asiago cheese, pesto, sun-dried tomatoes, and garlic. Fruit panettone, corn rye, and whole wheat are other possibilities, as are European hearth breads such as walnut rye, kalamata olive, ciabatta, and pain au Levain, using a starter that has no added yeast.

This is the place to go for breads shaped in holiday designs, such as shamrocks, pumpkins, hearts, and turkeys. The company also sells sourdough bagels, and several useful gift packages, such as sandwich rolls with BBQ fixings, a picnic basket of cheese, dried salame, mustard, baguettes, sparkling cider and biscotti, and all the elements for grilled cheese and turkey sandwiches and clam chowder. An up-to-the-minute gift package includes extra-virgin olive oil, glass dipping bowls, an oil bottle with pouring spout, and 4 baguettes.

There are also bread-of-the-month packages, and bread-bowl packages. A sourdough sampler of a 1-pound long loaf, a 1.5-pound round loaf, and 3 sandwich rolls is $22.95, plus shipping. Shipping costs for the sampler are $7.95, and vary with the cost of the order. The bread freezes well, so you can order more than you'll use immediately.

The company now has 40 bakery cafes, where bread is sold along with sandwiches, soups, salads, pizza, and coffee drinks. Twenty-two of them are in northern California, but San Diego, Orange County, and Chicago now have branches. Interestingly enough, at first the California bakery had to send fresh starter to its remote locations every few weeks, because once out of San Francisco, the starter seemed to lose its will to live. That problem now has been solved, but San Francisco remains the premier place to buy or eat sourdough.

ORDERING ADDRESS
Boudin Gift Catalog
564 Hawthorne Street
San Francisco, CA 94105
415/913-1849
800/992-1849
www.boudinbakery.com
Credit cards accepted

VISITS
Boudin Fisherman's Wharf Bakery
156 Jefferson Street
San Francisco, CA 94113
415/928-1849
The wharf bakery is on Jefferson between Mason and Taylor Streets and features large picture windows through which visitors can watch bread being made.

FISHERMAN'S WHARF HOURS: *Monday–Thursday, 7:30 A.M.–7 P.M. Friday–Sunday, 7:30 A.M.–8 P.M. (During December and January, the bakery closes at 6 P.M.)*

CENTRAL BAKERY PORTUGUESE MUFFINS

Portuguese sweet bread is a rich, slightly sweet, eggy bread that elevates any sandwich or toast into something memorable. One of the best places to sample sweet bread is in Fall River, Massachusetts, a city that is home to about fifty thousand people of Portuguese descent who trace their roots to the Portuguese sailors employed by the whale and cod fisheries there in the 1800s.

Now, Fall River has many Portuguese businesses, among them Central Bakery, which makes *bolos levedos,* a cross between sweet bread and an English muffin. Made by Tiberio Lopes and his family since he opened the bakery in 1975, these have a word-of-mouth following that has spread nationwide. The family now sends boxes of muffins from the bakery, a most welcome service. There are six muffins in each package and the Lopes's send a minimum of 6 packages. The cost is $15, plus shipping costs. Shipping costs vary by geography, so call to find out the charges to your address.

Other Fall River Portuguese bakeries make sweet bread muffins, but they are more on the order of the sweet bread itself, only smaller. Central Bakery's muffins are different. They are flatter, with a browned top and bottom characteristic of English muffins. At about 4½ inches in diameter, they are hardly dainty. Chewy and substantial, they make superlative toast—or try them as hamburger buns.

The business is quintessentially family run, with Tiberio and his wife, Leonor, getting help from their three sons, ages 31, 30, and 26. The recipe for the muffins came from Leonor's mother, Beatriz Caetano, who was living in the United States and missed the muffins she used to eat for breakfast in Portugal. Tiberio, who was working in a market in Fall River, began experimenting with the muffins at home, selling some on the side. They were popular and remain the bakery's first and only product.

Beatriz returned to Portugal, but her muffin recipe remained to be enjoyed by more and more Americans. The bakery is getting busier all the time, but you still are likely to have the phone answered by Tiberio, who unfailingly requests all callers to "have a nice day" in his cheerful, sincere way. It is cultural cross-fertilization at work: we trade a colloquialism for unique, outstanding muffins. We get the better deal.

ORDERING ADDRESS
Central Bakery
711 Pleasant Street
Fall River, MA 02723
508/675-7620
800/588-5523
No credit cards

VISITS: **Fall River is in southeastern Massachusetts, near the Rhode Island border on I-195. Central Bakery is in the heart of the downtown Portuguese area. Coming from the west on I-195, take exit 7. Turn left on to Plymouth Avenue. At the second set of lights, turn right onto Pleasant Street. The bakery is half a mile down Pleasant Street, on the right.**
Monday–Friday, 7 a.m.–5 p.m. Saturday, 8 a.m.–1 p.m.

DI CAMILLO'S BAKED GOODS

The Di Camillo bakery has become a legend in the food world. It is a first-class family-owned firm that serves as a neighborhood bakery, at the same time it has triumphed in gourmet markets with its unusual biscuits and cookies packaged in breathtakingly beautiful canisters and boxes. Its wine and champagne biscuits, cheese crisps, biscotti, almond macaroons, Italian flat breads, and Christmas cakes are all superlative.

There is true family pride throughout this 80-year-old operation. If the Di Camillo bakery had a letterhead in the style of a Park Avenue law firm, you'd see Di Camillo after Di Camillo after Di Camillo, because this is a family that works together. Much of the credit for the arresting graphics and packaging, as well as the pursuit of new products, goes to Michael Di Camillo, age 49, grandson of the founders, Thomas and Addotorato Di Camillo.

Grandfather Di Camillo worked as a caterer in Italy and hired on at Nabisco when he first emigrated to the United States. The Di Camillos then began their own bakery, with the help of their 11 children.

Michael, a former English teacher, rejoined his father, mother, brothers, cousins, aunts, and uncles in the business 22 years ago. "We knew we had food in Niagara Falls that was better than what was in the New York food stores," said Michael. "Now outsiders know it, too."

His brother, Tom, is a bread artist, making St. Joseph Day alter displays of wheat staffs, cornucopias, and fruits for neighborhood churches. Michael's father, now 88, still handles all of the books. His mother, 88, also is active in the business.

Modern shipping has meant the business can expand beyond the busy foot traffic in the local bakeries. It also means outsiders have a chance to experience excellent bread.

It's a five-hour process to make the bakery's venerable Italian curly bread. Now, the company will air ship three 14-ounce loaves, double-bagged in a decorated tin, for $33, delivered.

Among the many good biscuits, we particularly like the Biscotti di Vino (wine biscuit), with its slightly sweet taste. These squat cubes are sprinkled with sesame seeds and have centers that are moist for the biscuit world and wine-purple in color. They are best eaten for dessert with fruit and, of course, wine. "This isn't pure Italian because the taste is sweeter," explained Michael. "But the palates of Italians in America have changed, and since World War II this is the taste people like."

The Di Camillos' offerings make special gifts because the presentation—often with softly colored tissue, wheat stalks, and Renaissance drawings—amplifies the beauty of the food. Many of the company's early tins featured Niagara Falls. They're now collector's items.

The current tins of the wine or champagne biscuits are wonderful hostess or holiday gifts. A banquet gift tin of sweet cookies—butter wafers, walnut biscotti, and almond macaroons—is $40, delivered, and can serve 16 to 20. There are chocolate-covered biscotti, and beautiful hand-painted ceramic jars from Deruta, Italy, filled with a medley of individually wrapped biscuits and cookies.

If you visit the bakery, line up with the neighbors to buy loaves of fragrant, crusty pepper and herb breads, cracked wheat, and, of course, Italian bread. Bring along the coupon from the bakery's website, which reduces your cost to $4.60 for two large loaves of bread.

Residents of Niagara Falls don't know how fortunate they are to have four branches of a superlative hometown bakery, let alone an enterprise that is in its ninth decade.

ORDERING ADDRESS

Di Camillo Baking Company, Inc.
811 Linwood Avenue
Niagara Falls, NY 14305
716/282-2341
800/634-4363
FAX: 716/282-7236
e-mail: dicamillo@dicamillobakery.com
www.dicamillobakery.com
Credit cards accepted

VISITS: The bakery is in Niagara Falls' north end. From I-90 (New York State Thruway), take exit 50 (I-290) to I-190 North. Cross the Grand Island Bridges and exit at the Robert Moses Parkway. Take the Quay Street exit, and follow Quay Street to the end. Turn left onto Niagara Street, then right onto 3rd Street. Follow 3rd Street. It merges with Whirlpool Street. Turn right onto Linwood Avenue. Di Camillo Bakery is on the right. Every day, 7 A.M.–7 P.M.

There are other Di Camillo bakeries at: 7927 Niagara Falls Boulevard, Niagara Falls, NY, tel. 716/236-0111, daily 6 A.M.–10 P.M.; 1700 Pine Avenue, Niagara Falls, NY, tel. 716/284-8131, daily 7 A.M.–9 P.M.; 535 Center Street, Lewiston, NY, tel. 716/754-2218, daily 7 A.M.–9 P.M.

H & H BAGELS

Before overnight delivery became common, bagel-starved eaters who lived far from a decent bakery were out of luck. Judging from the number of requests we receive for a bagel bakery that ships, good bagels are second only to good corned beef and pastrami in the "wish I could get it" category. Well, go ahead. Move to What Cheer, Iowa, or Warsaw, South Carolina. H & H Bagel will find you.

This New York City bakery produces more than 200 million bagels a year, and a big chunk of those travel to wholesale and retail accounts around the globe. "We send to delis in Hawaii and delis in Amsterdam," said Helmer Toro, one of the partners in the family business. "We go to restaurants here in New York and restaurants around the country. We like to say if it is not from H & H Bagel, it is not a bagel."

H&H BAGELS

Like no other bagel in the world.

We wouldn't go that far. There are quite a few great bagel bakeries in northeastern cities, Chicago, and elsewhere, and buying them fresh and warm at the source is one of life's more satisfying shopping excursions. But few of them ship. And we don't know anyone else who has so refined the shipping details. H & H Bagel takes orders from 9 A.M. to 5 P.M., Eastern Standard Time, on weekdays and offers a toll-free number (800/NY BAGEL) to make it easy to order.

H & H makes its bagels the old-fashioned way, boiling them in water. Lately, some bakeries have been steaming bagels to improve the shelf life, but the result is not the same. The H & H method produces the definitive bagel, with a chewy crust and a dense interior. There is real flavor here. The most popular variety is plain, which says a lot for how well the bakery executes the basics. Next is cinnamon-raisin, then sesame and poppy varieties. Other possibilities are onion, salt, garlic, pumpernickel, whole wheat, blueberry, sourdough, and bagels with "everything" on them. Mini bagels and bialys (bagel-like buns baked with chopped onions) also are available. All are certified kosher. The bagels are thick and generous and arrive unsliced. If you plan to freeze them, the bakery suggests slicing them before returning them to their plastic bags. That way you won't be sawing through a frozen bagel so it can fit in the toaster.

We tried six of H & H's varieties and found them all terrific. The bakery doesn't stint on ingredients. The poppy and sesame bagels are heavily coated with seeds, instead of a perfunctory sprinkle, and the cinnamon-raisin has a good number of plump raisins.

H & H sends a minimum of 24 bagels, shipped overnight, for $45 within the continental United States. The bagels are packaged in units of 4, which allows you to choose up to six different varieties to make the minimum.

Add $15 for Alaska, Hawaii, and Puerto Rico delivery. Saturday delivery is an additional $10, and each additional dozen bagels is $10. (The bulk of the charge is shipping, so it makes sense to order in quantity; they freeze well.) H & H will ship worldwide, so call for prices to far-flung locations.

The company offers a gift package called A Taste of New York that includes 24 bagels, 2 H & H coffee mugs, 6 ounces of salmon, and 6 ounces of cream cheese, delivered overnight for $85.95.

Helmer Toro, age 50, who has been working in bakeries since shortly after he arrived here from his native Puerto Rico at the age of 9, began H & H bakery with a partner in 1972. When they began, customers used to lament that they couldn't get good bagels outside New York. When delivery services started guaranteeing next morning delivery, said Toro, H & H began shipping bagels.

Thank goodness.

ORDERING ADDRESS
H & H Bagel
639 West 46th Street
New York, NY 10036-1906
212/595-8000
800/692-2435
FAX: 212/765-7391
www.hhbagels.com
Credit cards accepted

VISITS: The original bakery is on the Upper West Side, next door to Zabar's, at 2239 Broadway, New York, NY 10024. The cross street is West 80th. A second retail location is at the company's main office, 639 West 46th Street. The cross street is 12th Avenue. The hours are the same at both stores—they never close.
Every day, 24 hours a day

KNODEL'S SHORTENING BREAD

In 1988, the University of Missouri published a catalog of farm-based food producers in the state. Titled "Best of Missouri Farms: A Taste of Rural Missouri," it had profiles and pictures and ordering instructions—sort of a statewide *Food Finds*. We thought it was a positive, tangible boost to the state's economy that could be successfully copied by other states. An updated edition featuring forty-one small food makers came out in 1989.

One of the companies we learned about by reading the catalog is not farm based, or even rural. But we are glad the editors included it. It is Knodel's Bakery and Catering in suburban St. Louis, a family-run business in operation since 1901 that makes, among many other good things, an authentic shortening bread. Other than hearing Daffy Duck sing about shortnin' bread, we really didn't know what it was before we ordered some. What arrived was a moist, crumbly, sweet corn bread that was buttery in flavor and golden in color. It had a finer texture than corn bread, almost like cake.

The ingredients are simple: milk, honey, eggs, flour, cornmeal, corn sugar, and butter. The recipe came after quite a bit of tinkering by Ned English, who owns the bakery with his wife, Marlene. (The Knodel name came from Marlene's side of the family. Her grandfather, who was Swiss, opened the bakery in its original downtown St. Louis location at the turn of the century.) Ned, a Missouri native, said he remembered his aunts and grandmother talking about shortening bread. "Long ago, they said when you were living high on the hog, you had shortening bread. It had shortening in it, and corn bread didn't." Ned's aunt, Maude Hudson of Tipton, Missouri, gave suggestions on ingredient proportions and tasted for authenticity. One reason Knodel's shortening bread stays moist is that the batter sits for a while before it is baked, allowing the cornmeal to soak up the honey and butter.

The bakery sends 1-pound loaves in special paperboard containers from Italy that can go from freezer to oven. The container does not get hot, even in a conventional oven. Each loaf is $2.50, and there is a minimum order of four loaves. Shipping costs are additional, so buyers should write or call before ordering to get the exact charges.

Another specialty of this full-service bakery is gingerbread houses. Amazingly, the Inglishes send these around the country, as far away as California. We ordered one, and it arrived miraculously intact. We were surprised, but the Inglishes weren't. "They're pretty durable things," said Ned.

The houses sit on a paper-covered cardboard base and are about 9 inches high from their piped icing base to the miniature plastic Santa and sleigh on the roof. There are gumdrops and peppermint candies on the roof, and red and green clear icing decorations. They cost an extremely reasonable $34, plus shipping—far less than we've seen them in fancy department store catalogs.

ORDERING ADDRESS
Knodel's Bakery and Catering
6621 West Florissant
Jennings, MO 63136
314/385-2000
FAX: 314/385-2001
e-mail: Knodels@aol.com
Credit cards accepted

VISITS: Same address. Jennings is in northern St. Louis. From I-70, take Jennings Station Road and go north to West Florissant Avenue. Turn right and drive 3 blocks, and look for the bakery on your left.
Monday–Saturday, 7 A.M.–7 P.M. Sunday, 9 A.M.–3 P.M.

ORRELL'S MARYLAND BEATEN BISCUITS

For a definitive history of the Maryland beaten biscuit, you need to study the career of Ruth Orrell, age 98, who lives in the town of Wye Mills in the eastern part of the state. For most of her adult life Mrs. Orrell baked the historic, dense biscuits. She has now turned the business over to her granddaughter Betsy Skinner, her daughter-in-law Margaret Orrell, and Ruth Orrell's son, Herman. They work in a special added-on kitchen in her home two days a week, turning out hundreds of dozens of biscuits for local stores and for shipment around the country.

A history of the hand-shaped biscuit, written and prepared by Herman Orrell, says they originated in southern Maryland and the Eastern Shore during plantation days. The idea of beating the dough to help it rise, however, could have come from an Indian method of beating corn.

At first, biscuit dough was beaten on stumps of hardwood trees, which were either left in the ground or mounted on legs and taken into the kitchen. The dough was beaten with a special ax used only for this purpose, either a blacksmith's hammer or a wooden mallet. Later, the dough was compressed in homemade rolling machines, which were little more than a roller mounted to a slab of wood or marble.

Mrs. Orrell used machines to beat her biscuit dough, but after exploring various ways to shape the biscuit by machine, she realized that nothing but human hands could give a satisfactory smooth surface on all sides. The round, nuggetlike biscuits are about 2 inches long and 1½ inches high. Their browned top is pricked so it doesn't blister and burn. When Mrs. Orrell began making biscuits, she used the tines of a fork for the job. But copying the tradition of long-ago cooks who had specially made picks fashioned with individual designs, the company's bakers now use a pick with an "0" and a cross on the top of each biscuit.

These are the perfect biscuits to sell in a supermarket or to ship, since they keep well. They are not eaten hot. They were a weekend bread, the biscuit history states, kept for Sundays and visitors.

Some say beaten biscuits are an acquired taste, but we don't think they take much introduction. They are heavy biscuits, made simply with lard, flour, water, salt, sugar, and baking powder. But the taste is unusual enough to warrant eating them plain. They are soft and doughy on the inside and hard on the outside. Many first-time eaters think the biscuits are stale, judging from the feel of the crust. But don't give up on them until they mold, the Orrells say.

"Under normal storage the biscuits become extremely hard but are still very much edible," the company tells purchasers. "In fact, some people desire them in this condition."

It is evident that stale is not a word to be used lightly at Orrell's. The instructions that come with the biscuits continue: "After becoming hard or what some consider stale, the biscuit can be ground for crumbs."

Above all, beaten biscuits are culinary history, and we recommend them to anyone who wants a distinctive bread and an authentic bit of America's past.

The company sells regular beaten biscuits and honey beaten biscuits, as well as trail biscuits, large, flat biscuits favored by hikers, for $3 per dozen. The company's other products are flat biscuits, about the size of a quarter, in plain, Cheddar, and cayenne pepper cheese flavors. Two dozen of the flat biscuits sell for $3.

There is a $1.50 handling fee, plus shipping costs, added to each order.

ORDERING ADDRESS
Orrell's Maryland Beaten Biscuits
Box 7
Wye Mills, MD 21679
410/827-6244
e-mail: b.skinner@iname.com
No credit cards

VISITS
14124 Old Wye Mills Road
Wye Mills, MD 21679
Wye Mills is on the east side of the Chesapeake Bay. Take the Bay Bridge east and follow Route 50 south. After you pass Kent Island, take Route 662 to Wye Mills. At the stoplight at Chesapeake College, turn right and drive until you come to Wye Oak's famous oak tree. The Orrell house is next door to Old Wye Parish.
Tuesday–Wednesday, 7 A.M.–until finished baking (Call in advance for more specific hours. Schedule changes, depending upon demand.)

PINAHS CRUNCHY BREAD CHIPS

Dorothy Austin, the now-retired food editor of the *Milwaukee Sentinel,* has observed the successful history of the Pinahs Bakery, a city landmark since 1917, for many years. She remembers the story she wrote 25 years ago about Marge and George Pinahs, the second generation to operate the company: "They were putting in fifty- and sixty-hour weeks, living above their bakery and raising two well-scrubbed sons. The boys came home from school every day for lunch, the only time the family could be together except for Sunday dinners. Yet they had a strong and unified family life." The two boys, Carl and Chris, took over the business in 1981, and as Austin noted, "are maintaining the family traditions of hard work, long hours, and good bread."

In 1998, Chris bought out his brother and became the sole owner.

The bakery is a sterling example of how a single product, if it is done extremely well, can make a business thrive. The product that has become synonymous with the Pinahs name (pronounced *pie*-nahs) in Milwaukee is rye chips—cooked circles of Vienna rye bread. Marge Pinahs created the chips as a way to use up old bread. Starting with her husband's Vienna Rye bread, she fried slices with a bit of garlic. Soon, her chips were outselling everything else in the bakery.

The key to the excellent flavor is excellent bread. The dark bread starts with a sponge dough that rises three times before it is baked. After the five-hour baking process, the bread is cooled, dried, sliced, cooked in soybean oil, and packed in cartons. No preservatives are used. The plain unsalted variety lets the good taste of quality rye bread shine through, but the varieties salted with garlic, sour cream, and jalapeño flavorings do not overwhelm the bread's flavor. The garlic chips are the largest seller. Crunchy, with slightly curled edges, the 2-inch-diameter chips are very good used as a base for hot cheese, with soup, or for appetizer dips. The company also makes sweet flavors, such as triple berry and cinnamon swirl, but all flavors are not available at all times. Check the website to see what flavors are currently available.

The Pinahses used to make a full line of baked goods, but in the 1960s began concentrating on supplying bread to bakery departments of supermarkets. Demand for the chips grew to the point that in 1965, the Pinahs closed their retail bakery and made only chips. They continued to bake their own bread for chips, but rye-loving Milwaukeans could no longer buy it by the loaf.

The company has expanded several times, but has never lost a day of production during its moves. The current plant, in the Milwaukee suburb of Waukesha, is 59,000 square feet.

A 7-ounce box of chips, any flavor, retails for about $1.69. If they are unavailable in your area, and the company cannot locate a convenient retail outlet, it will send them by UPS, with a 1-case (12-box) minimum order. The price of a case, delivered, ranges from $21 to $23, depending on your location. At the plant, a case is $18.

Traditionally, the chips have been sold only in Wisconsin, Michigan, and Illinois. Chris Pinahs is aiming toward more bulk distribution of the chips, but the recipe and time-consuming method will never change, the company promises.

ORDERING ADDRESS
Pinahs Company, Inc.
N8 W22100 Johnson Drive
Waukesha, WI 53186
262/547-2447
800/967-2447
FAX: 262/547-2047
www.pinahs.com
e-mail: info@pinahs.com
No credit cards

VISITS: From downtown Milwaukee, take I-894 west toward Madison. Take the exit marked Highway 18-JJ-Blue Mound and Barker Road. Drive straight on the exit alongside the interstate. The road becomes Highway 18. At the first light, take a right. Proceed to the first stop sign, and turn left onto Blue Mound Road. At the next light, turn right onto Springdale. At the bottom of a hill you will see the Beatrice cheese company. Johnson Drive is across the street, just before the bridge for the interstate. Pinahs is in the large white building on the right.
Monday–Friday, 8 A.M.–5 P.M. (No factory tours or retail store, but it is possible to buy cases of chips at the plant.)

VERMONT COMMON CRACKERS

If you ever wonder how distinctive a lowly cracker can be, try a Vermont Common Cracker, made at the Vermont Country Store. In 1980 the store rescued this historic Vermont cracker from culinary extinction. First made in 1828 and a mainstay in general stores, where they were dispensed from a barrel, the crackers now are available by mail in bags or in an unusual, five-color art nouveau tin. The machinery used to bake the crackers is nearly as antique as the recipe and operates at the North Clarendon, Vermont, location of the company's warehouse and bakery.

The crackers are made today much as they were when Civil War troops carried them to battle (to eat, not as weapons). Puffy and round, they taste yeasty, almost breadlike, with a faint aroma of potatoes. Potato flakes are in the dough, along with flour, water, vegetable shortening, salt, lecithin, yeast, and baking soda. A no-salt version is available, but the regular crackers are salted sparingly. They are easily split—aficionados like to butter and toast them under a broiler. Common crackers are excellent with pâté or Vermont Cheddar. They also fit neatly into small children's hands, making a good first cracker. A recipe booklet printed by the store suggests other possibilities, such as a hearty cracker pudding, cracker apple crisp, and scalloped oysters using cracker crumbs. Sixteen ounces of common crackers, bagged, sell for $4.50 by mail. In the tin, they are $11.95. Shipping charges are extra.

It's dangerous to change an original, but the company has succeeded in adding a logical new flavor with a common cheese cracker containing Vermont Cheddar. A wonderful bite-size snack cracker with a hint of cayenne pepper, it is proof that a cheese cracker does not need to be salty or horribly orange. The cheese crackers come in 18-ounce bags for $6.50, or in a green, yellow, and orange art nouveau tin for $12.95, both plus shipping.

It is worthwhile to request the store's catalog, as it includes an array of other authentic New England foods. The family-run business, begun by Vrest Orton in 1946 and continued by his son, Lyman, is known for seeking out high-quality foods and rediscovering old favorites like horehound drops, chocolate Wilbur Buds, and Horlicks Malted Milk. Expected favorites such as excellent Vermont Cheddar cheeses and maple syrups are available, but so are many more unusual items such as real jellied mint, tomato preserves, beach plum jam, and sweet mustard pickles.

ORDERING ADDRESS
The Vermont Country Store
Mail Order Office
P.O. Box 1108
Manchester Center, VT 05255-1108
802/362-8440
FAX: 802/362-0285
www.vermontcountrystore.com
Credit cards accepted

VISITS: **Two stores: the Rockingham, Vermont, store is on Route 103, nearly at the New Hampshire border, about 25 miles north of Brattleboro.**
Monday–Saturday, 9 A.M.–5 P.M. Sunday, 10 A.M.–5 P.M.

The Weston store is northwest of Rockingham, about 15 miles away on Route 100.
Monday–Saturday, 9 A.M.–5 P.M. Closed Sunday

Cakes & Cookies

AUSTRIAN OBLATEN

In this era of "light" and "lite" there exists a dessert that is such a featherweight that, as one writer put it, "it threatens to float right out of your hand." Oblaten (pronounced oh-*blah*-ten), made in Minneapolis from a 600-year-old recipe and a German baking machine, are wedge-shaped, crisp almond wafers that are stunning in their design. They are truly waferthin (try 1/16 inch!) and each 7-inch round has a design and "Original Carlsbad Oblaten" stamped on its face. The rounds are cut into wedges, making them easy to serve with iced desserts, fruit, or champagne.

The almond taste is fleeting. In fact, they are such airy wafers that it is difficult to convince yourself you've eaten something. But there are actually two paper-thin wafer layers pressed together with ground almonds, confectioners' sugar, unsalted butter, and vanilla.

The oblaten have been baked in the Twin Cities area since 1950, two years after company founders Frank and Josephine Ullman escaped to this country from Karlouy Uury, which was in Austria but is now in the Czech Republic. The couple brought with them the oblaten recipe and the special baking irons, which Josephine wore strapped to her back. Carlsbad was the home of oblaten, which explains why the design on the wafer includes a geyser, representative of the famous geyser discovered there in 1349 by Emperor Carl IV. (The name Carlsbad translates to "Carl's Bath.")

The couple kept the business here small, using seven hand-operated baking irons, until the early 1970s. Frank Ullman sold the business unsuccessfully two times before he offered it to his neighbor, Marie Kennedy, in 1973. Kennedy bought the company with her mother, Dorothy Sisco, and later fulfilled Frank Ullman's dream of buying an automated oblaten baking machine.

A dozen years ago, the company updated its packaging with awardwinning graphics, and has seen its distribution soar. "People love it. It's a product you can't stop eating," said Marie. "It's so agreeable, and so good with lots of things." She introduced lemon-flavored oblaten and a version dipped in dark chocolate. The newest flavors of the wafers are chocolate and cinnamon.

The fan-wafer oblatens are tailor-made to accompany specialty coffees and teas, or to serve on the side with ice cream or sherbet. We have seen them on cheese trays and served with after-dinner liqueurs.

The company will send its original-flavor oblaten in two sizes of beautiful tins. The 6.75-ounce tin holds 48 wedges and is $8.95. The 13.5-ounce tin holds 90 wedges and is $13.95 Prices do not include shipping costs. We were amazed that the oblaten arrived perfectly intact when mailed.

The company now bakes biscotti in several flavors, and has changed its name to Award Baking International to reflect the fact that it produces more than oblaten. It is possible to order both oblaten and biscotti from its website.

ORDERING ADDRESS
Award Baking International
1101 Stinson Boulevard, N.E.
Minneapolis, MN 55413
612/331-3523
800/333-3523
FAX: 612/331-1685
www.oblaten.com
e-mail: awardbaking@oblaten.com
Credit cards accepted

VISITS: **The building is at the corner of 35W North and Stinson Boulevard in northeast Minneapolis. It is about 6 minutes from the Metrodome on 35W North.**
Monday–Friday, 9 A.M.–5 P.M. Saturday (September-December only), 9 A.M.–5 P.M.

CAFE BEAUJOLAIS PANFORTE DI MENDOCINO

Cafe Beaujolais, in Mendocino, on northern California's rugged coast, serves such wonderful food that the mere mention of the name makes us hungry for California. Margaret S. Fox, who founded the restaurant, and her husband, executive chef Christopher Kump, are well known in food circles. The restaurant, which first earned a reputation for its artful breakfasts, now is open only for dinner. But it has expanded the quality foods it will send by mail.

The original mail-order product is an Italian fruitcake, or panforte, which is made at the restaurant. Margaret named the round cake Panforte di Mendocino, since it is more a California or American-style cake than an Italian version. For one thing, it is not as dry, nor is it meant for dunking in coffee. It's a luscious, rich, moist, and chewy cake meant for serving in thin wedges with espresso, tea, dessert wines, or brandy.

There are two varieties: almond (the original), and hazelnut. Both are sold in 22-ounce wheels ($24.95) or 11-ounce quarters ($12) that are wrapped in colored cellophane—a classy touch. Inside, the wheels are quite lovely, dusted with confectioners' sugar, which makes a nice contrast to the dark cake. It is a dense, not overly sweet cake with nuts, candied citrus peel, a small bit of flour, sugar, honey, butter, and spices.

Margaret prefers to call the panforte (pronounced pan-*fort*-ay) a confection rather than a fruitcake. The bakery also produces a true fruitcake, "with no candied anything and nothing that's a weird color," she said. Her fruitcake, which is wrapped in a brandy-soaked cheesecloth and covered with colored cellophane, contains 20 ingredients, including such unexpected ones as blackberry jam, molasses, papaya, and apricots. It is a switch from the usual taste as well. A 1-pound rectangular loaf sells for $18.95. A chocolate fruitcake, flavored with Ghiradelli's bittersweet chocolate, is $20.75.

The panforte can be sent year-round. In the spring and fall the cafe sends out enticing mail-order catalogs that feature well-edited food selections, such as a pear barbecue sauce (two 1-pound jars for $19.50) made with pears from Chris and Margaret's orchard. Other treats include apricot and vanilla bean compote (two 1-pound jars for $22.75) and a wild blackberry jam (a 1-pound jar for $13.25) made from berries brought to the cafe by local berry pickers. Prices do not include delivery charges.

Chocolate almond toffee, chocolate-covered graham crackers, the cashew granola that was a mainstay of the restaurant's breakfast business, spicy gingersnaps, and a hot chocolate mix are other foods available from the cafe's catalog. This is also the place to find the three Cafe Beaujolais cookbooks. We've had the first one for years, and it has been well used. The second book, written by Margaret, focuses on morning food, and the third, written by Chris, is on evening food. They are $21.25 each.

ORDERING ADDRESS
Cafe Beaujolais Bakery
Box 730
Mendocino, CA 95460
707/937-0443
800/930-0443 (outside California)
FAX: 707/937-3656
www.cafebeaujolais.com
e-mail: cafebeau@mcn.org
Credit cards accepted

VISITS
961 Ukiah Street
Mendocino, CA 95460
Mendocino is a 150-mile trip from San Francisco, but winding roads make the trip take 3 ½ hours. From the San Francisco Bay Area, take Highway 101 north to Highway 128, just north of Cloverdale. Turn left (west) onto 128 and drive along this winding road to Highway 1. Continue north about 6 miles to Mendocino. Make a left into Mendocino at the Jackson Street-Business District turnoff, then take the first right (Evergreen) and then the first left (Ukiah). Cafe Beaujolais is the big yellow house near the corner on the south side of the street.
Every day, 11 A.M.–3 P.M.

THE CHARLESTON CAKE LADY

Whenever we got discouraged or overwhelmed while doing this book, we got ourselves back on track by thinking about the Charleston Cake Lady. Teresa Pregnall of Charleston began baking cakes to commemorate her colleagues' birthdays at the College of Charleston. During the first energy crisis of the 1970s, her reasoning was: why turn on the oven just to make one cake? So she would make two and take one to work. In 1983, her husband, William, built her a small commercial kitchen in what had been their carport. She and her husband were having fun, baking together in their leisure time and selling about eight cakes a week.

When *Food Finds* came out in 1984, she read the entry about Marge Murray in Oklahoma, who makes homemade pound cakes. So she sent us one of her Low Country Poppyseed Pound Cakes. (The area along the South Carolina coast is known as the Low Country because of the high water table.) We were instantly smitten. A few months later we described her cake in an article for the *Washington Post* about mail-order holiday treats, and the resulting flood of more than three hundred orders swamped Teresa and her son Wally, and made it a Christmas to remember. The next year Marian Burros of the *New York Times* included the Charleston Cake Lady in her list of by-mail Christmas goodies, and the Pregnalls were again up to their ears in orders.

After a few years of building up her business, Teresa received another unexpected honor. A national publisher wanted her to write a cookbook. Beset by doubts that she could do such a thing, Teresa created a charming, personal cookbook that is a joy to read and a delight to use. *Treasured Recipes from the Charleston Cake Lady* (Hearst Books, 1996) is a petite, pretty book, and one that preserves the author's distinctive voice. As *Southern Lady* magazine enthused, "Writing like she's talking to a friend, Teresa makes you feel comfortable as she introduces each recipe in her book—you can almost hear her rich Charleston accent."

Several of the recipes are of cakes she bakes and sells—a generous sharing of recipes that's quite remarkable. Even though we can make some of her cakes in our home kitchens, we—and hundreds of her customers—still prefer to eat the ones Teresa bakes. She sends personal notes, gift-wraps the cakes, and makes sure they arrive on schedule for special occasions. "Being able to maintain the personal touch is the most rewarding 'business' aspect of my lifelong hobby," she says.

In addition to a traditional Charleston Pound Cake and a German Chocolate Pound Cake, she offers an Eggnog Cake, a Sherry Nut Cake, three chocolate cakes, a Lemon and Cream Cheese and Mandarin Orange Victoria Cake, and a cake fashioned after a Toll House cookie.

The Charleston Cake Lady's cakes are baked in tube pans, and the large cakes weigh from 2½ to 4½ pounds. Most serve 12 generously. It is eminently possible to pass them off as your own homemade cakes, but we wouldn't suggest it, unless you want to deal with guests clamoring for the recipe.

All prices include regular UPS shipping costs. Teresa recommends that customers on the West Coast order their cakes using UPS second-day air service, at an additional cost.

"I've made so many, many friends around this country while sending the cakes," said Teresa, "and I can speak very highly of the American public." She, like many of the small entrepreneurs we interviewed, sometimes sends her product before payment is received. "I deal on trust, and I've had very, very few people not pay me," she said.

ORDERING ADDRESS
The Charleston Cake Lady
774 Woodward Road
Charleston, SC 29407
803/766-7173
800/488-0830
No credit cards
Visits by appointment only.

CONCORD TEACAKES, ENGLISH SCONES, AND EMILY DICKINSON'S RAISIN BRANDYCAKE

Ten years ago, Judy Fersch of Concord, Massachusetts, was given the recipe by friend Joel Porte, chairman of the English Department at Harvard, and she used it to produce what she calls a raisin brandycake. We like the description given it by Nancy Zerbey, writing in *Boston* magazine in 1987: "Resembling nothing so much as damp black brick . . . Fersch's brandy-and-raisin spice cake rises or falls on its taste alone."

The taste is raisinlike and rich with spices. There is an undercurrent of brandy, but it is just enough. This is a cake that can be enjoyed year-round, although many will find it especially welcome at holiday time, when it can serve as an alternative to fruitcake.

Fersch ages the cake before it is sold, and notes that it will keep well unrefrigerated for at least six months. A 12-ounce loaf, which will provide a dozen compact slices measuring less than 2 by 3 inches, is $12. It comes beautifully packaged in a small red box and makes a cheerful gift.

Most buyers are over the age of 40, notes Fersch. "Younger people don't have mincemeat memory and don't have raisin memory." For those deprived souls, she bakes other cakes. There's an almond-lemon cake, with ground almond and bits of citrus rind, in an 8-inch Bundt pan that she sends for $16, plus shipping. A chocolate cake with a semisweet chocolate glaze is the same price, as is a moist, dark gingerbread.

Fersch's signature product is a traditional English scone, offered in three varieties: plain, cinnamon, and currant. They are superlative and have become her biggest selling item. "Scones are everyday things, and people become addicted to them," she explains.

These scones are large, hand-formed oblongs about 2 inches high and 3 inches long. Golden in color, they are a sweet and buttery tidbit that is halfway between cake and biscuit. They are so tasty we can understand why people make regular treks to the company's store. A dozen scones are $19.50, plus second-day air shipping.

"People don't say our scones are like mother used to make," Fersch observed. "They say they are like grandmother used to make. Basically, that's what our business is. Bringing back memories."

ORDERING ADDRESS

Concord Teacakes Etcetera, Inc.
P.O. Box 1427
Concord, MA 01742
978/369-7644
www.concordteacakes.com
Credit cards accepted
Items are shipped from October to July only.

VISITS

59 Commonwealth Avenue
Concord, MA 01742
The shop is in West Concord. From Route 2 West, bear left on Route 62. Follow for seven-tenths of a mile. Bear right at the 99 Restaurant. The shop is at the end of the first block on the left-hand side. Look for the green-and-white awnings.

Monday–Friday, 6 A.M.–6 P.M. Saturday, 7 A.M.–5 P.M. Sunday, 7 A.M.–1 P.M.

CRANE'S FRUIT PIES

Of all the misleading descriptions found on restaurant menus, "homemade" pies is undoubtedly the most common. At roadside stands, the term most worthy of suspicion is "homegrown."

But at Crane Orchards, in western Michigan's rolling farm country, both words are used accurately. The family orchard yields a wealth of fruit from its 280 acres—sweet and sour cherries, blueberries, raspberries, peaches, Barlett and Bosc pears, and eight varieties of apples—and the Cranes sell truly homemade pies, dumplings, and tarts made from the fruits of their harvest. "If we don't raise it, we don't sell it," says Lue Crane, a youthful-looking grandmother who is uncharacteristically slim for a pie eater. She and a crew of seven local women make the pies in a large second-story kitchen in what once was the haymow of the farm's 1879 barn. Below them is a cold storage room where fresh fruit awaits customers and a restaurant where cider and pie by the slice are sold, along with light lunches, all made from scratch. There is cider in the batter for the fresh doughnuts, and the Cranes go as far as making homemade yeast buns for the sloppy joes and homemade bread for the sandwiches.

Although the remodeled barn has unabashed appeal to tourists, with old magazine advertisements on the wall and antiques at every turn, this is no ersatz "attraction." First and foremost it is a working farm, with all the ups and downs that implies. The restaurant, pie baking, and a "U-Pick" fruit operation all have been added in the last 20 years to counteract the declining fortunes of apple growers in the area. "You just can't run an orchard anymore without some sideline," says Lue.

Bob and Lue Crane have deep roots in the Fennville, Michigan, areas. Bob's grandmother was born here in 1862, and his family has owned farmland in the area since shortly thereafter. Now their five children, a daughter-in-law, and a son-in-law work with them at the orchard. In the kitchen, a high chair and crib stand ready for visiting grandchildren. "It's a family business even with the employees who aren't family," comments Lue. "I've been Aunt Lue to all the girls who have worked here."

During the fall apple harvest, the restaurant is mobbed, and visitors can wait up to two hours to sit down. But the orchard stays open year-round, and at other times the pace is not as hectic. The barn (which actually is two barns pushed together long ago) is an eminently cozy place to get acquainted with some of the best pie you'll ever taste. We were there during peach season, and the warm fresh peach pie was as aromatic and flavorful as it comes.

The pies are made several times a week. Each is heaped with fruit and weighs in at about 3 pounds. The crusts are rolled, crimped, and vented by hand, and the cherry pies even boast a hand-done lattice top. No preservatives, colorings, or artificial flavorings are used.

The apple pie is blue-ribbon material. The apples are sliced by hand (peeling is done by a machine, the only concession to mechanization) and retain a hint of crispness after baking. Tart Ida Red apples, a variety akin to Jonathan, are primarily used, resulting in a pie that resonates with apple flavor, not cinnamon.

Whole pies (apple, cherry, peach, and blueberry) are available frozen for $8.75, and frozen rhubarb tarts and apple dumplings (whole apples encased in pastry) sell for $2 each. Also available frozen is an excellent apple crisp and a cherry crisp, fragrant with spices and topped with sugar and rolled oats.

The pastries are not available by mail. So if you visit, buy in bulk. Nothing will make you more prepared for entertaining challenges than to have a row of Crane Pie Pantry pies stored on your freezer shelf.

ORDERING ADDRESS
Crane's Pie Pantry Restaurant
6054 124th Avenue
Fennville, MI 49408
616/561-2297
Credit cards accepted

VISITS: From I-196 in southwestern Michigan, take the Fennville exit (Highway 89) east. The orchard is 4 ½ miles east of the interstate on the right side. Look for the sign.

May–November: Monday–Saturday, 9 A.M.–7 P.M. Sunday, 11 A.M.–7 P.M.
November 1–April 30: Saturday–Sunday, 11 A.M.–7 P.M.

DANISH KRINGLE FROM RACINE

Philadelphia and pretzels. New Orleans and beignets. San Francisco and crab cocktails. Today's quiz question is: What is the famous food linked with Racine, Wisconsin? The answer (needed only for those who haven't been to Racine, where you are distracted by more than a dozen bakeries selling it) is kringle, a flat Danish pastry that resembles an oval racetrack.

Originally, kringle was made with a breadlike dough and shaped like a pretzel with an almond paste filling. Over the years, however, the Danes who immigrated to Racine added pecans, used a thin, almost filo-like dough, and flattened out the shape to an oval.

An endearing treat, it is the sort of pastry one would rarely attempt at home, welcome as a breakfast sweet or a dessert. The pecan kringle, with its thin wash of confectioners' sugar frosting, is the most popular, but Racine's bakeries never end their attempts to create new varieties. Some, like chocolate chip and chocolate turtle, are a bit jarring, especially when contemplated for breakfast. The fruit and nut versions are more successful.

Kringle ships extremely well because it is so flat—a mere 5/8 inch thick. It freezes beautifully, taking up little vertical space, which makes it an ideal food to order. Two Racine bakeries that do a brisk business shipping kringle are Lehmann's Bakery and O & H Danish Bakery (addresses follow). We've ordered from both with great success. The bakeries each began business about 50 years ago.

At O & H, the founding family—the Olesens—is still at the helm. They offer 14 kringle flavors and will also send their traditional pumpernickel bread, essential for Danish open-face sandwiches, upon request. We are indebted to Joseph Petreye of Prescott, Arizona, who grew up in Racine, who sent us the O & H brochure and his native-son endorsement of its kringles. "They are superb!"

Eric, Dale, and Mike Olesen and their parents, Ray and Myrna, make the most kringle of any of Racine's bakeries, shipping more than sixty thousand each Christmas season. As Eric wrote us: "My family prides itself on the quality of our bakery. Our customers confirm that by ordering time and time again." He explained that their pastry making is a three-day process, involving many layers of Wisconsin butter and fruit fillings that are made by O & H.

O & H prefers to send its kringle on Monday and Tuesday and sends orders via UPS second-day air. Cream cheese or chocolate-filled kringle are shipped from October through April only.

One kringle sent regular UPS is $17. It's cheaper to order in multiples (and the box still won't be very thick!). Two are $23.50, 3 are $30.00, and 4 are $36.50. The bakery also offers a kringle-of-the-month club.

Lehmann's Bakery was founded in 1950. The current owner, Charlie Palmer-Ball, makes a staggering 33 varieties of kringle, including such unusual fillings as almond-macaroon, cranberry-walnut, pineapple-pecan, blueberry cheese, maple-walnut, and chocolate chip. We tried almond-macaroon, cherry cheese, and a chocolate "turtle" kringle and began thinking about kringle as a dessert rather than a breakfast item. These special flavors are an additional $2 per kringle. Lehmann's has the more familiar flavors, such as almond, apricot, date, pecan, prune, raspberry, and walnut, and it is these flavors that actually ship best. For several years Lehmann's has been supplying the Neiman-Marcus mail-order service with kringle, further spreading the word about this regional treat.

Lehmann's will send a very pretty maple wood kringle platter with a kringle for $39.95. It makes an excellent housewarming gift or wedding present. The bakery also has a kringle-of-the-month plan, as well as strudel, coffeecake, and stollen by mail. Cheesecakes and kringle with cheese fillings are sent October through April only. One kringle with a traditional filling is $14.95, 2 are $21.95, and 3 are $27.95. All prices include shipping costs.

Thinly sliced and warmed, kringle is a superior alternative to the dull doughnuts and doughy Danishes that are standbys of so many meetings. A single kringle will yield twelve 2-inch slices. We've pulled them out of the freezer for church fellowship hour, for evening club meetings, for school parties, and for an afternoon open house—to appreciative audiences all.

ORDERING ADDRESS
O & H Danish Bakery
1841 Douglas Avenue
Racine, WI 53402
262/637-8895
800/227-6665
FAX: 262/637-4215
www.ohdanishbakery.com
e-mail: ohdanishe@mail:wi.net
Credit cards accepted

VISITING ADDRESS: **Same address, and a branch at 4006 Durand Avenue. Racine is on Lake Michigan, in southeastern Wisconsin, about 30 miles north of Chicago. To visit the main bakery on Douglas Avenue, take I-94 to Highway 20 (Washington Avenue) and go east to Highway 31. Go north on 31 to Highway MM. Stay on MM until it runs into Highway 38. Go east one block and take a left on Rapids Drive. Take Rapids Drive to Douglas Avenue, then turn left and look for the sign with the Viking ship.**
Monday–Friday, 5:30 A.M.–6 P.M. Saturday, 5 A.M.–5 P.M.

Lehmann's Bakery
2210 Sixteenth Street
Racine, WI 53405
262/632-4636
800/607-8721
FAX: 800/232-6315
www.lehmanns.com
Credit cards accepted
From I-94, go to Highway 20 (Washington Avenue) east to Highway 31. Turn right on Highway 31 and go to Sixteenth Street, where you will turn left. Lehmann's is at the corner of Taylor and Sixteenth Street.
Monday–Friday. 5:30 A.M.–6 P.M. Saturday, 5:30 A.M.–5:30 P.M.

DINKEL'S STOLLEN

If you're the type of holiday eater who automatically avoids stollen because of all the cavity-jarring candied fruit, the Dinkel family will convert you. Its rich, yeasty bread is a delight, the only fruits used being raisins and pineapple, neither in unnatural colors.

From the minute you unfold its gold foil wrapping you know this stollen is going to be different. Lightly dusted with confectioners' sugar, it's a satisfying moist cake with an abundance of nuts. The bakery triple-wraps its stollens, and the slight amount of rum and brandy added allow the loaf to stay fresh for at least two weeks. Its bakers even include directions on how best to slice it, to minimize crumbs.

Dinkel's, a German bakery in Chicago's Lake View neighborhood, north of downtown, was founded in 1922 by Joseph K. Dinkel. His son, Norman, ostensibly is retired from the business, but he continues to tinker with recipes, coming up with new products or variations on old ones. The Old World recipes for the bakery's longtime favorites—its stollen, strudels, tea breads, fruitcake, and fudge brownies—remain the same, however, with no preservatives.

The firm's current president, Norman Dinkel, Jr., now makes all of the aforementioned items, as well as several cookies, kuchen, and cakes available by mail. One item rarely seen elsewhere is Bavarian cheese tarts. They have lattice tops, and are filled with cream cheese and fruit toppings. Cherry-, apple-, or raspberry-apricot cheese tarts are $21.95 for a 1½-pound size.

But should you be in Chicago, it's infinitely more fun to stop in this neighborhood shop, buy a cup of coffee, and browse among the overflowing bins and cases. It's rare to find a neighborhood bakery carrying such a complete range of goods, and Norman Junior notes that full-line bakeries such as theirs are a dying breed. "It's far easier to specialize," he says.

The 2-pound confectioners' sugar stollen is $19.95, and arrives in excellent condition, always fresh. Prices do not include shipping charges.

ORDERING ADDRESS
Dinkel's Bakery
3329 North Lincoln Avenue
Chicago, IL 60657
773/281-7300
800/822-8817
FAX: 773/281-6169
www.dinkels.com
e-mail: norm@dinkels.com
Credit cards accepted

VISITS: Dinkel's is 10 minutes north of the downtown Loop. Driving north on Lakeshore Drive, take the Belmont exit and go west to Lincoln. Immediately past Ashland, turn right on Lincoln. You'll see the vertical neon "Dinkel's" sign on your right.

Monday–Friday, 6 a.m.–7 p.m. Saturday, 6 a.m.–6 p.m. Sunday, 9 a.m.–5 p.m.

ELI'S CHICAGO'S FINEST CHEESECAKES

Eli's gets our vote for the most careful packager. Its cheesecakes come in a thick cardboard box that holds a reusable foam cooler (personalized with "Eli's" on it) inside. Open the cooler and the individual cheesecakes are packed inside smaller corrugated boxes. The cheesecake itself is shrink-wrapped for freshness and kept frozen with dry ice. Tall cardboard collars protect the piped rosettes and decorations. Each cheesecake is presliced, with paper dividers between each slice. All this devoted attention is worth it. Eli's cheesecakes can travel hundreds of miles and arrive picture-perfect. Since they are presliced, they'll stay in top condition as they are served. Just thaw in the refrigerator overnight or at room temperature for three hours.

Eli's Chicago's Finest is one of a growing number of companies taking restaurant specialties and developing them into mail-order and grocery items. While some restaurants simply license their name and recipe to another firm, Eli's has stayed in the family. Marc Schulman, the son of restaurateur Eli Schulman, who developed the cheesecake more than 20 years ago, now runs both the cheesecake bakery and the restaurant that started it all, Eli's the Place for Steak.

Marc says his father was obsessed with creating a creamy cheesecake with a nicely browned top crust. He succeeded admirably. The ingredient list is simply cream cheese, sour cream, sugar, whole eggs, real vanilla, and a little flour. The thin cookie crust is flour, butter, sugar, and egg whites.

Since the Schulmans started baking their cheesecakes for consumption outside the restaurant 18 years ago, their popularity has soared. They are traditionally one of the largest sellers at the city's huge Taste of Chicago summer festival and are now found on the menu at dozens of Chicago restaurants. Of the thousands of cheesecakes baked daily at Eli's bakery, half go to Chicago restaurants and hotels. The rest are shipped out to gourmet shops, supermarket delis, and restaurants in other parts of the country.

If you can't find Eli's cheesecake in your area, the company will send them. The hardest part about ordering is deciding what flavor to select. Eli's has several categories of flavors—original favorites, Eli's dream team, candy crazy, cravings, and sensational seasonals. You can choose from the plain original for $25, plus shipping, or a one-of-a-kind cheesecake like brown cow—a chocolate cheesecake with spots of chocolate chip cheesecake for $43, plus shipping. Some offerings take cheesecake in new directions, such as the chocolate banana fusion, banana cheesecake layered with chocolate ganache, chocolate mousse, and banana mousse.

We sampled the twilight chocolate macadamia cheesecake, which had the following layers: a chocolate walnut cookie crust, chocolate cheesecake with chunks of white chocolate and roasted macadamia nuts, white chocolate mousse frosting, more macadamia nuts, and a drizzle of dark chocolate on top. Definitely party fare!

The company's website pictures all of its offerings, including noncheesecake treats such as tiramisù. It also has a 12-page color catalog.

It is one of life's contradictions that in this health-conscious age, sales of rich desserts and chocolates have never been better. To accommodate the interest in cheesecake, the company has opened Eli's Cheesecake World Café and Retail Store. Visitors can buy cheesecake, take tours (call ahead), and partake in special activities such as dessert-decorating demonstrations and seasonal promotions. The store is about 15 minutes from O'Hare International Airport.

ORDERING ADDRESS
The Eli's Cheesecake Company
6701 W. Forest Preserve Drive
Chicago, IL 60634-1470
773/736-3417
800/999-8300
FAX: 773/736-1169
www.elicheesecake.com
Credit cards accepted

VISITS: **The company, café, and retail store are located at the corner of Montrose and Forest Preserve Drive. From I-90 take the Montrose exit and go west. For information on its five different tour packages, call the tour coordinator at 773/736-3417.**

Monday–Friday, 8 a.m.–6 p.m. Saturday, 9 a.m.–5 p.m. Sunday, 11 a.m.–5 p.m.

ERICANN CANDY COMPANY COOKIES

Ericann Candy Company started as a seasonal operation during the Christmas holiday. The late Erich Hamburger, who lived in Grand Beach, Michigan, in the extreme southwestern part of the state, and learned baking and confectionery trades in Germany and Switzerland, would set up a kitchen every winter to make European treats.

He made lebkuchen, a rich German Christmas cookie with almonds, dried fruits, and spices; butter cookies; and a stollen (coffee cake) studded with almonds, pecans, and cashews. His one-of-a-kind desserts included marzipan or praline loaves, covered, respectively, with bittersweet and milk chocolate. His most incredible treat was chocolate leaf cookies, a confection so delicate that they were shipped with the caveat that he couldn't be responsible for breakage. We would order them even if they came as a pile of chips, but in five years of leaf-cookie orders, we've never had more than a few broken cookies in each tin.

The thin cookies are about 5 inches long and shaped like an oak leaf. They have an intense almond flavor, with the taste of the superlative bittersweet chocolate that covers the top and sides. They are unlike any cookie we've ever had.

Before he died, Hamburger passed his business secrets along to the brother and sister who ran the Ramberg Bakery in nearby Union Pier. Linda Stone and Chuck Stone had worked for Hamburger years ago during one of his holiday baking efforts. "We knew exactly what we were getting into and knew what was involved," said Linda. Since they live in a resort area, the winter months were always slow for the bakery. Having a mail-order holiday business was a perfect fit, she said.

Three years ago, Chuck bought his sister out and now is the sole owner of the candy company. His product line is much the same as Erich's was. He has extended the time the lebkuchen and chocolate leaf cookies are available, which is a positive change. This year, they were made until May 15.

Lebkuchen are available in 1-pound tins, either glazed and chocolate-dipped or plain. A mixed tin is $11, and an all-chocolate tin is $1 more.

Chocolate leaf cookies also come in a 1-pound tin for $13. Shipping costs are extra.

We smile at the thought of an Old World skill successfully being passed down from one generation to the next, and consider ourselves lucky that Chuck Stone is keeping this unique tradition going.

ORDERING ADDRESS
Ericann Candy Company
P.O. Box 225
Union Pier, M1 49129
616/469-1010
FAX: 616/469-0560
Credit cards accepted

VISITS: The bakery is located at 9811 Townline Road in Union Pier, a small town just over the Indiana border on Lake Michigan From I-94, take exit 7 for Union Pier and go downtown. Townline Road is the community's main street.

Tuesday–Thursday, 7 A.M.–2 P.M. Friday–Sunday, 7 A.M.–5 P.M.

FRALINGER'S MACAROONS AND CHOCOLATE PADDLES

Our favorite Fralinger's ad shows winged boxes flying around the world under the slogan: "Fralinger's taffies bound . . . the world around." It certainly is our simplistic version of world happiness, with everyone contentedly chewing a Fralinger's molasses taffy paddle. For us, these dark chocolate confections, and the incomparable golden macaroons also created by the Fralinger family, represent "vacation food nostalgia."

Almost every summer we'd visit what had then become unfashionable Atlantic City. We'd disregard everything but the magic boardwalk and our special stores: the Mr. Peanut Shop and Fralinger's, original home of the "pure cream chewing candy," as taffy was first billed. Years later you expect your memory to have played tricks on you, that the paddles and macaroons won't be as special as they were when you watched the diving horse or the lights on the Steel Pier. With hearts full of gratitude for Frank Glaser, president of the 115-year-old firm, we can report that they are being made as exquisitely as ever.

Everything about the paddles is special, from their Maxfield Parrish-esque box, featuring an Atlantic City sunset, to their ability to freeze well in case you're exceptionally disciplined and can save some. The molasses taffy base is never so sticky that it clings to the roof of your mouth (unlike a much-publicized imitator), and the bittersweet chocolate is so thick that it breaks off in chunks.

As is common with America's best-made foods, the price is a bargain. They are shipped by the dozen at $11.99, plus the 2-pound UPS rate.

The soft, beautifully baked almond macaroons have distinctive crackled crusts and are packed in individual bags. Their pristine condition, even when shipped, puts lie to the belief that bakery products must have stabilizers and preservatives in order to travel. Because of the fragility of the almond paste and the large number of egg whites used, Fralinger's mails the cookies out only hours after they're baked. They are packaged in their original maroon art deco box and sold in 1- or 2-dozen versions. Each cookie is 3 inches in diameter. The 1-dozen box costs $8.75, plus a 2-pound UPS rate. Two dozen cookies are $16.25, plus shipping.

And, in some very welcome news, Fralinger's now offers huge, soft coconut macaroons. They are packed in the same box, at the same price, as the almond macaroons.

ORDERING ADDRESS
Fralinger's Inc.
1325 Boardwalk
Atlantic City, NJ 08401-7287
609/345-2177
800/93-TAFFY (938-2339)
FAX: 609/345-3343
www.fralingers.com
e-mail: salesf@fralingers.com
Credit cards accepted

VISITS: There are two Fralinger's stores on the boardwalk: at 1325 (Tennessee Avenue) and at Bally's Park Place. There also is a store on the Ocean City, New Jersey, boardwalk, at 1100 Boardwalk (609/399-2202), and a store in the Victorian town of Cape May, New Jersey, on the Washington Street Mall at Jackson Avenue (609/884-5695). Both the Ocean City and Cape May stores have their own souvenir boxes.
Every day, Year-round except Thanksgiving and Christmas (Evening hours in summer) 9 A.M.–5 P.M.

GETHSEMANI MONKS FRUITCAKE, CHEESE, AND FUDGE

We say if you're going to eat a fruitcake, then make it the real thing. And if you want the real thing, with ample dark cake, cherries, raisins, pineapple, dates, quality nuts and redolent with bourbon, you should seek out the fruitcakes that have been made by the Trappist monks at Gethsemani Farms in central Kentucky for 35 years.

The oldest of the Trappist Cistercian monasteries in the United States, Gethsemani Farms sells fruitcake, a distinctive semisoft cheese, and bourbon fudge. All products are available all year long by mail.

Given their location, it is no surprise that Kentucky bourbon is used to flavor both their moist fruitcake and the butter walnut or chocolate fudge. In the past year the monastery has adopted new labels and packaging, and all of its foods are in beautifully rendered boxes and tins. Cheese wedges can be purchased in handmade round yellow poplar boxes that have been created for more than 30 years by Brother Julian Wallace.

The monastery's cheese, semisoft and creamy with an assertive flavor similar to that of a good brick or Port Salut, is made from a formula that goes back several centuries to Trappist monasteries in Europe. It is available in mild, aged, smoky, or basil pesto varieties.

Prices are extremely reasonable. A 2½-pound fruitcake is $24, postpaid. A 20-ounce mini fruitcake packed together with 12 ounces of mild cheese is $20, postage included. A 16-ounce gift box of either the chocolate bourbon fudge or the butter walnut bourbon fudge is $12, postpaid.

Two years ago, the monastery celebrated its 150th year in America. An illustrated gift book was produced to mark the milestone, *The Abbey of Gethsemani: Place of Peace and Paradox.* It is available for $35 postpaid.

ORDERING ADDRESS

Gethsemani Farms
3642 Monks Road
Trappist, KY 40051-6102
800/549-0912
www.monks.org
e-mail: brjoshua@bardstown.com
Credit cards accepted

VISITS: From Bardstown, take Highway 31E south about 7 miles to Highway 247 at Smith's Corners. Turn east (left) onto Highway 247, which goes directly to the monastery in about 3½ miles. There are no tours of the monastery, nor is food available for sale there, but visitors may attend services in the monastery church.

There usually are 7 services, varying in length, throughout the day, with the longer services at 5:45 A.M. and 5:30 P.M.

HELEN'S BLUEBERRY CREAM PIE

The best things in America's cuisine are simple—like Maine's wild low-bush blueberries and real whipped cream. Larry and Helen Mugnai made this combination famous in Machias, Maine, and rightfully so. The restaurant they founded, now run by David Barker and Judy Hanscom, specializes in an uncooked blueberry pie.

The restaurant's pies begin with a baked crust and whole blueberries. A hot blueberry gel is added and the fruit is topped with whipped cream. By 9 A.M., the pies are ready to be eaten.

The Mugnais, who have since passed away, had no idea their venture would be successful when they arrived in Machias from Bridgeport, Connecticut, in 1950 to help Mugnai's ailing father with his grocery store. The son added a soft-custard stand to the grocery, then knocked out a wall for a hot dog counter, and before long the couple was baking pies and running a restaurant.

"My wife would take a trip back to Connecticut and I would build on while she was gone," related Mugnai, who worked for a commercial bakery earlier in his career. "Finally, she said, 'Larry, the next time you build on, I'm going to leave you.' So I stopped."

Helen's was moved a short distance from its original location in 1983, and Judy and Gary Hanscom opened a second restaurant in 1997 in Ellsworth on Route 1 with the same menu as Helen's. In the summer, the bakery produces 110 pies per day and has to ration them because of demand from tourists passing through Machias on their way to Canada. Strawberry pies are made year-round because of the availability of California berries, but the native blueberry and raspberry pies are produced only in June–July (raspberry) and August–September (blueberry).

The 9-inch blueberry cream pies, cut in 6 generous slices, are $17. A plain blueberry pie is $12. They cannot be shipped.

VISITS
Helen's Restaurant
29 East Main Street
Machias, ME 04654
207/255-8423
e-mail: barker@remaine.com
From the Maine Turnpike, exit at Bangor. Take Route 1A to Ellsworth. Pick up Route 1 into Machias. This becomes Main Street.
June–September: Every day, 6 A.M.–9 P.M. October–May: Every day, 6 A.M.–8 P.M.

ITALIAN BAKERY POTICA

It may seem confusing, but the Italian Bakery in Virginia, Minnesota, makes a terrific Yugoslavian *potica*. Pronounced po-*teet*-sah, this holiday pastry roll of walnuts, butter, cream, and flour is at its best when thinly sliced and warmed, with a sliver of butter or ice cream on top.

Expert Old World cooks make potica at home, of course, and you can run into the long, square loaves at church fairs, provided the congregation is made up of Slovenians, Croatians, Serbians, or Yugoslavians. But absent a local source of supply, you can depend on the Italian Bakery's version, which is inexpensive and arrives fresh.

The rolled pastry has been made ever since the bakery opened in 1905, first in Eveleth and then in its current home of Virginia, an iron-ore city 60 miles north of Duluth. The recipe was developed by Mary Janezich, who thought her family's Yugoslavian dessert could find a place in her son-in-law's bakery. Her son-in-law, Gino Marcaccini, agreed, and the potica quickly became the bakery's most popular item, available year-round. Fourteen years ago, Marcaccini sold the operations to his co-owner, Joseph Prebonich, who has worked at the bakery for 35 years. Joseph and his wife, Betty, follow the original recipe.

As happy consumers we can attest that the effort is definitely worth it. The pastry stays fresh and is excellent warmed in the microwave or toasted, or even gilded with a complementary ice cream, like butter brickle.

A 1 -pound loaf currently is $18.50 ($27.50 for 2), including shipping, and a 1½ pound loaf is $22.50 ($37.00 for 2). A raisin potica is $27.50 for a 2-pound loaf ($46.50 for 2). The Preboniches have added an assortment of biscotti. One package of 6 almond biscotti is $12.50; 2 packages are a bargain at $15.50. They also sell chocolate almond biscotti for the same price. The bakery also will send very clean and crunchy wild rice that is hand-parched by Native Americans in Minnesota for $17.50 for a 1-pound package ($25.75 for a 2-pound package), including shipping.

ORDERING ADDRESS
Italian Bakery, Inc.
205 S. First Street
Virginia, MN 55792
218/741-3464
No credit cards

VISITS: **Virginia's streets are arranged by number and direction. The bakery is at the intersection of South First Street and Second Avenue.**
Monday–Saturday, 5:30 A.M.–5 P.M.

JAARSMA'S DUTCH LETTERS

Pella, Iowa, is a town that parades its Dutch heritage gracefully and honestly. About 90 percent of its population is of Dutch ancestry, with the telephone book having more Van Zees and Van Wyks than Smiths or Joneses. It is known for its gorgeous displays of tulips in its public square, along its main street, and in its parks, all timed to be at their showiest during the annual Tulip Festival the second weekend of May. Downtown has a European air, with a carillon pealing from a tower in the square and well-tended narrow brick stores with facades decorated with Delft tiles.

The town is equally famous for two Dutch food specialties, a ring bologna and an almond paste pastry shaped into alphabet letters. The smoked Dutch bologna, mostly beef with a little pork, is made fresh at In't Veld Bologna, on Main Street, and Ulrich's Pella Bologna, on Franklin. The letters are specialties of the Vander Ploeg Bakery and the Jaarsma Bakery, which still is run by the family that founded it. Herman Jaarsma, grandfather of the brothers who run the business today, came to Pella from Holland in 1893 and purchased an existing bakery five years later. The bakery has been at its present location since 1948.

There are a number of Dutch pastries that have remained in the Jaarsma line for decades, including egg buns, apple and raisin bread, spiced cookies, lace cookies, and homemade egg noodles, but the Dutch letters are the best known. The dough is puff pastry fashioned into a long, thin rope about an inch wide and 15 inches long. Inside is a strip of intensely flavored almond paste.

In Holland, the sugar-dusted pastry is shaped into letters only at Christmas, for gift giving, and is sold in straight lengths the rest of the year. Jaarsma's will take orders for specified letters during the holiday season but makes its everyday letters in the shape of an S, "mainly to create interest," says Ralph Jaarsma, who with his brother, Howard, runs the Pella bakery and one other in nearby Oskaloosa.

The letters, made fresh daily, are sweet, and one can easily satisfy two eaters. Despite their fragile nature, they can be sent by UPS. They arrive in mint condition, we can attest, packed two-by-two on Styrofoam trays. A dozen letters is $26, including shipping and packing. A dozen in the store is $16.

The bakery also makes a delicious almond butter cake that mails well. It comes in a 7- or 9-inch-diameter size, selling for $6.99 and $8.99, respectively, at the bakery. For mail orders, UPS charges and a $3 handling fee are added. The bakery ships several gift packages year-round, and customers are encouraged to write for a list of suggestions. A brochure of products is available.

ORDERING ADDRESS
Jaarsma Bakery
727 Franklin Street
Pella, IA 50219
515/628-2940
FAX: 515/628-9148
www.jaarsmabakery.com
Credit cards accepted

VISITS: **Pella is about 40 miles southeast of Des Moines on Highway 163. The bakery is on the square downtown, half a block west of Main Street and across from the "Tulip Tower."**
Monday–Saturday, 6 a.m.–5:30 p.m.

LUCY'S SWEET SURRENDER STRUDEL

On the east side of Cleveland is Lucy's Sweet Surrender, which is, in the words of its owner Michael Feigenbaum, "a small scratch bakery with a very large menu."

Feigenbaum merged his Sweet Surrender company with the storied Lucy's when he bought it from Lucy Ortelecan in 1994. Lucy had been making hand-stretched strudel dough in her Hungarian bakery for decades. Her apple, cherry, cheese, and poppyseed strudels had feathery, flaky pastry and intensely flavored fillings. Feigenbaum inherited some of Lucy's recipes and continues the tradition of creating fine Hungarian pastries. His strudel is made on Tuesdays, and the flavors include apple, cherry with cheese, apricot with cheese, cherry, cheese, poppyseed, and cabbage.

In addition, Lucy's Sweet Surrender's menu includes nut rolls and poppyseed rolls, 20 different kinds of tortes and cakes, and custom items. It's famous for its Dobos torte and produces 1,000 nut rolls for the holidays. In spring there's an entire Passover menu that is made without flour (matzo meal is used instead). The bakery's apple bread and raspberry bread is similar to Jewish *challah* in consistency. Although not a kosher bakery, it makes specialties from matzo, such as chocolate cakes, macaroons, and cheesecakes. Also at Easter the bakery makes nut rolls, poppyseed strudel, lamb cakes, and hot cross buns. From Thanksgiving to Christmas, a chestnut torte with chestnuts imported from Italy is available. This triangular cake with chestnut butter cream can't be shipped. Tortes are about $35.

Other items, however, can be shipped UPS by second-day air. Feigenbaum says the best products for shipping are the strudel and nut and poppyseed rolls. A strudel is $10. After years of waiting, we are thrilled to finally be able to order Lucy's Strudel long-distance. (Lucy Ortelecan was stubborn about not shipping.)

Feigenbaum grew up in Cleveland, patronizing Lucy's as a youth. He attended California Culinary Academy and worked at San Francisco bakeries and other restaurants, doing his apprenticeship at Fantasia Confections. He said, "I left when Cleveland was in the doldrums. I came back during its renaissance. I had always wanted to have a bakery in the old Broadway neighborhood. It once had fourteen bakeries on it, but the Hungarians moved out to the suburbs."

Although the neighborhood is not exclusively Hungarian, as it once was, the bakery and the Balaton restaurant across the street are places where Hungarian is spoken and a sense of community prevails. Cleveland is a mixture of such neighborhoods—Polish, Slovenian, Russian, Czech—and each has a few gemlike food makers. While in Cleveland, it's well worth seeking them out.

ORDERING ADDRESS
Lucy's Sweet Surrender
12516 Buckeye Road
Cleveland, OH 44120
216/752-0828
No credit cards

VISITS: From Public Square in downtown Cleveland it's 5.4 miles to the east. Take Ontario Rd. East. This becomes Broadway Ave. Make a slight left onto the I-77 South ramp. Take the first right onto Orange Ave. Make a slight left onto US 422 east. Turn right onto Woodland Ave. Take a right onto Buckeye Rd. The shop is just past E. 125 St.
Wednesday–Saturday, 7 A.M.–4 P.M.

MARIDEE'S POUND CAKES AND SAUCES

For about 20 years, Marge Murray's fragrant pound cakes were shipped from the separate kitchen her husband, Eric, built for her in the back of their home in Duncan, Oklahoma. Although the 86-year-old baker has been retired from the business for several years, she used to make every one of the 700 cakes she sold annually. That commitment to quality lives on in the pound cakes and sauces made at Maridee's Country Kitchen Cakes in Elmore City about 30 miles away. Owned by Marilou Munn and Dee Stout, two friends of more than 20 years, the women said Mrs. Murray was definitely a mentor and inspiration.

Raised on farms and ranches in the Texas Panhandle and northwestern Oklahoma, both women learned to cook for farmhands, ranch workers, and harvest crews. They formed their company in 1999 after many years of requests from friends and family to prepare special dishes for occasions. Their signature pound cake is Dee's grandmother's original recipe.

They feature 11 other flavors of cakes, including a devilish pound cake, orange cranberry, butter pecan, almond, citrus, coconut, and lemon poppyseed. Sauces such as pecan praline, buttermilk caramel glaze, Key lime, chocolate fudge, and strawberry, peach, and lemon are available for cake toppings. All sauces are in 8-ounce jars and sell for $4 to $5.50.

Their cakes come in three sizes: large (about 3½ pounds, serving 20 to 24), medium (about 1¾ pounds, serving 10 to 20), and baby (about 5 ounces, serving 1 to 2). Large cakes are $18 to $22; medium cakes are $9 to $11; baby cakes are $1.75 to $2. The cakes are made with no preservatives and will keep on the shelf for 2 to 3 weeks and freeze well. All flavors come in all sizes and in low-fat versions.

The company also features home canned cakes, which are baked and sealed in a jar, and can be kept on the shelf indefinitely. They are great in gift baskets, for unexpected company, or for camping trips. These cakes are $4 to $4.50.

The cakes and sauces come gift-wrapped with a gift card enclosure. They can be mailed anywhere in the country, and prices include the gift wrapping.

ORDERING ADDRESS
Maridee's Country Kitchen Cakes
P.O. Box 36
Elmore City, OK 73433
580/788-2209
800/798-7730
FAX: 580/788-2209
www.marideescakes.com
e-mail: mdcakes@hotmail.com
Credit cards accepted

VISITS
108 N. Main
Elmore City, OK 73433
The shop is located 1 block north of the intersection of highways 74 and 29 in Elmore City.
Monday–Friday, 9 A.M.–2 P.M.

MATTHEWS 1812 HOUSE LEMON RUM SUNSHINE CAKE

Pound cakes, which are still within the realm of most home cooks in America, must be exceptional to develop a mail-order following. Deanna Matthews, whose 20-year-old cottage industry in Cornwall Bridge, Connecticut, began with apricot and date fruitcakes but now includes cakes, tortes, bar cookies, candy, and nuts, has developed such a specialty.

Her Lemon Rum Sunshine Cake, which is baked in a Bundt pan, is soaked in a mixture of lemon juice and rum. Its heady aroma announces the cake as you open its cream and brown tin. It is an extremely moist, dense cake with a strong lemon flavor. Your mouth is left with a slight tingle of rum, just enough to keep this cake for adults.

Matthews, who grew up on a farm in Kansas and studied home economics at Kansas State University, ended a career in retailing in New York City to develop a home business that would allow her and her husband, Blaine, to spend more time with their two children. Through her insistence on top-quality ingredients and handling most of the production herself, the reputation of her home bakery has grown quickly. In the fall of 1990 she moved into a new kitchen, with a retail shop, located less than a mile down the hill from her home. Her small staff has joined her there, not only to help bake and package her cakes but also to answer questions from callers and help customers select gifts.

In addition to the two light, creamy fruitcakes, Matthews offers brownies, a chocolate raspberry liqueur pound cake, a variety of tortes, trifles, and other items. The Lemon Rum Sunshine Cake, which weighs 1¾ pounds and comes in a gift tin with ribbon, is $23. The chocolate raspberry cake is $24.50 gift-wrapped. A selection of dessert sauces and hand-dipped chocolates, candies, nuts, and maple syrup also are available. Shipping is additional and varies with the amount of the order.

ORDERING ADDRESS
Matthews 1812 House
P.O. Box 15, 250 Kent Road
Cornwall Bridge, CT 06754-0015
860/672-0149
800/666-1812
www.matthews1812house.com
e-mail: info@matthews1812house.com
Credit cards accepted

VISITS: Cornwall Bridge is in northwestern Connecticut, west of Torrington near the New York border. The new retail store and kitchen are on Route 7, less than a mile from the 1812 farmhouse.
Monday–Friday, 9 A.M.–5 P.M.

MRS. HANES' MORAVIAN COOKIES

The 45 women who bake the six specialties of Moravian Sugar Crisp, Inc., arrive at 6:30 A.M. to begin the sifting, mixing, and hand-rolling that the cookies require. The aroma at baking time is heady: ginger, sugar, chocolate, lemon, butterscotch, and black walnut cookies are baked daily and mailed to the thousands of people who have discovered the high-quality treats.

Despite the overwhelming success Evva Hanes has had in selling the cookies from her mother's Moravian recipes, the cookies still are cut and packaged by hand. This is not just sentimentality, but necessity, as the paper-thin rounds are too fragile for any machine to handle.

Stacked vertically in slender cardboard tubes, or cushioned in round tins, the spicy ginger cookies arrive with only one or two broken, a remarkable record for so crisp a product. These are much milder than a ginger snap and are the perfect accompaniment to ice cream or fruit slices. The delicate cookies also come in chocolate, lemon, butterscotch, sugar, and, most recently, black walnut with crushed walnuts.

Moravia once was part of Czechoslovakia. Persecuted for their religious beliefs, Moravians found refuge first in Germany, then in the United States. Although many settled in Pennsylvania, a contingent traveled to Winston-Salem, North Carolina. The Moravian church that Evva Hanes attends there is 227 years old. The Moravian community roots are strong and Hanes runs her bakery to serve her local customers. "When customers hunger for cookies after hours, they call us at home and we meet them at the bakery," she said. Hanes understands that substitutes just won't do.

Two 8-ounce tubes of ginger cookies or two 7-ounce tubes of sugar cookies and all 1-pound tins cost $15.50 plus $4.75 for shipping and handling. All

2-pound tins cost $26 plus $6 shipping and handling. Mrs. Hanes's cookbook, *Supper's at Six & We're Not Waiting!* is $16 plus $4.75 shipping and handling.

At the bakery, the cookies are sold in cellophane bags for $8 per pound or $4.50 per ½ pound. Tubes at the bakery are $6.50, pound tins are $12.50, and 2-pound tins are $23.

ORDERING ADDRESS
Mrs. Hanes' Moravian Cookies
Moravian Sugar Crisp Co., Inc.
4643 Friedberg Church Road
Clemmons, NC 27012
336/764-1402
888/764-1402
FAX: 336/764-8637
www.hanescookies.com
e-mail: hanes@hanescookies.com
Credit cards accepted

VISITS: From Winston-Salem, take Highway 150 west to Friedberg Church Road. Take a right and continue for 4 miles. The bakery in on the left, in a beige building. Tours are available and viewing windows have been added, so before 2 p.m. on weekdays you can observe the cookies being rolled, cut, baked, and packed by hand.
Monday–Friday, 6:30 A.M.–5 P.M.

NEW GLARUS BAKERY CHRISTMAS STOLLEN

Bakeries that are not dependent on frozen dough and mixes are a rare breed, and it is rarer still to discover one in the rural Midwest, operating in a town of 1,700 people. Yet in New Glarus, Wisconsin, there is just such a place. Continuing much as it has since 1916, the New Glarus Bakery turns out superlative pastries, cookies, and European-style breads, all made from scratch.

Howard and Nancy Weber bought the bakery in this little town known as America's Little Switzerland in 1978, two weeks after they first spied it on a visit. Howard had worked at bakeries since he was 15 and had attended various baking schools in the United States and Switzerland. Nancy purchased Howard's half in 1996 and has been running it herself since then with few major changes, except to keep expanding the business. (The tea room the

couple used to run is now closed to make space for, among other things, cake decorating.)

The fancy pastries stop window shoppers in their tracks, but even the more pedestrian goods receive careful attention. The doughnuts, for example, are made from scratch, as are the buttermilk fry cakes. Known for its stollen, the bakery will send by mail during November and December. The stollen is made with whole almonds, dark and light raisins soaked in rum, and decorated with marzipan. It costs $21, including shipping.

Available all year is raisin pumpernickel bread, a coarse, raisin-filled bread with natural sourdough and no fat. This bread is one of four (along with sourdough, farmer's rye, and potato) the bakery offers for $23—you have to take your chances on what variety is baked on shipping day. The bakery's Swiss breads, which generally are available only at the bakery, spark memories of the old country among the Swiss clientele: Burebrot (farmer's rye), a natural sour rye; Eir Zopf, a rich, hand-braided bread often reserved for Sunday breakfast; and Schweizerbrot (Swiss bread), a long-fermentation loaf made from white flour and baked directly on the hearth with added steam to form a hard crust. Available by mail during cooler weather is Beinenstich Kuchen, with its honey-almond topping and gooey butter filling.

ORDERING ADDRESS
New Glarus Bakery
534 First Street
New Glarus, WI 53574
608/527-2916
FAX: 608/527-5799
www.newglarusbakery.com
e-mail: ngbakery@aol.com
Credit cards accepted

VISITS: New Glarus is about 22 miles southwest of Madison, Wisconsin. From Highway 69, turn onto Highway 39. Drive 2 blocks to First Street and turn right.
Mid-May–November: Every day, 8 a.m.–5 p.m.
December–Mid-May: Closed Sunday and Monday

NEW ORLEANS KING CAKES

Wherever you are, you can celebrate Mardi Gras vicariously with a king cake. These braided yeast rings, iced and decorated with purple, green, and gold sugars, are a New Orleans tradition, available from January 6, or Three Kings' Day, until Fat Tuesday, or Mardi Gras, the day before Ash Wednesday. During these five or six weeks, New Orleans bakeries will produce more than a quarter of a million king cakes!

The cakes mirror European and Latin American traditions, where Twelfth Night or Feast of the Epiphany celebrations are held 12 days after Christmas to commemorate the coming of the Three Wise Men bearing gifts to the Christ child. Cakes baked for those celebrations have a small ceramic figure or bean hidden inside. Some cultures say the figure represents the Christ child; others dictate that the finder must portray one of the kings. In New Orleans, the hidden object may be a tiny plastic baby. King cake parties are a tradition, and custom has it that whoever finds the baby in his or her piece of cake is obligated to host the next king cake party.

King cakes are basically coffeecakes, enriched with decoration. They taste best heated and served warm. Bakers in New Orleans have taken to cluttering the menu with myriad choices of fillings and flavors, but the traditional cinnamon-flavored dough is most popular. The colored sugars on the icing are symbolic, representing the colors associated with Mardi Gras since the 1870s. The gold stands for power, the green for faith, and purple for justice.

Thanks to overnight shipping and improved packing, the cakes now are sent to Mardi Gras revelers around the world. We ordered from four longtime New Orleans bakeries that send king cakes by air, offering toll-free ordering numbers, and all were good. The icing and sugars are messy, of course, so don't expect otherwise.

The two we liked best were the cakes from Haydel's Bakery and Maurice French Pastries.

Haydel's Bakery is the largest shipper of king cakes in Louisiana, said co-owner Gary Haydel. He saw the market potential in shipping king cakes, and 16 years ago helped Federal Express design a special decorated box to fit the king cakes. Other New Orleans bakeries use the box, but Haydel has broken his ties to Federal Express, upset because the shipper took the concept and box to bakeries in other states. "I pleaded with them not to. I said I'm your best customer but I'm going to be your worst enemy," said Haydel. Haydel's ships UPS now. His king cake box is even fancier than the Federal Express box, with a four-color scene on its cover designed by Mardi Gras artist Michael Hunt.

For $30.95, Haydel's will send a king cake, *Arthur Hardy's Mardi Gras Guide,* 2 packs of Café du Monde coffee, and colored beads and doubloons by overnight delivery. If you want a cake with either plain or strawberry cream cheese, German chocolate, or chocolate rum topping, add $4. The cake comes on a gold foil board, and a tiny replica of an antique porcelain king cake doll is enclosed, as well as the plastic baby in the cake. A king cake scroll also comes in the package, giving the religious and historic background of the treat.

Haydel's also offers a variety of baked goods, such as praline cheesecake, chocolate doberge cake, pecan pie, Cajun kringle, and gourmet chocolate chip cookies. Regional products including coffee, seasonings, and olive oils round out its selection.

Maurice French Pastries is in Metairie, a New Orleans suburb. Owner Jean-Luc Albin will send his bakery's king cakes nationwide by next-day air, using UPS and its special king cake box.

There are three kinds of cakes: traditional, filled, and French, and they all give the king cake a bit more of a French accent. You have a choice of several fillings, from cream cheese and praline to piña colada, chocolate bourbon pecan, and a variety of fruits. The French cake's filling is a creamy almond-flavored custard. It is magnificent in appearance and taste—truly the sort of pastry one would rarely, if ever, attempt at home. It is most suitable for dessert, and would be a crowning finish to a meal of any persuasion. It serves about 20.

All king cakes come with a tiny plastic figure of a baby embedded inside. The finder of the trinket is rewarded with a gold paper crown—also enclosed with the cakes. Customers can be assured they are getting the genuine article. The cakes come in four sizes: small (serves 6 to 8), medium (serves 8 to 12), large (serves 12 to 20), and extra-large (serves 16 and more). Traditional cakes range from $8.50 for small to $29 for extra large. Filled cakes run from $10.50 for small to $36 for extra large. French cakes range from $9.50 for small and $34 for extra large.

Albin, age 49, is definitely French, from the town of Briançon, in the French Alps. A chef by trade, he had worked in top-flight hotels in New Orleans and Dallas and then for MGM in Los Angeles. When he returned to New Orleans to hotel work, he learned that the bakery's owner and namesake, Maurice Ravet, was going to be retiring. Albin began working with Ravet in December 1988 and bought the bakery the following May.

Ask about having your cakes shipped with beads, doubloons, and king cake history.

ORDERING ADDRESS
Haydel's Bakery
4037 Jefferson Highway
New Orleans, LA 70121
800/442-1342
FAX: 504/837-5512
www.haydelbakery.com
Credit cards accepted

Maurice French Pastries
3501 Hessmer Avenue
Metairie, LA 70002
504/885-1526
888/285-8261
FAX: 504/885-1527
www.mauricefrenchpastries.com
To order: www.mardigraskingcakes.net
Credit cards accepted

VISITS: Metairie is between the airport and downtown New Orleans. From I-10 take the Causeway North exit and go to Veterans Boulevard. Turn west and drive 5 blocks to Hessmer Avenue. Turn right, and the bakery is up half a block.

Sunday–Thursday, 7 A.M.–6 P.M. Friday–Saturday, 7 A.M.–8 P.M. Holidays, 7 A.M.–noon. Closed Mardi Gras Day and New Year's Day

NORMAN'S NORDIC KRINGLE

In the upper Midwest, and anywhere else Norwegians gather, kringle is found. Nordic kringle is quite different from Danish kringle, although both are coffee-time pastries that take time and skill to produce. Danish kringle is a flat, oval pastry filled with fruit or nuts. The mecca for this version of kringle is Racine, Wisconsin. Nordic kringle (pronounced *kring-la*) is a sweet, bland, unfilled pastry shaped like a fat pretzel.

Home bakers in Norwegian areas around the Midwest have sealed their reputations on the basis of their kringle-twisting skill, which reaches its apex at Christmas. Their kringle has a plain taste that some prefer to supplement with a smear of butter. Mostly, however, it is eaten plain. It is homey and homely—the sort of holiday food that quickly becomes a tradition.

Norman Storvick, formerly of Nevada, Iowa, began making kringle commercially in that central Iowa town in 1989. A former bus driver, he suffered a heart attack five years earlier and had been a house husband while his wife managed a grocery deli. He did a little woodworking and began baking for friends to keep busy. He experimented with kringle, adapting a recipe from a centennial cookbook from the nearby town of Huxley and began selling it to area groceries.

Norman's Nordic kringle began in a Nevada storefront with Norman, his wife, Melisse, their daughters, Christine and Suzanne, and son, Nathan, all helping. Now it is made according to Norman's recipe by Field Foods in the nearby town of Story City. Hundreds of dozens of kringle are hand twisted each day by a staff of 15. The kringle comes in lemon or almond-flavored versions, as well as the original plain, but they are so lightly flavored that there's not a tremendous difference among them.

They are light and can be mailed easily. The packaging is utilitarian (6 kringle in a quart-sized zip-top bag, with 2 bags per box), and the price is reasonable. A dozen is $4, plus shipping and handling charges. They also can be purchased at Field Foods.

Kringle freeze well. They are real comfort food any time of year and any time of day.

ORDERING ADDRESS
Norman's Nordic Kringle
c/o Field Foods
620 Penny Avenue
Story City, IA 50248
515/733-5329
FAX: 515/733-5329
No credit cards

VISITS: **The retail shop is in the center of town,**
1 block north of Story City's main street, which is Broad Street.
Monday–Thursday, 8:30 A.M.–4:30 P.M.

NUNS OF NEW SKETE CHEESECAKE

Of all the monasteries that produce superior, carefully made foods, New Skete in Cambridge, New York, is the home of the widest range of products. Smoked hams and poultry, nitrite-free bacon, smoked turkey and chicken breast, whole-grain pancake mix, cheese spreads, and smoked cheeses (Cheddar and Gruyère)—the monks and nuns make them all. They get their award-winning maple syrup from a neighbor. All products can be mailed.

The monastery of the Orthodox Church in America, high in the Taconic Mountains, just shy of the Vermont border, is a local landmark, with its traditional onion-shaped domes covered in gold leaf. The domes are a reminder of the Russian influence in the religion. The community is relatively small—10 nuns, 12 monks, and 8 lay members—but efficient, with several diverse and flexible small business enterprises. In addition to the food products, they reproduce religious icons and raise gentle German shepherd dogs, which they sell for guide dog service and search and rescue work. They also produce and sell all-natural dog biscuits in both small and large sizes. The price is $19.50 per pound, plus shipping and handling.

We tried the bacon (which the government insists be labeled "pork strips" because it has little salt and no nitrite) and were pleased; it loses little with the omission of the preserving agents and has an intriguing sweet-salty taste from the dry-rubbed cure.

But if you could order just one thing from New Skete you might want to consider the cream cheese cheesecakes made by the nuns. They ship amazingly well in deep metal tins with plastic lids and arrive still half-frozen. We sampled a dense, New York-style cheesecake with a sweet crumb crust and figured the 2-pound cake (about 8 inches in diameter) could serve 10. The filling simply is cream cheese, sugar, eggs, cream, flour, and natural flavoring, and is properly rich and silky. (We do wonder why the cooks aren't as careful in their choice of ingredients for the crumb, which contains several tongue-twisting chemicals. However, they don't seem to affect the taste.)

The nuns also make the following cheesecakes: Kahlua with a chocolate crumb crust, chocolate, white chocolate, amaretto, raspberry, Key lime, Irish cream, apple walnut, pumpkin, and eggnog (the last three are seasonal). All are offered in large (4 pounds, 40 ounces) and whole or presliced into 16 slices. Several are offered in the smaller 2-pound size. Prices range from $14.85 to $17.50 for the 2-pound size, and $23.50 to $28.50 for the larger size (add $2 for sliced of the larger size). All prices are without shipping costs.

Any of the foods can be sent as a gift, and the monks and nuns will enclose a handsome gift card with a photograph of their onion-domed monastery.

ORDERING ADDRESS

New Skete Farms
P.O. Box 128
Cambridge, NY 12816
518/677-3928
FAX: 518/677-2373
www.newskete.com
e-mail: monks@newskete.com

VISITS

New Skete Lane
Cambridge, NY 12816
The monastery is 7 miles east of Cambridge, which is in extreme eastern New York State, northeast of Albany and almost to the Vermont border. From Highway 22 going north, turn right at the traffic light in Cambridge and continue until you cross Highway 313. From there, it is another 4 miles until you see the sign for the monastery.
Tuesday–Saturday, 9 A.M.–5 P.M. Sunday, 2 P.M.–5 P.M.

OUR LADY OF GUADALUPE FRUITCAKE AND GINGER DATE-NUT CAKE

In the late 1970s, when the Trappist monks at Our Lady of Guadalupe Abbey in Lafayette, Oregon, were casting about for a project to help sustain themselves, they considered such diverse activities as raising racehorses, warehousing wine, and processing frogs legs. Luckily for us they decided to bake fruitcakes. Although other monasteries around the country make fruitcakes, the products from Our Lady of Guadalupe are in a class by themselves. Extremely dense and moist, a 1-pound cake fits into a box that is but 3¾ inches square. The cakes are very rich, and a small sliver will satisfy.

Guadalupe Abbey fruitcakes are dark and heavy and studded with pecan halves, chopped walnuts, and cherries. After baking, each cake is immersed in 120-proof brandy and then aged for at least two months. The cake has little in common with the light, flour-filled commercial varieties, and, as the abbey's business manager at the time, put it: "It is a solid mass of fruit and nuts. When you slice our fruitcake and hold it up to the light, it looks like stained glass."

The monks also make a ginger date-nut cake that is prepared the same way, including the soak in brandy, but does not contain any fruit except dates and is topped with chopped walnuts. It makes an unusual dessert at any time of year, and, indeed, the monks began baking the date-nut cake in an attempt to extend the appeal of their cakes beyond the Christmas holiday season. We are particularly fond of the date-nut cake, and like it with a dollop of unsweetened whipped cream. (But our tastes are contrary, as the fruitcake outsells the date-nut cake by about four to one.)

The cakes are available as a box of two 1-pound cakes and a single 3-pound cake for $18.50 and $24, respectively. A box of three 1-pound cakes is $25.50 and there are further savings for large orders. Shipping is not included.

The cakes are made in a cheerful kitchen with a blue and white tile floor that was built 17 years ago on the abbey grounds. A team of three brothers turns out ninety 3-pound cakes six mornings a week, scooping dough into parchment-lined tins, decorating the tops with fruits and nuts, soaking the cakes, and boxing them all by hand. The kitchen is absolutely spotless.

The abbey is located in rolling foothills of spectacular appeal in a state filled with exceptional natural beauty. Driving on a winding rural road from the small town of Lafayette, you can see berries growing wild in the roadside ditches and postcard-perfect farmland and timber. Set into a heavily wooded hillside are the beige frame buildings of the monastery, with its chapel, book bindery, living quarters, reception lodge, and other structures. Although the abbey dates from 1955, its well-planned setting makes it look as if it has always been part of the landscape.

ORDERING ADDRESS
Trappist Abbey
Box 97
Lafayette, OR 97127
503/852-7174
800/294-0105
www.trappistabbey.org
e-mail: bakery@trappistabbey.org
Credit cards accepted

VISITS
9200 N.E. Abbey Road
Lafayette, OR 97127
Fruitcakes can be purchased at the porter's lodge on the monastery grounds. Drive to Lafayette, which is just east of McMinnville, in northern Oregon, on Highway 99W. On Highway 99W in downtown Lafayette, find Bill's Market. Directly across the street is a paved road and sign for the abbey. Take the road nearly 3 miles, following the abbey signs. At the entrance, turn right to the visitor's parking area.
Every day, Daylight hours

PATTI'S PLUM PUDDINGS

Why are there no plums in plum pudding? We don't know, but Patti Garrity gives a plausible explanation in the hand-lettered booklet that comes with each of her festive puddings. "Plum" has been used as a generic term for raisins, she writes, and her puddings abound with those. They contain other dried fruits (but no bitter citrus peel), beef suet, brown sugar, nuts, eggs, unbleached flour (and whole wheat bread crumbs), and spices. These moist, molded cakes are steamed and wrapped in brandy-soaked cheesecloth for several months. They can be kept indefinitely as long as they are refrigerated, waiting for a proper occasion to heat them up and flame with warm brandy.

Garrity makes each of the puddings herself, starting sometimes as early as August or even continuing the season into January and cold-storing them. Her original inspiration was Dickens ("The pudding . . . blazing in ignited brandy . . . with Christmas holly stuck in the top. . . . Oh, what a wonderful pudding!"), but it took her eight years of experimenting before she perfected her recipe.

She has been especially successful at creating an airy confection. "Most plum puddings could act as door stops," she observed. Hers is a robust, not-too-sweet cake, satisfying in small slices even without the addition of hard sauce, foamy sauce, or hot cinnamon sauce, whose recipes she thoughtfully provides. (The booklet also clearly describes how to ignite brandy so that even the most inept server can pull off a showy presentation.)

Garrity knows a thing or two about presentation, and her packaging makes the puddings a great choice for a gift. The large and jumbo puddings are wrapped in red or green cellophane and tied with metallic cord, and the smaller ones come in sturdy red gift boxes that ship well. The large puddings, which serve 8 to 12, are available in handsome pewter tins that are a welcome change from the Currier and Ives variety. Her largest puddings, the jumbo-sized, serve up to 24 people. The extra-large size will serve 15. A medium size serves 4 to 6.

Many of Garrity's puddings are sold to restaurants and hotels where picky pastry chefs serve her creation alongside their fancy cakes and desserts. The Ahwahnee Hotel in Yosemite National Park, served her pudding at its spectacular Bracebridge Dinner for 18 consecutive years.

For your own spectacular dinners at home, Patti's Plum Puddings are as close to foolproof as desserts come.

ORDERING ADDRESS
Patti's Plum Puddings, Inc.
301 North Poinsettia
Manhattan Beach, CA 90266
310/376-1463
FAX: 310/372-4132
www.patti'splumpuddings.com
No credit cards

SAMADI SWEETS BAKLAVA AND PASTRIES

Allow us a bit of nepotism as we quote our older sister, Joan Horwitt, who when she was a restaurant reviewer for the *Washington Post,* wrote about the Middle Eastern pastries at Samadi Sweets Cafe in northern Virginia: "The star here is the baklava, ten varieties of different shapes (squares, diamonds, rolls) and flavors (pistachio, cashew, pine nut). And what makes them so good is the handmade phyllo, parchmentlike sheets of pastry coated with clarified butter and stacked sixteen deep to make exquisitely rich desserts. Fortunately, the pastry syrup is light, lending a gentle sweetness."

Samadi Sweets creates baklava in the Lebanese tradition, reflecting the French influence on the pastry, which, unlike Greek varieties, is light, crispy, and not too sweet. This is the first American venture featuring Lebanese-style baklava, and it has been thriving since it opened in 1987. Samadi Sweets, which ships authentic pastries to homesick Lebanese and others all across the country, is planning to expand into other states. With the success of its pastries, the café has increased its customer base nationwide and will soon be introducing a website and full-color mail-order catalog.

Samadi Sweets owner Nora Burgan said, "The chef, who apprenticed with Samadi Sweets in Lebanon, has a love affair with every pastry he puts out." To foster that, Burgan imports pure butters, sweet cheeses, and specialty doughs from the Middle East. In 1998, to complement its line of sweets, the café introduced an expanded menu with sophisticated Lebanese cuisine. On Sundays, you can find a full house at Samadi during brunch, which features more than 20 dishes, an extensive pastry bar, mint tea, and coffee, all for one price. Hanging trays used by the waiters provide an interesting ethnic display, and the large colorful murals of Lebanese scenes add life to the café.

Samadi Sweets has its packaging down pat, and its baklava is not sticky or cloyingly sweet. Its syrup is restrained, with just a hint of rosewater. Samadi ships its baklava in 3- or 5-pound tins, and will send an assortment of flavors, or all of one variety. There are about 14 pieces to the pound, so a 3-pound assortment will yield about four samples of each variety made.

The golden tins are then wrapped in Samadi Sweets' pink patterned paper, complete with Arabic writing, and tied with a bow. Most of the baklava sells for $9.50 a pound. An exception is *asabe'a* (or ladyfingers), small, delicate rolls of filo stuffed with chopped pine nuts and sprinkled with crushed pistachios. A pound, which yields about 20 of the pretty tidbits, is $10.50. The ladyfingers, and the café's other baklava treats, would be standouts on a dessert or tea tray. The pieces are dainty, not overwhelming. We particularly liked the cashew versions, which use toasted nuts.

Samadi also ships other Middle Eastern pastries, including *maamoul,* which are individually wrapped tartlets in various shapes stuffed with ground walnuts, pistachios, or dates. They are buttery and rich. *Maamoul med* is a pastry square made with semolina and farina, filled with dates, and baked until golden. It is a moist, comforting sweet. Sesame cookies are large (5 inches in diameter), but paper-thin, with chopped pistachios in the dough and toasted sesame seeds paving the top. The cookies and the *maamoul* are $10.50 per dozen and the *maamoul med* is $8.50 a pound. Upon request, for an additional $4.50, the café will include personalized cards and special occasion gift wrap.

Shipping costs, via UPS, are added to the above prices. The café has a helpful price sheet that describes its pastries. All but the ones using cheese and cream can be shipped. The café is doing more shipping of its tins nationwide for gift giving, as well as more catering in the Washington, D.C., area.

ORDERING ADDRESS
Samadi Sweets Cafe
5916 Leesburg Pike
Falls Church, VA 22043
703/578-0606
FAX: 703/578-1757
Credit cards accepted

VISITS: **The café is between I-395 and the Seven Corners area on Leesburg Pike (Highway 7), a major road.**
Monday–Saturday, 10:30 A.M.–11 P.M. Sunday, 10:30 A.M.–8 P.M.

A SOUTHERN SEASON'S CAROLINA HIGHLAND SHORTBREAD

When we visit our mom in Chapel Hill, North Carolina, there is one stop we always make: A Southern Season in the Eastgate Shopping Center. It's first and foremost an emporium of fine foods, but that description falls short of its wall-to-wall attractions. It's a restaurant, with so many imaginative choices that we want to order everything. It's a coffee bar, a fine chocolate shop, a wine store, a cookware shop, and a cookbook store. It's a place to get in the seasonal spirit, no matter what that season happens to be. And it is a champion of Southern cooking. Although there are food items from around the world for sale, the emphasis is always on great regional specialties.

For 26 years, founder Michael Barefoot and his savvy staff have scoured the backroads of North Carolina, bringing to wider acclaim such marvels as artichoke sweet pepper relish from Hamilton, handmade chocolates from Hendersonville, peach preserves from the Grandy Greenhouse and Farm Market, and country hams that have been salt- and sugar-cured by Barefoot's parents, Jean and Everette of Four Oaks, North Carolina.

Among our favorites are its Carolina Highland shortbread cookies. They've been featured at the store since it opened. The basic shortbread has a brief ingredient list: rice flour, butter, and sugar. They literally melt in your mouth. Original or chocolate shortbread cookies are packed in a more than 1-pound tin for $14.95. At the winter holidays, A Southern Season offers a 24-ounce sampler of lemon, raspberry, chocolate, almond, caramel nut, apple pie, and orange chocolate chip shortbreads in a silver gift tin for $15.95.

It is easy to order from A Southern Season by telephone or from its well-organized website. If you are anywhere near Chapel Hill, however, make a visit. It's hard to recognize that this artistic, neon-decorated store was a bowling alley in one of its former lives. Now, instead of fries and a Coke, you are tempted by red pepper pizza and moist pound cake topped with lemon curd. The atmosphere is warm and welcoming. A Southern Season is simply one of the best places to buy food and cookware in the country. It also is unsurpassed in the gift basket department. Not only are there dozens of choices and price ranges, but they truly are a notch above most in their visual appeal. The containers, the trimmings, and the contents all are first-class. In a thoughtful touch, several baskets come in an alcoholic and non-alcoholic version. For example, a pretzel sampler gift assortment comes with either Virgil's Root Beer or a microbrewery beer, for $29.95.

Its full-color mail-order catalog is the equal of a luxury New York food emporium, yet the prices reflect North Carolina. Smoked turkey (the Tarheel state is the nation's top turkey producer), smoked trout, peanut brittle, and a Swamp Sauce (for grilling and use as a marinade) are some of the reasonably priced local foods that are worth ordering.

ORDERING ADDRESS
A Southern Season
Eastgate
Chapel Hill, NC 27514
919/942-9274
800/253-3663
FAX: 800/646-1118
www.southernseason.com
Credit cards accepted

VISITS: **Eastgate is a shopping center at the intersection of Franklin Street (which is Chapel Hill's main street) and the 15/501 Bypass. As you enter the shopping center from 15/501, turn right. Eastgate is about 2 miles south of I-40.**

Monday–Saturday, 10 A.M.–7 P.M. Sunday, noon–6 P.M.

SPALDING BAKERY HONEY-GLAZED DOUGHNUTS

When Bowman Spalding started this family bakery in Lexington, Kentucky, in 1929 with $200 he borrowed against an insurance policy, he already had a long history of hard work. When he was in the fourth grade, his father was thrown from a bread wagon and was paralyzed, and the young boy began to support the family. Bowman passed away in 1991, but three generations of Spaldings still work in the bakery: Bowman's son James, his daughter Joyce Spalding Leverett, and granddaughters Martha Leverett Edwards and Catherine Leverett Barton. The next generation of potential bakers varies in age from 3 to 15 years.

Doughnuts—crispy honey-glazed ones with large, irregular centers—are the bakery's best-known item, and the long lines that form outside the door the four mornings a week the bakery is open attest to their goodness. On Sundays the bakery is closed but continues to supply doughnuts to area churches, some of which have been customers for more than 50 years.

The Spaldings do not ship their products, but the bakery is well worth a detour if you are in the area. The 1928 oven, cash register, wooden display cases, mixers, and Victorian building all are vintage. The fact that so little has changed over the years is part of the shop's uniqueness, said Joyce. "It's fun to have customers say, 'My grandparents brought me here when I was a child, and now I'd like you to meet my grandchildren.'"

The honey-glazed doughnuts are $4.20 a dozen. Other items are old-fashioned cinnamon rolls (also $4.20 a dozen), raisin bar cookies, cream horns, individual fruit tarts, raspberry-filled and cream-filled doughnuts, a variety of cupcakes, and chocolate fudge brownies.

Light yellow butter cake with butterscotch fudge icing, chocolate cake with chocolate fudge icing, and white cake with vanilla cream icing are available on Fridays and Saturdays.

Seasonal items are carrot cake with cream cheese icing in springtime, blueberry cake doughnuts in summer, apple cider cake doughnuts in fall, and spice cake with fudge icing in winter.

ORDERING ADDRESS
B. J. Spalding Bakery
574 North Limestone Street
Lexington, KY 40508
606/252-3737
No credit cards

VISITS: The bakery is just north of downtown near the Transylvania University campus, at the corner of Sixth Street and North Limestone.
Wednesday–Saturday, 7 A.M.–2 P.M.

ST. JULIEN MACAROONS

Macaroons are wonderful cookies that should be rediscovered because they contain no fat or cholesterol and are relatively low in calories. They're made in the French style, simply, with crushed almonds, egg whites, sugar, and flavorings. Because they must be kept cold to stay fresh, they have fallen out of favor in America's bakeries, so we are doubly grateful to the Price family for rescuing two special macaroon recipes—honey almond and chocolate almond.

In 1974, Elizabeth Price and her family purchased the recipe for these confections from a fellow churchgoer and started their mail-order business from their Massachusetts home, naming it St. Julien Macaroons after a 14-century English mystic. Her youngest son, James, now runs the business from the quaint town of Sandown, New Hampshire.

The delicious, soft, chewy macaroons are still baked in small batches in brick-lined ovens and hand-packed into tissue-lined tubs. The customer mailing list now totals 10,000 macaroon fans and continues to grow.

The delectable confections are popular as the perfect gift for all occasions, especially Christmas. A personal gift card is included with each gift. Many packages are sent to convalescents and nursing homes because the cookies have no fat and are easy to eat. The macaroons are of particular interest to people suffering from a condition called celiac sprue, which renders them unable to digest wheat, oats, rye, barley, and probably millet.

The Prices' beautiful, chewy cookies also are a special accompaniment to fresh fruit and ice cream and are perfect for snacking, tea time, or dessert. They freeze well, for up to a year, can be refrozen with no ill effects, and can stay refrigerated for up to a month—longer than our willpower lasts.

The macaroons are shipped anywhere, and both the honey almond and cocoa-almond are available in two sizes: a 7.5-ounce half-tub of approximately 18 macaroons and a 15-ounce tub of approximately 3 dozen macaroons. For shipping outside the Northeast United States, the cost for the large tub and half tub of the cocoa-almond version is $22.50 and $19, respectively. The honey almond version is a dollar less for each size.

The prices are slightly lower for shipments to the Northeast. The company's website explains the charges, and it's possible to order from the site.

The company prefers to ship on Mondays and Tuesdays, for delivery later in the week.

ORDERING ADDRESS
White Oak Farms Inc.
343 Main Street
Sandown, NH 03873
603/887-2233
800/473-8869
FAX: 603/887-2880
www.macaroons.cc
e-mail: info@stjulienmacaroons.com
Credit cards accepted

VISITS: From Manchester, take I-93 south. Turn left (north) on Rt. 102. At the town of Chester, turn right on Rt. 121 going east. After 100 yards, the road forks. Take 121A straight. The shop is on the left and shares a parking lot with the Sandown post office.

September–May: Monday–Friday, 10 A.M.–5 P.M.

SUNRISE GOURMET FOODS PASTRIES

Bakery owner Virginia Forti (pronounced fór-tee) is of Italian origin, but her bakery in Hibbing, Minnesota, represents many of the more than 40 countries with roots in the northeast part of the state known as the Mesabi iron range. Her most famous product, *potica,* is Yugoslavian—a jelly-roll-like pastry that is a staple at weddings and special events. Our explanation for its specialness is that potica is an absolute killer to make at home. You have to roll the dough extremely thin (we counted nine tightly coiled turns of dough in the bakery's 3-inch-thick potica), and the filling takes no little skill as well. Our Christmas at-home efforts were tasty, as anything with sweet dough, walnuts, and brown sugar would be, but awfully crude in comparison to Sunrise's version, which is picture perfect. At $9.95 for a 1-pound roll, plus shipping, it is a steal.

The bakery also will ship its excellent apple strudel, which is everything true strudel should be. It has paper-thin, flaky crust, tart and spicy filling, and an honest, hand-rolled look. They are about 15 inches long and weigh about 3 pounds. One would make a dozen co-workers very happy at coffeetime. It is $21.99, plus shipping, and a cream cheese version is also available.

Sunrise also offers Scandinavian *kaage* (coffee cake with citron and white raisins), cardamom biscuits, almond and chocolate dipping biscotti, and Scandinavian dipping cookies, made with whole toasted almonds, cardamom, butter, and sour cream. The bakery also offers an assortment of gourmet foods, including porketta, porketta sausage, Polish sausage, pasties, and fixings for a pasta dinner, wild rice, and spaghetti sauces.

"The Italian bread was the original item in the bakery and has been made for almost ninety years," said Virginia. She sends 6 "brown-and-serve" loaves for $11.99. Hard rolls, in packages of 6, are $11.99 for 6 packages. An unusual Romano cheese bread also is available.

Most of Sunrise's products are sent UPS second-day air to preserve freshness, and they arrive in good form. Even with the minimum $5 UPS charge per order, the products are very reasonable.

Hibbing itself is worth a pilgrimage, not only to the bakery but also to the nearby Ironworld Discovery Center in Chisholm, a cultural center depicting the life and times of the area's open-pit iron miners. Ironworld's displays include a kitchen where local women prepare foods unique to the region, such as potica and Cornish pasties. If you're visiting, stop by Hibbing High School, built in 1920 by United States Steel and other mining companies, and see the murals painted there by nationally known artists.

ORDERING ADDRESS
Sunrise Gourmet Foods
1813 Third Avenue East
Hibbing, MN 55746
218/263-4985
800/782-6736
www.Sunrisegourmet.com
Credit cards accepted

VISITS: Hibbing is in northern Minnesota, northwest of Duluth on Highway 169. The bakery is 2 blocks north of Main Street downtown.
Monday–Friday, 9 A.M.–5 P.M.

TASTYKAKE CHOCOLATE CUPCAKES

Everyone has a sentimental connection to some foods, and in our family, the bond is strong with Tastykakes. Small packaged cakes are found in nearly every grocery store and filling station throughout America, but most aren't worth eating. But the Tasty Baking Company, which has been operating in Philadelphia for 95 years, knows how to mass-produce cakes. Our favorites are its butterscotch krimpets and the 1-ounce chocolate cupcakes, frosted with the best commercial chocolate frosting we've encountered. The cakes are extra-moist and dense and are sold in packages of 3. Most packaged cakes have the texture of cotton, but these cakes have genuine substance. They also are sold in grocery stores in family-packs of 12 cupcakes, which lowers the price per cake.

The company was founded when Pittsburgh baker Phillip J. Bauer and bakery supplier Herbert C. Morris of Boston joined forces to improve the grocer's standard time-consuming practice of cutting and wrapping slices from a whole cake. The company's slogan was "the cake that made mother stop baking." They established their company in Philadelphia out of respect for Bauer's family bakery in Pittsburgh, as his relatives asked that his venture be located at least 300 miles away. (The two cities are 301 miles apart.)

The cake's unique taste has remained throughout the years, even with the recent considerate substitution of canola and cottonseed oils for their more saturated cousins.

The firm has added a lot of new flavors in recent years, but we tend to stick with the originals. We are in good company, because we note that Atlantic City's famed White House Sub Shop, where the dessert choices are only Tastykake products, also sticks with butterscotch krimpets, chocolate cupcakes, and juniors, which are small, square layer cakes in chocolate, coconut or "koffee kake" flavors.

The company's website describes all its products, and lists several Tastykake Packages that can be ordered. We like the nostalgia tin, with 10 packages of butterscotch krimpets, chocolate cupcakes, peanut butter kandykakes, and chocolate juniors, for $24.95 postpaid.

There's also a collegiate care package (28 packages for $39.95 postpaid), chocolate and vanilla gift assortments, and the Philadelphia collection that includes 22 Tastykake packages and a Tasty T-shirt. Each of these gift packs is $39.95 postpaid.

ORDERING ADDRESS
Tastykake Gift Department
The Tasty Baking Company
2801 Hunting Park Avenue
Philadelphia, PA 19129-1392
800/338-2789
FAX:800/348-2789
www.tastykake.com
Credit cards accepted

WICK'S SUGAR-CREAM PIE

If Indiana had a state pie, it would be the sugar-cream. Not a custard pie (it has no eggs), it is a cousin to the chess pie or the Southern specialty known as transparent pie. But sugar-cream pie is unique—so unique, in fact, that its sole manufacturer, Wick's Pies, Inc., of Winchester, Indiana, had both the method and formula patented in 1962, a process that involved the owner, Duane Wickersham, going pie in hand to Washington, D.C., to confer with patent attorneys. It was the first patent ever awarded for a pie.

The pie, which has been made at home by Indiana farm wives for years and is sometimes referred to as Indiana Farm Pie, has as its primary ingredient cream containing a whopping 40 percent butterfat. At the factory, the ingredients have to be blended by a dairy pump because a conventional mixer would quickly turn the cream to butter. The other ingredients are sugar, flour, shortening, vanilla, nutmeg, and salt, blended and baked in a lard crust.

As a trade publication, *Bakers Weekly,* described it: "Slightly less firm than custard, with an almost translucent appearance something like starch, with a little of the flavor of the hot sauce often poured over puddings and a little of true custard, but with a much richer butter-creamy base than either." It is sweet, no doubt about it. But after sampling several sugar-cream pies at Indiana restaurants famed for their pastries, we concluded that the Wick's pie—although a little firmer in texture—is even richer and better than the café versions.

It is an original, this cream pie with the nicely browned top that is baked in its shell. Another distinction is that the pie does not spoil if unrefrigerated, incredible as that may seem for a cream pie, and one made without preservatives. "The high sugar content prevents spoilage," says Wickersham, who has had bacteria tests run on the pie to confirm it. The pie also can be frozen with no loss of quality.

Although the company makes a number of other pies, including pecan, peanut butter cream, German chocolate, pumpkin, and eight varieties of fruit, the sugar-cream is the undisputed best-seller. In Indiana, it is one of the best-selling items of any kind in grocery freezer cases.

Duane Wickersham, who is known simply as Wick, started in the restaurant business and began having local women make pies in their home kitchens. He then concentrated on pies and in the early sixties moved his operation to a wonderful restored red-brick factory that became vacant because of a change in burial fashions. It formerly housed the J. W. McCamish Company, makers of burial slippers, but when the vogue in caskets changed from full-view to half-view, the slipper business sagged.

"Wick" again is running a restaurant, Mrs. Wick's Pie Shoppe, that is also the factory store. The youngest of his seven children, Mike Wickersham, is president of the company and runs the plant. A daughter and daughter-in-law also are involved in the business full time and another son consults for the firm.

The company has expanded and now has some distribution in 22 states. The company will ship its frozen pies by next-day air service, with a minimum order of a case of 6 of the 9-inch pies. A case of the sugar-cream is $14.45, plus $29.25 for shipping. A case of pecan pies is $17.80 and 6 German chocolate pies are $16.55. The pies may be just starting to thaw when they arrive, but may be refrozen. In the restaurant, the pies come in 8- or 9-inch diameters and range in price from $1.70 for the pumpkin to $2.15 for the German chocolate. The sugar-cream at the restaurant is $1.80 for the 8-inch and $2.20 for the 9-inch pie.

ORDERING ADDRESS
Wick's Pies, Inc.
217 Greenville Avenue
Winchester, IN 47394
317/584-8401
www.wickspies.com
e-mail: wickspies@wickspies.com
No credit cards

VISITS
Mrs. Wick's Pie Shoppe
100 North Cherry Street
Winchester, IN 47394
317/584-7437
e-mail: rstaurant@wickspies.com
Winchester is in eastern Indiana, near the Ohio border, on Highway 32. At the courthouse square in the center of town, continue on Highway 32 (East Washington Street) for 2 miles to Greenville Avenue. Turn right and look for Wick's sign on the left. Mrs. Wick's Pie Shoppe is on Cherry and Washington Streets, and also serves soup, sandwiches, and salads.
Monday–Thursday, 6 A.M.–7 P.M. Friday, 6 A.M.–8 P.M. Saturday, 6 A.M.–2 P.M.

CANDIES

ALINOSI'S CHOCOLATES

How could we have overlooked Detroit's oldest chocolatier? Thank goodness for the inventive store, Pure Detroit, that assembles the city's best books, photographs, sports memorabilia, and products. There, we tasted Alinosi's exquisite chocolate bars and made a beeline for this vintage candymaker's downtown plant.

Known equally for its fine Italian ices, premium ice creams, and French-style chocolate, this 1921 firm does so many labor-intensive products well. There used to be 11 Alinosi shops and soda fountains throughout Detroit. There is only one retail outlet now, a lovely soda fountain and candy shop in Grosse Pointe Woods that dispenses 32 flavors of ice cream, 16 flavors of cake, and dozens of unusual chocolates.

Most of the company's new business is in beautiful foil-wrapped chocolates for airport shops, corporations, the city's stunning Fox Theatre, and for the governor. The packaging is deluxe—black velvet, jewel-toned foils, and gold wire ribbon. But it's the content of the chocolate that shines. It's stealth chocolate—it has a very light mouth feel. It has more milk solids than most, imparting a creamy taste that vanishes without leaving a coated, heavy feeling.

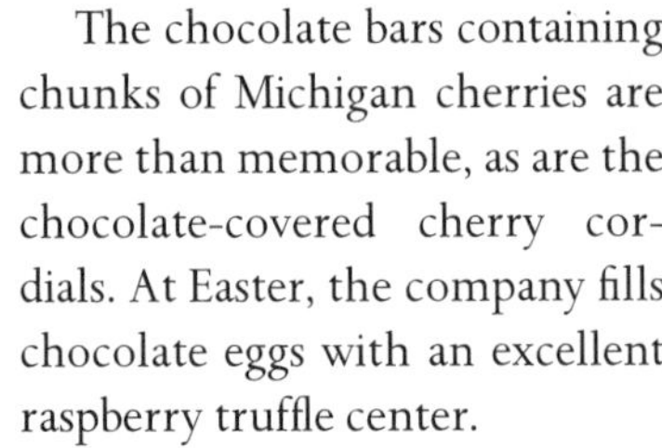

The chocolate bars containing chunks of Michigan cherries are more than memorable, as are the chocolate-covered cherry cordials. At Easter, the company fills chocolate eggs with an excellent raspberry truffle center.

Nancy DiMaggio, the daughter of owner Louis Alinosi, still hand-dips her chocolates. Her sons, Steve and Joe DiMaggio, handle the frozen confections. Chocolate maker Dave Tessman grew up with the DiMaggios and started working as an ice cream dipper in a fountain at age 14. He works now in that same now-closed location, with a crystal chandelier, pink and blue neon on the wall, and the vintage soda counter used as a wrapping area. "We love creating new candy bars for people—we just did a chocolate CD for a jazz festival," Tessman said.

We were bowled over to find out Alinosi's still makes three-layered spumoni—a process that has nearly disappeared from the American food landscape. Real spumoni has a top layer of pistachio ice cream, followed by a layer of rum ice cream laced with chopped fruits and nuts. The bottom layer is chocolate ice cream. If you've had spumoni at all, most likely it's been a rum-like ice cream with fruits in it.

This tri-layered beauty uses equipment that is no longer sold. Alinosi's sells the spumoni in rounds that customers slice at home for a showy dessert, or in pre-sliced quart box that serves 8.

The spumoni and ice cream can be found at gourmet shops throughout the Detroit area. Pure Detroit, 1551 Woodward Avenue, Detroit, sells the chocolate bars, chocolate-covered cookies, and an assortment of other confections. The 2-ounce chocolate bars are $1.75. At the company's retail outlet, the chocolate covered cherries are $19.50 for an 18-piece box.

ORDERING ADDRESS AND VISITS
Alinosi's
20737 Mack Avenue
Grosse Pointe Woods, MI 48236
313/884-1993
www.alinosi.com
Credit cards accepted
Tuesday–Thursday, 11 A.M.–8 P.M. Friday–Saturday, 11 A.M.–9 P.M. Sunday, 1 P.M.–8 P.M.

ATKINSON'S CHICK-O-STICK

Chick-O-Stick candy has a wonderful name, no? When it was introduced in 1938, it was called Chicken Bone, a name that'll stick in your throat. But for more than 40 years, this toasted-coconut–covered peanut butter stick has been Chick-O-Stick. The name change made it possible for it to be enshrined, along with approximately 3,000 other items, in Shrine O'Stuff, a collection of items whose names have the letter "O" in the middle, set off by dashes or with an apostrophe. That's "O" as in House O'Weenies hot dogs, Roll-O-Paper office supplies, and Bag O' Catnip cat toy. The collection is the brainchild of longtime friends Rich Szabo and Richard Crater, of Livingston, New Jersey. The two maintain the "shrine" underground in the Crater family's bomb shelter, a relic of the 1950s. Since they began their collection 18 years ago, at least 1,000 otherwise normal Americans have been moved to write the duo, offering suggestions for inclusion in the collection.

Which brings us back to Chick-O-Stick, made by Atkinson Candy Company of Lufkin, Texas, located 120 miles northeast of Houston. "Fresh from the heart of Texas" is an Atkinson slogan, and all its products have a star on the label, prompting another corporate phrase: "The candy with the star is better by far."

The company was established in 1932 and is perhaps best known for its peanut butter bars. But Chick-O-Stick has its legions of fans, and the company supplies them in five sizes.

The orange cylinders have a taste similar to that of a Butterfinger bar. They are chewy and messy and great. They have less than 3 ounces of fat, none of it saturated. Legally, it could be called a low-fat food.

The company got started by Basil Atkinson, a lathe operator in a local foundry. He got laid off, borrowed cash from relatives, and started selling candy. Chicken bones was a traditional name for this form of candy in the 1920s. Since someone else had that name, Atkinson decided his version looked a little like fried chicken. Ironically, the company is located near a poultry processor.

His grandson, Eric Atkinson, now runs the company. "We're staunchly a family company and built to stay that way," said Eric, noting he has a 17-year-old daughter and 6-year-old son who are candy fans.

Chick-O-Sticks are sold in bite-size pieces now. Chick o' Nuggets come individually wrapped in 6- and 12-ounce bags. At candy counters, they are 3¢ each. Currently, minimum shipping orders are 100 pounds, but Atkinson is working on Internet ordering for individuals wanting to order less.

We have ordered by the case successfully. We were awash in Chick-O-Sticks for a while, but co-workers, children at elementary-school parties, and Halloween trick-or-treaters cleaned us out. If you call the company, you'll be told where in your area the candy is sold.

ORDERING ADDRESS
Atkinson Candy Co.
P.O. Box 150220
Lufkin, TX 75915-0220
936/639-2333
800/231-1203
FAX: 936/639-2337
www.atkinsoncandy.com
No credit cards

VISITS
1608 Frank Avenue
Lutkin, TX 75915
It's on the west side of town. Take Loop 287, John Ritter Drive.
The plant is at Frank Avenue and Highway 94.
Monday–Friday, 8 A.M.–4:30 P.M.

BRIGITTINE MONKS FUDGE

Like other religious orders that support themselves by the labors of their hands, the Brigittines see fudge making not as a business but as a way to continue their life of prayer. Candy making appeals to them because it can be done without leaving the premises. The cooking is arranged to fit into a day that begins at 4:45 A.M. and involves at least six and a half hours of prayer.

The Brigittines are a very old order, started in 1370. The monks died out over a hundred years ago, largely because of wars in Europe, and only in the last 24 years has a monastery been established in the United States.

The 10 hooded and robed monks, who eschew all but necessary conversation during the day, take great pride in their candy making. It was their profits from the fudge that allowed them to purchase their permanent monastery and confectionery on 44 acres in Amity, Oregon, in 1986.

One measure of how popular their fudge has become is that look-alike recipes for Brigittine Monks Fudge have started cropping up in school and service club cookbooks around the country. We've tried a few of the imitators, however, and they are just that.

The monks' fudge is remarkable for its excellent flavor and its creamy consistency. One reason could be that the monks make their own mazetta, or marshmallow cream, from egg white and corn syrup and use butter and real vanilla. For their chocolate fudges, they blend two varieties of Guittard chocolate. No preservatives are used.

Four flavors are available: chocolate with nuts, chocolate without nuts, chocolate amaretto, and pecan praline. The fudge is $9.95 per pound. From October 1 through March 31, the monks also produce hand-dipped truffles filled with their silky, truffle ganache. The flavors are chocolate, chocolate amaretto, chocolate cherry, chocolate mint, chocolate maple, chocolate raspberry, chocolate butter rum, and milk chocolate. They are sold 6 to a 7.5-ounce package for $10.95. For all orders, add $4 in the United States. For 2 or more items within the continental United States, add $5 for shipping. For Alaska and Hawaii, the shipping charge for 2 or more items is $6. Contact the monastery for rates outside the United States.

The candy is packed in an attractive box. It is available by mail and in some department stores and catalogs. At the monastery is a sheaf of unsolicited endorsements from satisfied customers. "I can honestly say it is the most delicious I've ever tasted," wrote one fan. We have to agree. This is the most heavenly, the most divine fudge made. It is hard to resist eating it all in one sitting.

ORDERING ADDRESS
The Brigittine Monks Gourmet Confections
23300 Walker Lane
Amity, OR 97101
503/835-8080
FAX: 503/835-9662
e-mail: fudge@brigittine.org
www.brigittine.org
Credit cards accepted

CHOCOLATES BY MR. ROBERTS

If we had to choose one box of assorted chocolates from one candy maker in America to give as a gift to a sophisticated eater, it would be the maroon felt box with the gold ribbon from Chocolates by Mr. Roberts in Boca Raton, Florida. Handmade by Heinz Robert Goldschneider, a Swiss tailor turned chocolatier, the chocolates and truffles are elegant and refined. The centers are exceedingly rich, the garnishes unusual (crushed candied violets and mocha beans, for example), and the combinations inspired. Try dark chocolate covering a center of ground walnuts with a hint of rum. Or pistachio praline. Or a hand-rolled milk chocolate with a bit of Cointreau and a confectioners' sugar coating. The truffles are small, with thin outer shells. Each is a joy to be savored and mused over. Charlyne Varkonyi, former food editor of the *Fort Lauderdale News-Sun-Sentinel,* who told us about Mr. Roberts, said these are the chocolates she would most like to be locked in a room with.

Goldschneider started his candy making on New York's Upper East Side, making chocolates for friends, drawing upon professional skills he learned with top chocolatiers in Switzerland. Soon, the chocolates overtook his tailoring business, and he opened a retail chocolate shop, Le Chocolatier. In the early 1980s, he sold Le Chocolatier and retired to Boca Raton. However, seeing an empty storefront there rekindled his candy-making urges.

Goldschneider will send his chocolates by mail between November and May only. In addition to his assorted chocolates ($25 postpaid per pound), we would recommend the candied ginger dipped in dark chocolate ($16 per pound, postpaid). The bite of the ginger is tempered by the chocolate. Pass a small plate of this confection with fruit, and you have an unusual, elegant dessert. Pass up the nut barks, which were surprisingly ungainly, but give thanks that Mr. Roberts has seen fit to turn Florida's touristy coconut patty into a candy worth eating. He offers 2-inch circles of coconut paste whose sides and bottom are dipped in bittersweet chocolate ($16 postpaid for a 1-pound box) that are daintier and more delicious cousins to the thick slabs found at every area fruit stand.

In keeping with his tropical location, Goldschneider offers milk- or dark-chocolate-dipped orange slices, orange peel, prunes, figs, dates, and glazed apricots or pineapple slices.

ORDERING ADDRESS
Chocolates by Mr. Roberts
505 Northeast 20th Street
Boca Raton, FL 33431
560/392-3007
Credit cards accepted

CHOCOLATERIE STAM BONBONS

Visitors may be permitted a double-take when they look at the window of Chocolaterie Stam's jewel box of a shop on a main street in Iowa's capital city. There, printed in gold letters, are the company's locations—Amsterdam and Des Moines.

Finding authentic fine Dutch chocolates in the middle of Iowa seems like a stretch, but it's true. Co-owner Ton Stam grew up in the Netherlands, in a family of fine chocolatiers that has been making candy and pastries since 1817. He literally grew up surrounded by chocolate, living above the various Stam stores. Twelve years ago, when Ton was recruited to this country to become a financial planner, he quickly realized that the fine chocolates that were at the heart of his life in Europe were virtually unknown here. When he moved to Des Moines with his partner, David Clem, a hotel food and beverage manager, the two decided to begin a chocolate business. They started modestly in 1997, with a kiosk in a mall. Today, there are two Chocolaterie Stam stores in Des Moines and six in the Netherlands run by members of Ton's family.

They specialize in fresh cream bonbons, made with high-butterfat chocolate and fillings of crème fraiche, fruits, and caramel. These are fine chocolates, beautifully molded into dainty shapes (a butterfly, a miniature log, a bas-relief rectangle that spells out "Stam.") One of the most popular pieces is shaped like a hedgehog.

Most of the chocolates are flown in from Holland from one of the four shops run by Ton's older brother, Ad. Thanks to time zone differences, the Iowans can fax an order one afternoon and receive it the next day. So the chocolates are very fresh, which is absolutely critical to good chocolate, says Ton. "All of the best chocolate shops are small, artisan-run shops," he says. "If you get too large, you can't keep anything fresh."

Virtually nothing in their shops is older than four to six weeks. They have begun making several of the bonbons in their Des Moines shop, and hope to continually expand the number of locally made pieces.

We adore its cream caramel shaped like a tiny tower, the hazelnut creams, and the coconut ganache. These are chocolates to eat slowly and savor. Consider its cocoa truffle, a heavenly creation made with 68 percent butterfat whipping cream, and a dark chocolate shell made with puur, a dense cocoa mixture that has 52 percent cocoa fat. "This is high quality fat," explains Ton. "If you are going to have something sweet, why not the best?"

The prices, to put it bluntly, are a steal. A pound of chocolates, approximately 25 pieces, is $15.95. That's half the cost of Godiva chocolates and less even than small boxes of the Fannie Farmer brand.

Not surprisingly, the company has a thriving national mail-order business among those who appreciate the craft and quality involved in Stam chocolates. This past Christmas they were shipping 100 boxes a day from their tiny store. "It was wild," said David.

They offer 45 different kinds of bonbons, and will pack boxes to order. A 1½-pound fancy gold box of chocolates is $26.95, and bonbons in a wooden box is $19.95 for 1 pound and $35.95 for 2 pounds. There is a $3 handling fee, plus shipping costs, added to these prices. During the summer, the company adds gel packs to its boxes and sends by overnight delivery. Gift wrapping is available at no extra charge. On its website, the firm pictures some of its specialties, such as a chocolate log filled with about a dozen bonbons.

Once you have tasted Stam exquisite chocolates, it's impossible to be satisfied with a run-of-the-mill candy bar. We're grateful we live in Des Moines.

ORDERING ADDRESS
Chocolaterie Stam
2210 Ingersoll Avenue
Des Moines, IA 50312
515/282-9575
FAX: 515/282-9763
www.stamchocolate.com
Credit cards accepted

VISITS: Ingersoll Avenue is a major east-west street in Des Moines. From I-235, take the Martin Luther King exit south to Ingersoll. Turn right. The easy-to-miss storefront is about one-fourth mile away, on your left. It is next to a larger store, VanGinkel Athletic Manufacturing Co. Chocolaterie Stam also has a store at Valley West Mall in West Des Moines, located off I-235 at the 35th Street/Valley West exit. The shop is on the second level in the center of the mall.

Ingersoll store: Monday–Friday, 9 A.M.–6 P.M. Saturday, 9 A.M.–5 P.M.

CHOWARD'S MINTS AND SCENTED GUM

If Superman had been using his X-ray vision 50 years ago to peer into ladies' handbags, we would bet that he would have seen mints or scented gum from the C. Howard Company in a good number of them. The company still makes its unique products today, but it would be easy, looking at their labels, to think otherwise. The reasons include the flowing script logo, the old-fashioned foil wrappers, and the slightly stilted copy: "A Delicious Confection. Fragrance That Refreshes After Eating, Smoking or Drink."

We were charmed by the foil rectangles of flavored mints and the dainty cardboard box of violet-scented gum, and gave a silent thanks that the company had not been seduced by postmodern splashes and lowercase scrawls. Arthur Pratz, the vice president for sales and one of the owners, said the only changes in the packaging over the past five decades have been slight accommodations to new government regulations and UPC codes.

C. Howard's most famous product is its Choward's violet mints and the violet-scented gum; both remind us of no-nonsense treats that our grandmother would have stashed in her handbag next to a flowered cotton handkerchief. The violet mints are ⅝ of an inch square and are violet in color. You either adore them or hate them. There's no in between. In truth, they taste a bit like eating floral perfume. The violet-scented gum is milder. The small, shiny dark violet squares come in nifty 2½-inch-long boxes that hold 8 tablets.

MINTS & GUM

We particularly liked the lemon-flavored mints in the yellow-and-black foil package and the spearmint variety in the green and silver pack. They are full flavored and unusual. A fourth flavor of mints, peppermint, is labeled "extra strong," and it is. Peppermint fans will want to know about these.

Choward's mints and gum are distributed in the New York metropolitan area, Pennsylvania, New Orleans, South Florida, Chicago, and the West Coast. "We are not in the mail-order business," said Pratz. "However, we do sell our products by mail as a courtesy to customers who relocate or live in areas where our products are not distributed." There is a 2-box minimum for mail-order. Two dozen packages of mints (there are 15 mints to a package) is $11.50 postpaid. The gum is the same price for 24 boxes.

ORDERING ADDRESS
C. Howard Co., Inc.
1007 Station Road
North Bellport, NY 11713
631/286-7940
800/49-MINTS (496-4687)
No credit cards

CRANBERRY SWEETS

Cranberries grown in Oregon are prized for their superior deep red color. However, most of the state's production is shipped to New England, where it is mixed with local berries to improve their appearance. But some Oregon-grown berries find their way to Coos Bay, Oregon, to be made into jellied candies at a 40-year-old company called Cranberry Sweets.

The company, in what surely must be the most exhaustive inventory of its type, makes 27 kinds of cranberry candies. It recently has added various chocolate candies, but the company's reputation has grown on the strength of its first product—sugared, jellied cubes known as Cranberry Sweets. Cranberry Sweets come in plain cranberry and apple cranberry flavors, and each contains chopped walnuts. They are tangy, chewy confections covered with a thin layer of granulated sugar. Need we add how refreshing it is to see a red candy that contains no food coloring? There are no preservatives or artificial flavors used, either.

The unusual candies were devised by one Dorothy Johnson, a cook who experimented for quite a while before coming up with the recipe and method for making the jellied candy. She made only the two kinds of sweets and worked from her Bandon home. The current owners of the business, Clayton Shaw and his mother, Margaret Shaw, won't get specific about how the sweets are made, but admit that it takes a good while to make them.

Cranberry Sweets & more

Sixteen years ago, the family moved the business from its cramped confines to the historic Bandon Hotel, across the street, one of three buildings in town that survived a devastating 1936 fire. In 1988, with the business continuing to expand, they moved the factory to Coos Bay. Still, "we just can't make enough to supply everyone," said Margaret. "We have to limit our wholesale customers."

Eaters are drawn to the company's unique offerings, like the cranberry nut jelly candies flavored with lemon, almond, orange, raspberry and plum, all lightly dusted with sugar. They give a pure, concentrated burst of berry flavor. The 20-ounce assortment is $19.95, including shipping and gift wrapping.

The company makes 15 kinds of jellied candies, plus cranberry nougat, several kinds of chocolate-dipped cranberry confections, lemon meringue pie candy, chocolate creams, and truffles. Exquisite cranberry cordials are sold at the Christmas holidays. A 12-ounce box of cranberry or apple-cranberry Cranberry Sweets is $15.95, including postage and wrapping. The company has a color catalog it will send upon request.

ORDERING ADDRESS
Cranberry Sweets Company
1005 Newmark
Coos Bay, OR 97420
541/888-9824
800/527-5748
FAX: 541/888-2824
e-mail: info@cranberrysweets.com
www.cranberrysweetsandmore.com
Credit cards accepted

VISITS: The factory and retail store are in Coos Bay. A second store is south of Coos Bay in Bandon, on the coast in southern Oregon. The Bandon shop is at the corner of First and Chicago Streets downtown, across from the city's boat basin.

Coos Bay store: Monday–Saturday, 9 A.M.–5:30 P.M. Sunday, 11 A.M.–4 P.M.

CRAND'S CANDY

It is disheartening to see candy companies, even those that still hand-dip their chocolates, use coatings that have the interloper lecithin added. Lecithin, a waxy stabilizer, either takes the place of cocoa butter entirely or is added to it for the purpose of prolonging shelf life and shine. The trouble is, chocolate containing lecithin has a taste that is slightly off and doesn't react quite the same way as unadulterated chocolate.

The Crand family, responsible for unsurpassed chocolate creations in Enfield, Connecticut, refuses to even consider using chocolate with lecithin. This is a company that is even fussy about the kind of corn syrup it uses, insisting on a hard-to-obtain 43 Regular that makes the fluffiest candy centers. This is a company that hand-pulls its own candy canes at Christmas, and the result is a substantial piece of candy that weighs twice as much as the common puffed-up variety. And this is a company whose ingredient list on boxes of chocolate is a joy to read: chocolate, fresh cream, pure butter, sugar, corn syrup, cocoa butter, fresh eggs, fruits and nuts, and pure fruit flavor.

It has been that way since John Crand, who emigrated from Greece in 1911, taught himself fine candy making by trial and error. Mr. Crand was a determined man who started his business in the basement of a cousin's ice cream parlor, lost everything in the Crash of 1929, and came back to open his own candy shop in 1935. Mr. Crand died in 1966, but not before teaching his sons Robert and Thomas his own way of making high-quality candy. Robert and his wife, Nancy, now run the enterprise.

It is fitting that Crand's is located in a home—an impressive 1820 Federal-style dwelling known as "The Chimneys" owing to its four massive chimneys, two at either end—because it is the quintessential family-run business. A drawing of "The Chimneys" graces each candy box.

Crand's Special Assortment chocolates, at an incredibly low price of $10.50 a pound, give a sample of the family's wide range of candy-making skill: various chocolates, butter crunch, snow flakes (dark chocolate split open to reveal sweetened coconut), French roll (a Crand exclusive that's a cross between a fudge and a caramel rolled in nuts), and pecan roll. The latter is one of Crand's many standouts: a thick stab of chewy nougat covered with caramel and then rolled in pecan pieces. The nougat recipe sounds simple—three dozen egg whites and corn syrup—but timing and humidity are critical.

Crand's will mail its candies all year long, insulating them with paper in the summer months. We ordered cherry cordials in July and they arrived without disappointment. For a typed list of its specialties and their prices, write the company. All of the candies are extremely reasonable, with the most expensive, cordials, at $11.95 a pound, excluding shipping.

ORDERING ADDRESS
Crand's Candy Castle, Inc.
Route 5, P.O. Box 3023
Enfield, CT 06082
860/623-5515
e-mail: crandcandies@aol.com
Credit cards accepted

VISITS
1684 King Street.
Enfield, CT 06082
Enfield is in the north-central part of the state, about 15 miles north of Hartford. "The Chimneys" is located in a partly residential area directly on Highway 5 just south of the city. Visitors can see the kitchen from the sales area.
Sunday–Tuesday, 10 A.M.–6 P.M. Wednesday–Saturday, 10 A.M.–8 P.M.

CUMMINGS STUDIO OPERA CREAMS

We love the coy propaganda that Paul and Marion Cummings include in every order: facts like "Confections do not add many calories" and "Large quantities of candy and chocolate help fight driving fatigue" and "Businessmen are learning that confections can help both plant and office workers keep alert and are providing their employees with a mid-morning and mid-afternoon candy break." Those are employers we'd like to meet, especially if they are considerate enough to offer their workers the Cummings' opera creams.

The name refers to the delicacies eaten while listening to arias, not drill presses, of course. These chocolates are elegant cousins to buttercreams. Their creamy centers contain delicately flavored cream of 48 percent butterfat that's been cooked and then hand-rolled before being dipped in chocolate. We prefer the plain Boston cream, but customers have 60 flavors to choose from!

The Cummings family has been making the opera creams, as well as dozens of other confections, since 1924. Paul's father, Victor Clyde Cummings, first learned about candy after getting interested in a classmate at Salt Lake City High School and deciding that the best way to woo her was to join her home economics class. The romance didn't endure, but the candy making did, first in his mother's basement, then, with the backing of a friend who owned the local Franklin auto dealership, in the downtown shop still in use today.

The company now enrobes 250,000 California strawberries and 30,000 cups of raspberries in chocolate each year. These fragile delicacies must be eaten with 24 hours and are. They are not shipped.

The candy is well priced at $15.25 per pound for chocolates, plus shipping.

ORDERING ADDRESS
Cummings Studio Candies
679 East Ninth South
Salt Lake City, UT 34105
801/328-4858
800/537-3957
FAX 801/328-4801
e-mail: candy@xmission.com
http://utah.citysearch.com
Credit cards accepted

VISITS: From the Mormon Temple, travel 9 blocks south. Turn east on Ninth Street for 7 more blocks.
Monday–Saturday, 9 A.M.–6:30 P.M.

DINSTUHL'S CHOCOLATE-COVERED STRAWBERRIES

Eight decades before department stores and cookware emporiums found it politic to hold shoppers in thrall with the sight of someone dipping fruit in chocolate, the Dinstuhl family of Memphis was creating an enduring tradition of hand-dipped strawberries.

It is a rite of spring in Memphis to visit one of the five Dinstuhl stores and buy chocolate-covered strawberries. Only fresh Louisiana berries are used, so the season is short—usually from mid-March through Mother's Day. During the rest of the year, however, the family has more than enough other outstanding sweets to divert an eater's attention. There are chocolate-dipped cherries for the holidays that have been soaked in brandy for three months. There is cashew crunch, exceedingly tasty nuggets of a brittle-type candy rolled in ground coconut. Figaros, a European-type sweet of filbert paste and chocolate, also have a loyal following.

A third and fourth generation of Dinstuhl (pronounced Din-stool) is now running the business. Chairman Gene Dinstuhl's grandfather founded the company in 1902, and it began, like many candy shops, as an ice cream parlor. Only top-quality ingredients are used, cooked in vintage copper kettles, and then hand-dipped in good chocolate.

Gene's son, Gary, the company's president, explained that it's a common problem that some of the young women who work as dippers find they can no longer eat candy bars out of machines. They write to the Dinstuhls from college and say, "Please send chocolate."

The company prides itself on personal service and is happy to fill out-of-the-ordinary requests such as matching the color of wedding mints to fabric swatches or making up special gift boxes.

All indications are that Dinstuhl's will remain a charming part of Memphis for years to come. The firm has a fifth generation growing up and has moved its candy making to a large, new kitchen.

The prices are good. Assorted boxed chocolates are $15 a pound. Cashew crunch is $8.25 per pound, and strawberries, which vary according to the price of the fruit, most recently were $12.99 per pound. For years, the company drew the line at shipping the strawberries. "Too perishable," said Gary Dinstuhl. But now, as befitting a company based in Nashville, Federal Express's hometown, it will send them via overnight delivery. Dinstuhl's doesn't guarantee the strawberries will arrive in perfect condition, but that caveat has not deterred faithful eaters.

ORDERING ADDRESS
Dinstuhl's
5280 Pleasant View Road
Memphis, TN 38124
901/377-2639
e-mail: dinstuhls@juno.com
www.dinstuhls.com
Credit cards accepted

VISITS: There are three Dinstuhl's locations around Memphis, plus there are Dinstuhl candies, including the strawberries, in 14 Seessel's grocery stores throughout the city. The kitchen and store is on Pleasant View Road in the northern part of the city. Take Covington Pike to the Pleasant View exit and turn right.

Monday–Friday, 8 A.M.–5:30 P.M. Saturday, 9 A.M.–5:30 P.M.

DOROTHY TIMBERLAKE'S BARLEY CANDY

It was the memory of the long-lasting barley-candy lollipops she used to buy at Fiske's Candy Shop in Harvard Square that launched Dorothy Timberlake into the candy business at age 55. When her husband bought her three antique candy molds for her birthday 30 years ago, neither guessed it would result in a full-time business for Timberlake and her daughter, Faith Timberlake-Alves.

Their collection of antique molds has grown, too, to more than 10,000 shapes. The Timberlakes do not use any of the old pewter molds directly, as they contain lead, but have them reproduced in aluminum and medical-grade silicone. The molds are displayed on the walls of the four candy rooms in the Eaton Center, New Hampshire, house in which Timberlake was born. It was due to the overwhelming popularity of her rainbow-colored lollipops that Timberlake created the candy kitchen in her family home.

By boiling pearl barley in water from a 210-foot artesian well, the Timberlakes achieve the candy's thick water base. Sugar and corn syrup and flavorings as ordinary as lemon and as exotic as fig, cantaloupe, kiwi, and custard are added. There is much hand labor involved. To unmold the clear candies, the Timberlakes use a clam shucker or a dentist's pick, then hand-file any roughness at the seams. The candy is strong flavored and not as sweet as traditional lollipops.

Buying from this company is not for the indecisive. Like a Chinese menu with unlimited columns, you can order nearly any color, flavor, and shape imaginable. The mold collection offers buyers very large shapes (Charlie Chaplin, tall policeman, teddy bear with collar); large shapes (accordion, chimney sweep, 5 varieties of elephant, and 16 types of rabbit-with saxophone, mandolin, or "egg in forepaws"), and small shapes (dinosaurs of the sphenodon, stegosaurus, and tyrannosaurus families), among others. You even can select Hamlet holding Yorick's skull! All can be ordered with or without lollipop sticks. Easter, Thanksgiving, Halloween, Valentine's Day, and weddings have their own assortments.

Christmas is special, with "tin" soldiers and rainbows of hanging tree ornaments. She also can make thin, barley-candy shells of medium-size clear toys, filled with chocolate. Hostesses frequently order candy baskets for centerpieces.

The candy "is like glass to ship," as Timberlake relates, but great care is taken in its packaging. Our candy arrived beautifully intact. She will ship a minimum of one dozen. A box of 6 lollipops is $10 and a dozen are $19.50. There's a $6 minimum shipping fee. Customers may have nearly any shape reproduced, as long as the Timberlakes are able to make a mold from it. Customers may ask to have pictures of shapes they are interested in sent to them first.

ORDERING ADDRESS
Dorothy Timberlake Candies
Main Street, Route 153
Eaton Center, NH 03832
603/447-2221
e-mail: barleycandy@landmarknet.net
Credit cards accepted

VISITS: The Timberlake house is on Main Street (Route 153), 2 houses from the village church and across the street from the Palmer House Hotel. Call first to see if a visit is convenient.

DR. PETERS PEPPERMINT CRUNCH

A confession. When Dr. Peters is around, we self-medicate. These pillows of peppermint are covered, and we do mean covered, in the softest-tasting bittersweet chocolate we've found. The individually-wrapped candies come in a tin with a picture of the good doctor just encouraging you to eat more.

Nearly all of the candy sold by Jo's Candies, a 54-year-old Torrance, California, company, is double-dipped. The menu board contains a hit parade of comfort confections—chocolate-covered graham crackers, honeycomb, peanut butter meltaways, rocky road, cream eggs, and chocolate-covered cherries.

Tom King, president of the company, now sells the candies only by mail and in high-end food stores. All the chocolate used is Swiss, with no tropical oils. For most candies, customers have a choice of milk or bittersweet chocolate. Some items, like eggnog bark, are seasonal.

The peppermint crunch is $15.50 for a 13-ounce tin. Shipping is extra.

ORDERING ADDRESS
Jo's Candies
2530 W. 237th Street
Torrance, CA 90505
310/257-0260
800/770-1946
FAX: 310/257-0266
Credit cards accepted

DUNDEE CANDY SHOP MODJESKAS

Did you know that when Henrik Ibsen's play *A Doll's House* premiered in this country, its heroine was called Thora, not Nora, and that Ibsen was forced to rewrite Act III so that Thora reconciled with her husband instead of finding liberation on her own? This surprising historic footnote came to light while doing research on the Modjeska—a caramel-coated soft marshmallow candy created to honor Polish actress Madame Modjeska, who starred in the Ibsen play's first American production, which was in Louisville, Kentucky, in 1883.

An article in the *Louisville Courier-Journal* that gave the history of the candy said it was the brainchild of Anton Busath, who came to Louisville from Alsace and opened a popular candy shop and soda fountain on Fourth Street. Mrs. F. S. Koestel, a great niece of Anton Busath, was quoted as saying that "not only was the Modjeska a best-seller in Louisville, it was shipped all over the world. Every other candy store in Louisville attempted to copy the Modjeska, in name as well as appearance."

In 1947, Busath's shop was destroyed by fire. Later, his copyright on the Modjeska name expired and other candy makers were able to use the name. Today, there are a number of shops in northern Kentucky and southern Indiana where Modjeskas are available. If you want to try one in its home territory, we suggest Dundee Candy Shops, a local favorite for nearly five decades. The business is now operated by Volindah Costabell. The original shop is dainty and decorative, from its maroon-and-white-striped awning to the geraniums, salvia, pansies, and ageratum growing outside.

The Modjeskas are puffy, individually wrapped rectangles that are about twice the size of a conventional caramel. They are soft, sweet, and chewy. Pure delight. Modjeskas can be shipped year-round. Summer shipments and those west of the Mississippi require next or second day air. They are $10.80 a pound.

Some of Dundee's more unusual offerings are cordials filled with tangerine, crème brûlée flavoring, and almond, among others. They are $10.60 per pound. Chocolate boxes are made in many sizes and tailored to customer's wishes. A popular version is a round 2-inch box with a horsehead lid. Inside are a candy horseshoe and rose. A sampler of assorted chocolates is $11.20 a pound. Shipping costs are additional.

Dundee gift-wraps everything that is shipped from its stores, at no additional charge, in a choice of embossed white, coated maroon, or gold and silver abstract . The shop has long been known for its beautiful wrappings and ribbons, which are extraordinary.

ORDERING ADDRESS
Dundee Candy Shop
2212 Dundee Road
Louisville, KY 40205
502/452-9266
FAX: 502/459-7319
Credit cards accepted

VISITS: **The Dundee Road shop is southeast of downtown in a neighborhood called The Highlands. From I-264, exit north at Bardstown Road. Go through the intersection of Trevilian and Taylorsville Roads. Then continue through 3 traffic lights to the Douglas loop (where 5 streets come together in a circle). The first street to the left is Dundee Road. Take Dundee Road and look to your right in the first block for the sign.**
Monday–Saturday, 9 A.M.–5 P.M.

ENSTROM'S ALMOND TOFFEE

The holiday rush is so hectic at Enstrom Candies that local firefighters provide the muscle each year to package and ship the thousands of pounds of toffee loyal customers demand.

Enstrom's started shipping their toffee because it couldn't bear to hear grown-ups whine, plead, and beg. It's the only one of their dozens of fine homemade candies that the family will ship—a decision based on the demands of travelers no longer near Colorado.

The late Chet Enstrom, an ice cream manufacturer in Grand Junction, began making the buttery toffee nearly 70 years ago. It's a medium-hard butter toffee that is covered with pale chocolate and packed with finely ground almonds. Perhaps because the chocolate is so mild, the flavors seem better blended than other combinations of its type. The toffee is made in large sheets and broken into pieces to fit into its handsome boxes.

It is delicious candy. Our Iowa friend, the late Judy Klemesrud, a pioneering writer on women's issues for the *New York Times,* first alerted us to Enstroms with a warning that she couldn't be responsible if we got hooked. We did. The candy can be frozen for six to eight months, but you'd have to have an iron will to do it.

"We'll tell anyone who asks what goes into the toffee," said Jamee Enstrorn Simons, granddaughter of the founder. "Yet no one has ever been able to duplicate the taste and we haven't the slightest idea why."

The toffee has four main ingredients: sugar, butter from Colorado, nonpareil almonds from orchards near Sacramento, and Guittard chocolate. The Enstroms surmise that the altitude and lack of humidity in the high desert climate may contribute to the toffee's uniqueness. "When Doug, my husband, was attending candy-makers' school back in the flatlands, he noticed that butter scorched at a much lower temperature than we cook our butter," said Simons.

The company truly is a family business. It will ship 1 pound of the toffee for $11.95, plus $4.55 shipping. But why not go for broke—get 5 pounds for $51.95, plus $5.35 shipping—and make five households happy? There are two stores in Denver; at Second and University, in the Cherry Creek Mall area and 14415 West Colfax, in Denver's West Village (Lakewood). The Lakewood store, which is just off I-70, has a kosher kitchen.

ORDERING ADDRESS
Enstrom Candies
P.O. Box 1088
Grand Junction, CO 81502
970/242-1655
800/ENSTROM (367-8766)
e-mail: toffee@enstrom.com
www.enstrom.com
Credit cards accepted

VISITS: **The company is at 200 South Seventh Street in Grand Junction. From 1-70 West, exit at Horizon Drive. Turn left onto Seventh Street and drive south through town. Cross Main Street, then Colorado Avenue, and Enstrom's is the building on the left. Visitors may watch the toffee makers at work.**

Monday–Saturday, 8:30 A.M.–5 P.M.

EUPHORIA TRUFFLES

Never underestimate the power of chocolate. On the strength of Euphoria Truffles' confections, what was once a tiny shop is now a five-store empire in Eugene, Oregon. Owner Bob Bury, Jr., is a third-generation chocolatier. His mother and grandmother both dipped chocolates at the late, highly esteemed San Francisco candy shop Princess Delight. "I grew up in a house were there were boxes and large blocks of chocolate around," said Bob. "I couldn't foresee the possibility of a life without large quantities of chocolate around."

His 20-year-old company is best known for its hand-dipped truffles, which have creamy ganache in well-thought-out flavors. The best-seller is the double chocolate. The firm has added raspberry, strawberry, coconut, Kona coffee, and a seasonal cherries jubilee. Truffles remain $1.75 each and can be purchased in tiny red gift boxes that hold a single piece. The truffles are refrigerated and are shipped in the winter months, although there are plans to ship year-round.

Less than perfect "oddballs" are sold in the shops at a discount. Discounts also are given at all times to customers over the age of 60.

In a nod to its hometown, the company makes a gourmet gorp, a designer trail mix of "good old raisins and peanuts." The mixture includes milk-chocolate-covered raisins and peanuts, dark-chocolate-covered almonds and pistachios, and unadorned large cashews.

Euphoria truffles can be bought at nearly 100 outlets in Oregon and Washington, mostly bakeries and delicatessens.

ORDERING ADDRESS
Euphoria Chocolate Company
6 West 17th Avenue
Eugene, OR 97401
541/343-9223
www.euphoriachocolate.com
Credit cards accepted

VISITS: **The company is at the corner of Willamette Avenue (a major street) and West 17th Street. From downtown, take Willamette south to 17th, or take Pearl Street to 17th, turn right and drive 2 blocks. The store is on the left. Another store is at 401 Center Street Northeast in Salem, in the Salem Center.**

Eugene Location: Monday–Friday, 10 A.M.–6 P.M. Saturday, 11 A.M.–5 P.M.

GOO-GOO CLUSTERS AND KING LEO STICK CANDY

If you're not from the South, you may never have tasted a gooey confection aptly named Goo-Goo Cluster. It's been a favorite candy bar there since 1912, when Howell H. Campbell mixed up a batch of chocolate, marshmallow, caramel, and peanuts in his kitchen. Still sold by the Standard Candy Company, which Campbell founded, the cluster is moving north. The cluster was named by a Nashville woman to whom Campbell related his difficulty in choosing a title. She suggested naming it after the only words Campbell's infant son could then pronounce.

It's also changing size, with new Goo-Goo babies. These are .7-ounce miniatures. They fit in with the craze of downsizing all of our favorite candies so we can eat more of them, guilt free.

With fans like Howard Baker, Pat Boone, and William F. Buckley (who wrote in *The New Yorker* that he found out about the candy from reading our first edition), the clusters are finding their way into a sprinkling of stores in New York and California. Vroman Foods, a Toledo, Ohio, maker of ice cream specialties, even has devised a frozen ice cream Goo-Goo bar with chocolate—marshmallow ice cream, caramel, and peanuts. We've seen a Safeway variety, too. But for most people north of the Mason-Dixon line, their only source of supply is a mail-order delivery of a 24-cluster box, postpaid at $17.95.

The company also makes a Goo-Goo Supreme, wrapped in gold and containing more chocolates and pecans instead of peanuts. It retails for 60¢ at southern candy counters.

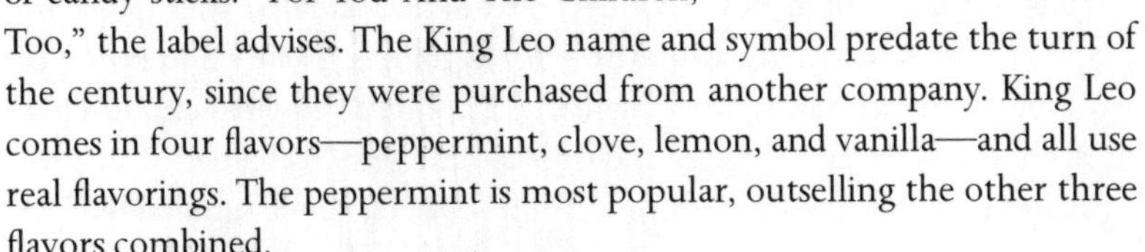

The firm's King Leo stick candy is even older than Goo-Goo Clusters, having been the company's first product when it began in 1901. "Pure King Leo," states the dark-blue tin canister that depicts a full maned lion standing on his hind legs, with his front legs resting on a pile of candy sticks. "For You And The Children, Too," the label advises. The King Leo name and symbol predate the turn of the century, since they were purchased from another company. King Leo comes in four flavors—peppermint, clove, lemon, and vanilla—and all use real flavorings. The peppermint is most popular, outselling the other three flavors combined.

The sticks, handmade in 90-pound batches, have a pulled white center that is softer than the exterior. After stripes are added on the outside, the sticks are twisted, giving a slightly uneven surface. Each stick is about 3½ inches long and, nestled into a tin, will keep fresh for months. The flavors are strong and stay with the stick from one end to the other.

Nearly everything about King Leo has remained the same for decades—the lettering on the can, the slogans, production methods, and flavors—with one exception. The drawing of King Leo on the can was retouched 15 years ago to give him longer legs and a more lion like face. "He looked like a dog!" we were told. Now more kingly than ever, King Leo and his candy can be ordered by mail in a 1.5-pound tin. Four tins are sent for $29.95, shipping included.

ORDERING ADDRESS
Standard Candy Company
Mail Order Department Box 101025
Nashville, TN 37210
615/889-6360
e-mail: scc@standardcandy.com
www.googoo.com
Credit cards accepted

VISITS
715 Massman Drive.
Nashville, TN 37210
The plant is in east Nashville.
Monday–Friday
8 A.M.–5 P.M.

HARBOR SWEETS CHOCOLATES

Ben Strohecker earned a reputation as an innovative, flexible manager. Business-school classes, community service organizations, and church groups seek out his advice. He also takes his own counsel. He mentored a college student, Phyllis LeBlanc, decades ago and now she owns the Salem, Massachusetts, company he founded, Harbor Sweets.

He built the company from a basement enterprise 26 years ago, gaining national attention because of its mix of employees. More than half of Harbor Sweet's 140 employees are elderly, students, disabled, or new immigrants. There is a wide mix of ethnic backgrounds. Nearly all employees work part time, choosing their own schedules to fit in with school schedules, child-care commitments, and other home responsibilities.

All that would mean nothing if the products weren't first rate. Customers care most about taste, not enlightened management and noble hiring goals. Happily, Strohecker came to the realization early on that the world did not need one more chocolate company. To succeed, he would have to be unique and offer only top-notch products unavailable elsewhere. He and LeBlanc have kept the product line small—just a few special chocolate pieces—and created beautiful packaging and an efficient shipping department.

Strohecker has managed to impart a sense of wonder, even childishness, in his creations. That alone is worthy of praise. The company's signature piece is the Sweet Sloop, a white-chocolate-covered triangle of almond butter crunch with one side dipped in dark chocolate and dusted with chopped nuts. He created it while trying to do something different with almond butter crunch, a confection that he discovered was at the top of several candy makers' list of favorites. While working as the marketing director of Schrafft's, the late confectionery-restaurant chain, Strohecker polled top candy makers and consultants. He used their wish lists of best candies as a jumping off point for his own candy-making experiments, coming up with six candies.

All were given nautical themes appropriate to his seacoast location. In addition to the Sweet Sloop there is a soft caramel, chocolate, and pecan sand dollar; a chocolate-mint round with a yacht molded in relief on the face (dubbed Marblehead for the nearby city that is home to a great number of yachts); an orange and chocolate molded sea shell; a toasted almond and chocolate oval named Barque Sarah for the 1850-esque sailing ship molded on its face; and miniature periwinkle snail shells. The emphasis is on bittersweet chocolate, although several items are made in milk chocolate as well.

A new line, Dark Horse Chocolates, was created by LeBlanc, inspired by her own black horse. Our favorite is Peppermint Ponies, which are dark chocolate rounds covering a thin layer of peppermint crunch. An 18-piece assortment is $14.95, plus shipping. There's also a line of golf candies—Sweet Shots, Fairways, and TournaMints.

Harbor Sweets are not hand-dipped, but the hand of an individual with a vision is evident. The company's chocolate rabbit epitomizes the firm's quirky, personal approach. It is the Robert L. Strohecker Assorted Rabbit (certainly the longest name for an individual candy we've heard), named in honor of Strohecker's grandfather, who was believed to be this country's first promoter of chocolate rabbits. The molded bunny, which traps assorted Harbor Sweets candies inside the chocolate, was four years in the making, as the mold maker and Strohecker struggled to re-create the proper shape of a rabbit his grandfather posed with in 1890.

The rabbits are a dainty 5 inches tall. They come in dark or milk chocolate and are split down the middle. The innards are surprises—toasted almonds, caramel, almond butter crunch, and peanut almond butter crunch. Each side is wrapped in gold foil and the two are joined by a ribbon around the bunny's neck. Available only in the spring, a single rabbit is $15.50 and two are $25, plus shipping.

Harbor Sweets will undoubtedly continue to chart new waters in hiring practices, work practices, community involvement, and product development. Recently, Ben Strohecker has been working on AIDS education in the workplace.

We like the way his workplace works.

ORDERING ADDRESS
Harbor Sweets, Inc.
Mail Orders
c/o New England 800 Company
251 Jefferson Street MS4
Waldoboro, ME 04572–6011
978/745-7648
800/234-4860
FAX: 978/741-7811
e-mail: steph@harborsweets.com
www.harborsweets.com
Credit cards accepted

VISITS
85 Leavitt Street
Salem, MA 01970
Salem is 35 minutes east of Boston. Take Route 128, exiting at Route 114. Harbor Sweets is about 4 miles from the exit, on Leavitt Street.
Monday–Friday, 8:30 a.m.–4:30 p.m. Saturday, 9 A.M.–3 P.M.

HAMMOND'S HARD CANDIES

The hardest thing about describing Hammond's is deciding what candy to feature. We could have given the headline to its hand-dipped toffee. Or to the delicious caramels that include flavors like licorice, strawberry, vanilla pecan, and chocolate. Or to the company's popular Golden Nutty Korn, a glazed popcorn snack studded with cashews, pecans, and almonds. Or its Honey KoKo's, a coconut-honey cream rolled in chocolate and coconut whose recipe dates to the company's founding by Carl T. Hammond in 1920. But we're slighting the jelly squares (apricot, orange, lemon, and raspberry). And the ground-nut candy known as Mija that fans buy in pound bags to sprinkle over pies and puddings. And the cherry cordials, barks, brittles, and fudges. There's more, but you grasp the dilemma.

This is one of those rare shops that is a virtual edible museum of longtime favorite candies. We are forever in the debt of Joanne Holcomb, a Denver resident who knows the city inside out, for taking us there—twice. Each holiday provides a compelling reason to swing by for a visit. We were there at Easter and were charmed by rustic-looking chocolate eggs and baskets.

But it is at Christmas, with its hard candies, that Hammond's indulges in unmatched food nostalgia. When we returned to the store in December it was like stepping back in time. There was delicate ribbon candy in two sizes: miniature satiny peppermint pillows in gold and white, green and white; or red and white stripes, each with exactly 16 stripes. The price is a bargain $12 per pound. Flavorful hand-formed candy canes that come in vivid combinations, such as red and green stripes or gold and white stripes, are substantial enough to hang out of a Christmas stocking and pretty enough to use as decorations. A set of 6 canes is $10.50.

Hammond's is one of the few stores we know where good-quality, hard art candy is made. This "cut rock," which was once a common item in candy shops, is not yet another endangered species. At Hammond's, the art candy was made for years by Bud DePry, who knew 35 different designs and taught Emery Dorsey his secrets before retiring several years ago. Emery, age 40, who apprenticed under DePry and his late father-in-law, Carl "Tom" Hammond, Jr., has been the chief candy maker for 15 years.

Art candy is formed by hand-kneading, coloring, and pulling heated sugar and corn syrup into long ropes. To make a lime slice, for example, "seeds" of white ropes are wrapped in green triangular wedges. Six wedges are formed in a cylinder that is wrapped in another white layer, then in an outer green layer. The resulting thick rope is pulled to a smaller and smaller diameter, taking care not to squash the picture elements inside. Just as the candy begins to harden, the rope is sliced into half-inch pieces, with each slice revealing the lime pattern on both sides.

Every year a dozen or so designs are made for the holidays, and Emery usually creates a new one as well. One year it was a snowman encased in blue "ice." One pound of the art candy is $11. Some of the other special Hammond hard candy treats are red satin cream-filled straws, satin jewels with soft coconut filling, and elegant-looking black walnut rectangles. These are so far removed from the crude designs that pass for Christmas candy these days that they are in a class by themselves. One pound of the Christmas straws is $8 and they come with a choice of fillings.

Hammond's also offers hand-formed "whirl" lollipops that are made in ropes and then stuck on a stick. A set of 6 is $9.

Hammond's brochure has enough temptations to make your choices agonizing ones. At Christmas, Valentine's Day, and Easter, Hammond's has a holiday cart at Park Meadows Mall, south of the city.

ORDERING ADDRESS
Hammond Candy Company
4969 Colorado Boulevard
Denver, CO 80216
303/333-5588
888-CANDY99 (226-3999)
FAX: 303/333-5622
www.hammondscandies.com
Credit cards accepted

VISITS: **The Hammond's kitchen and store is about 1½ blocks off I-70. Exit at Colorado Boulevard and drive north to 48th Avenue. Turn left on 48th and immediately turn right onto the frontage road. Hammond's is on the frontage road, between 48th and 50th Avenues.**
Monday–Friday, 9 A.M.–4 P.M.

IDAHO SPUD CANDY BAR

We are fans of old-fashioned candy bars and always scan the candy counter offerings in other cities. But too many retail outfits take the lazy way out, carrying the same old national brands.

Anyone who lives in Idaho is fortunate, because there's a living candy museum more than pulling its own weight in the historic candy bar department. The Owyhee (oh-*wy*-hee) Company is a national treasure.

First, it makes the Idaho Spud, America's only candy bar designed to look like a potato. The Spud is about 3 inches long, shaped in an oval, and covered in dark chocolate. Toasted coconut is scattered on the top, perhaps to suggest potato eyes. The inside is marshmallow. The wrapper, which lists a copyright of 1931, is dark brown with little orange eyes. The Spud's motto, "The Candy Bar That Makes Idaho Famous," appears below the name. It's a tasty bar that's fun to eat, and a sentimental favorite with a definite sense of place.

The candy company is responsible for two other old-fashioned candy bars that are also distinctive. The Old Faithful peanut cluster is a bumpy milk chocolate and peanut coating over a creamy nougat center. The Cherry Cocktail bar is a mound of chopped cherries and pink cream covered with chocolate.

Every city and region used to have several candy bars, as author Ray Broekel described in his well-researched *The Great American Candy Bar Book* (Boston: Houghton Mifflin, 1982). Gone are the Chicken Dinner, Denver Sandwich, Baby Lobster, and No Jelly bars. There are still a few old-time regional holdouts, like the Idaho Spud, and a very few new entries such as the Wisconsin Cow Pie, from the Wiscandy Corporation in Wisconsin Dells.

In Idaho, the Owyhee Candy Company is now owned by the Idaho Candy Company in Boise. The offices are in a modern building near the airport, but the large vintage factory is still downtown. "We're still using equipment that goes back one hundred years, with wooden pulleys and leather belts," said company chairman John Wagers. His son, David, now runs the company.

The company allows walk-in customers in its 1909 building, the first one in Idaho with skylights and a "welfare room," (employee lounge). Let your children see how turn-of-the-last-century companies looked.

The Wagers have owned the company for 17 years, and were delighted to discover that it came with vintage employees as well as equipment. Violet (Vi) Brewer, for example, only retired when she turned 95 years old, after working for the company for 82 years. Her granddaughter now works there.

Don't miss Owyhee Toffee, an amazing candy that is shipped year-round but is especially popular at Christmas. The name comes from the Sandwich Island Indians, or Owhyees, who gave their name to a river, mountains, and county in Idaho. A 1 -pound box is a very reasonable $10.99, which includes shipping costs. A 2-pound box is $17.99. The toffee comes in three versions—bite, chunk, and chocolate coated. All are rich toffees covered with finely ground almonds. The bite size is daintier eating. Be sure to specify which type you prefer.

The company will send a carton of 24 of its Idaho Spuds for $16. A carton of 36 Old Faithful bars is $22. Both prices include packaging and shipping charges. We'd recommend that first-timers get the $18.99 variety pack, which includes 6 Idaho Spud bars, 4 Cherry Cocktails, 4 Old Faithfuls, and 1 pound of Owyhee Butter Toffee bite. Shipping is included.

ORDERING ADDRESS
Idaho Candy Company
P.O. Box 1217
Boise, ID 83701-1217
208/342-5505
800/8-YUM YUM (800-898-6986)
FAX: 208/384-5310
e-mail: info@idahospud.com
www.idahospud.com
Credit cards accepted

Owyhee Butter Toffee
IDAHO CANDY CO.
BOISE, IDAHO.

VISITS
412 South Eighth Street
Boise, ID
The plant is one block south of Rt. 20 and 3 blocks north of the Boise River. It's between S. Capitol Blvd. and South 9th St. at Broad Street downtown Boise.
Monday–Friday, 9 A.M.–3 P.M.

KEHR'S KANDY KITCHEN HOMEMADE CANDIES

Kehr's Kandy Kitchen has provided a sweet anchor to a downtown Milwaukee neighborhood for 70 years. Faithful customers who have moved away still seek it out, and locals have appreciated the reasonable prices and large selection.

Kehr's is one of a handful of old-fashioned candy and ice cream parlors around the country that have stayed true to their roots, despite the changing surroundings. Crown Candy Kitchen, in St. Louis, the nation's best place to have a banana malt, comes to mind. Stores like these deserve to be supported for not fleeing to the suburbs and giving up on decades of culinary history.

Kehr's used to have a thriving fountain with homemade ice cream, but it was taken out 20 years ago. The candy-making operation, however, has changed little over the decades, relying on memorized recipes and hand-stirring. The company is now run by Paul Martinka, a longtime employee who bought the business in 1996 from Bill Kehr. The company's slogan is "Made With Care-by Kehr," and the hand labor shows on its signature candies, such as its chocolate and caramel patties. So often the nuts on these candies seem apportioned by computer. At Kehr's, they are slathered on.

A pound of assorted milk and dark chocolate patties, available with cashews or pecans, is a reasonable $11.95, which includes wrapping in white paper with a brown grosgrain ribbon bow. The assorted chocolates are $12.95 a pound, which seems absurdly inexpensive for the rich mix of chocolate-covered cashews, Brazil nuts, dates, creams, and cherry cordials. It is possible to order boxes of assorted chocolate-covered nuts, assorted creams, assorted fruit and nut centers, or hard and chewy centered chocolates. Kehr's chocolate is first rate, especially the dark.

A Kehr's tradition is fairy food, a chocolate-covered candy that looks a bit ungainly in the box (individual pieces are large 2-inch nuggets) but has an appealing burnt-sugar sponge interior. This is food for fairies with strong teeth, it should be noted. The sponge is quite crunchy. It comes in milk or dark chocolate, at $10.95 a pound. UPS charges are added to all the above prices.

Kehr's has an extensive repertoire, including toffees, peanut butter melt-away squares, nut cups, nougats, cherry cordials, dipped pretzels, nut barks, and mints. From the vintage graphics to the huge assortment of "penny" candies to the helpful suggestions of its longtime employees, Kehr's abounds with honest charm. For many years, we have argued that our country should designate national culinary landmarks the way it does architectural and historic landmarks. If that day ever comes, Kehr's should be one of the first to be awarded the honor.

ORDERING ADDRESS
Kehr's Kandy Kitchen
3533 West Lisbon Avenue
Milwaukee, WI 53208
414/344-4305
No credit cards

VISITS
From Highway 41, take the Lloyd Street exit. Drive on Lloyd to Lisbon Avenue and turn right. Stay on Lisbon a few blocks until you hit 36th Street. Kehr's is on the corner of Lisbon and 36th.
Late September–April: Tuesday–Friday, 10 A.M.–4 P.M. Saturday, 10 A.M.–3 P.M.

LAGOMARCINO'S FILLED EASTER EGGS

How could we have lived a mere hour away from Lagomarcino's for years and been unaware of this sterling monument to fine chocolates and soda fountain classics? This is no reproduction soda shop, suffering from the cutes. This is a bonafide turn-of-the-century sweet shop, still run by descendents of the founders, that turns out high-quality chocolates and one of the best hot fudge sauces made.

"The Michelangelo of Fruitland and Candyland" is its slogan, which doesn't quite fit. That image calls up an oversized tourist trap, yet Lagomarcino's is a quiet and modest sort of place, located in the altogether too-quiet downtown of Moline, Illinois. Moline is one of the Quad Cities on the Illinois-Iowa border, and Interstates 80 and 74 slice through just a few miles from Lagomarcino's. When we think of all the unsuspecting travelers zipping by, not knowing what waits just a short detour away, we want to persuade Lagomarcino's to invest in highway billboards.

Lagomarcino's does have a vintage neon sign outside ("Our Own Ice Cream"), a white tin ceiling, blue snowflake tile, mahogany booths, and Tiffany-style lamps that date from 1918. At the luncheonette you can order a real turkey sandwich on homemade rye bread, a phosphate, salad served with crackers that remind you of the Forties, and any number of sundaes and sodas made with the store's homemade ice creams. The names recall the years when the store was surrounded by seven theaters. Bachelor's Kiss, Sweetheart Sundae, Hawaiian Twilight, and C'est Si Bon conjure up date nights and corsages. You can order a Green-River, fruit lemonade, or a glass of Lago, a fruit-flavored soda pop that was popular decades ago and re-created for the shop's 75th anniversary.

The hot fudge, served in little glass pitchers on the side, still is made using the recipe that the late Angelo Lagomarcino bought from a traveling candy salesman in 1918 for $25. His wife, Luigia, was appalled that her husband would be so extravagant, and they argued about it. Angelo prevailed and the hot fudge sauce has drawn people back to Lagomarcino's for years. Despite many pleas for the family to bottle the sauce, it is available only at the soda fountain. "It wouldn't be the same in a can," said Betsy Lagomarcino, the wife of Angelo and Luigia's son, Tom.

The company will send its handmade candy by mail year-round (weather permitting on some chocolate items); its English toffee ($14.95 a pound), golden sponge candy ($14.95), and hand-rolled creams in various flavors ($13.95) are especially recommended. As is true with many small candy shops, the chocolates are almost embarrassingly inexpensive. Betsy Lagomarcino explained that most of their business is the walk-in trade, so the prices must fit Moline's idea of a good value. Big-city chocolatiers might charge twice as much for an inferior factory produced chocolate, but smaller shops can't charge more than the local traffic will bear.

If all this weren't enticement enough, Lagomarcino's also makes unique filled chocolate Easter eggs, which it will ship around the country. Very few chocolate shops make these eggs, whose roots are European, because they involve so much hand labor. Opening one is not unlike breaking apart a piñata. The large eggs, which come in five sizes, break apart to reveal between 20 to 70 pieces of Lagomarcino's homemade candy, each one wrapped in white tissue. One variety of the large eggs contains pecan dainty candies. The smaller "children's eggs" have foil-wrapped chocolate eggs, jelly beans, and M&M candies inside. Both kinds of eggs are made of halves of molded chocolate that are welded together with chocolate and given a bumpy chocolate exterior.

The small eggs come in a decorated Easter box, with shredded cellophane grass, while the larger eggs come in a plain box. Both arrive wrapped in gift paper, at no additional charge. They are memorable additions to an Easter basket. In many families, they are an annual tradition. Large eggs cost from $22.95 to $51.95. Children's eggs vary from $5.95 to $7.50. All prices quoted are without shipping.

ORDERING ADDRESS
Lagomarcino's
1422 Fifth Avenue
Moline, IL 61265
309/764-1814
FAX: 309/736-5423
www.lagomarcinos.com
Credit cards accepted

VISITS: From I-74, take the Seventh Avenue exit and turn west. Go to 15th Street and turn right. Go 2 blocks to Fifth Avenue. Lagomarcino's is by the First National Bank Building. There is a second location in the Village of East Davenport, Iowa, at 2133 E. 11th Street, telephone 319/324-6137.

Monday–Friday, 8:30 A.M.–5 P.M. Saturday, 8:30 A.M.–4:30 P.M.
From Mother's Day through October: Closed Monday

LI-LAC CHOCOLATES

Li-Lac's tiny, 1923-era shop in Manhattan's Greenwich Village reminds you of tearoom lunches and sachet. Beautiful, faded-looking drawings of lilacs cover its boxes and walls. No one knows why the store's name originally was pronounced "lee-lock," but the lilac motif has effectively changed its name.

A similar, pleasant confusion revolves around its celebrated truffle, which is unlike others. Li-Lac's chocolate-dipped truffle is a tiny square, a praline French truffle with ribbons of ground hazelnut butter interspersed with dark chocolate. It is fragile and melts easily, but can be shipped.

Martha Bond runs the shop, having purchased it from her brother, Edward, in 1988. Edward, a former caterer with a fondness for his native New Orleans cooking, bought Li-Lac after founder George Demitro died and passed on the operation to an employee, Margaret Watt, who asked for Bond's help. To his dismay, Bond discovered that Demitro's unique recipes had never been written down. He spent several anxious months recording the instructions of an elderly employee who was in ill health.

The recipes are now recorded, a fortunate thing for Li-Lac fans. There are several distinctive sweets that may be irreplaceable, such as its chocolate cream rolls and its coconut patties, whose fresh coconut cream filling has just the right amount of moisture and sweetness.

The small shop has a variety that far exceeds its size. Few chocolatiers of any dimension still make large and complicated assortment boxes. Li-Lac's

49-piece French Assortment is an exception and uses many of the delicate imprints (strawberry, a coffee bean) from the German metal molds the Bonds inherited from Demitro.

The kitchen is a living museum of candy production, with its wooden ice chest still in use (now electrified), the 76-year-old French water bath machines, and the aged copper kettles, dented from years of use. The wrapping room contains two hand-dipping stations where employees individualize such delights as the maple walnut creams (former Governor Thomas Dewey's favorite).

Because it is a neighborhood shop, located near five schools, Li-Lac continues its tradition of producing inexpensive after-school treats, such as chocolate steamships and roadsters, made from Demitro's molds from the art deco era. The choices of solid molded chocolates are many, including an Empire State Building, Statue of Liberty, computers, and typewriters (remember them?).

One pound of the truffles, which are gift-boxed, is $27, plus shipping. They are mailed all year, but in summer customers must pay extra for next-day air shipments. The French Assortment is $27, which is a pound of hand-dipped chocolate. The shop's chocolate creams are $18 per pound.

ORDERING ADDRESS

Li-Lac Chocolates
120 Christopher Street
New York, NY 10014
212/242-7374
800/624-4874
FAX: 212/366-5874
Credit cards accepted

VISITS

The shop is located between Bedford and Bleecker Streets, across the street from the Lucille Lortel Theater. There is a second shop in the Market Hall at Grand Central Station, tel. 212/370-4866.

Christopher Street store: Monday–Friday, 10 A.M.–8 P.M.
Saturday, Noon–8 P.M. Sunday, Noon–5 P.M.
Grand Central Station Marketplace store: Monday–Friday, 7 A.M.–9 P.M.
Saturday, 10 A.M.–7 P.M. Sunday, 10 A.M.–5 P.M.

MALLEY'S NUTMALLOW

Malley's is in no danger of losing the family-run touch. It is loaded with family. Mike Malley opened his first candy kitchen in Lakewood, Ohio, in 1935, after working in a confectionery in Meadville, Pennsylvania, while growing up. A host of relatives have kept the standards high at this full-service candy empire, which has spread to 12 Cleveland-area stores, including one in the concourse of Hopkins International Airport.

No matter where the store is located, Malley's nutmallow is the favorite. We understand why. It is a delicious, 2-inch-high mixture of walnuts, blocks of homemade marshmallow, and milk chocolate. It's not for idle nibbling and is sold in a 1-pound piece, packed in a gift box. The price is $10.95 plus shipping, but the cost is reduced each October, after Sweetest Day, to commemorate the anniversary of the business. Because of the chocolate used, it is not shipped between Memorial Day and Labor Day.

Five of the Malley's stores contain old-fashioned ice cream parlors, serving tin roof sundaes, black and whites, and a memorable hot fudge sundae. At the plant's retail store, and at the store in the Premium Outlets in Aurora, customers may buy slightly imperfect candies at a discount.

ORDERING ADDRESS
Malley's Chocolates
13400 Brookpark Road
Cleveland, OH 44142
216/362-8700
800/835-5684
FAX: 216/265-2989
www.malleys.com
Credit cards accepted

VISITS: Thirty-minute tours are given at the candy kitchen, for $3, at the above address. Please make reservations first. There are 11 other Malley's shops in the Cleveland area.
Candy Kitchen: Monday–Friday. 9 A.M.–3 P.M.

MARSHALL'S FUDGE AND CANDY KITCHEN

Mackinac Island, that anomaly in northern Michigan where no cars or trucks are allowed, is a lovely place to visit, if just to see streets uncluttered with motor traffic. It is the business district that is in danger of being overrun with fudge shops.

There always has been a cachet connected with Mackinac Island fudge, and usually several shops to choose from. Now, however, there are at least 11 stores fighting for attention on the tiny island, with about half of them claiming to be the original.

Keith Wunderlich, who founded Detroit Sampler Company, a firm that sends gift baskets of foods made in Detroit and around Michigan, had done some research on the issue, and steered us to Marshall's Fudge and Candy Kitchen in Mackinaw City, saying it had the original recipe and had stuck with it. When we tried to sort out the history of Marshall's, we learned that the original candy shop on the island was founded in 1887 by a Mr. Murdick but did not offer fudge. That came after the turn of the century. Beyond that, we became tangled in a web of Murdick heirs, friends, rivals, and successors. According to Dean, a son of Jim Marshall, who started his candy-making career with the Murdicks, only two companies now use the original recipe—and neither is on Mackinac Island. They are Marshall's Fudge and Candy Kitchen in Mackinaw City and a fudge shop run by Murdick descendants in Charlevoix, Michigan, to the southwest.

The recipe is "an old-fashioned recipe from someone's grandmother" and is kept a secret, even to most of the Marshall's employees. Only Dean and a few others know the formula. The fudge is cooked in copper kettles, poured onto marble slabs, and flipped into a loaf, which is then cut into slabs. Customers are encouraged to watch—an irresistible invitation.

"There are lots of different ways to make fudge," said Jeannie, Dean's wife. "Many other fudge makers use mixes, loaf shaped forms, or add preservatives" to shorten the manufacturing process and prolong shelf life. "We have kept it truly old fashioned, with no preservatives and good ingredients. Three-fourths of our business is repeat customers, so we are concerned beyond selling you a box of fudge one time." It remains a family business, with two daughters and their husbands representing the third generation of fudge makers.

In the summer, the company makes as many as 35 flavors of fudge, including chocolate caramel, German chocolate, chocolate almond, and a triple chip. Many, such as rocky road, black walnut, and chocolate chip, were developed 40 and 50 years ago by Dean's mother, Oradelle Marshall. The most popular variety is the original one, chocolate with pecans. All flavors sell for $11 per pound, plus shipping. It is a very creamy fudge with a short shelf life that reflects the quality ingredients. It is sold in half-pound slices and can be frozen for up to 12 months. The company also makes distinctive sweet crème caramel kisses, as well as homemade divinity, penuche, and caramel corn. Fudge and other hand-made candies can be ordered by mail or via the Internet year-round.

ORDERING ADDRESS
Marshall's Fudge and Candy Kitchen
308 East Central Avenue
Mackinaw City, MI 49701
800/34 FUDGE (343-8343)
e-mail: shop@marshallsfudge.com
www.marshallsfudge.com
Credit cards accepted

VISITS: The Straits of Mackinac separate Michigan's Upper Peninsula from the rest of the state, and Marshall's Candy Kitchen is located at the south end of the connecting Mackinac Bridge, next to the Mackinaw City post office.
Every day. June–September, 8 A.M.–11 P.M. November–May, 9 A.M.–6 P.M.

MOUNT SAINT MARY'S BUTTER NUT MUNCH

When you order candy from the sisters of Mount Saint Mary's Abbey, near Wrentham, Massachusetts, you receive more than a box of sweets. Enclosed in each order is a thoughtful note about the true importance of giving and receiving gifts. Another enclosure describes the joy of candy: "Candy is made to enjoy—take time to taste it. Candy is made to share—make it into a bond of laughter and exchange. Candy is made for remembrance—give it with love and thoughtfulness." Conclude the sisters: "We have made it with joyful care, because care and joy are part of the monastic way of life. We hope it shows."

Anyone who has tasted the sisters' specialty, butter nut munch, would agree that it does. It's a buttery, chopped-almond brittle coated with milk chocolate, with roasted filberts hand-patted into the chocolate. It is very, very good. "People get addicted," said one nun.

The Trappistine sisters' first venture into foods was making and selling bread, but the operation was physically draining and difficult because of the quick perishability of the bread. The sisters turned to candy in 1956, learning their craft from John Crand, an old-school candy maker whose family candy business thrives today in Connecticut (see entry in this section).

Mount Saint Mary's is the "mother house" for a second abbey, established in Dubuque, Iowa. The two abbeys each make caramels, but their other products differ. Unique to the Massachusetts nuns are the munch, chocolate fudge, and penuche, and an almond and milk-chocolate "bark." The penuche and fudge are sold in 1-pound, 8-ounce packages for $9.65. The barks, sold in ¾-pound amounts, are $6.50 by mail order. A 1¼-pound box of the munch is $11. Shipping is extra.

The abbey, founded in 1949 by the late Cardinal Cushing, is located in a wooded setting in the low granite hills near the Rhode Island border. It is largely a self-sufficient convent, and the 52 sisters milk an 85-head dairy herd, put up hay, sew their clothes, repair their own shoes, and even print their own newsletter. It is possible to buy candy directly from the cloistered abbey, as well as bread, which is baked primarily for the sister's own needs but sold on baking days (Wednesdays and Saturdays) at the door. However, "it is often gone within an hour," the nuns report.

Most candy sales are by mail and the nuns request that Christmas orders be in by December 6.

ORDERING ADDRESS
Trappistine Quality Candy
Mount Saint Mary's Abbey
300 Arnold Street
Wrentham, MA 02093-1799
508/528-1282
FAX: 508/528-1409
www.trappistinecandy.com
Credit cards accepted

VISITS: **Wrentham is 40 miles southwest of Boston. The abbey is west of Wrentham and actually is closer to the town of West Wrentham. Go west on Highway 121 through Wrentham and Sheldonville. Just past Sheldonville, you will see a sign for the Big Apple Farm. After the sign, take the next road to the right, which leads to the abbey. Visitors are welcome in the chapel and can visit the grounds, but cannot enter the convent itself.**

Every day, 9 A.M.–5 P.M.

THE OAKS CANDY CANES

There are but a handful of candy shops in the country that still hand-form candy canes. It is a time-consuming process, and most manufacturers are content to paint on the barber-pole stripes instead of twisting in strips of red or green candy. Making candy canes by hand also takes muscles to pull the cooked candy on a taffy hook until it turns from amber color to stark white. In addition, making canes requires skill to form a nice-looking crook.

But every fall when the weather turns crisp (usually around Thanksgiving), the family-owned and -run Oaks Candy Corner, in Oshkosh, Wisconsin, produces more than 50,000 hand-pulled and -formed candy canes. They come in 7 flavors (peppermint, wintergreen, anise, cinnamon, clove, lemon, and cherry), as well as a variety of sizes, from the popular 6-inch length to canes weighing 2 pounds and more.

The candy shop has been run by the Oaks family since 1890 and candy canes have been part of the repertoire from the beginning. Today, owner Charlotte Oaks, three of her five children, and several of their children's children work in the business. All are recruited to help with the canes, because it takes a crew of seven to make them. It's a marvelous process to watch, with the molten syrup first becoming a satiny taffy, then a large white watermelon with colors pressed into its sides. The canes are then pulled out and twisted. An assortment box of 24 canes is $14. Christmas orders should be placed by December 1.

The Oakses will now mail their fragile canes, but it is worth a personal visit to the family's 1920-era Tudor-style shop, with leaded-glass windows and solid-wood display cabinets. If a trip to Wisconsin is not in the offing for you, the Oakses are also willing to mail their popular assorted hand-dipped chocolates or boxes of the store's perennial best-seller, hand-dipped chocolate meltaways. Small rectangles with a whipped-chocolate center, meltaways "have been in the family almost forever," said Charlotte. They come in several choices of coating, but we favor the ones dipped in either milk or dark chocolate. Meltaways are $10.75 per pound, exclusive of shipping costs, and can be ordered in gift-wrapped boxes at no extra charge.

The company also makes molasses sponge candy, mint wafers, a malt candy bar, and a sugar-free chocolate assortment. If you are sending chocolate to a location that is 70 degrees or warmer, chilled shipping is recommended.

ORDERING ADDRESS
Oaks Candies
1206 Oregon Street
Oshkosh, WI 54902
920/231-3660
Credit cards accepted

VISITS: **Oshkosh is in eastern Wisconsin, south of Green Bay. The Oakses operate 2 candy stores downtown: the main shop at the corner of Twelfth Avenue and Oregon Street and a smaller shop at 9 Waugoo Avenue, just off Main Street. The first shop is where all the candy is made. Oregon Street is parallel to Main Street and a few blocks to the west.**
Monday–Thursday, 9 A.M.–8 P.M. Friday, 9 A.M.–9 P.M. Saturday, 9 A.M.–6 P.M. Sunday, 11 A.M.–6 P.M.

OUR LADY OF THE MISSISSIPPI ABBEY CARAMELS

The visits to the small food factories and showrooms dotting America's countryside can be as rewarding as the purchases. Should you happen to be driving south of Dubuque, Iowa, on Highway 52, you might see a small sign near a gravel road marking the entrance to the abbey that is home to 22 Trappistine nuns and some of the best handmade caramels ever made.

Following the rule of St. Benedict that their living should be made by the labor of their hands, the nuns of Our Lady of the Mississippi Abbey have been turning out their carefully made vanilla, chocolate, and hand-dipped creamy caramels for 35 years. Their lovely stone abbey is nestled on a bluff overlooking the Mississippi River, and the spectacular view and tranquil, tree-filled setting adds to the feeling that this is a special place. The nuns sell by mail and wholesale, but if you happen by, it is possible to buy the candy at the abbey. Several times a day the nuns sing their prayers in the sunlit chapel adjoining the abbey, and if you are there at an opportune time, it is possible to listen and pray there as well.

The candy kitchen is a snug, spotless building down the lane from the abbey, and the cooking takes place generally six mornings a week during the September–December candy season. The recipe originally came from their mother house, Mount Saint Mary's Abbey in Wrentham, Massachusetts, which also makes caramels and other candy, but years of adjustments have given the Iowa candies their own formula. The other offerings are chocolate-coated caramels and mint squares in creamy green and Swiss chocolate varieties. The coated caramels and Swiss mint squares cannot be shipped from May 15 to September 15 because they'll melt.

It's worth the wait for cooler weather to try the vanilla caramels dipped in chocolate. The caramels, dipped or plain, are soft, creamy, and rich, with an abundance of butter flavor. After you have tasted these, most other caramels will seem bland.

Prices are extremely reasonable: a 1-pound sampler box of vanilla, chocolate, and light and dark chocolate-dipped caramels is $11.60, including postage. A 22-ounce gift box of chocolate-covered caramels is $15.95, including shipping. Twenty-four ounces of individually wrapped vanilla caramels are $12.20, including shipping. Many assortments are possible, including Swiss and Irish mints. Christmas orders must be received by December 8.

The nuns are using the proceeds from the candy sales to re-establish the Cistercian way of life in Norway, on the island of Tautra in the Trondheim fjord. They're raising money to build a monastery near the ruins of a Cistercian monastery that existed there from 1207 to 1537. It's not often that indulging in something so sweet can pay off in spiritual rewards.

ORDERING ADDRESS
Trappistine Creamy Caramels
Mississippi Abbey
8325 Abbey Hill
Dubuque, IA 52003
319/556-6330
FAX: 319/582-5511
e-mail: monasterycandy@mcleodusa.net
www.monasterycandy.com
Credit cards accepted
(It's best to call between 8:30 A.M. and 11:30 A.M. Iowa time.
If no answer in the candy shop, call the abbey at 319/582-2595.)

VISITS: From the intersection of Highways 61 and 151 south of Dubuque, take 52 south about 5½ miles. Turn left on Hilken Hill and drive a half-mile. Turn left between 2 stone pillars onto the entrance to the property. Visitors may purchase candy or use the chapel but are not permitted to watch the candy making.

PEARSON'S NUT GOODIE

Edward Pearson and his four brothers would be pleased, finally, that the company they founded in 1909 has survived the hazards of corporate America and now is rescuing other vintage candies.

The existance of Pearson's nut goodie is an especially sweet celebration for its fans. In the late 1960s, the St. Paul, Minnesota, firm had been sold to ITT/Continental Baking and the quality of their products, particularly the Nut Goodie, which is distributed only in the upper Midwest, had fallen. The distinctive red and green wrapper was scrapped and the ingredients were cheapened.

After 10 years, ITT/Continental sold the candy company to a partnership that was primarily interested in distributing bulk food items. Nut Goodie lovers had trouble finding the candy bars, and many thought the company had stopped making the distinctive maple-flavored milk chocolate and peanut bars.

Enter Larry Hassler and Judy Johnston, two Pearson employees. In the mid–1980s, they bought the candy business and returned the Nut Goodie and other Pearson products to the quality that had made them famous. The Nut Goodie's original wrapper and recipe returned, and so did loyal customers. Garrison Keillor wrote about Pearson's Peanut Nut Roll. The Wireless Catalog, purveyor of wonderful music and wacky gifts from the world of National Public Radio in St. Paul, began to feature Nut Goodie. "It's paid off," said Pearson public relations representative Debbie Eskins, referring to the decision to resurrect the original candy recipes. "We're now getting lots of requests for us to bring back candy bars that we haven't made for years, like the 7Up bar."

Other early Pearson candies sound equally enticing: the Cherry Oval, Club Sandwich, New Recruit, Log Cabin in Fudge. Bring 'em all back, we say. Happily, the company has bought the Bun Bar Cluster trademark from Clark Bar America and now makes those wonderful chocolate-covered Bun patties in maple, vanilla, and caramel flavors.

Pearson's Peanut Nut Roll (formerly the Salted Nut Roll), mint patties, and Chocolate Nut Roll can be found nationwide, and they are well worth seeking out. Pearson's uses real chocolate, not compound coverings, and its peanuts are fresh and crunchy. The Nut Roll has a white nougat center covered with caramel and then salted peanut halves. The chocolate version simply adds a final layer of milk chocolate. The mints use dark chocolate.

The Nut Goodie, small but mighty, is distributed only in Minnesota and four contiguous states. It is a round patty about 2 inches in diameter, covered with milk chocolate. Underneath are unsalted peanuts and a maple-flavored cream center. If you grew up in Iowa, Minnesota, Wisconsin, or the Dakotas, Nut Goodie was part of your childhood.

Relive those memories. You can order a box of 24 Nut Goodies or Nut Rolls directly from Pearson Candy Company for $15, including shipping.

ORDERING ADDRESS
Pearson Candy Company
P.O. Box 64459
St. Paul, MN 55164
651/698-0356
No credit cards. However, you can order Nut Goodie through The Wireless Catalog at 800/669-9999 and use a credit card. A box of twenty-four is $16.95, plus shipping.

PHILLIPS TAFFY

As a candy type, saltwater taffy has a terrible reputation, thanks to the boxes of lurid-colored, poor-quality pieces that are sold at every rest stop and tourist attraction. Rock-hard, tasteless, and grainy, the dismal merchandise has given the entire taffy industry a bad name. The standard-bearer should be the taffy from Phillips Candies of Seaside, Oregon, a shop that was established in 1898 and has been run by the Phillips family for the past 61 years.

In addition to some of the softest saltwater taffy we've ever tasted, Phillips makes two taffies, a cinnamon and a butter, that are unlike any we've ever had. All their taffies include butter and cream, which makes for a softer consistency, but the butter and cinnamon, whose recipes go back to the founding of the store, use a lot of butter: a 50-pound batch will have 5 pounds of butter in it. They are not pulled on a hook, as the other taffies are, but cut with a knife, like caramels. The butter is a translucent caramel-colored candy with a distinctive, not-quite butterscotch taste. The cinnamon is bright red (a pretty Christmas or Valentine's candy), also translucent, and tastes like an uncommonly good, chewy, cinnamon red-hot. Both are best when fresh and soft. "Our taffy is not meant for a shelf life," explained Marguerite Phillips, who bought the shop with her late husband, John, in 1939. "We use no preservatives."

The shop's history reflects that of Seaside, a resort town of 5,000 that used to see tourists only in the summer. Marguerite grew up there, and her first summer job was behind the counter of what then was Pool's Confectionery in 1926. She kept returning each summer, and she and her husband, a teacher, eventually bought the business.

Marguerite, who has now retired, remembered the war years and food rationing. "We could only stay open an hour or an hour and a half at the most. People would be lined up a block in each direction, holding their money. They were so hungry for candy because it wasn't in the grocery stores. We would try to make the candies we could make the most of, and not worry about making creams or others that took a lot of ingredients." It was then that the couple changed the store name from Pool's to Phillips. "People didn't care what the name was," said Marguerite. "They just wanted candy."

All the confections except the hard candies are made in the shop, and many of the chocolates still are hand-dipped. The Phillipses make a staggering variety of candies for a small shop, and the day we were there, Steve Phillips, the couple's youngest son, who is now the owner and manager, was making tray after tray of beautiful, fluffy divinity.

Steve, age 52, an outgoing, civic-minded man, puts in long hours at the shop. It is open 12 hours a day in the summer, and he spends many of those hours stirring candy in hefty copper kettles in a kitchen area that often reaches 100 degrees.

After the taffies, Phillips' biggest seller is rocky road candy—a mixture of handmade marshmallow, whipped milk chocolate, and walnuts that is sold by the pound in large slabs and is so far superior to any we've had before that we believe it deserves another name. They make their own marshmallow. There is a sugar-free line of taffies for diabetics and children on low-sugar diets.

Phillips will send taffy by mail anytime, but chocolates can be mailed only in cool weather. Prices are more than reasonable. The taffy is $4 a pound (there are 10 flavors besides cinnamon and butter); the rocky road, $8.50 a pound. Shipping costs are extra.

ORDERING ADDRESS
Phillips Candies
217 Broadway
Seaside, OR 97138
503/738-5402
FAX: 503/738-8326
e-mail: candy@seasurf.net
Credit cards accepted

VISITS: Seaside is about 83 miles northwest of Portland on the Pacific coast. From Highway 101, take the "City Center-To Beach" exit, which takes you to Broadway, Seaside's main street. Phillips Candies is 2 blocks east of the ocean and the "turn-around," where there is a marker commemorating the end of the Lewis and Clark Trail.

Every day, After Labor Day–June: 10 A.M.–5 P.M. June–Labor Day: 10 A.M.–10 P.M.

PRIESTER'S PECANS SOUTHERN KERNELS

In 1935, the way Lee C. Priester made money as a youth was to sell little bags of shelled pecans to motorists who stopped for gas at his father's filling station, conveniently located on Route 31 in Fort Deposit, Alabama, a major north-south thoroughfare of the day.

His pecan business has stayed at the site of his humble beginnings, but now the company employs up to 200 people in the busy fall season following the pecan harvest, selling high-quality nut and chocolate confections to armchair travelers all over the country.

The company's president is Ned Ellis, whose father was a partner of Lee Priester. Ellis is a stickler for properly packing his goods. After you make your way through two separate boxes and a padded mailbag to reach the glossy red box containing your treats, you'll doubt that any customer finds a need to fill out the Priester's refund for those not 100 percent satisfied.

Given the popular combination of pecans, caramel, and chocolate, it's no surprise that Priester's makes a version, the Southern Kernel. We like to think of it as a box turtle, as it's completely square, with everything hidden under light or dark chocolate. They are neat, crunchy cubes that arrive with a few of their numbers foil wrapped to provide visual interest in the candy box, an old-fashioned nicety that we appreciate. The company also makes a pecan fiddlestick, a 4-inch bar of pecans covered with caramel, its edges dipped part way in chocolate.

The Kernels are $23.50, plus shipping, for a 1-pound, 4-ounce box. The fiddlesticks are $22.95, plus shipping, for a 2-pound size.

ORDERING ADDRESS

Priester's Pecans
208 Old Fort Road East
Fort Deposit, AL 36032
334/227-4301
800/277-3226
Credit cards accepted

VISITS

Priester's Pecans Retail Store
Interstate 65 and Alabama Highway 185
Fort Deposit, AL 36032
334/227-8355
The store is 35 miles south of Montgomery, Alabama. From T-65, take the Fort Deposit exit. Turn left, cross the bridge. Take the first left when you see the Priester's sign.

Every day, 8 A.M.–6 P.M.

TREMBLAY'S FUDGE

One of the reasons Karen Engman of Des Moines, Iowa, enjoyed summer camp as a child in northwestern Wisconsin so much was the annual pilgrimage to Tremblay's Sweet Shop in Hayward to buy fudge. "It was the best," she recalls fondly. A sampling confirmed her enthusiasm. The fudges—chocolate (the best-seller), vanilla, maple, and peanut butter—are smooth and loaded with nuts. They are solid, not soft, but without a hint of graininess. And the prices at the 26-year-old establishment are of a bygone era: $5.49 a pound, plus shipping.

Dennis and Marlene Tremblay will mail their fudge and other products, such as homemade fresh "turtles" with caramel and nuts, excellent cashew or peanut brittle, almond bark, and pecan logs and marshmallow fondant filling.

The bulk of their business comes from the fishermen and campers who journey to the hundreds of beautiful lakes hidden in the woods. For tourists and natives alike, the glassed-in kitchens at Tremblay's, where customers can see every step of the candy making, are irresistible. "That's the story of our success," said Marlene. "Everybody sees everything."

The company ships four days a week, from May through December.

ORDERING ADDRESS
Tremblay's Sweet Shop
P.O. Box 228
Hayward, WI 54843
715/634-2785
800/40-FUDGE (403-8343)
No credit cards

VISITS
221 Main Street
Hayward, WI 54843
Hayward is about 30 miles east of the Minnesota border, at the junction of Highways 63, 27, and 77 in the northwest part of the state. There is another store in Eagle River, Wisconsin, and one operated by the Tremblay's daughter, Marcy, in the Cedar Mall in Rice Lake, Wisconsin, that is open year-round. (Telephone 715/234-4474).
May–December 31: Every day, 9 A.M.–5 P.M.

QUEEN BEE GARDENS HONEY CANDIES

The Zeller family began bee keeping in Lovell, Wyoming, in 1920, using ornery bees, named Little Johnnies, that have a propensity to sting as well as to produce an extra-sweet honey.

Clarence Zeller inherited the business from his father. His wife, Bessie, who's cooked strictly with honey for 50 years, has developed many of the recipes. There are now pralines, truffles, and English toffee. No sugar is used in any of the confections, as one would expect with an abundant supply of homegrown sweetener. The candies contain no colorings or preservatives and are attractively packaged in boxes in a variety of shapes.

Although the factory is on Main Street in Lovell, the office remains on the Zeller farm, nine miles distant.

The pralines, like all the candies, are inexpensive. Six ounces are $3.90. A pound is $10.25. Shipping is $6 extra.

ORDERING ADDRESS
Queen Bee Gardens
1863 Lane 11½
Lovell, WY 82431
307/548-2543
800/225-7553
No credit cards

VISITS
270 East Main Street
Lowell, WY 82431
Lovell is 9 miles south of the Montana border and 90 miles east of Yellowstone Park. From Yellowstone, take 14A east toward Sheridan. The shop is in downtown Lovell.
Monday–Friday, 9 A.M.–4:30 P.M.

SCHWARTZ CHOCOLATE-COVERED MARSHMALLOWS

There are some confections that are so special that you pray for their survival. The marshmallows made by Schwartz Candies fit that bill. Fans weathered some scary months when a fire destroyed the kitchen recently. Thankfully, the company has rebuilt.

When Schwartz calls its products "Out of this World Chocolates," it isn't exaggerating in the least. Its star attraction is chocolate-covered marshmallows, which have been made for 60 blessed years. The wise Schwartz family has kept its circa–1939 lettering and logo, so the entire box, inside and out, looks like a treat from another era. When you open the red-and-white checkerboard box, you are greeted by 20 fat squares of semisweet chocolate. Each square is a good inch and a half high and is filled with toothsome marshmallow in one of eight flavors.

Schwartz marshmallow filling is airy and light, a very distant relative to the sticky, heavy marshmallow cream or tasteless marshmallows that most eaters settle for these days. In this case, ignorance isn't bliss. The unadorned vanilla is all you could hope for, but the Schwartz's go one better by also offering it with a caramel bottom. The caramel-bottom marshmallow is candy perfection. The coffee is appealing, as is the chocolate, strawberry, and banana. We've never been much of maple or mint fans when it comes to chocolates, but for those who are, they've got them. The chocolate is exemplary, and they don't stint on it. One of these marshmallows goes a long way.

The company offers other boxed candy, such as miniature assorted chocolates and butter crunch, with all chocolates and centers handmade on the premises.

The company was founded as a candy shop on Manhattan's Upper West Side by Allen Schwartz. In 1979, it moved to Long Island, to Nassau County, where it is run by Allen's daughter, Rhoda Schwartz Boskoff, and her husband, Ira.

A 1-pound, 2-ounce box of assorted flavors of "Out of this World" Marshmallows is $29.50. (All prices include shipping costs.) A 2-pound, 4-ounce box is $49.25. The caramel-bottom marshmallows are the most popular of the individual flavors, confirmed Ira Boskoff, and are sold in two sizes: 1-pound, 6-ounce for $40.25 and 2-pound, 4-ounce for $64.50.

As a charming gesture, Schwartz Candies will gift-wrap all its chocolates at no extra charge. With tollfree and fax numbers, free gift wrapping, and the best marshmallow candy in America, your gift-giving angst is over. If you're lucky enough to visit, there's an outlet shop open to the public.

ORDERING ADDRESS
Schwartz Candies
31 Denton Avenue
New Hyde Park, NY 11040
516/358-0940
800/522-CHOC (2462)
FAX: 516/358-0950
Credit cards accepted

VISITS: New Hyde Park is in Nassau County, Long Island. From the Long Island Expressway, take exit 34. Go to the first light and turn right, which will be New Hyde Park Road. Go to the first major intersection, which is Marcus Avenue, and turn left. Take Marcus through the intersection of Hillside Avenue and you will be on Denton Avenue. The candy company is on the right.
Monday–Friday, 10 A.M.–5:30 P.M. Saturday, 10 A.M.–4:30 P.M.

SHANE'S CINNAMON POTATOES

Tell your children you're serving them potatoes and delight them with tiny white lumps of Shane's Cinnamon Potatoes.

Imagine a smooth, cooked, coconut-cream candy (dusted with cinnamon powder) and you have the delicacy that makes this Philadelphia institution famous, even without advertising. Sold only from January through St. Patrick's Day, the potatoes are risky to mail-order, but owner Barry Shane, a third-generation candy maker, will send them as long as customers realize that an occasional shipment will run together and resemble mashed potatoes instead.

There's been candy made within Shane's storefront, located by Penn's Landing along the Delaware River, since 1876, when H. T. Wescott ran the place. Shane's grandfather bought the operation in 1911, and Shane hands have been cooking and dipping confections ever since. Luckily, Barry's son, Ryan, while working as a chemist, is accomplished in all phases of candymaking.

All cooking is done on the second floor of the historic row house, which has all the original accoutrements of an old-time candy parlor: pressed-tin ceiling, curved glass display cases, and leaded windows.

Although best known for its unusual potatoes, Shane's also makes exceptional marshmallows—moist, substantial squares that are hand-dipped in dark chocolate. The company's best-seller, buttercreams, also are standouts. The vanilla buttercreams covered in dark chocolate are the favorites—with good reason. Buttercreams are tricky. Without first-rate ingredients or careful blending, the filling easily is made too sweet or even pasty. These are delicious, well-made chocolates that sell for $8.95 per pound. The potatoes are $7.50 per pound; the marshmallows are $8.95 per pound. Shipping is extra. Shane's continues to provide free gift wrapping if you request it.

ORDERING ADDRESS
Shane Candies
110 Market Street
Philadelphia, PA 19106
215/922-1048
No credit cards

VISITS: **Shane's is east of center-city Philadelphia on Market Street, which divides the city into north and south. It is between First and Second Streets and is a 5-minute walk from Penn's Landing.**
Monday–Saturday, 9 A.M.–5:30 P.M.

SIFERS VALOMILK

Get out your handkerchiefs. Here's a happy ending to bring tears to the eyes of all culinary anthropologists. Actually, it's a happy new beginning, because Russell Sifers has brought Valomilk, "The Original 'Flowing Center' Candy Cups," back from the dead.

Valomilk was a Kansas City tradition from at least as far back as 1931, and possibly before. Harry Sifers, Russell's grandfather, had moved to Kansas City in 1916, bringing candy-making skills he had learned from his father, who started the unbroken chain of Sifers candy makers with a bulk penny-candy factory in Iola, Kansas, in 1903.

Harry and his wife, Cecil, began making some of the Midwest's first nickel candy bars, and what picturesque names they had! There was Old King Tut, Rough Neck, Subway Sadie, Ozark Ridge, and Jersey Cow, among others.

They also made penny marshmallow candy. The story goes that an employee named Tommy was known to take a few snorts of the alcohol-laden vanilla. One day he got carried away and ruined a batch of marshmallow, leaving it runny. Harry Sifers found the ruined batch and, loath to waste the ingredients, dipped scoops of the marshmallow into chocolate cups. Although the result was messy, Sifers realized it tasted delicious. He asked Tommy to re-create his mistake. Tommy pleaded ignorance. After several swigs of vanilla, the memory of his error returned and the recipe was developed. The candy was called Valomilk Dips. The etymology? "V" stood for real vanilla (from Tommy's point of view, the critical ingredient!), "alo" from marshmallow, "milk" to describe the creamy white center, and "Dip" because it was hand-dipped.

Harry's sons, Clarence and Samuel, joined him in the business, helping run the factories in Iola and Kansas City. In its post–World War II heyday, Valomilk spread throughout the Midwest.

In 1970, the candy company was sold to Hoffman Candy Company, in Los Angeles. The plan was to make Valomilk a national product, but the merger of the two companies was troubled. Eventually, the last batch of Valomilk was made in 1980 and the division was closed in 1981. A half-century of eating pleasure was brought to an end.

By that time Clarence had retired. His son, Russell, who had run the company for Hoffman until it closed, was working at a General Motors plant in Kansas when he got a call from the Hoffman Company in 1985. The Kansas City building where Valomilk had been made was being sold, Sifers was told, and if he would clear out the leftover "old junk," he could keep anything he could salvage.

Before agreeing to the job, Sifers asked for and received the rights to the Valomilk and Sifers candy names. His motive? He had discovered, in the coal bin of the downtown building, the original copper kettles, cookers, and bowls his grandfather had used to make Valomilk. There had been automated equipment later, but that had all been sent to California when the company was sold. "I had never seen this equipment run," said Russell, "but I knew that if I could figure out how it worked, I could make Valomilk again."

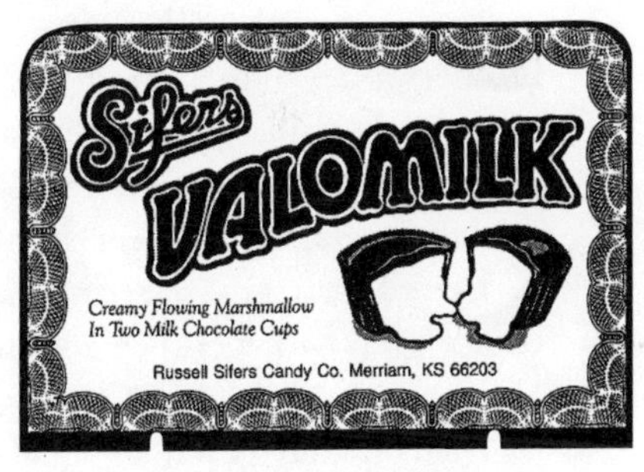

It took Sifers and his son, Dave, one year to rebuild the old equipment. Many parts had to be created because spares no longer existed. Clarence Sifers told his son as much as he recalled about the original recipe but died before the first batch of Valomilk was re-created in September 1987.

Of the first three cases Russell Sifers made, he threw one away. He knew he had succeeded when a woman in his church tasted one of the new Valomilks and said it was better than the ones she used to buy in the thirties.

The milk-chocolate candies are on the order of a peanut butter cup in size and outward appearance, but the "flowing center" sets them apart. The center is made from simple ingredients—corn syrup, sugar, egg whites, salt, water, and vanilla—and it is sweet and runny. Biting into a Valomilk is just plain fun.

The public response has been overwhelming, and Sifers is expanding. Valomilk is now available in Kansas and parts of Missouri, Iowa, and Nebraska. As Sifers searches for rare automated equipment from the 1950s to update his original equipment a few decades, he has also taken on the task of sending Valomilk by mail to the fans who have begun writing the company.

To order a box of 24 packages (there are 2 cups to a package), send a check for $21.95 to the company. They are delivered UPS, weather permitting.

ORDERING ADDRESS
Sifers Valomilk Candy Company
5112 Merriam Drive
Merriam, KS 66203
913/722-0991
No credit cards

TURKEY JOINTS

Confectioners are creative. No further proof is needed than to see Rome, New York's, treasured turkey joints. These look like candy bones—knobby silver stalks that are filled with chocolate and Brazil nuts, coconut and almonds, or peanut butter.

These unusual candies were introduced in 1919 by the four Haritatos brothers, who sold them at their Candyland restaurant. They were first made by their uncle, Harry Haritatos, in Syracuse. The restaurant closed in 1972, but thankfully, Nora's Candy Shop continues the turkey tradition, with Spero Haritatos, son of the original owners, carrying on production.

These 5-inch stalks are handmade and are fun to eat. The thin silver shell breaks open with a crunch and the soft insides are nutty and unusual. We like the original chocolate and Brazil nut filling, but all are good.

The company gets many mail-order requests, thanks to soldiers at the former Air Force base in Rome, who sent the treats around the globe. They are shipped in 1-pound amounts in tall glass jars and arrive in great shape. One jar is $14.40, plus shipping. These would be fun conversation candies for kids' birthday, Halloween, or Thanksgiving parties.

You may also buy them, and other confections, at the candy shop.

ORDERING ADDRESS
Nora's Candy Shop
321 N. Doxtator Street
Rome, NY 13440
315/337-4530
888/544-8224 (toll-free)
FAX 315/339-1054
www.turkeyjoints.com
Credit cards accepted

VISITS: **The shop is in the west end of Rome, New York.**
Monday–Friday, 10 A.M.–5 P.M. Saturday, 10 A.M.–3 P.M.

WHITE CROW CULINARY CHOCOLATES

The culinary talents of Neika Soisson, age 46, are the epitome of personal service. For 18 years she has been making custom chocolates, drawing upon her artistic background to create beautiful and dainty food art. She is a caterer, a pastry chef, and a winner of the Chocolatier of the Year award. Neika is also a trained artist, and has done cheese sculptures, ice sculptures, and chocolate sculptures, as well as one-of-a-kind chocolate centerpieces.

She makes wondrous chocolate baskets with lids, hand-woven from chocolate piped through a parchment cone, and fills them with her assorted handmade chocolates. Large baskets, approximately 5 inches in diameter, are $75. Baskets that are 3½ inches in diameter are $50.

We were charmed by her dark-chocolate roses carefully attached to green floral stems and leaves. There are long-stemmed roses with baby's breath and ribbons in a floral gift box and are $10 each. She also makes a small, short-stemmed version tied with a sprig of baby's breath that is used primarily by caterers. We visualized a host of uses for them, such as party favors and package decorations.

Other offerings are "mini gifts" of two to four exquisite pieces of candy in clever little lock-top boxes, in gold or silver. Just the ticket when a standard box of chocolates would overwhelm! They are $4.50 each. If you order 6 or more, the price drops to $4 each.

True to her Missouri location, Neika makes use of native black walnuts for an assortment of black walnut candies dipped in milk and dark chocolate.

Neika, who has a Greek first name, a French last name, and is American, says she notices that people are becoming more particular about the sweets they eat. "If they are going to eat something sweet, they want it to be really good and they are willing to pay for it." Echoing our long-held sentiments, she said: "if there are the same number of calories, why waste it on a Twinkie?"

As for her own food favorites, Neika confessed to being unable to resist the chocolate ganache cake she makes for local restaurants. "That's my weakness." Luckily for us, the cake can't be shipped.

Chocolates can be mailed from October through May only.

ORDERING ADDRESS
White Crow Culinary Productions, Inc.
9396 Golden Gate Road
St. Louis, MO 63144
314/963-0316
www.bestparties.com
Credit cards accepted

VISITS: **By appointment only**

VATORE'S CARAMELS

Tim and Janet Beyer are postal workers and we are thrilled about their most important delivery—they have rescued Washington, D.C.'s, famed caramels from oblivion.

Our nation's capitol is known for making laws, not food, so its distinctive crumbly caramels, made for more than a century under the Velati's name, were a beloved downtown fixture. Devised by Salvatore Velati in 1866, from a recipe from his native Italy, the caramels were part of most downtown shopping excursions for decades.

When the Velati store closed in 1972, the Woodward and Lothrop department store kept them going, under the tutelage of Tim Beyer, great-grandson of the founder. When Beyer retired in 1986, caramel lovers were out in the cold. Woodward and Lothrop later shuttered its doors.

Fast forward to 1999. Beyer's son, also named Tim, persuaded his father to teach him and his wife the recipes. The name had been sold, but once the candies were back in production, devising a new name based on "Salvatore" seemed logical.

Our friend, food maven, and D.C. native Rory Zuckerman, alerted us that the famous caramels were back from the dead. "It's bringing back my childhood," she said, echoing the happy reaction of many. The response has been so overwhelming, that Janet has left her postal duties and works as a candy maker full time in Vatore's new shop in Salisbury. "We've been getting orders from every state, including Alaska and Hawaii," she said. "We are going to carry this on to our children."

Nestled in pink-and-gold 1-pound boxes are these most unusual caramels. Forget sticky. These come in two forms—crumbly (or sugared) and a hard, chewy variety. Each kind comes in chocolate or vanilla. Vanilla caramels, of either kind, are $9.95 per pound. Chocolate is $11.95. There also is a chocolate almond caramel and a butter rum, which cost $12.95 per pound. Shipping is extra.

ORDERING ADDRESS
Vatore's Caramels, Inc.
P.O. Box 2861
Salisbury, MD 21802
410/341-3177
877/828-6737 (toll-free)
FAX: 410/341-3177
e-mail: vatores@aol.com
www.vatores.com
Credit cards accepted

VISITS: **717 Roland Street Salisbury, MD 21802. From Route 50, take Business 13 South. Drive .9 mile to a Giant Food store. Turn left. The shop is adjacent to the Giant store in the Goliath Shopping Center.**
Monday–Friday, 8 A.M.–4:30 P.M.

WISTERIA CANDY COTTAGE CANDIES

Lynne Branson of Lakeside, California, was the first to write us about southern California's Wisteria Candy Cottage: "This place has been in the mountains here for years and years! I first went there when I was fifteen years old. [She's now fifty-five.] It is a family operation and everything is of wonderful quality. They have seventeen different types of divinity alone!" Then, Art Hall of San Marcos, California, sent us a Wisteria brochure, appropriately printed on violet-colored paper. "Here is one you missed. Very good to best!"

Then, we ordered a box of Wisteria's old-fashioned mix of fudges, divinities, brittles, English toffee, and caramels—an assortment that has been popular since the shop opened for business 78 years ago. ("World Famous since 1921," the stationery declares.) When the package arrived, it looked as if it had been sent in 1921. Not that the candy wasn't fresh—it was—but the violet-colored box, the grosgrain ribbon bow, and the curliqued lettering made the package look like a period piece.

Another assortment, the "Supreme" box, is an even better introduction to Wisteria's charms, for it includes some of the shop's superlative pecan roll, which has a buttercream and caramel center. The Supreme box also holds hand-dipped chocolates, cherry cordials, light and dark toffee, and one of Wisteria's imposing caramel turtles. The Old-fashioned and Supreme boxes can be ordered in 1-, 2-, 3-, or 5-pound sizes. One pound of the Old-fashioned box is $12.95. The Supreme 1-pound box is $12.95.

LuzCelia Rankin, Wisteria's owner, sent us an unordered treat: a small gold box tied with a violet ribbon filled with 8 large turtles of various types. Surely, no turtle lover could ask for more. The box includes milk-, dark-, and white-chocolate turtles. Some are made with the traditional pecans, but others use whole California almonds or salted cashews, both inventive and successful substitutes. The cashews, particularly, provide a savory counterpoint to the caramel and chocolate. Each turtle is about 3 inches long and comes individually wrapped in cellophane. A 1-pound box of turtles (from 7 to 9) is $14.95.

If you are a divinity fan, we know of no other place that makes as many varieties. While we must admit that none comes close to the divinity made by Robert Kirkpatrick, Allison's father-in-law, every Christmas, the Wisteria versions are smooth, nongrainy, and available year-round. Unusual choices include pineapple, apricot, coconut, cashew, black walnut, and mixed fruit. It's possible to order a pound (or more) of assorted divinity, if you'd like to sample them all before settling on a favorite. A pound is $10.95.

Nut roll, either pecan or brazil nut, is available by the pound at $13.95. We also recommend the cashew brittle, peanut brittle, or chop suey brittle, made with noodles and nuts. A pound of any variety sells for $7.90. A special "Wisteria brittle" with 7 different kinds of nuts, sliced coconut, and cherries is $8 a pound. If you can't make up your mind on the brittles, a popular solution is the brittle assortment, ½ pound of each of the 4 varieties, for $17.90.

Chocolates are sent from October through May only. Shipping and handling costs for all orders are $4.50 to $8.50 for up to 5 pounds of candy.

LuzCelia Rankin and her mother had worked for Wisteria's previous owner for several years before they bought the shop 24 years ago. Since he retired, LuzCelia's husband, Gordon, has worked with her. The shop has been family owned for 40 years.

The store began as a roadside business for travelers on their way to San Diego, and its reputation survived changes in highway geography that rerouted tourist traffic to the interstate several years ago. The cottage originally was a one-room schoolhouse, "and we're bursting at the seams" with seven employees, said LuzCelia. There are lilac bushes out front and, of course, twining wisteria shrubs.

ORDERING ADDRESS

Wisteria Candy Cottage
P.O. Box 985
Boulevard, CA 92005
619/766-4453
800/458-8246
e-mail: candy@candycottage.com
www.candycottage.com
Credit cards accepted

VISITS

39961 Old Highway 80
Boulevard, CA 92005
Boulevard is 65 miles east of San Diego on I-8. Take the Boulevard-Campo exit off I-8 to Old Highway 80. The candy shop is ⅓ mile from the freeway.
Every day, 7 A.M.–6 P.M.

CHEESE

BLYTHEDALE FARM CAMEMBERT AND BRIE

In the 1980s and early 90s, Craigston was a Wenham, Massachusetts, cheesemaker known for producing a fine Camembert that compared favorably with those made in France.

The Craigston company is no more, but its two cheesemakers, Karen Galayda and Tom Gilbert, began making Camembert and other cheeses in Vermont in 1992. Their farmstead cheese company is called Blythedale Farm. It began in Springfield, but in 1995, they moved their Jersey herd to 50 acres near Corinth, Vermont, a town in the central part of the state that doesn't show up on highway maps. The two do all the work themselves, milking cows and making cheese from 5 in the morning until 8 in the evening. They make two soft cheeses, Camembert and brie; a Stilton style blue medium-hard cheese called Jersey Blue; and two aged cheeses, Green Mountain Gruyère and Parmesan.

Milk from Jersey cows has a higher content of solids than most, which makes for richer, more flavorable cheeses. The couple know each of their 20 milking cows personally, and is careful about what the cows eat. Their good stewardship has earned the farm a "dairy of distinction" award from the Vermont Department of Agriculture for each of the past three years.

The brie is the best seller, perhaps because the cheese variety itself is well known. It is excellent brie, but we suggest trying the Camembert as well. If you want a mild cheese, eat it immediately when it is firm in texture. If you want a deeper flavor, let it ripen in your refrigerator. It softens as it ages, and takes on more of its distinctive mushroomlike taste. It should always be served at room temperature. Sliced in wedges and served with fruit, it is a satisfying way to end a meal.

Blythedale Farms doesn't operate a retail business, but its cheeses can be ordered by mail from Vermont's historic Taftsville Country Store, in business since 1840. There, two 8-ounce, foil-wrapped wheels of either brie or Camembert are $19.75, plus shipping. The Jersey Blue, Green Mountain Gruyère, and Parmesan are cut off large wheels in wedges, and are sold in approximate amounts. That means if you want a 1-pound wedge, country store proprietor Charlie Wilson will try hard to get close to 1 pound, but may be slightly over or under, and will charge accordingly.

At various times of year, the store offers free shipping. You can view the catalog on the website (address below) and see the current details.

ORDERING ADDRESS
Taftsville Country Store
Route 4
Taftsville, VT 05073
800/854-0013

FAX: 802/457-5173
www.taftsville.com
Credit cards accepted

VISITS: Blythedale Farm in Corinth is not open for visits. The Taftsville Country Store is in east-central Vermont, outside Woodstock. The store is 3½ miles east of Woodstock's village green on Route 4.
Monday–Saturday, 8 A.M.–6 P.M. Sunday, 8 A.M.–5 P.M. (In the summer, the store is open longer in the evenings.)

BRIER RUN FARM CERTIFIED ORGANIC CHÈVRE

The fitness magazines have been full of references to quark, but when you try to find it, be prepared for odd looks. Although it is very popular in Europe, where its consumption vies with that of yogurt, it is the rare cheesemaker who produces it here.

A soft, white cheese that's usually made from skim milk, quark finds favor with the body-conscious because it is low-calorie, low-fat, low-cholesterol, low-sodium, and nutritious. On a farm in central West Virginia, about an hour northeast of Charleston, cheesemakers Greg and Verena Sava make a version with whole goat's milk that they say is even more easily digested than cow's milk quark. Their recipe is one used by Swiss goatherds, courtesy of a Swiss Alps cheese inspector.

The Savas send a list of suggestions for using their quark, such as spreading it on toast, muffins, and bagels; mixing it with berries, peaches, pineapple, and applesauce; or making "a heavenly cheesecake that won't leave you feeling guilty." Quark substitutes for cream cheese, sour cream, or yogurt, and can be used on tacos, stirred into tomato soup, or mixed with hot pasta.

It is sent in 8-ounce plastic tubs for $4, plus shipping. It can be frozen, so your order doesn't need to be geared toward immediate consumption.

The Savas also make a goat's milk fromage blanc, a French standby that is a bit like smooth cottage cheese. It is close to the quark in taste and appearance but is slightly more compact. It also is used in cooking or can be flavored and sweetened and served with fruit. One especially delicious way to use it is to add sugar and rum and spoon the mixture over sliced bananas. Sprinkle with chopped nuts and you have a zippy, unique dessert. Fromage blanc is sent in 6- or 8-ounce containers for $3 or $4, plus shipping.

Greg, age 53, a native New Yorker, and Swiss-born Verena, 56, have lived on their 160-acre West Virginia farm for 25 years. Fifteen years ago, they began commercial production of their soft goat cheeses after discovering, as many fledgling cheesemakers have in this country in the last decades, that soft cheeses involve less work and aging time and are more readily accepted by American consumers. West Virginia's famed Greenbrier Hotel was one of its first customers. The farm has been a certified organic-cheese producer since 1990. Since April 1999, the Savas have cut back on production so they can handle the whole operation by themselves. They now concentrate on selling to restaurants, hotels, and private customers.

Brier Run offers a host of goat-cheese flavors and ages. Its 6-ounce banon, which is a dense, disc-shaped cheese, and the cylinder-shaped chabis, a young, mild cheese, come in several flavors, including Java black pepper, Italian, basil, herbes de Provence (with herbs imported from a French farm), and garlic and herb. Log-shaped cheeses can be sliced in rounds and come plain, flavored, or ash-coated.

Brier Run also produces aged, mold-ripened chèvre, with blue (Roquefort) or white mold. These cheeses are harder and more pungent than the soft ones. As goat cheese becomes a basic part of our food vocabulary, it stands to reason that more of us will come to appreciate these mature cheeses.

Brier Run also makes a goat-cheese product that appeals to all eaters, sophisticated or plain. Chocolate fudge, using their chèvre as a base, can be ordered for $2.50 a ¼ pound, plus shipping. The cheese is unsalted, so the fudge is very low in sodium—and lower in fat than traditional fudge.

Call or write Brier Run for its complete product list and shipping prices. There is a $25 minimum for ordering.

The farm is not open for visits.

ORDERING ADDRESS

Brier Run Farm
HC32, Box 73
Birch River, VW 26610
304/649-2975
Credit cards accepted

CABOT CREAMERY AGED CHEDDAR

If you eat a sharp Cheddar labeled Vermont, chances are it came from the Cabot Farmer's Cooperative Creamery in Cabot, where an estimated 90 percent of the sharp Vermont Cheddar cheese sold in this country is produced. Although the cooperative is the largest cheesemaker in New England, with 1,500 farmer-owners supplying milk, it is able to produce a superior hard, aged Cheddar that involves much hand labor. The cheese is aged slowly—as long as two years for the extra-sharp Cheddar that is the true Vermont Cheddar, with a fierce bite. Cabot's Cheddar also comes in private stock, sharp, mild, and many specialty flavors such as tomato basil, with aging time from 9 to 18 months.

The critical step of "cheddaring," which involves flipping and stacking the slabs of cheese curds to expel moisture, is done by stainless-steel forks. The process is repeated over and over for at least an hour, to allow the milk acid to develop, and is one of the reasons that Cabot cheese has such a good texture. Rich Stammer, president of the cooperative, explained, "The hand attention and timing make a big difference in the finished product. Enzymes to speed up flavor can't replace them."

The waxing of the Cheddar wheels and blocks is all done by hand, with each piece dipped three times. Color varies, according to the cheese type, and an uncolored wax is available for 32-pound wheels.

The cooperative's handsome 3-pound wheels, covered with clear or black wax and stamped with the lot number, are the company's handmade specialty, and we prefer them sharp. A sharp wheel costs $21, including UPS shipping. At the co-op, the wheel sells for $15. Call for special prices on larger wheels of 12 and 38 pounds, or check out the website.

The well-regarded light cheddar is a high-moisture cheese with half the fat and cholesterol and 30 percent fewer calories than Cheddar. It's a natural-colored cheese that tastes like medium Cheddar and melts well for cooking, when used in recipes that do not call for the cheese to be in direct contact with heat. One ounce contains 5 g of fat and 15 mg of cholesterol, compared to Cheddar's 10 g of fat and 30 mg of cholesterol. It is sold in 8-ounce ($5.50, including shipping), 1-pound ($8.50, including shipping), or 5-pound ($23.75, including shipping) sizes and also comes in a jalapeño pepper variety.

ORDERING ADDRESS
Cabot Farmer's Co-op
P.O. Box 128
Cabot, VT 05647
802/563-2231
800/639-3198
www.cabotcheese.com
Credit cards accepted

VISITING ADDRESS
Visitor's Center
Main Street
Cabot, VT 05647
Cabot, a town of less than 1,000, is just west of St. Johnsbury, Vermont, in the northeastern part of the state. From Highway 2, turn north at Marshfield and drive about 5 miles. The creamery is on Main Street, which is Rt. 215.

Daily: June–October, 9 A.M.–5 P.M. Winter hours: Monday–Saturday, 9 A.M.–4 P.M. Closed during January

CALEF'S SNAPPY OLD CHEESE

Austin Lea Forest Calef, the son of a rugged New Hampshire woman who spurned convention and founded a country store in Barrington more than 130 years ago, gave a pithy description of the store's best-known product, its Cheddar cheese: "It's snappy," said Austin. "Makes a man sit up and take notice. All you have to do is give a customer a sample and a cracker from the barrel, and he's sold."

The cheese gets its snap from its long aging, which averages two years. It came about, the story goes, when young Austin long ago discovered some cheese in the cellar that had been hidden and forgotten under some merchandise. The forgotten cheese, it seems, had developed an unusually good flavor in the process. Now Calef's Country Store sends the cheese all over the world, in its traditional sky-blue wrapping paper with the time-honored logo copied from Austin Calef's handwriting and the slogan: "Every Bite Tastes Right."

The Calef family sold the store in August 1996 to Cleve and Lindy Horton, formerly of Concord, Massachusetts. They continue to market raw-milk Cheddar as Snappy Old Cheese. They also still prepare a smoked version. It is indeed a sharp snappy cheese, with a firm texture that we prefer to the younger, more bland Cheddars. The smoked version is particularly good. Snappy Old Cheese is available in a red wax-covered 1½-pound brick for $10.99, a 2½-pound brick for $16.99, or a 5-pound brick for $29.99. A 3-pound black-wax–covered round is $21.99. Shipping costs are added to all orders, based on the retail value of the order. Cheese is not sent in July and August unless a customer requests second-day air shipment.

The store today still sells crackers in a barrel, dry goods, brooms, ammunition, china, ice cream, fertilizer, paints, poultry feed, seeds, tobacco, pearl tapioca, penny candies, molasses, and wallpaper, among numerous other wares. The store also offers maple syrup, hams, and unusual homemade jams and jellies, including such varieties as quince and cherry-grapefruit, by mail. The jams, which come in 60 flavors, are made by a small army of women throughout New England who cook the products exclusively for the store.

ORDERING ADDRESS
Calef's Country Store
P.O. Box 57
Barrington, NH 03825
603/664-2231
800/462-2118
e-mail: CALEFS@aol.com (checked infrequently)
Credit cards accepted

VISITING ADDRESS
149 Route 9
Barrington, NH 03825
Barrington is just south of Rochester, New Hampshire. Calef's is directly on Highway 9, west of the intersection with Highway 125.
Every day, 8 A.M.–5 P.M.

COUGAR GOLD CHEESE

It was a new idea in the 1940s, sealing fresh cheese in cans, and it enjoyed a brief bit of popularity during World War II, when the military bought cheese to ship overseas. But canning cheese never really caught on, even though it allows the cheese to be made without preservatives. Today, it is done only in one place, the school where the process was developed, Washington State University at Pullman. The creamery there continues to give canning the old college try, producing five varieties of cheese in distinctive striped round tins. Happily, the quality of the cheeses inside makes them more than mere conversation pieces.

Decades ago, nearly every land-grant or technical college had a working creamery on campus, producing dairy products for sale, but the number has dwindled in recent years to a dozen or so around the nation. Those that remain generally produce notable cheese, usually with a cheese or two that is unique to the school, generally named after the sports team or school mascot. At Washington State, the most distinctive cheese is Cougar Gold, named not only for the WSU mascot ("Butch"), but also for Dr. N. S. Golding, a professor who developed the cheese. It is not gold in color but is even lighter than Gouda, to which it has been compared in taste. It is an aged cheese, one year in the making, with a mellow and full-bodied flavor and a judicious amount of tang. We found it a bit like England's Lancashire, although not as crumbly. It toasts well and is excellent with fruit. Popular for at least 50 years at WSU, it is the creamery's best seller.

The other variety unique to Washington State is Viking cheese, a soft, white cheese that is aged four months and is creamier and milder than Cougar Gold. Viking cheese also comes in a reduced-fat version. Seven other flavors are available: American Cheddar, smoky Cheddar, hot pepper, dill garlic, sweet basil, Italian, and cracked pepper and chive.

Mark Bates, creamery manager, said the increasing popularity of the cheeses can be credited to a desire by Americans to eat a wider variety of cheese.

On campus, the cheeses, milk, and the creamery's celebrated ice cream and milk shakes are dispensed at a hole-in-the-wall known as Ferdinand's, located in a classroom building in the south part of the grounds. The name, chosen during a campuswide name contest in the 1950s, refers to the peace-loving bull of the storybook fame.

The school sells by mail nationwide to WSU alumni and others who have discovered the unusual cheese in the funny cans. A 30-ounce can of any of the 5 varieties is $13, plus shipping ($4 per address, plus $1 per tin).

ORDERING ADDRESS
WSU Creamery
Washington State University
P.O. Box 641122
Pullman, WA 99164–1122
509/335-4014
800/457-5442
FAX: 509/335-6775
www.wsu.edu/creamery
e-mail: creamery@wsu.edu
Credit cards accepted

VISITING ADDRESS
Ferdinand's
Washington State University
101 Food Quality
Pullman, WA 99164–1122
Ferdinand's is at 101 Food Quality on the southern part of the campus.
Monday–Friday, 9:30 A.M.–4:30 P.M.

GRAFTON VILLAGE CHEESE COMPANY CHEDDAR

The Windham Foundation, created in 1963 by a longtime summer resident of Grafton, Vermont, pledged itself to acquiring properties in order to preserve the existing charm of the small Green Mountain village. It began by purchasing and renovating the defunct Village Store, a former 1801 stagecoach inn, which is now a choice tourist destination. Then, in 1968, the foundation turned its sights to preserving an edible Vermont heritage—white raw-milk Cheddar cheese. The cheese, which is available at the small factory just south of Grafton, by mail, and through the Internet, is aged one year.

Grafton Cheddar, like most cheeses, is at its full-flavored best when served at room temperature. It is a soft Cheddar with a richer, less sharp taste than, say, Cabot's longer-aged cheeses. The company produces three aged Cheddars: a one-year Premium, a two-year Classic Reserve, and three-year Grafton Gold. Three flavored Vermont cheddars are available: maple smoked, garlic Cheddar, and sage Cheddar.

A 2-pound block of Premium Cheddar is $11.95, plus shipping. The same size of the Classic Reserve is $14.50, plus shipping. Two 1-pound blocks of the smoked Cheddar is $15.25, plus shipping. If you are having the cheese sent to the West Coast or to the South during hot weather, add $7 for second-day air shipments. The company also will send out apple boxes and gift packages, which are described in its catalog.

ORDERING ADDRESS
Grafton Village Cheese Company
P.O. Box 87
Grafton, VT 05146
802/843-2221
800/GRA-FTON (800/472-3866)
www.graftonvillagecheese.com
e-mail: info@graftonvillagecheese.com
Credit cards accepted

VISITING ADDRESS
533 Townshend Road
Grafton, VT 05146
Grafton is south of Springfield, Vermont, in the southeast part of the state. Take Route 35 south to Grafton, and at The Old Tavern, in the town center, turn left onto Townshend Road. Drive about a half mile to the cheese company, which is in a modern building. *Monday–Friday, 8:00 A.M.–4:00 P.M. Saturday-Sunday, 10 A.M.–4:00 P.M.*

HOOK'S COLBY

We approach awards with a certain wariness. Travel to enough sausage shops, candy makers, and cheese factories, and you'll see enough ribbons and plaques to keep a trophy maker in business for life. But we were impressed when we read an article in *Farm Wife News* about a woman in Mineral Point, Wisconsin, who was honored with the "World Championship Cheesemaker Award" for her Colby cheese late in 1982. She was the first woman in the competition's history to win the award, and her cheese won over 394 entries from 14 countries and 12 U.S. cheese-producing states.

After years of living above their cheese factory in a rural setting, 13 years ago Julie Hook and her husband, Tony, moved their operation to a building in downtown Mineral Point that had once housed a cheese maker. They bought a home in town, "and it's nice to get away from cheesemaking once in a while," Julie admitted. The two work hard, rising at 4 A.M. on cheesemaking days, and Tony spends afternoons collecting milk from area dairy farmers.

Tony, 48, has been making cheese for 33 years. Julie, 46, a former beautician, learned from Tony. Their output is relatively small, perhaps 1 million pounds a year. "Some big places can turn that out in a day or two," notes Julie. The cheese is distributed in some stores and supermarkets in Wisconsin and northern Illinois, and the couple sells directly from their factory, in sealed random 1-pound packages. They also will send cheese.

The operation may be an international award winner, but it certainly is not fancy. The "brochure" consists of half a sheet of paper with the prices home-typed, and the price is a reasonable $3.25 per pound for the Colby and Monterey Jack, and the mild Cheddar. They also make a medium Cheddar; 1-year, 3-year, and 5-year Cheddars; a variety of flavored Cheddars, such as tomato basil and smoked; and a variety of Jacks, including Muenster-pesto and dill. A baby Swiss, Hook's blue cheese, and cheese curds also are available. The marble and flavored cheeses and curds are $3.25 per pound. Other prices range from $3.75 per pound for the medium Cheddar to $6.25 per pound for the 5-year Cheddar. Shipping charges via UPS or U.S. mail and a $2 handling charge per order are extra.

Their cheeses do have a marvelous, even texture. The Colby, particularly, is fine-grained and firm and has character, in marked contrast to the blandness of mass-produced Colbys.

Mineral Point is an interesting, historic town that got its start as a lead-mining village, and it is a civic asset to have Hook's cheese company downtown. The town attracts tourists drawn to its many stone dwellings, its picturesque names, like "Shake Rag Street" (so named because miner's wives would shake washrags to alert their husbands working on the opposite hill that a meal was ready), and remnants of its English history brought by hard-rock miners from Cornwall in the mid 1800s.

Every Saturday from the end of April until the first of November the Hooks sell their cheese at Dane County Farmer's Market in Madison. It is set around the sidewalk encircling the state capitol and offers regional goodies, including these cheeses.

ORDERING ADDRESS
Hook's Cheese Company, Inc.
320 Commerce Street
Mineral Point, WI 53565
608/987-3259
e-mail: amh@chorus.net
No credit cards

VISITING ADDRESS
Mineral Point is in the southwest corner of Wisconsin, about 45 miles southwest of Madison. The cheese company is in downtown Mineral Point, at the five-point corner, on Commerce Street.
Monday–Friday, 4 A.M.–2 P.M.

KENDALL CHEESE COMPANY CRÈME FRAÎCHE

Sadie Kendall might be called the Queen of Crème Fraîche. Previously known for her goat cheeses, she has seen interest in the crème fraîche she makes from cow's milk grow so consistently over the years that she has decided to concentrate on that one item. From her dairy in Atascadero, California, she will send crème fraîche around the country.

Crème fraîche is a thick, slightly sour heavy cream that is popular for cooking and for topping fruit. It is called for increasingly in recipes, but it can be difficult to find in stores.

"I've always had it in abundance," said Sadie, "and over the years I've figured out lots of interesting things to do with it." So in 1990, she wrote *The Crème Fraîche Cookbook,* which was published by Ridgeview Publishing Company. Her husband, Jeffrey Sicha, runs Ridgeview, so it was a true team effort.

Sadie has a college degree in philosophy and intended to go to law school. Goat raising, a hobby, led her to earn a degree in dairy manufacturing at Cal Poly in San Luis Obispo and then to open a dairy about two decades ago.

She will send a half-gallon (4 pounds) of crème fraîche for $14, plus shipping. If you want smaller containers, 9-ounce tubs are $2.50. There is a $10 minimum purchase, however.

She also will send her cookbook for $14, which includes tax and shipping.

ORDERING ADDRESS
Kendall Cheese Company
P.O. Box 686
Atascadero, CA 93423
805/466-7252 or -7271
No credit cards

VISITING ADDRESS
Same address. Atascardero is in central California, near the coast. It is about 15 miles north of San Luis Obispo. The dairy is on the grounds of the state hospital, but rather difficult to find, since the roads are unmarked. Sadie Kendall suggests calling ahead for hours and directions.

KOLB-LENA CHEESE COMPANY

Those who insist that the best Bries, Camemberts, and double creams are imported should try the soft ripened cheeses made by the Kolb-Lena Cheese Company in the small town of Lena, Illinois.

The business was started by immigrant Fred Kolb in 1925 and has been run, in turn, by his son-in-law, Karl Renter, Renter's wife, Freida, and her son-in-law, James Demeter. In June 1987, the Kolb-Lena Cheese Company was bought by the Bongrain group.

The company's soft ripened cheeses are sold under the Alouette and Délice de France brands. They are creamy, luscious cheeses with an interior that properly turns from chalky white to butter-colored as it ripens, becoming softer in the process. They have a rich, mushroomlike flavor that develops a tang at their peak.

The company also is known for its best-selling Delico Baby Swiss cheese, which it developed 45 years ago with the help of Iowa State University dairy scientists.

VISITING ADDRESS
Kolb-Lena Cheese Company
3990 North Sunnyside Road
Lena, IL 61048
815/369-4577
No credit cards
Lena is in northwest Illinois, about 30 miles west of Rockford and 10 miles south of the Wisconsin border. The cheese shop is on Highway 20, just 5 miles west of Lena.
Tuesday–Saturday, 9 A.M.–4 P.M. Sunday, 10 A.M.–4 P.M.

LAURA CHENEL'S CHÈVRE

There was an American goat-cheese industry before Laura Chenel turned her goat-raising hobby into a nationally recognized business 20 years ago, but we never heard much about it. It was a low-profile, geographically scattered industry, in places such as the southern Colorado towns of Trinidad and Pueblo, where goat cheeses have been made for more than a hundred years. Some of the goat cheeses there are left to harden in straw baskets and incorporate wild mushrooms and local red peppers, and all are sold out the farmhouse door. Cheesemaking skills, passed down from parent to child, are in danger of becoming extinct, as the few remaining cheesemakers are elderly or have very limited production.

Laura Chenel is no conglomerate, but she does produce enough cheese to supply top restaurants and gourmet shops nationwide. Six years ago the company moved from Santa Rosa, California, to an old dairy in Sonoma, where there is more space to make cheese. With two cookbooks out on cheese, and a raft of national attention given her business, she has become one of the most visible symbols of American goat cheese.

Laura makes cheese in the French style, which is why she calls her product *chèvre* (French for "goat"). She learned how to make her cheese from the source, when she apprenticed herself to four cheesemakers in France in 1979. Her product may in one respect be even better than the imported varieties.

Laura buys milk only from goat raisers she knows personally. The milk is pasteurized and the curds are formed into a variety of shapes, using traditional French cheese molds. There are logs and pyramids, disks and chabis, which are small circles about 1½ inches high. She is best known for light, mild cheeses. But she has developed several aged cheeses over the years and offers a wide variety of these cheeses as well.

The chabis, an all-round cheese, is dense, with a consistency a little softer than cream cheese. It is good served warmed on salad greens or mixed in a soufflé. Goat cheese is more pungent than cow's milk cheese, but this is a gentle introduction. Others of her mild chèvre cheeses come coated with pepper, dill, paprika, or fresh herbs.

The cheese is not sent by mail. However, there are distributors throughout the country. Laura Chenel suggests calling either Cheese Works, in

New Jersey (973/962-1202) or Domestic Cheese, in San Francisco (415/826-7080) to find the nearest sales outlet. The price for the chabis, for example, averages $3.50 for a 5-ounce round.

Laura Chenel's Chèvre, Inc.
4310 Fremont Drive
Sonoma, CA 95476
707/996-4477
FAX: 707/996-1816

MAYTAG BLUE CHEESE

The folks who make Maytag Blue Cheese have heard all the jokes about its being mixed in washing machines. They take them good-naturedly because you can afford to be sanguine about slights when you produce what many believe is the best blue cheese in the country. Cheese writers George Kovatch and Bob Wiskotzil, in their syndicated newspaper column, "About Cheese," wrote in 1980: "We honestly believe that we can say without any fear of contradiction, that it is the finest blue cheese made in the United States. We will even go further and state that Maytag Blue ranks with Roquefort, Stilton, and Gorgonzola as one of the four greatest blue cheeses in the world."

What makes Maytag Blue superior is: (1) fresh, unpasteurized milk from Iowa Holstein herds near the Maytag Dairy Farms cheese plant at Newton, Iowa; (2) longer aging, about twice as long as most other American blues, making it creamy and spreadable. The cheese is aged in a man-made cave dug into the side of a hill and covered with 8 feet of earth. As for the taste, to quote Kovatch and Wiskotzil, "The taste is extraordinarily sharp, yet, contradictorily, so absolutely mellow that it never tires the palate. You can eat it plain with bread, in a salad dressing, for dessert with ripe fruit or make it into a wonderful blue cheese soup."

Wrapped in a blue and silver foil with a smiling Holstein head on the label, the cheese comes in wheels, wedges, and spreads. A 2-pound wheel is $20.65, plus a $5 delivery charge per address. During warm months and for shipments to warm states, the company recommends shipment by air, which is an additional $3 for up to two items.

The Maytags got into the cheese business via a circuitous route. E. H. Maytag, the son of F. L. Maytag, the appliance company founder, raised a prize-winning herd of Holstein Friesian cattle on the family farms and was known throughout the country for them. There was a milk bottling plant on the farm, but the herd primarily was a hobby, not a business. But when E. H. Maytag died, in 1940, the farms were left as a corporation and needed to pay their way. E. H.'s oldest son, Fred, went to Iowa State University, where dairy scientists had developed a patented, new method for making American Blue cheese. In return for helping subsidize the development of the cheese, the Maytags were given permission to make it.

It is still a family operation, with brothers Fritz Maytag and Ken Maytag being co-chairman of the board. Fritz Maytag also owns the historic Anchor Steam Beer Brewery in San Francisco. Jim Stevens, the company president, joined the Maytags as an assistant cheesemaker in 1945 and has been with the Maytag Dairy Farms for over 50 years.

ORDERING ADDRESS
Maytag Dairy Farms
P.O. Box 806
Newton, IA 50208
515/792-1133
800/247-2458 (outside Iowa)
FAX: 515/792-1567
Credit cards accepted

VISITING ADDRESS
2282 East 8th Street, North
Newton, IA 50208
Newton is in central Iowa, about 35 miles east of Des Moines on I-80. From I-80 just west of Newton, take exit 164 and follow Iowa Highway 14 north about 3 miles, then follow our signs. Or, from I-80 just east of Newton, take exit 168, go north and follow the belt line road about 4 miles until you see the company's sign.
Monday–Friday, 8 A.M.–5 P.M. Saturday, 9 A.M.–1 P.M.

MORNINGLAND DAIRY RAW-MILK CHEESES

Margie and Jim Reiners have a small farm in the Missouri Ozarks, but they are well known nationwide in health-food circles. To make their raw-milk cheeses, they start by worrying about the kind of pasture their Holsteins have. They want it pesticide-free and enriched with organic fertilizers. They worry about their cows' nutrition and grind their own feed weekly, using organic corn, soybean meal, and minerals. They worry about insect control, and shun sprays. All this worrying and care brings them at last to the milk, which was Grade A bonus quality when they used to sell it to a large dairy. Since 1981, however, the Reinerses have been making cheese from their own milk in an effort to have more control over the final product and to achieve self-sufficiency.

The Reinerses are concerned with keeping the natural digestive enzymes from the milk intact in the cheese, so it is not pasteurized and is heated only to 99 degrees—the body temperature of the cow.

After the cheese is pressed, it ages for at least 60 days, as is required of all raw-milk cheeses. All the cheeses are uncolored, and Cheddar is available unsalted. Some Cheddars include dill and are mild, medium sharp, and sharp. Colby cheeses come in plain, hot pepper, Italian, and garlic. Goat cheese and washed curd cheese also can be ordered.

The cheese is packed in vacuum-seated bags and sent by UPS. Cheese is sent Monday and Tuesday, and insulated boxes are used during hot weather to ensure safe shipment. Cheese can be ordered in bulk, ranging from 5- to 40-pound blocks, or in smaller pieces. The no-salt mild Cheddar is $3 per pound for a like amount. There is a $2.75 handling charge per order in winter and $4 per order in summer, plus shipping costs.

There is no visiting.

ORDERING ADDRESS
Morningland Dairy
6248 County Road 2980
Mountain View, MO 65548
417/469-3817
FAX: 417/469-5086
No credit cards

MOSSHOLDER'S FARMSTEAD CHEESE

The past decades have not been kind to small, family-run cheesemaking operations. In Wisconsin alone, scores have gone out of business, victims of consumer acceptance of nondescript cheeses and ever more concentration of cheesemaking in large dairies and cooperatives. Although the last few years have been marked by a modest resurgence of family cheesemakers, it is quite unusual to find farmers who have been making cheese for more than half a century in the basement of their farmhouse, using milk from their own dairy cows.

North of Appleton, Wisconsin, is such a cheesemaking family. At the farm of Larry and Lois Mossholder, a distinctively American brick-style semisoft cheese has been made from raw milk from their family's registered Holstein cows for more than 70 years. Larry's cousin, David, left the business in March 1994, and today Larry, Lois, and their three grown daughters, Bonnie, Lisa, and Becky, run the complete business. Described as having the characteristics of Swiss, brick, and Colby rolled into one, the lightly colored cheese has a taste all its own and was developed by Larry's grandfather, Otto Mossholder. Creamy and mild, it has a rich milk flavor and a fine texture with small holes dispersed evenly throughout. Variations include caraway seed, jalapeño pepper, crushed red pepper, chopped onion, and dill.

Larry and Lois make four different ages of this one cheese and use only the family's own milk from the 40 milking cows in the white barn a few hundred yards away. Since the milk is unpasteurized, the cheese is required to be aged 60 days before it is sold. The family still molds the cheese in stainless-steel blocks, known as hoops. In the cool green-and-white-tiled basement, creamy blocks of cheese rest on aging tables. In a separate room, the morning's production sits in the hoops, weighted with bricks. A retail store is on the ground-floor level.

The cheese is sold from their house year-round and shipped throughout the United States from September through May. It is easy to spot the tidy farmstead, for the suburbs of Appleton have moved out to surround the Mossholders' barns, making the operation seem even more of an anachronism. Customers should heed the small sign by the door, which says: "Ring doorbell for cheese." As you watch, your cheese will be wrapped and cut. The cost is an extremely modest $3.64 per pound for the mild cheese (aged 2 to 4 months). The medium cheese, aged from 6 to 9 months, is $3.84 per pound; 9- to 14-month-aged cheese is $4.04 per pound, and the extra-aged (over 14 months old) is $4.44 per pound. Cheese gift boxes also are available.

The Mossholders' way of cheesemaking is clearly threatened by increasing land taxes and urban sprawl. It exists now as a poignant example of history slipping away. We have long advocated preservation of American culinary specialties, and some jurisdictions have given tax relief to long-established food landmarks threatened by growth. We hope that spirit will grow and protect this fourth-generation family operation.

ORDERING ADDRESS

Mossholder Farm Cheese Factory
4017 North Richmond Street
Appleton, WI 54913
920/734-7575
www.mossholdercheese.homestead.com
e-mail: lalomo@athenet.net
Credit cards accepted

VISITING ADDRESS

Located on Highway 47, at 4007 North Richmond, a quarter mile north of the junction with Highway 41. Watch for the signs.

Monday–Friday, 9 A.M.–5 P.M. Saturday, 9 A.M.–12 P.M. Closed Sunday and major holidays

MOZZARELLA COMPANY HANDMADE CHEESES

It seems that every other recipe we see in a food magazine calls for fresh ricotta, mascarpone, or mozzarella. If you don't have access to one of the Old World cheesemakers who operate quietly in a few urban ethnic neighborhoods around this country, you are generally out of luck. Unless you know about Mozzarella Company of Dallas, that is.

Paula Lambert, like countless others who have spent time in Italy, wondered why it was nearly impossible to find fresh mozzarella cheese in America. Unlike the others, she did something about it. In 1982, she and two other Dallas women founded a company to produce handmade fresh mozzarella. Paula had spent time learning cheesemaking at a plant near Assisi, Italy, and she prevailed upon an Italian cheese professor to spend part of his summer vacation in Dallas, furthering her cheese education.

Fresh mozzarella bears little resemblance to the solid, rubbery cheese that's a staple on pizza. It is soft, moist, and elastic. It is still good on pizza, but it is even better at room temperature in a fresh tomato and basil salad or simply served with fruit.

The company sells retail and wholesale at the cheese factory in a renovated neighborhood near downtown Dallas, but it has earned a nationwide reputation for its willingness to ship its cheeses, even the very perishable ones, to hotels, restaurants, cheese shops, and individuals. Over the years its repertoire has expanded to include more than 35 varieties of cow-milk cheeses and 16 varieties of goat cheeses.

Some of the tempting ingredient items it offers are hand-churned unsalted butter ($6 a pound), triple-creme cheese ($13 a pound), fluffy fresh cream cheese (without added gums, alleluia!) at $7.50 a pound, salt-free fresh ricotta ($5 a pound), and mascarpone, an unsalted, thick cow-milk product that is reminiscent of clotted cream ($13 a pound). These perishables must be sent via overnight delivery (unless you live within 300 miles of Dallas).

Mozzarella Company is best known for the southwestern twist it puts on its cheeses. Mozzarella is shaped, jelly-roll style, around jalapeño chiles or sun-dried tomatoes. Mascarpone is layered in tortas with ancho chiles or pecan pralines. Its semisoft aged caciotta cheeses come waxed, in cow- or goat-milk versions. The cow and goat caciottas are available with a number of Tex-Mex seasonings: Texas basil, Mexican marigold mint, Mexican oregano-garlic, or various chiles, such as ancho, chipotle, or serrano. One version brings to mind the soda fountain treat known as "suicide" (one of every flavor of syrup on the counter). It is La Cocina ("the kitchen"), which includes all the previously named chiles.

We sampled the ancho-chile caciotta (cow milk), a warm beige-colored cheese with flecks of red pepper and green cilantro, and were delighted by its mellow but zippy taste. Goat-milk caciotta had the consistency of Meunster, with small holes, and was pleasantly tangy. These savory cheeses will never be confused with Colby or American!

The tomato-basil mascarpone torta was picturesque, with pine nuts and sun-dried tomatoes on the top of its 2-inch-high cone and alternating layers of basil, tomato, and cheese. You can discard the cheese-ball recipes if you have a few of these charming tortas on hand.

Mozzarella Company requires a minimum order of 1 pound of cheese, but allows you to select as little as ½-pound increments of individual varieties. The company offers a number of gift baskets, ranging from $25 to $125, and always includes recipe cards with orders. The overnight delivery is not as expensive as you might imagine. For 1 to 4 pounds of cheese, it is $15 and for 4 to 6 pounds, it is $20.

ORDERING ADDRESS
Mozzarella Company
2944 Elm Street
Dallas, TX 75226
214/741-4072
800/798-2954
www.mozzco.com
e-mail: MozzCo@aol.com
Credit cards accepted

VISITING ADDRESS: The company is in the Deep Ellum section of Dallas, east of downtown. From downtown, take Commerce Street, which is one way to the east, and go under the bridges past Oakland Street until Walton Street. Take a left on Walton and go 2 blocks. The cheese company is on the left corner of Elm and Walton.
Monday–Friday, 9 A.M.–5 P.M. Saturday, 9 A.M.–3 P.M.

NAUVOO BLUE CHEESE

In the marketing of out-of-the-ordinary foods, there is an almost religious reverence given to what we have come to refer to as the "In the beginning" story. Usually found in mail-order catalogs or brochures available at the factory, the stories are inevitably without footnote or credit, and often involve a mistake that turns out to be the fortuitous start of a brilliant enterprise.

At Beatrice Cheese, in Nauvoo, Illinois, the "In the beginning" story concerns a young shepherd boy who forgot his lunch of bread and curds in a limestone cave in southwestern France centuries ago. When the boy found his lunch some weeks after he had left it in the cave, the curds had acquired a "delectable and delicate flavor," to quote the Nauvoo brochure. He took it to the monks in a nearby monastery, who began making blue cheese from sheep milk, returning to the same cave to age the cheese.

Nauvoo, an intriguing town that was the site of an ill-fated communal living experiment by French Icarians and a settlement for Brigham Young, Joseph Smith, and other Mormons in the mid-1800s, is in the west-central part of Illinois along the Mississippi River. Another unique Nauvoo feature is the limestone caves high on a hill overlooking the river. Once used to age beer for the extinct Schenk Brewery, the caves were rediscovered in 1937 by the late Oscar Rohde, who found that they provided the consistent temperatures needed for the proper aging of blue cheese. Rohde (pronounced "Road-y") began making cheese, and his family continued to operate the plant until December 1987, when it was sold to Raskas Foods, Inc. Today, the cheese factory is an operating unit of Beatrice Cheese of Waukesha, Wisconsin.

The methods have remained the same, however, and the cheese continues to be as flavorful as ever. It is available in wheels or crumbled and packed in plastic bags, for use on salads and hamburgers. Tangy and nicely marbled with blue veins, the cheese is an American treasure.

Cheese also is shipped in whole wheels, half wheels, and wedges. Shipping is done November through March. Their holiday gift catalog includes the Nauvoo Mill and Bakery's own whole wheat corn bread and pancake mixes.

ORDERING ADDRESS
Nauvoo Mill and Bakery
1530 Mulholland Street
Nauvoo, IL 62354
217/453-6734
888/453-6734
www.visitnauvoo.org
e-mail: naumibak@nauvoo.net
Credit cards accepted

VISITING ADDRESS: Nauvoo is on Illinois Highway 96, across the river and south of Burlington, Iowa. The Nauvoo Mill and Bakery is on Highway 96, 2 blocks east of downtown. The cheese plant is in the center of town, but there are no sales or tours at the plant. Cheese is available in town, however, at the Nauvoo Mill and Bakery, Duck's Foods, Baxter's Vineyards, John A. Kraus Co., and Dottie's Red Front.
Monday–Saturday, 8 a.m–5 P.M.

PLYMOUTH CHEESE

It's unusual to find a cheese that's still kneaded by hand, as machines have taken over the aching task of breaking up the curds. Historically, of course, all cheese was made this way, and if any cheese can claim to be historic, it is this one. Made since 1890 in the cheese factory in Plymouth, Vermont, founded by President Calvin Coolidge's father, was owned by the president's son, John. The raw-milk uncolored cheese, which is similar to but less compact than a Cheddar, is hand-stirred and kneaded, salted, pressed into molds, wrapped in cheesecloth, and dipped in four coats of wax before aging, much as it always has been.

When it arrives by mail, it gives a good reflection of the sparse, "waste not, want not" Coolidge image. The wheel of cheese is wrapped in foil, placed in a plain bag, and then wrapped again in newspaper. In our case, it was John Coolidge's copy of the *Rutland Herald.*

Plymouth cheese is moist, with lots of small holes and a slightly sour, rich taste. It is one of our favorites of all the cheeses we tasted for this book. The cheese comes in mild or medium-sharp, or with sage, pimiento, or caraway added.

The company will ship cheese, as well as maple syrup, Indian pudding, brown bread, and other Vermont products, all year long. Three-pound wheels are $16 plain and $16.15 in the flavored varieties, including postage to addresses east of the Mississippi River. West of the river, the prices are $17.25 and $17.40, respectively. The cheese also is available in 5-pound wheels for $27 per wheel, delivered ($28.60 west of the Mississippi and 25 cents more for the flavored varieties). Please specify mild or sharp.

John Coolidge, 94, died as this book was going to press. There is ample Coolidge memorabilia in Plymouth, with the Coolidge Homestead nearby.

ORDERING ADDRESS
The Plymouth Cheese Corporation
Box 1
Plymouth, VT 05056
802/672-3650
No credit cards

VISITING ADDRESS: **Plymouth is east of Rutland, not far from the New Hampshire border. From Highway 4, take Highway 100A south to Plymouth and turn right at the road just before the Coolidge Foundation parking lot. (There isn't a sign for the cheese factory.)**
Monday–Saturday, 8 A.M.–5:30 P.M.
Sunday (Memorial Day weekend–December 1): 9 A.M.–5:30 P.M.

ROUGE ET NOIR CHEESE

When Jefferson Thompson came west from Illinois and started his cheese business in 1865, he gained experience in making Camembert, having been taught by his neighbor, who was from France. Coincidentally, Thompson kept in contact with another early maker of soft cheese, Fred Kolb, in Lena, Illinois (see entry in this section), and the families have copies of old letters in which the two traded information.

Since 1998, new owners James and Christine Boyce have run the Marin French Cheese Company in its same rural location, west of Petaluma, in a part of Marin County that outsiders hear little about. The fancy homes and chic shopping areas disappear and you find yourself in dairy country, driving through the state's beloved "Golden Hills" past white farmhouses and grazing cows. The cheese factory and sales room are in an idyllic setting: a red-roofed frame building with red shutters on well-landscaped grounds with covered picnic tables overlooking a duck-filled lake. Free tours are scheduled regularly, and since cheese is made four mornings a week, there is usually something to see.

Although the building has undergone extensive remodeling, the original curing room in the basement has been left as is (with the damage from the 1906 earthquake visible), because the mold on the walls produces a valuable flora that makes the cheese change from acid to alkaline and produces its distinctive flavors. The late Ed Thompson, grandson of the founder, told us that his grandfather once scrubbed the walls and temporarily lost the flora, a mistake that has not been repeated.

The company now makes four cheeses: Brie; Camembert; schloss (*schlosskaese*, or castle cheese, a strong-flavored German cheese similar to Kolb-Lena's Old Heidelberg); and breakfast cheese, a milder, soft white cheese that is eaten fresh. Flavored Bries are also available.

Brie and Camembert, although from separate cultures, are both made by heating raw milk and adding mold culture, starter, and rennet. The curds and whey are separated and the cheeses, in metal molds, are cured in a salt brine and then left to drain in a succession of basement rooms. About 12 days after it enters the plant as milk, the cheese is wrapped. Then it ripens for about eight weeks to yield the creamy, yellow color and nutty flavor.

Marin French Cheese Company cheeses are available by mail year-round. Six 4-ounce half wheels of either Brie or Camembert are $14, postpaid.

ORDERING ADDRESS
Marin French Cheese Company
7500 Red Hill Road
Petaluma, CA 94953
707/762-6001
800/292-6001
www.sfnet.net/cheesefactory
e-mail: cheesefactory@sfnet.net
Credit cards accepted

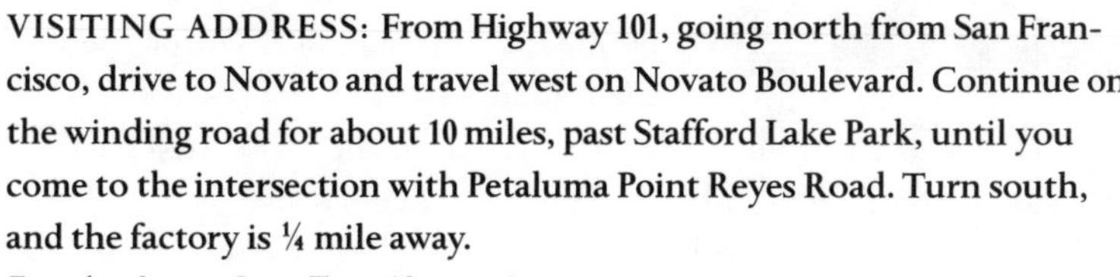
VISITING ADDRESS: **From Highway 101, going north from San Francisco, drive to Novato and travel west on Novato Boulevard. Continue on the winding road for about 10 miles, past Stafford Lake Park, until you come to the intersection with Petaluma Point Reyes Road. Turn south, and the factory is ¼ mile away.**
Every day, 9 A.M.–5 P.M. Tours: 10 A.M.–4 P.M.

SHELBURNE FARMS CHEDDAR CHEESE

Shelburne Farms, on the shores of Lake Champlain, is not easily classified. It is a historic inn with noteworthy cuisine. It is a 1,400-acre working farm with a herd of Brown Swiss cows, managed woodlots, and grass pastureland. It is a dairy and cheese plant, and a commercial bakery. It is the site of numerous concerts and other cultural events. It is a nurturer of small Vermont businesses and of new agricultural efforts for the state. And it is a mail-order source for its own superb cheeses and breads, and for maple syrup. Summed up, Shelburne Farms is an attempt to find contemporary uses for a showplace estate without caving in to development pressures. Its diversified approach is a model for other farms, historic houses, and businesses attempting to find meaning in the coming decades.

This nonprofit institution places a strong emphasis on quality. Its choice of products, its packaging, the professionalism of its employees—all reflect simple things done well. Our first encounter with Shelburne Farms was with its Cheddar cheese, which remains our favorite product. The master cheesemaker at the farms is Ross Gagnon, and he and his assistants produce a true handmade farmhouse cheese, using milk from the farm's Brown Swiss herd, which is fed primarily with the farm's grass and silage.

The cheese is available aged 6 months (medium sharp), 1 year (sharp), over 2 years (extra sharp), and smoked. A sampler package of 1 pound of each variety is $40. Purchased individually, they range from $9 per pound for the medium to $13 per pound for the smoked. We tried the sharp and found it clean-tasting and crumbly. Such a far cry from the rubberized blocks that are usually passed off as Cheddar! This is excellent cheese.

The bread Shelburne sells is a product of O'Bread Bakery, operated by Chuck and Carla Conway, and is housed in the Farm Barn at Shelburne Farms. It is spontaneously leavened, which means no yeast or yeast-based starters. The dough requires more time to proof and demands more skill of the baker, since no two risings are alike. The ingredients are the minimal three—flour, water, salt—that have been used for bread for centuries but are nearly impossible to find in a loaf today without the addition of sugar, yeast, flavorings, or conditioners. The bakers use red spring wheat and rye grown in the Champlain Valley and milled as needed on stone mills at the bakery.

The wrapper on the loaf of sourdough we ordered said it does not go stale. It's true. We kept the heel of the loaf in the refrigerator for several weeks and then reheated it in the oven, as directed. It was just as good as the first fresh slices. This is crusty, chewy bread that makes superior sandwiches and French toast.

A 1-pound loaf of the sourdough and a 2-pound block of sharp Cheddar are sold together for $21. For topping that French toast, you can't go wrong with the medium-amber maple syrup Shelburne Farms offers from David Marvin of Butternut Mountain in central Vermont. Delicate in color and taste, it comes in pint, quart, and half-gallon tins that have Shelburne Farms' understated deep-red label with gold printing. They sell for $12, $19, and $31, respectively.

The handsome packaging extends to the farm's raspberry, wild blueberry, blackberry, and strawberry jams, honey, and honey mustard. These items are made for the farms but with evident care. There are no pectins or flavorings added, and the makers don't stint with the fruit. The honey has a particularly light, lovely flavor. A set of four 8-ounce jars of the jams is $19.

Shipping is additional. Second-day air delivery is required when sending bread outside New England or when sending cheese and hams in warm weather.

ORDERING ADDRESS
Shelburne Farms
1611 Harbor Road
Shelburne, VT 05482
802/985-8686 (Telephone orders weekdays only)
FAX: 802/985-8123
www.shelburnefarms.org
Credit cards accepted

VISITING ADDRESS: **Shelburne is 7 miles south of Burlington, in western Vermont. Turn west off Route 7 at the traffic light in Shelburne and continue 1½ miles to the farm entrance at the intersection of Bay and Harbor Roads. There is a store and a visitor center from which tours of the farm leave hourly from June through mid-October.**
May–December: Every day, 9 A.M.–5 P.M.

SUGARBUSH FARM SYRUP AND CRACKER-SIZED CHEESE

Just listing the daily responsibilities of Larry and Betsy Luce and family makes us tired. The couple has 125 head of cattle and milk 55. That alone is enough for most farmers, because dairying is unrelenting, confining work. But they've got haying and corn production as well. Then there's the maple-syrup operation that involves tapping 4,500 trees, some with pipelines and some with buckets. Boiling down sap can mean all night at the sugarhouse in early spring. Each 25 gallons of syrup takes about a cord of firewood, so add woodcutting to the regular chores.

We have yet to mention the business that has given the Luces' Sugarbush Farm a national reputation—a nationwide but very personal mail-order retail cheese business that is just beginning to employ its fourth generation of family members. The Luces' son Jeff is in charge of all cheese smoking and aging, as well as sales to selected stores. Son Ralph is active in the farm part of the business. And Jeff's children are giving maple sugaring tours and learning to run the cash register.

Fifty-four years ago, Betsy Luce's parents, Marion and Jack Ayres, improved upon the traditional way of marketing fine Vermont cheese. Instead of sending tourists home with unwieldy wedges of cheese that needed immediate refrigeration, the Ayreses cut down the cheese into cracker-sized bars. The cheese is aged and smoked at the farm, tightly wrapped in foil, and then dipped twice into wax to keep the cheese from drying out. Having one wax pot for all the cheese varieties would be easier, but Sugarbush gives each cheese its own wax color. Thus, sage cheese has green wax, sharp Cheddar is red, blue cheese is blue, and so on.

The Ayreses and the Luces never have made the cheese, but the family has always made the rounds of the best Vermont cheesemakers, tasting each wheel individually before purchase. Their goal is "cheese like it was." As their longtime slogan goes: "Not processed, not colored, not pasteurized, not fussed with."

We were taken with these uncolored, handy-to-slice cheeses, blessedly free of the gimmicks and extraneous additions that proliferate in gift cheese catalogs. The smoked Cheddar has a robust smoked flavor throughout the cheese, unlike many "smoked" cheeses that owe their flavor to smoke flavoring sprayed on the rind. Sugarbush smokes the cheese for three days and three nights over hickory chips and maple in its own smokehouse. (Marion died in 1993, but in her retirement, it was her job to watch over the smokehouse at night, keeping it smoldering but not hot enough to start a fire. In the sixties, an earlier smokehouse burned, taking half of Marion's house with it. Betsy Ayres, who was alone at home at the time, ran in the house and saved the company's mailing list.)

Sugarbush specializes in aged Vermont Cheddar and offers a mellow Cheddar (aged 6 to 10 months) and a sharp Cheddar (approximately 2½ to 3 years old), both superlative. The younger cheese is creamier, and the older cheese has more character—sharp, but not biting. New cheeses include a low-fat Cheddar and a smoked Cheddar with onion. A fine soft blue cheese is also offered, as well as an old-fashioned New England favorite—sage Cheddar. We were smitten with the sage, which is added with a light hand. (Don't expect green polka-dotted cheese, in other words.) On a turkey sandwich, nothing could be better.

There is an abundance of gift packages of cheese available, and they are particularly festive, thanks to the brightly colored wax coverings. The most popular package is the one with six ½-pound bars of cheese—your choice of flavors—for $37.25, postpaid.

Ordering from Sugarbush is charming. First of all, Betsy Luce types a personal note with every order that goes out. The family writes a letter on the front of each seasonal brochure that explains what's going on at the farm. The Ayreses and Luces have longstanding relationships with customers. The farm has more than 13,000 customers, and Betsy Luce estimates that she has a personal connection to at least 2,000 of them. She stresses: "Our small family atmosphere makes for careful attention to quality and to service."

Half-gallon, quart, and pint tins of maple syrup can be ordered in three grades: light amber (the first syrup made each season, and often limited in availability), medium amber (the syrup made during the bulk of the season), and dark amber (very maple-y syrup made at the end of the season that's often favored for cooking). A quart of any grade in 2000 was $24.20 postpaid. It is hard to think of any gift more welcome than good maple syrup, especially in areas where real maple syrup is available only in tiny, shockingly expensive bottles in gourmet shops.

With all their other activities, the owners of Sugarbush actually encourage visitors to come and spend some time. In fact, the visiting part of the farm has grown the fastest in the past five years, with about 36,000 visitors in 1999. "Our beautiful farm is a lovely quiet place to visit, sample our products, and learn in general about Vermont maple syrup and farming," concludes Betsy.

ORDERING ADDRESS
591 Sugarbush Farm Road
Woodstock, VT 05091
802/457-1757
800/281-1757
www.sugarbushfarm.com
e-mail: sugarbsh@sover.net
Credit cards accepted

VISITING ADDRESS: **Turn off U.S. Route 4 at Taftsville, which is 3 miles east of Woodstock. Cross the red covered bridge, go to the top of the hill, and turn left onto Hillside Road. Follow the yellow signs 2½ miles up Hillside Road.**
Monday–Friday, 7:30 A.M.–5 P.M. Weekends and holidays, 9 A.M.–5 P.M.
Call ahead for hours and road conditions

VELLA MONTEREY JACK CHEESE

When at last a U.S. Food Hall of Fame is created, which is a terrifically good idea, one of the first inductees would have to be the Vella Cheese Company in Sonoma, California. Long before that wine-producing area north of San Francisco became the food mecca that it is today, Tom Vella made a commitment to produce extraordinary cheese. Today, his son Ignazio (Ig), 71, continues to oversee the making of legendary Monterey Jack and Cheddar cheeses.

The company is the only one in the world making dry Monterey Jack. An aged hard cheese that compares favorably with Italy's Parmesano Reggiano, it melts and grates easily but can stand alone as an eating cheese. *New York Daily News* food writer Suzanne Hamlin calls it "the best all-purpose cheese I've ever encountered." The company sells it in large wheels or grated. The wheels have a hard, coated rind and demand a sharp, heavy knife for cutting. Because it is a low-moisture cheese, it keeps well without refrigeration, as countless backpackers have discovered. A fan letter from a member of the 1986 American Kangtega Thamserku Expedition in Nepal was a sterling testimonial: "During the three months

we had your cheese, we subjected it to more abuse than I care to remember," wrote Jay Smith. "It never spoiled or lost its flavor. By far and away it was the best food we carried throughout our entire expedition."

The grated version can be substituted for Parmesan, with an added benefit—an extremely low salt content. Try it on popcorn instead of salt. A 2-pound bag is $20.

Another original with Vella is its extra-dry Monterey Jack aged at least 2 years. Known as "California Gold," it is sold only in 6-pound wheels, which are about $60 over the counter.

In the 1930s, there were as many as 60 California cheesemakers producing dry Jack cheese—a result of tight supplies of Italian Parmesan and Romano cheeses. All of them, save Vella, have quit the labor-intensive enterprise.

Monterey Jack has been around since Gold Rush days. Its name came from its creator, a Scottsman named David Jacks. It is Vella's signature cheese, and the original high-moisture variety, made from whole milk, continues to be one of its best-sellers. Vella's wheels of cheese are hand-rolled and shaped, and wrapped in muslin. The high-moisture Jack also comes in blocks, which are a little firmer than the wheels, to make it easier to grate or slice for sandwiches. A 5-pound wheel is $33; a 5-pound block, $31.

Vella's Jack cheeses are creamy and mild, but not insipid, like many imitators. The wheels seem to be particularly well suited to buffet tables. Recognizing this, Vella offers 3-pound wheels seasoned with garlic, pesto, or red and green jalapeño peppers that sell for $29 each.

An alternative for those concerned with cholesterol is Vella's partly skimmed Monterey Jack. Still a creamy, rich-tasting cheese, it has 30 percent less fat than the high-moisture Jack. It can be used like mozzarella, and melts nicely. A 2½-pound block is $22.

The company also makes extraordinary Cheddar cheese, which comes in sharp (lightly colored with annatto seed pulp), mild, and sharp and mild raw-milk versions. The sharp raw-milk Cheddar we sampled seemed creamier and less biting than its New England cousins. A 2½-pound block is $30. Cheese is shipped year-round by UPS, and all prices include shipping costs.

If you are in the wine country, it would be a shame not to visit Vella's cheese plant. Its pre-earthquake building, made from stone quarried in the surrounding hills, is as distinctive as its cheeses. Vella keeps California history alive with its Bear Flag Brand name (referring to the grizzly bear flag that flew over the short-lived Republic of California in 1846), and keeps food history alive with its dry Monterey Jack.

ORDERING ADDRESS
Vella Cheese Company
315 Second Street East
Sonoma, CA 95476
707/938-3232
800/848-0505
FAX: 707/938-4307
www.vellacheese.com
e-mail: Dana@vom.com
Credit cards accepted

VISITING ADDRESS: Sonoma is about an hour north of San Francisco. From Highway 101, exit east on Highway 37 to Novato. At the intersection with Highway 121 at Sears Point, follow 121 into Sonoma. Turn right at the plaza, then left on Second Street East.
Monday–Wednesday, 12:30 P.M.–2:30 P.M.

WESTFIELD FARM CAPRI CHEESE

Letty Kilmoyer was the first of New England's goat-cheesemakers, and for 15 years she tended a herd of 80 goats, and made cheese. In 1996, she and her husband sold their farm to Bob and Debby Stetson, who continue to make all the cheeses the Kilmoyers did, using milk purchased from local farms. Fresh cheeses are in stores (or in the mail) within days of being made.

The original cheese—the plain, fresh Capri goat cheese—is still the most popular, but the aged blue goat cheese also has a loyal following. The plain cheese is an excellent choice for first-time goat-cheese eaters because it is exceedingly mild. It is a soft, creamy cheese that can be spread on toast slices grilled with olive oil, melted on homemade pizza, or used in sauces or even in cheesecake. An herb-garlic version of the Capri is delicious on savory breads or on warm vegetables. The blue cheese is covered with a surface blue mold, which is edible. It is not nearly as intense in flavor as, say, Maytag blue, which is made with cow milk and has blue veining throughout. It is a delicate blue, not at all salty like some, and one that tastes fresh and light. Westfield Farm's other offerings are pepper Capri (white cheese coated with ground black pepper) and Camembert.

The farm packages its cheeses well for shipping, sending them in foam boxes with reusable ice packs to keep them chilled. The container charge is $4. Delivery by UPS is free to northeastern states if the order is $15 or more. Outside the Northeast, orders of $15 or more are shipped via Federal Express second-day air at an additional cost of approximately $10.

The 5-ounce wheels of plain Capri are $3.39 each, and the pepper or herb varieties sell for $3.49. A 7-ounce log of blue cheese is $4.98, and a like amount of Camembert is $4.24.

ORDERING ADDRESS
Westfield Farm
28 Worcester Road
Hubbardston, MA 01452
978/928-5110
FAX: 978/928-5745
www.chevre.com
e-mail: Stetson@tiac.net
No credit cards

VISITING ADDRESS: **Hubbardston is 50 miles west of Boston. From Route 2, turn south onto Route 68 at the Hubbardston exit. Westfield Farm is ½ mile south of Hubbardston Center on Route 68.**
Self-service cheese selection: Every day, 24 hours a day!

CONDIMENTS

ALPINE TOUCH SEASONING

We are suckers for the endorsement letters that appear in food catalogs and brochures. We've never personally known M. R. from Octonto, Wisconsin, who writes that "your product is out of this world," or P. W. from Westbrook, Connecticut, who doubles his order from last year because his family and friends like it so much, but we are drawn to these confessional letters and would be crushed to discover, as some cynics have said, that they are fictitious.

We know that Russell and Mary Jane Street, who founded Alpine Touch All-Purpose Seasoning in Whitefish, Montana, did not have to invent letters from enthusiastic customers. As proof, we offer an unsolicited testimonial we received some years ago from Mary Vant Hull in Bozeman, Montana: "A gift I have carried with me when visiting friends in other states is Alpine Touch, a seasoning which is very good sprinkled on salads if you don't want to use a salad dressing. It's very good, with few or no calories, on eggs, soups, meats, etc."

Russell originated the mixture 40 years ago while cutting meat in his small Northwestern Montana grocery store. It was a "mom-and-pop" store he built after discharge from the service following World War II, and there he became well known for his seasoned rolled roasts. Customers started taking brown bags of the seasoning mix home and urged the Streets to market it. They did, reducing the grocery store to just that one offering. It was a homey operation: they blended the mixture in a cement mixer and on the weekends, gave out bites of steak, popcorn, or celery dipped in Alpine Touch to potential customers.

It is a seasoning salt (salt, monosodium glutamate, and spices constitute the ingredients list), and it has a pronounced peppery tang. We like it on eggs, fresh tomatoes, and cucumbers, and in place of garlic salt on beef.

The Streets retired from the business in January 1989, but their customers were fortunate that they sold it to Mark and Vicki Southard, who are continuing to prepare the seasoning using the same recipes and care. They have now added a light, but full-bodied low-salt alternative, a tart and tangy lemon pepper, and a bold pepper blend to their line of special spices. In 1993, the Southard's moved from the original store to Choteau, Montana, located about 50 miles west of Great Falls, where they have a small retail shop with the spice bottling operation in the back.

The Southards are still getting the same kinds of letters from satisfied customers. "It's like everyone you sell to is your friend," Vicki Southard related. "It's a nice feeling to make someone you don't even know happy. . . . The checks come from every corner of the country and there has never been a bad one. That's a pretty good record."

The seasoning comes in 4-ounce bottles with a shaker top. The first bottle of any Alpine Touch Spice is $6.95; the second bottle is an additional $3, shipping included. Mark says that many individuals order in bulk, and the couple is happy to send as many pounds as people want. A 1-pound bag is $8, each additional bag is $3.75 including shipping.

With luck the Alpine Touch story will continue, with cooks like N. R., of Great Falls, Montana, enthusing, "My first bottle of Alpine Touch came as a bridal shower gift from my mom and grandmother, who both swore by it. . . . It's been sixteen years since that bridal shower and I'm still using Alpine Touch. Keep up the good work. Three generations of cooks are depending on you."

ORDERING ADDRESS
Alpine Touch, Inc.
P.O. Box 864
Choteau, MT 59422
406/466-2063
877/755-2525
FAX: 406/466-2076
www.alpinetouch.com
e-mail: mrspice@3rivers.net
Credit cards accepted

VISITS: Choteau is in the northwestern part of the state, west of Great Falls at the junction of highways 89 and 287. Alpine Touch is located at 714 Main Avenue right across from the Old Trail Museum.
Monday–Friday, 8:30 A.M.–5 P.M.

BERTMAN'S ORIGINAL BALLPARK MUSTARD

Our hometown of Cleveland, Ohio, now has everything a baseball fan could want—a fabulous new downtown ballpark, a winning team, and the right mustard on the hot dogs. Forget the lurid yellow condiment that most ballparks pass off as mustard. Give us the good stuff!

We first parted company with Ralph Nader on the issue of hot dogs. Without having grown up in Cleveland with the tough assignment of being an Indians fan, how could he know that the ballpark's mustard-slathered hot dogs offered one of the few rewards on many disappointing nights in the old Municipal Stadium?

We were shocked to learn later in life that some cities have bad teams *and* bad mustard. It hardly seems fair.

Joe Bertman's Original Ballpark Mustard, a smooth brown mustard with bite, is celebrating its 75th year in business. His daughter, Pat Bertman Mazoh, carries on her late father's business with gusto. You can get this wonderful mustard throughout Cleveland's Jacobs Field, which also has the wisdom to carry pirogis, soft tacos, and Pierre's ice cream, a very good regional brand.

Bertman's mustard has won several national mustard awards and is now available in the Williams-Sonoma catalog. Pat will send a 9-ounce squeeze bottle to most parts of the country for $9.50, delivered. It also is sold in 16-ounce squeeze bottles for $10.50, delivered. Cases are more popular—a dozen bottles of either size are offered. For a case of a dozen of the 9-ounce bottles, the cost is from $26 to $32, depending on your address. Check with her on the shipping costs to your address.

A new horseradish sauce has just been introduced and will be available for limited mail order, too. Its label has a balloon with a "wow" on it and we agree with the customer who wrote her, "The WOW isn't big enough!"

"I don't care if I don't sell the most mustard in the world, just the best," says Pat, an endlessly enthusiastic former teacher and social worker.

The company now shares space, appropriately, with the local Orlando Bakery, which makes hot dog buns. It's housed in the former Van Dorn foundry building, where Pat's aunt once worked 85 years ago.

ORDERING ADDRESS
Joe Bertman Foods, Inc.
P.O. Box 6562
Cleveland, OH 44101-1562
800/749-4460
No credit cards; checks OK

VISITS
Orlando Bakery Building
7777 Grand Avenue
Cleveland, OH 44104
216/431-4460
From downtown Cleveland, drive east on Woodlawn Avenue to 79th Street. Take a right. Cross the Rapid Transit tracks. Take a right on Grand Avenue. At the first driveway, take a right. The guard in the entry station will direct you to Bertman's.
Monday–Thursday. 9 A.M.–noon

BOETJE DUTCH MUSTARD

One of the delights of Boetje (boat-chee) mustard is how it drubs the high-priced competition in blind tastings. Eight and a half ounces of this stone-ground Dutch mustard sells for about $1.50 in stores both near its home in Rock Island, Illinois, and in 26 other states.

A dark-brown mustard peppered with marinated, ground mustard seeds, it has been made there since 1893, when Fred Boetje created it and sold refills door to door. Leon Wernentin, who had eaten the mustard since childhood, bought the firm in 1971 upon the death of the owner. In 1985, the 82-year-old Wernentin sold the firm to his neighbors, Robert and Dorothy Kropp, whose son, Will Kropp, is now the general manager.

The factory is tiny—only three employees—and scrupulously tidy. Although its neighbors take the mustard for granted, outsiders discovering it do not. The chef at Washington's exclusive hotel, The Madison, is one such fan, buying eight 1-gallon jugs every year to create his special sauce for fish. Mustard gravy is another use some cooks have devised.

The mustard is sold by the gallon to schools in the area and appears under a few private labels such as The Machine Shed Restaurant. Recently, Boetje's expanded its product line to add an all-natural seafood cocktail sauce, which it calls sea sauce. It is a fabulous cocktail sauce—more horse-radish than tomato.

The Kropps have kept the mail-order price a bargain: $20 for 6 or $28 for twelve 8½-ounce jars of mustard or sea sauce, including packing and UPS charges. Customers may buy the mustard or sea sauce at the plant, in a 12-jar pack, for $18.

ORDERING ADDRESS
Boetje Foods, Inc.
2736 12th Street
Rock Island, IL 61201
309/788-4352
877/726-3853
FAX: 309/788-4365
www.boetjefoods.com
Credit cards accepted

VISITS: The plant is in southern Rock Island, 6 minutes south of downtown. It is 2 miles north of I-280. From I-280, go east on Illinois Route 92 for three-quarters of a mile. Take a right on the 31st Avenue exit and continue to 12th Street. Turn left onto 12th Street and drive three and a half blocks. The plant is on your left.
Monday–Friday, 8 A.M.–4 P.M.

BRASWELL'S ARTICHOKE PICKLES AND RELISH

Artichoke pickle is such an obscure product that buyers figure it's undoubtedly made by the handful of firms that offer it. But the truth is, for at least two of the better-known purveyors of this hot pickle, the real manufacturer is the A. M. Braswell Company, of Statesboro, Georgia.

A 55-year-old firm that specializes in regional favorites such as fig preserves, pear preserves, and onion relish, Braswell's has been making a crunchy artichoke pickle since World War II. A combination of vinegar and onions gives the artichoke a tingling aftertaste. The amber chunks of artichoke soak up the spiciness while packed in a sweet-sour bath.

The company keeps a low profile and doesn't seem to mind that the labels of firms in Charleston and in Georgia that it applies to some jars are more recognized than its own brand. But the Braswell name has continued to grow in popularity in the past 10 years. With Braswell's not only are prices lower but you can also be assured the pickle and relish recipes really did come "from grandmother"—Albert M. Braswell's grandmother, to be exact.

The company charges $2 for a 8½-ounce jar of the pickle relish. It is sold by the case for mail orders and by the case or jar at the plant.

ORDERING ADDRESS
A. M. Braswell Food Company
P.O. Box 485
Statesboro, GA 30459
912/764-6191
800/673-9388
FAX: 912/489-1572
www.braswells.com
e-mail: braswell@bulloch.com
Credit cards accepted

VISITS: Statesboro is 50 miles west of Savannah. From Savannah, take I-16. Exit on U.S. 67 and drive north for 12 miles. Once in Statesboro, turn right onto Zetterower. The plant is at 226 Zetterower Avenue.
Monday–Friday, 8:30 A.M.–5 P.M.

CASADOS FARMS CHILES AND SPICES

The corn is roasted on the cob, in large adobe ovens called *hornos,* which are sealed with mud and left to smolder overnight. The dry white corn (*posole*) is boiled with lime in open kettles. Locally grown Chimayo chiles are available coarsely ground, finely ground, crushed, whole, in the pod, or as seeds.

If you are looking for authentic ingredients for southwestern foods, it would be hard to find a better source than Casados Farms, run by Pete and Juanita Casados, in the small northern New Mexico town of El Guique. The Casados, chile farmers who both come from families of chile farmers, have been selling their chiles and blue and white corn for 45 years. Casados Farms always has sold its ingredients by mail and now also advertises nationally. A mail-order brochure with color photographs lets you see exactly the difference between roasted blue cornmeal (*atole*) and roasted white cornmeal (*chaquegue*). The company is a partnership with friends who live in Albuquerque, and the Casados children also help in grinding, roasting, and packaging the more than 30 ingredients they offer.

The Casadoses grow 5 acres of chiles themselves and 15 acres of corn, buying the rest locally. Five acres may not sound like much, but the chiles are hand-planted, thinned, hoed, and picked. One acre can yield as much as 10 tons of fresh chiles, so individual acreages remain small. The smaller, hotter Chimayo chile is a specialty of the northern New Mexico area bordering the Rio Grande River, where the climate is arid, with warm days and cool nights. Says Juanita Casados, "People get used to Chimayo chiles and they want to cook only with them."

The short local growing season makes it impossible to dry the chiles on the vine, so the pods are tied together by the stems and hung in strings (*ristras*) from the eaves of buildings. *Ristras* are available from the farm in lengths from 18 to 60 inches from November until mid-April, or when supplies run out.

In addition to raw ingredients, Casados Farms sells mixes designed for cooking Mexican foods. *Sopaipilla* mix can be used with or without yeast to make a reasonably authentic deep-fried square of bread, to be eaten hot with butter and honey. The taco and enchilada sauce mixes are a blessing for those who consider the Schilling and Ortega brands too mild. The taco sauce, especially, is infinitely hotter. Made to be mixed with tomato sauce, it also is coarser than the pulverized supermarket versions.

Casados Farms products can be purchased at the farm, from the packing shed where all the items are ground, labeled, and sealed, or in grocery stores around the state, or by mail. The taco and enchilada mixes are $2.50 each for 1 ounce and *sopaipilla* mix is $2.50 for 12 ounces. *Ristras* cost approximately $5 per foot. Prices do not include shipping.

ORDERING ADDRESS
Casados Farms
P.O. Box 1269
San Juan Pueblo, NM 87566
505/852-2433
No credit cards

VISITS: El Guique is a small town near San Juan Pueblo, which is about 25 miles north of Santa Fe on Highway 285. From 285, drive to Highway 91, turn right, then look for the sign for Casados Farms.
Every day, No set hours

CHICAMA VINEYARDS WINE VINEGARS

Surprisingly enough, there was never a commercial vineyard on Martha's Vineyard until Catherine and George Mathiesen founded theirs in 1971. The island got its name from the wild grapevines that grow in profusion. The couple, with six grown children, started Chicama Vineyards to produce high-quality wines, and the winery does have a good reputation for its Cabernets, Merlots, Zinfandels, Chenin Blancs, and a Champagne-method sparkling wine.

A small present in George's Christmas stocking 24 years ago led to a second business, wine vinegars, which has sent the vineyard's products all over the country—even to California. Catherine said she bought a pint of vinegar culture for her husband because "I liked to eat a lot of salads and thought it would be fun to try making vinegar."

The two businesses, however, are not as compatible as they may seem. Although Chicama wines are used for the vinegar, the Mathiesens must be careful to keep a good distance between the vinegars and the wine, so that bacteria do not disperse through the air, turning all the wine on the premises to vinegar.

The business soon branched out to herb vinegars, using many herbs grown by the family, and to fruit vinegars—just in time to take advantage of a phenomenal national interest in raspberry wine vinegar. Crushed fruit is added to a basic vinegar, Catherine explains, and then the mixture is cooked down, added to a large quantity of vinegar, and left to steep. In addition to raspberry, the company makes Cape Cod cranberry, wild blueberry, and spicy orange wine vinegars. Many of the berries also are grown on the farm.

The vinegars are not aged chemically, but left to turn in 50-gallon oak barrels. The herb-flavored vinegars are especially beautiful, and cry out for display on a sunlit shelf. Several of the herb varieties are unique to Chicama, such as a lemon and ginger vinegar, with a large slice of lemon floating in the bottle; parsley, sage, rosemary, and thyme (inspired by the song, of course); and chive and cracked peppercorn. We are particularly fond of the opal basil, which turned out to be exactly "the most beautiful shade of cerise" that Catherine promised. It is the critical ingredient in Fire and Ice Tomatoes, a Mathiesen recipe for sliced tomatoes, green peppers, red onions, and cucumbers served cold on a platter—a show-stopping salad.

The family also produces two unusual mustards, a raspberry-honey-poppyseed and a spicy orange, as well as unique cooking oils—Cajun, Thai, and Moroccan varieties. A Thai paste, designed as a rub for meat or as a flavoring for stir-fry dishes, is $7.25 for a 4-ounce container. Two salad dressings are sold: the raspberry-honey-poppyseed combination and a classic vinaigrette.

Vinegars sell for $4.75 for a 375-milliliter bottle, plus shipping. The mustards are $4.15 for 8 ounces; the oils are $5.25 for 375 milliliters; and the salad dressings are $6.85 for 375 milliliters. Shipping is extra.

The availability of certain vinegars changes from time to time, but Chicama Vineyards usually has at least 18 choices.

ORDERING ADDRESS
Chicama Vineyards
P.O. Box 430
West Tisbury, MA 02575
508/693-0309
888/244-2262
FAX: 508/693-5628
www.chicamavineyards.com
e-mail: info@chicamavineyards.com
Credit cards accepted

VISITS: The ferry to Martha's Vineyard arrives at Vineyard Haven. From there, take State Road west toward Gay Head. After 2¼ miles, you will see a sign for the vineyard, which is located on Stoney Hill Road, on your left.

June 1–October 15: Monday–Saturday, 11 A.M.–5 P.M. (tours at noon, 2 and 4 P.M.)
Sunday, 1–5 P.M. (tours at 2 and 4 P.M.)

CINNABAR JAMAICAN JERK SPICE AND CHUTNEYS

Jerked meat is: (1) a meat dish prepared by comedian Steve Martin, (2) a relative of beef jerky, or (3) a Caribbean dish made with a highly spiced grilling paste. The answer, known to growing numbers of Americans looking for hot taste sensations beyond jalapeño, is (3).

Caribbean, Thai, Indian, South American cuisines—all are getting an eager reception in this country by eaters intrigued by their unusual combinations of sweet and hot, fruits and spices. One company that is helping to bring these new flavors to the American kitchen is Cinnabar Specialty Foods, in Prescott, Arizona, run by Indian-born Neera Tandon and partner Ted Schleicher. We were told about Cinnabar by the *Arizona Republic's* Jean Novotny, one of the country's best food writers, who has managed to research and write an exhaustive guide to all the unusual markets and restaurants in the Phoenix area.

In 1985, Cinnabar got its start making chutneys, and they are ample reason to send away to the company pronto. Tandon, a caterer, had approached Schleicher, whose father owned a gourmet grocery, about making a chutney. Schleicher took a jar of chutney off the shelf and challenged Tandon to do better. She did so, and her sweet and spicy mango chutney is one of the firm's best-sellers.

The basic definition of chutney is a condiment made from fruits cooked slowly with vinegar, sugar, and spices, but there are as many different versions as there are cooks. Cinnabar makes a pear cardamom chutney that is an excellent introduction to the family. It is a sweet mix of raisins, pears, cashews, oranges, green chiles, cardamom, vinegar, and spices that can be spooned directly from the jar. Unlike many of the company's products, the recipe was not adapted from those Tandon collected in India. She created this one from scratch.

The tomato-mint chutney is more savory and hot, with garlic, ginger, and other spices flavoring a tomato and oil mixture. It gives a new dimension to lamb and wakes up grilled bread. Peach, mango, ginger-pineapple, hot vegetable, and tomato round out the company's chutney selection. Try any of them in chicken salad, on sandwiches, mixed with sour cream as a dip, or in stir-fried vegetables.

But back to jerked meat. Tandon developed Cinnabar's jerk spice grilling paste after a trip to Jamaica, where she partook of jerked meat at roadside stands. Her version is not as hot or as salty as the Jamaican originals, and for that we say thank goodness. It is plenty spicy, but you can control the hotness by the amount you use. Heat a little with vegetable oil, hulled pumpkin seeds, and slivered almonds and you have a spicy partner for chilled drinks.

Cinnabar (its name came from the street where Tandon lived when she was in Phoenix) sells an array of exotic ingredients used in cuisines from around the world. From a spicy Thai seafood marinade to Japanese sushi-making items, Cinnabar's products have been described as "versatile" and "intriguing."

Tandon points out that Cinnabar's products allow people to cut out oils and butters and still have flavorful foods. Even the tandoori grilling paste, normally extended with oil, can be mixed with low-fat yogurt, she said. "People are definitely changing their eating habits, and it has been very good for our business."

If you shy away from spicy foods, Cinnabar has products that Tandon promises are "not hot at all." One is an Asian tamarind sauce used for marinating and tenderizing all kinds of meat. A second offering is Barbados Honey Pepper Sauce, designed as a dipping sauce for fried foods. Or, says Tandon, you can add rum and use it as a fish marinade.

Cinnabar offers a wide variety of chutneys, sauces, and marinades. Nine-ounce jars of the chutneys ranging from tomato to mango are $5.75 to $6.50. Six-ounce chutneys and sauces such as ginger/garlic Kashmiri Marinade and Southwest Sizzler, a hot barbecue sauce that features the exotic juice of prickly pear cactus, are $4.75. Jamaican jerk spice and Tandoori Indian grilling paste come in 4-ounce jars, at $4.25. Shipping and handling charges are $4.95 for orders up to $15 and $5.95 for orders up to $25. Add $1 for each additional $10 order or fraction thereof. All of Cinnabar's products are available in quart-size, for quantity cooking.

ORDERING ADDRESS
Cinnabar Specialty Foods, Inc.
1134 West Haining Street
Prescott, AZ 86305
520/778-3687
FAX: 520/778-4289
www.cinnabarfoods.com
e-mail: info@cinnabarfoods.com
Credit cards accepted

VISITS: Same address. The company is north of downtown, near the Ponderosa Shopping Mall.
Monday–Friday, 9 A.M.–4 P.M.

CLANCY'S FANCY HOT SAUCE

Twenty years ago, when Colleen Clancy began making her Clancy's Fancy Hot Sauce, it was safe to say that it was the hottest sauce around. Tabasco type hot sauces were the standard. Asian and Mexican sauces were available in ethnic groceries, but were unfamiliar to the mass audience.

But now, with the fiery food craze, there are literally hundreds of sauces made with habanero peppers and oleo resins of peppers. "Some of them are dangerous and are labeled as such," says Colleen. "Many are novelty items with names like Sudden Death and my personal least appealing, Heine Hurtin' Hot Sauce. You get the idea."

Clancy's Fancy, on the other hand, is a flavorful condiment that adds complexity and heat without overpowering a dish.

Fans add Clancy's to all sorts of dishes, using it as an ingredient and on the table for those who like to spice things up. It may not be the hottest sauce on the market these days, but it does pack a wallop. Each 8-ounce bottle contains five whole peeled garlic cloves, plus a generous amount of cayenne pepper and freshly squeezed ginger. A dab will do you. Colleen, who is blessed with red hair, as any maker of hot sauce should be, says she likes to watch people try her sauce. "Their eyes stare out as they adjust to it. Beads of sweat come out on their foreheads and upper lips."

The cayenne in the sauce makes your heart beat strong, Colleen says, and she insists Clancy's Fancy is powerful enough to chase away her hay fever. "When a spell of it is on me, I take a big hit of my hot sauce. A teaspoon or two in the morning, and my hay fever's gone!"

Colleen, who lives in Ann Arbor, Michigan, concocted the mixture in 1978 and used to take it to potluck suppers. ("I was being lazy," she said. "It was an easy thing to take.") People started asking for "the fancy sauce that Clancy makes," and the name and business were launched.

Fans use the sauce on everything from tuna salad to popcorn, sautéed fruits, and goat cheese on crackers. "We still mix it with maple syrup to put on French toast and blue cornmeal pancakes," Colleen says. She refers to it as a type of Far Eastern or Jamaican sauce, rather than South American, and the thick reddish-brown sauce does not have much in common with fiery tomato-based sauces. For one thing, it's much hotter. At the risk of sounding like the Department of Redundancy Department, we stress again that this is a hot sauce that brings new meaning to the term. Although it's hard to believe, for the diehards who insisted the original wasn't hot enough, Clancy developed an extra-hot, using even more incendiary peppers. Fortunately, for those wanting a little relief, she also has introduced a "mild" version.

Word-of-mouth has resulted in good distribution in Michigan and in selected stores across the country. The sauces also are available by mail, with a minimum order of 2 bottles. Two 8-ounce bottles (7.5 fluid ounces of sauce) are $17. Two 4-ounce bottles (3.75 fluid ounces of sauce) are $13.40. These prices include shipping and handling. Mail-order customers should note whether they want extra-hot, original, or mild.

ORDERING ADDRESS
Clancy's Fancy, Inc.
410 West Washington
Ann Arbor, MI 48103
734/663-4338 (24-hour "hot"-line)
e-mail: clancysfancy@hotmail.com
No credit cards

DOROTHY LYNCH HOME-STYLE DRESSING

If American culinary historians organize themselves to the point of issuing plaques, we hope they install one at the American Legion Club in St. Paul, Nebraska, where Dorothy Lynch was head cook. It was there that she developed her delicious and innovative salad dressing, one of the best America has to offer. Its slogan: "Tastes Like You Made It Yourself," is absolutely true.

The fame of her peppery, pale-orange dressing caused Mac Hull, of Columbus, Nebraska, to buy the recipe in the early 1960s. He formed a company, Tasty Toppings, Inc., to bottle it. Similar to a sweet French dressing, the thick dressing has tomato as its main ingredient. It is flavored with vinegar, sugar, salt, celery seed, and lots of coarsely ground black pepper. This dressing also is popular as a ham glaze, in meat loaves, and on pasta salad. We realize this betrays our Midwestern roots, but we like it on cottage cheese, too.

The dressing, in both original and 100 percent fat-free style, is available in parts of the Midwest, South, and West. The company will ship dressing to individuals in areas not served by a distributor. The minimum order is a case of a dozen 16-ounce jars. Write or call for an exact price.

ORDERING ADDRESS
Tasty Toppings, Inc.
P.O. Box 728
Columbus, Nebraska 68602-0728
800/228-4148
No credit cards

GAZIN'S SALT-FREE CAJUN SPICE BLENDS

New Orleans has its own food vocabulary. Beignets. Shrimp remoulade. King cakes. Jambalaya. Andouille sausage. Muffuletta. And on and on.

Gazin's, a venerable New Orleans mail-order company, is a one-stop source for all of the above, and just about any other Creole or Cajun specialty associated with the city. You can order fully prepared foods, such as turtle soup or crawfish étouffée, sent by air. Or you can order any of the specialized ingredients to make your own New Orleans cuisine.

Its four-color catalog is definitely worth ordering. Owner Earl Robinson has items that you won't find elsewhere, such as muffuletta bread, café brûlot mix, pure chicory, wild pecan rice, Blue Runner okra, shrimp gumbo, and alligator sausage.

Some of our favorite Gazin's products are its salt-free Cajun spices, packed in shaker jars. There are salt-free blends for seafood, poultry, beef, pork, and veal. They more than adequately replace the salt, and are well balanced, pungent seasoning. Each shaker is $3.50, or you can order all five for $16.95 and receive a collection of Cajun recipes. Shipping costs are extra.

In the catalog, we also were delighted to find bouquet garnis, the traditional French blend of spices that can make a stew or braised meats unforgettable. Gazin's sells 10 bouquets for $9.98.

There's one more charming thing about this company. If your order totals $40 or more, Gazin's sends a *lagniappe*—French for something extra.

ORDERING ADDRESS

Gazin's
P.O. Box 19221
New Orleans, LA 70179-0221
504/482-0302
800/262-6410
FAX: 504/488-6239
www.gazins.com
e-mail: gazins@aol.com
Credit cards accepted

VISITS

2910 Toulouse Street
New Orleans, LA 70119
Open by appointment only

HERMAN VALDEZ FRUIT STAND'S CHILES

When we saw a grocery store employee dusting with spray wax strings of dried chiles that had been hung over the produce section, we had grave doubts about their food value. While garlic braids, popcorn on the cob, and chile ropes now are popular in decorating, it shouldn't be forgotten that their original purpose is for cooking.

One place that manages to respect both the culinary and the decorative qualities of chiles is the Herman Valdez Fruit Stand, in Velarde, New Mexico, where the Valdez family has dispensed its own plums, peaches, nectarines, cherries, apricots, pears, and apples for 38 years, as well as strings of garlic, chiles, corns, gourds, pine cones, and other dried plants.

The stand may be best known for its chiles, and when they are harvested in the fall in the southern part of the state and brought to Velarde, the family hangs them to dry everywhere on their combination fruit stand and home—from the eaves and on chainlink fences—transforming the structure into a blaze of red.

HERMAN VALDEZ FRUIT STAND
P.O. BOX 218
VELARDE, NEW MEXICO 87582-0218

Loretta and Herman Valdez started their business as a weekend hobby for Herman, who works at the Los Alamos laboratory, but Loretta works at it full time "because I enjoy the people contact," she said. Years ago, she used to make chokecherry, wild plum, apple, and green and red chile jelly to sell at the stand, turning out as many as 100 dozen jars a season in her home kitchen. When she stopped doing that, she started creating dried arrangements, and now the stand has become so well known for its wreaths of native grasses and plants that tour buses often stop there.

Many of her special Christmas wreaths must be ordered by the end of October, but plain chile wreaths are available through December 1. They are about 18 inches in diameter and cost $45, including shipping. Chile strands (*ristras*) can be ordered in lengths from 1 foot ($25) to 4 feet ($45). *Pequin ristras* are available in 9-inch lengths ($22), 12-inch ($30), 18-inch ($45), 24-inch ($50), and 48-inch ($65). All prices include shipping.

The future of this unique stand is uncertain. Loretta and Herman say it is for sale, because they would like to retire and spend time with their eight grandchildren. Let's hope they are able to find someone who will continue to make the stand a mecca for authentic locally grown produce.

ORDERING ADDRESS
Herman Valdez Fruit Stand
P.O. Box 218
Velarde, NM 87582
505/852-2129
Credit cards accepted

VISITS: Velarde is halfway between Santa Fe and Taos. The fruit stand is directly on Highway 68, and the sign can be seen from the road.
Every day, 9 A.M.–5 P.M.

HICKIN'S MAPLE ICICLE PICKLE CHIPS

A mom-and-pop operation usually conjures up thoughts of the corner grocery store. But Mary, her late husband Frank, and now her son Randy Hickin of Dummerston Center, Vermont, have made farming, cooking, baking, plant propagating, plus a substantial retail and mail-order business their own mom-and-pop venture for 52 years.

They raise their own vegetables and fruit for their jams, pickles, relishes, and fruit butters. A small home bakery is used for the pies, breads, and fruitcakes they sell. Now in her late seventies, Mary still harvests and sells their goods seven days a week from their Black Mountain farm and greenhouses. Talk about a living definition of the American work ethic!

"It's still about sixteen-hour days, mostly," said Mary, who in her spare time grows potted perennials for her customers. She started this cornucopia innocently enough by making strawberry jam for the neighbors. Now there's hardly a food they don't produce. They continue to add new plants and products, such as a beautiful, pure yellow raspberry jam. Although they don't sell the plant, the jam is $6.50 for 6 ounces.

Their pickles are standouts. They are thick cut and, what is a rarity in the business, are firm and crisp. The sweetener used is their own maple syrup, which gives a pleasant aftertaste quite unlike the sugar-coated, artificially green versions found across the land. These are sweet pickles one actually can enjoy eating plain. They're more expensive than supermarket varieties ($5 for 9 ounces, plus shipping), but infinitely worth it.

The Hickins encourage travelers to visit their farm and pick their own raspberries, blackberries, and blueberries. The raspberries are available from late June until October.

ORDERING ADDRESS
Hickin's Mountain Mowings Farm
1999 Black Mountain Road
Brattleboro, VT 05301-9535
802/254-2146
No credit cards

VISITS: From Brattleboro, take I-91 north to exit 3. Turn left (north) on Route 5. About 2 miles up the road, a directional sign points you to the left, onto Middle Road, heading for Dummerston Center. At the first crossroad (in front of a church), turn left onto East-West Road. Drive 1 mile through Dummerston Center until the Hickin's sign directs you to take a left onto Black Mountain Road. The farm is 1 mile down the gravel road.
Every day, 9 A.M.–5 P.M.

JASMINE & BREAD CONDIMENTS

There's been lots written about how food labels are including more nutrition information, but we haven't seen much comment about a parallel phenomenon—the trend toward more personal information on food labels. Some of the labels we've seen lately are mini-novels, with quotes and credits. Some include biographies of the makers, histories of the product, or explanations of the ingredients or methods. All are efforts to bridge the gap between producer and consumer, to infuse some individuality into inanimate objects.

Sherrie Maurer's labels are well worth reading. She explains her products' unusual names (Beyond Catsup, Spicy Mango Jazz, Serious Sauce), tells how they can be used, and gives reactions to earlier food efforts. About the only thing she doesn't explain is her company's name, which is Jasmine & Bread, Inc. (It comes from a Mideastern fable that said jasmine was for the soul and bread for the body.) We especially are taken with her prose on the Serious Sauce. It's a barbecue sauce, and the name comes from "the highest compliment given to the cooks at the outdoor gatherings of my youth," which was: "This is some serious barbecue!" Sherrie signed her name on the label, and then added: "To Pops, whose secret sauce has been my guiding light."

"Pops" is her stepfather, Poppa Harvey, she told us, and his sauce was indeed secret. "It wasn't until after I had my labels printed and had my sauce that he told me what was in his," she said. "It turned out they were similar, but I had put in a few more ingredients. " It is a thin, tomato-based sauce, with vinegar, honey, plum puree, horseradish, and several spices. It is hot, but not torrid, and sweet, but not cloying.

Sherrie Maurer has been running Jasmine & Bread for 16 years, and it has grown with the constant, loving help of friends and family, particularly her husband, Hugh.

Jasmine & Bread's best-selling products are the ones with horseradish. The Beyond Horseradish Mustard lifts itself above the crowded field of specialty mustards by dint of its crunchy whole mustard seeds and sweet-hot flavor. So many mustards are acrid-tasting and can't stand alone. Beyond Horseradish Mustard is a thick, well-balanced blend that's tops for pretzel or cheese or vegetable dipping. With wine vinegar and oil, it makes a salad dressing that won't get overlooked.

Sweet Lightning Horseradish Jelly is clear, with bits of horseradish and red peppers suspended in the sweet jelly. It can be spread on cream cheese and crackers or used to baste meats and poultry. Stir it briskly and use it as a dipping sauce for chicken wings. It also serves as the base for an excellent salad dressing, with the addition of wine vinegar and oil.

Sherrie's first product was Beyond Catsup, which is a sweet condiment made with apples and tomatoes. It's a fairly straightforward sauce, used to replace regular catsup when you want something different but not too obscure. A more assertive, hotter choice is her Beyond Belief Tomato-Pear-Pepper Salsa. Think of it as a Vermont salsa, since it is sweetened with maple syrup.

Jasmine & Bread, Inc.

Of all her products, we find ourselves gravitating to the Serious Barbecue Sauce and the Beyond Horseradish Mustard. Both are made without salt, by the way, as is the Beyond Belief Sauce. Two 14-ounce jars of Serious Sauce are $13.50, as are two 6½-ounce jars of Beyond Horseradish Mustard. All prices include shipping. Gift boxes and baskets are available with selections of Jasmine & Bread's various condiments.

Sherrie is always innovating, and some of her newer products are spicy hot ones. There's Balsamic-Habanero Sauce, which is excellent over cooked greens, and Spicy Mango Jazz, a mango, ginger, and wine sauce that turns cubed fish, pork, or poultry into a sophisticated stir-fry. We also are fond of the Three Onion Bliss Jelly, made from red onions, Vidalia onions, and chives. It is great with corn chips and exactly right as the dipping sauce for egg rolls.

Call or write for an order sheet that describes all the products.

Sherrie Maurer's sauces have received plaudits from their inception, and she has been a recipient of New England's Minority Small Businessperson of the Year award. Her latest honor was being chosen as one of the "Women of Taste" to be immortalized in a quilt. This was a book project linking 50 quilt artists with women chefs and culinary entrepreneurs. Sherrie's quilt, "Lighting the Flame," was designed by Ed Johnetta Miller of Hartford, Connecticut. It is a crazy-quilt design, including vintage flour sacks and 1940s food fabrics. All the quilts and stories about the women who inspired them were collected in a book, *Women of Taste,* published by C&T Publishing.

ORDERING ADDRESS
Jasmine & Bread, Inc.
R.R. #2, Box 256
South Royalton, VT 05068
802/763-7115
Credit cards accepted

KELCHNER'S HORSERADISH

We're constantly amazed at the strange twists and turns that keep small American businesses afloat. The Kelchner story is full of them—a middle-aged couple, far removed from the horseradish field, who stepped in to save a struggling family business.

More than a quarter century ago, Walt and Janet Slaymaker of Dublin, Pennsylvania, were looking for an opportunity when Walt hit his fifties and his employer, a pharmaceutical company, did what has become depressingly familiar to older salesmen in America—made life difficult in order to force him out. By coincidence, the fate of a respected horseradish first made by Preston Kelchner, a Mennonite, in his Bucks County kitchen in 1938, also was in flux. After the death of Kelchner, the company was sold to a couple who decided within the year that they were not cut out for the vigorous life of horseradish cleaning.

The Slaymakers saw the firm advertised in the local paper and, with the help of one of the Kelchner daughters, started producing the natural, chunky horseradish that is an honor to its distinguished past. "We used the recipes exactly as we found them in the box of three-by-five cards passed through the Kelchner family," said Janet Slaymaker.

Today, their son John Slaymaker and his wife Mimi run the company, as Walt and Janet have retired. The firm has 18 employees and relocated just around the corner from the original building in 1991. John reports that the processing is still done in the same manner at the new location, "there's just more room to breathe which is a valued commodity when grinding horseradish."

With the demise of the Pennsylvania horseradish growers, the company has turned to farmers who till the sandy, loamy soil of New Jersey, Canada, and St. Louis, Missouri. Each locale produces a different variety of the piquant root, whose hotness lies in the roots' fingers, far beneath the innocent-looking ground cover, which slightly resembles tobacco leaves.

The result of the Slaymakers' care is a tart, substantial horseradish with very little water. It does not simply blend into sour cream unnoticed: its texture and taste demand attention, leaving its pablum-smooth competitors far behind.

The Slaymakers also bottle their horseradish with beets, a traditional combination, and add it to their cocktail sauce, tartar sauce, and hot mustard. As their plain black label solemnly states: "When it can be made better, we will make it."

The firm's small fleet of trucks carry their products to stores from Rhode Island to the Carolinas. The company also will ship a case of any combination of their horseradish and sauces. A dozen 6½-ounce glass jars is $27.60, plus shipping; $33.60 west of the Mississippi.

ORDERING ADDRESS
Kelchner's
P.O. Box 245
Dublin, PA 18917
215/249-3439
800/424-1952
www.PA-foods.com
Credit cards accepted

KITCHEN KETTLE CHOW CHOW

"Chow chow" is pidgin English for a relish of chopped mixed vegetables. Originally, the *Cook's & Diner's Dictionary* tells us, it was a Chinese dish with orange peel, ginger, and other ingredients in a sweet syrup. The modern version of chow chow, it says, should be strongly flavored with mustard.

The folks at Kitchen Kettle Foods, in Lancaster County, Pennsylvania, who have been making a highly acclaimed chow chow for 45 years, were surprised to hear that. Their chow chow has no mustard in it whatsoever, but it is sweet. The ingredients are mostly vegetables: green and wax beans, lima and kidney beans, carrots, red peppers, sweet pickles, cauliflower, and onions. You can imagine how colorful it is.

Said founder Pat Burnley: "Outside of Lancaster County, chow chow often has a mustard base to it. In Ohio, they call it 'end of the garden pickle' because you put in everything that's left. I've often wondered if there was any connection with the Italian 'ciao' for good-bye and 'chow chow' meaning 'end of the garden.'

"Although there is vinegar in the brine, the taste is sweeter than sweet and sour. Maybe for that reason, it can be eaten out of the jar much more readily than other marinated or vinaigrette-covered vegetables. The vegetables are intact and firm, and the relish is a cheery addition to a plate. It's no wonder it has been one of the company's best-sellers for years.

When Pat and Bob Burnley began their jelly business in 1954, tourism was not a mainstay in the county. As their business and product line grew, so did the tourist appeal of the Pennsylvania Dutch region where Kitchen Kettle Foods is part of a collection of shops in Kitchen Kettle Village. If you have no Pennsylvania travel plans, there is a toll-free number to order the company's staggering line of relishes, dressings, and preserves (78 at last count).

The family offers items rarely made these days, like tomato jam, a sweet and tangy spread that includes the seeds, fig jam, quince jelly, pickled watermelon rind, pepper cabbage, and pickled red beets. A red pepper jam is wonderful draped over cream cheese and then spread on crackers.

For those who can't abide seeds, Kitchen Kettle has seedless versions of several fruit jams, such as blackberry, black raspberry, boysenberry, red raspberry, and strawberry. All-fruit (sweetened with white grape juice) spreads include five blends: blueberry, peach, pepper, red raspberry, and strawberry.

Prices are reasonable. Pints of chow chow are $3.95, and quarts are $8. The jams range from $3.29 to $3.87 a half-pint. Shipping is additional. Discounts are available at the company store.

If you are free on the third Friday and Saturday in May, you might be interested to know that Kitchen Kettle Village hosts an annual rhubarb festival on those days. Events include a rhubarb derby, with tiny drag racers fashioned from rhubarb stalks, a pie-baking contest, and a kid's rhubarb arcade of games. This generally neglected plant deserves a celebration. If you can't make the party, raise a glass of rhubarb punch, using Kitchen Kettle's strawberry-rhubarb jam.

ORDERING ADDRESS
Kitchen Kettle Village
Box 380
Intercourse, PA 17534
717/768-8261
800/732-3538
Credit cards accepted
www.kitchenkettle.com
e-mail: kkvl@kitchenkettle.com

VISITS: Intercourse is in eastern Pennsylvania, 10 miles east of Lancaster. The Kitchen Kettle Village is on Route 340, east. There are large signs in the heart of town to direct you.
Monday–Saturday, 9 A.M.–5 P.M.

LE SAUCIER CONDIMENTS AND SAUCES

A bouquet to Lisa Lammé of Boston, the Sauce Lady. In one fell swoop, she became a white knight to many a small food company and improved the lot of eaters everywhere. She did so by starting a retail and mail-order company that sells a well-edited selection of the best hot sauces, mustards, sweet sauces, dressings, marinades, and curries available. Many are from small companies whose wares rarely show up on supermarket shelves. Often, these companies can't be bothered with sending a bottle or two to individuals, so Lammé becomes the only source for those who want less than a case of, say, Scorned Woman Hot Sauce.

Le Saucier

Gourmet Sauces
From Around The World

While Le Saucier offers approximately 800 sweet and savory sauces both domestic and imported, Lammé specializes in hot sauces and barbecue. There are many sauces that were new to us, such as Inner Beauty Hot Sauce from the East Coast Grill in Cambridge, Massachusetts. The label couldn't be trendier—Jamaican voodoo colors and insouciant attitude: "Keep away from pets, open flames, unsupervised children and bad advice. This is not a toy. This is serious. Stand up straight, sit right and stop mumbling." It calls itself the hottest sauce in North America and it is one corker of a hot sauce. We declined to try an imported sauce—MP West Indian Hot Flambeau Sauce from Trinidad—that Lammé says is hotter still. Just flipping through the pages of her catalog can make you break into a sweat as you peruse the products under headings like "Hot," "Hot Hot Hot," and "Killer Hot."

Le Saucier's condiments come from every corner of the United States and 45 countries around the world. French lemon honey imported from France is a sweet delight. A 12¼-ounce jar retails for $9.99. Rice Vinegar, from Paramount, California, is a gentle vinegar that, with sesame oil and soy sauce, makes a standout Chinese dressing for green salad. Indonesian-style Bali BBQ sauce is slightly sweet and mildly hot. Or try its horseradish mustard, meant for pretzels, poultry, or potato salad, from Blue Crab Bay Company, in Onancock, Virginia.

The least overwhelming way to deal with Le Saucier is to call or send a fax and order a catalog so you can browse its many discoveries. If you are in the Boston area, LeSaucier's fun store is open to the public seven days a week, with spoons and crackers for sampling.

ORDERING ADDRESS
Le Saucier, Inc.
Faneuil Hall Market Place
Boston, MA 02109
617/227-9649
FAX: 617/474-9713
www.drhot.net
e-mail: drdrhot@aol.com
Credit cards accepted

VISITS: *Monday–Saturday, 10 A.M.–9 P.M. Sunday, 11 A.M.–6 P.M.*

NICK SCIABICA & SONS OLIVE OILS

When you talk about quality olive oils, by and large you are talking about imports. There are only a few olive-oil producers left in America, and nearly all are salvage operations, using olives that have fallen from the tree or are otherwise unsuitable for canning. The labor-intensive olive-pressing business, which flourished here around the turn of the century, has declined steadily since the 1940s, when many small producers folded under the pressure of less expensive imports.

One exception to this sorry state of affairs is Nick Sciabica & Sons (pronounced sha-beek-a) of Modesto, California, founded in 1936. The company is notable because it presses varietal oils, much like a vintner would crush varietal grapes. The Sciabicas also have their own 50-acre orchard, where they hand-harvest about half the olives the operation consumes.

Begun by Nichola Sciabica and his son Joseph, who is 84 and still goes to work daily, it is run today by Joseph and his sons, Dan and Nick. Joseph's wife, Gemma, is "the final authority" on the oils' taste and develops the many recipes the company makes available with its products. She has written two cookbooks, one on biscotti and one on family favorites.

The family's original label was Marsala brand, in honor of the Sicilian city where Nick Sciabica was born, but the company also bottles oils under its family name.

"We are the only U.S. producer who presses by variety and season," says Dan Sciabica. The company offers oils from three varieties of olives: Mission, Manzanillo, and Sevillano. Mission olives, the first type planted in California, have a high oil content and are the most commonly used for oil.

Manzanillo olives, a larger-sized Spanish variety, produce oil with a fruitier flavor. The firm's newest oil variety comes from Sevillano olives, which yield a delicate oil with a flavor reminiscent of artichokes.

The company offers a "fall harvest" version of each variety of oil. The Mission Variety Fall Harvest is the firm's tangiest, a darker-green oil with a pronounced olive taste. The Manzanillo Fall Harvest is a lighter oil, both in taste and color. The Sevillano also is light and is wonderful on salads. Also available is Mission Variety Natural (a blend of the greener oil from fruit picked early in the harvest and the thinner, more golden oil from the late harvest), an organic version of the Mission and Manzanillo varieties, a limited-release Mission variety oil that is not available every season, and the original Marsala-brand oil, which is a blend of Mission and Manzanillo varieties.

All Sciabica oils are virgin, cold-pressed, and unrefined. So what does that mean? Olive-oil terminology is nothing but confusing to consumers, and rightly so. Olive oil labeled "pure" is often highly refined oil mixed with small amounts of virgin oil. (Refining oil is akin to refining flour, and strips it of many natural vitamins, minerals, and enzymes.) The operative word is "virgin," and you need to see that on a label to be assured of decent quality. Virgin oil basically means oil with less than 3 percent acid content that has been crushed and pressed instead of processed with solvents. "Extra virgin" oil generally refers to crushed oils with less than 1 percent acid, but the term does not legally apply to U.S. oils.

The company constantly battles misinformation about olive oils. There's a widespread, but inaccurate, belief that you can't cook with extra-virgin olive oil. It is ideally suited for cooking, Dan Sciabica says. Since it never has been heated, you get nice flavors released when it cooks.

Another dilemma for olive-oil users has been the introduction of "lite" olive oils. This onslaught "is misguiding consumers into using the lowest-grade of olive oil which has been refined to the point of being completely flavorless and in many cases colorless," the Sciabicas warn.

The company will mail its oils, as well as a very good red wine vinegar, aged in oak casks, which is made by the Solano Wine Vinegar Company, which the Sciabicas own. For a salad-lover, consider a gift crate of 16.9 ounces of Marsala Extra Virgin olive oil and a like amount of Marsala red wine vinegar for $27, plus shipping. A gift pack of 12.7 ounces each of Manzanillo Fall Harvest, Mission Organic, and Sevillano Fall olive oils in a wooden crate is $40, plus shipping. Or try a sample of six olive oil varieties. The "6-pack carry out" contains 5-ounce bottles of Mission Winter, Mission

Organic, Sevillano Fall, Sevillano Winter, Manzanillo Fall, and Marsala oils for $35. Shipping is additional.

Corti Brothers, the Sacramento grocers and wine mechants known nationwide for their acumen and high standards, have sold olive oil from Sciabica & Son almost as long as they have been in business, and offer oils bottled by Sciabica under the Corti label—a first. Wrote Daniel Corti at the time of their unveiling: "Never having been a great appreciator of California oils, I am proud to have found these two lots which I think can stand up to fine oils anywhere . . . Perhaps if we produce more oils like these—by selecting the varieties and locations, being careful in production, and improving quality—one day our oil will be as respected as our wines."

ORDERING ADDRESS
Nick Sciabica & Sons
P.O. Box 1246
Modesto, CA 95353-1246
209/577-5067
800/551-9612, ext. 23
FAX: 209/524-5367
www.sciabica.com
e-mail: nsciabica@yahoo.com
Credit cards accepted

VISITS
2150 Yosemite Boulevard
Modesto, CA 95354
Monday–Friday, 8 A.M.–5:30 P.M. Saturday (October through Christmas), 9 A.M.–5 P.M.

RED PELICAN MUSTARD

We're really angry at the conglomerate concessionaires who run America's sports stadiums. Instead of celebrating the superlative regional foods that mean something to hometown crowds, the move is to bland, tasteless foods patterned after the fast-food chains. Nearly every city has several excellent sausage and meat vendors, but they are usually ignored by concessionaires in favor of hot dogs that are entirely ordinary, or worse. We really lost our patience upon learning that Red Pelican Mustard, for decades the official mustard at the Detroit Tigers stadium, had been replaced by the lurid yellow mustard found in every chain restaurant.

Although Tigers fans lost their beautiful, historic stadium in the mid-1990s, thankfully, Red Pelican continues to produce its mustard, in both cream style and hot, for home consumption. We like the hot version—a speckled, tan colored mustard with a decided vinegar tang. It has but a few ingredients: mustard seed, vinegar, salt, and spices. The many ethnic groups in Detroit favor it as a Düsseldorf-style brown mustard. It is widely used by home cooks to baste meat loaf and pot roast.

A new ballpark, Comerica Park, opened in Detroit this spring, but it is unclear whether Red Pelican's products will be reinstated. We were at the ballpark on opening day and talked to the food manager, and he said it is a possibility. So there's hope.

Stadium or no, the company keeps its traditions alive by continuing to use its pelican label. We've lost track of the number of labels that have humans, animals, and inanimate objects wearing chef's hats. On the Red Pelican jar, the proud-looking bird of the label appears again on a lid, a little less dignified, in a large *toque blanche.*

This condiment has been made by the same family since 1923, when Henry Sabbe, a Belgian immigrant, created a cream-style and a hot mustard. Sabbe spent his first 11 years in America working for a grocery store, then began importing foodstuffs from the Old Country. He later decided to make the mustard he grew up on in his new home. "Henry's Best," a hot honey mustard named after the company founder, is the company's newest addition. Bud Cornillie, who is Sabbe's son-in-law, currently directs plant operations.

Six-ounce jars of the mustard are found on supermarket shelves for a bargain 59 to 69 cents. The company will ship a case of two dozen of its 8-ounce plastic jars for $20, shipping included.

ORDERING ADDRESS
Red Pelican Food Products, Inc.
5650 St. Jean Avenue
Detroit, MI 48213
313/921-2500
No credit cards

VISITS: From downtown Detroit, take I-94 east to the Conner exit. The plant is 1 block west of Conner. Make a right onto St. Jean Avenue.
Monday–Friday, 8 A.M.–4 P.M.

RILEY'S SEASONING

Riley's Seasoning, the brainchild of Griggsville, Illinois, farmer Wayne Riley, has enjoyed great success since he created it in the mid-1970s to spice up the hogs he barbecued for celebrations. The usual seasoning was simply garlic powder and fine black pepper, he said, "and if you got a piece of the skin with that on it, watch out!" He made up his own blend of spices and started using it. When he did, "I imagine there were fifty women come back and want to know where I got my spice. They was hard to say no to," said Riley. "About six of them just about got nasty."

Riley had started cooking hogs by accident. He used to raise them, but knew nothing about cooking. He volunteered to help cook a pig at a college football game and that got him interested. For years, his 50 hand-built pig roasters and a crew of helpers fanned out around the state to prepare dinners for as many as six thousand people. At the World Pork Expo in Des Moines, Iowa, in 1988, he had all 50 roasters lined up and in use at one time.

Of course, at all these hog roasts, the number of customers for Riley's Seasoning grew. He mixed it—and a no-salt version—on his farm, in an addition he built on his shop building. In 1995, Riley sold the business to Rick and Madelyn Orr, who moved it about eight miles south to their home in the small town of Pittsfield. Here the Orrs continue to hand-mix and bottle the spice. They now sell 33 other spices as well as the original, all-purpose seasoning blend.

Riley's Seasoning is available at some retail stores and by mail order. A 12-ounce jar is $5.99, and the 3½-ounce size is $2.99 per bottle, plus shipping.

It is a pungent, salty blend that is very good on pork or any meat that is cooked for a while. We especially like it on hamburgers. But it is also terrific on popcorn or in scrambled eggs. Founder Riley, like any good seasoning salesman, used to claim he ate it "on everything but ice cream."

ORDERING ADDRESS
Riley's Seasoning and Spices
802 West Washington Street
Pittsfield, IL 62363
800/690-7720
FAX: 217/285-4474
www.rileys-seasonings.com
No credit cards

SANTA BARBARA OLIVE COMPANY

Commercial black olives represent one of the longest-running food hoaxes ever pulled off on a gullible public. They are not black at all, or ripe, when the large processors pick them. In truth, they are taken green and, like a distressing number of other fruits, are chemically treated to give them the desired appearance. Add to that the ludicrous grading system, with infinite variations on the word "jumbo," and you have a good food done wrong.

There are a few small domestic companies that give you an honest olive that has been left to ripen and turn black on the tree, such as Old Rancher and Graber brands in California and a company in Santa Ynez that sells not only tree-ripened black olives but a fine array of marinated green ones as well.

The company was founded by Larry Callahan, Nancy Schneider, and Karen Klussman in 1982 and was sold to Craig and Cynthia Makela in mid-1984. The company uses all five types of olives grown in California—Barouni, Sevellano, Ascalano, Manzanillo, and Mission. They have lined up olive growers in the San Joaquin Valley and in Santa Barbara County and found a small processor to cure the olives. The company buys back the best olives from the processor, adds the spices, then packs and distributes the olives.

The "country-style" green olive, the company's most popular, is a peppery Barouni olive surrounded by whole garlic cloves, peppercorns, chopped oregano, and other spices. The country-style olives and Mexican olives undergo a Spanish cure—a short lye bath, followed by a three-month stay in a brine cure, and then packing in spiced solutions. The black olives follow the same curing process, but then are packed in the "mother" brine. They are not as sharp as Greek olives, but definitely have more of a pucker than the prevailing type on the market. They are not shiny black like the pretenders, and could easily be called dark brown. Their surface is matte, and the inside color more nearly matches the exterior. The company sells a pitted version, a rarity in the natural black olive market.

A Sicilian olive, the company's fourth variation, sits in a brine cure without lye for at least six months and sometimes even longer. It is aromatic and crunchy and a new taste in olives for us.

Visually, the company wins friends before its jars are opened. A box containing four varieties of olives and a bottle of its own cold-pressed olive oil showcases the company's distinctive four-color label that's reminiscent of old fruitcrate labels. A heavily laden olive branch is center front, and olive trees, the Santa Barbara Mission, and the Santa Ynez Mountains figure prominently. The olives are packed in glass jars, the better to show how fat and meaty they are. The Sicilian variety has a huge bay leaf and bright red pepper inside; the Mexican style is awash in red spices. Other varieties include a martini olive soaked in vermouth, a cerrano pepper-stuffed Sevellano olive cured in a jalapeño brine, and almond-, anchovy-, mushroom-, garlic-, and onion-stuffed olives. The company also sells specialty and herbed oils, pasta sauces and salsas, Turkish capers, and a wide variety of delicious hand packed, pickled vegetables.

The company will send gift boxes anywhere. The box of four 5-ounce spiced olive jars plus one 12.75-ounce bottle of extra-virgin olive oil is $23 plus shipping and handling. Gift sets are also available for the cooking oils and salsas.

ORDERING ADDRESS
Santa Barbara Olive Company, Inc.
P.O. Box 1570
3280 Calzaza Road
Santa Ynez, CA 93460
805/688-9917
800/624-4896
FAX: 805/686-1659
www.sbolive.com
e-mail: sbolive@thegrid.net
Credit cards accepted

SPRUCE MOUNTAIN BLUEBERRY CHUTNEY

Spruce Mountain Blueberries is a true farm-to-market operation that has just two employees, who in addition to owner Molly Sholes, handle all facets of production in the kitchen of her 150-year-old farmhouse in Maine. Molly, a spry 70, *is* Spruce Mountain Blueberries. She described herself for many years as a one-person cottage industry, stating, "I grew the blueberries, processed them in a blueberry shed attached to the house, and froze the fresh berries. At the appropriate time, I made the chutney and conserve in small batches." Today, along with her helpers, she follows the same process and continues to label, market, ship, and sometimes deliver.

Molly began testing her products in 1985 and began full production one year later, when electricity was put into the house she had purchased as a retirement home. The house came with the blueberry land, so it made good sense to do something with the berries. A spurt of orders after some national publicity, has meant steady growth for the formerly one-woman operation.

Her product list includes a wild blueberry chutney made with home roasted and ground North Indian-style garam masala. It's an unusual combination of sweet berries and raisins, vinegar, almonds, fresh ginger, red pepper, and other spices. Molly suggests using it to perk up sandwiches or to spice poultry or other meats. Some cook with it, stirring it into rice dishes or using it to improve curries. The plain blueberry chutney omits the almonds and raisins. She also offers a mild Maine cranberry chutney and a whole-blueberry topping—great for ice cream or breakfast goodies. Her conserve has a sweet-and-sour flavor and is slightly spicy but not hot. It can be spooned over ice cream or pancakes, or on a cracker with mild cheese. A reduced-sugar, pure blueberry jam and a beautiful infusion vinegar round out Spruce Mountain's old-fashioned product line.

Molly will send a gift box with three 10-ounce jars of her blueberry products for $19 plus shipping and handling. The blueberry chutneys and conserve are also available in very reasonably priced 6- and 16-ounce sizes. An *East Meets West Cookbook* filled with tempting Indian and Western recipes using Spruce Mountain Blueberry products can be purchased for $8.

ORDERING ADDRESS
Spruce Mountain Blueberries
P.O. Box 68
West Rockport, ME 04865
207/236-3538
FAX: 207/236-8545
e-mail: sprucemtn@worldnet.att.net
No credit cards

STADIUM MUSTARD

Cleveland has a new football stadium and a relatively new baseball stadium. Each has its own distinctive mustard with a history that goes back to the original stadiums.

Stadium Mustard has a half-century of association with Cleveland's football sports stadium. When the majestic Cleveland Browns Stadium replaced Municipal Stadium in 1999, Stadium Mustard was chosen to remain the only mustard served. The brown mustard has a sharp, vinegary tingle in addition to a smoothness that makes it a very versatile recipe ingredient. Customers continually send the company personal kudos and new recipes. The most concise one we saw said "mix sour cream and the best mustard in the world—then dip chips, pretzels, whatever!"

David Dwoskin currently runs Stadium Mustard. A longtime fan of the mustard served at the stadium, Dwoskin is a man driven by a condiment. "Everyone has a food they love, a taste that's always good to them. For me, it's this mustard I had when I was twelve years old at the baseball game." He not only eats the mustard straight, his wife uses it in meat loaf and mixes it with orange marmalade for a chicken glaze.

His firm will mail-order a minimum order of twelve 9-ounce squeeze bottles of the mustard for $24 including shipping and handling charges anywhere in the United States.

This is a mustard worthy of any game.

ORDERING ADDRESS
Davis Food Company
1230 Bonnie Lane
Mayfield Heights, OH 44124
440/461-2885
FAX: 440/461-2261
www.stadiummustard.com
e-mail: ddwoskin@stadiummustard.com
No credit cards

TAKOMA KITCHENS CONDIMENTS AND BREADS

In past years, many homemakers were Renaissance cooks. They could bake, can, preserve foods, and undertake exquisite meal preparations. Today, if people have time for any culinary endeavors, they specialize.

Louise Swartzwalder, the founder of Takoma Kitchens, is the food equivalent of a utility outfielder. Her 17-year-old firm started out with unique pies; moved into condiments, tea cakes, cookies, and preserves; and now offers unusual breads and muffins and handles full-event catering. A former journalist and political operative, Louise draws on her culinary roots, having grown up in a farm family in central Ohio. Her mother, Beatrice, taught her the basics of baking, sausage making, preserving, and feeding farm hands. Her daughter's customers throughout the Washington, D.C., area are now the fortunate beneficiaries of those lessons.

Although the pies—All American Apple, Perfect Pecan, and (seasonally) a wonderful Pear-Cranberry—cannot be shipped, smaller 4-inch tarts can. A wide variety of breads (Honey Oatmeal Whole Wheat, Cinnamon Raisin, Maple Walnut, and Amish-style Holmes Country White) travel well, as do a variety of tea cakes, scones, breadsticks, focaccia, and muffins. Takoma Kitchens also features pan dulce and quezadilla, Central American favorites, bowing to the skills of some of its Latino bakers.

The emphasis at Takoma Kitchens is on unusual flavors, achieved with ingredients fresh from the many local farmers markets. A Firehouse Tomato Chutney ($4.50 for an 8-ounce jar) is chunky and unusual without being incendiary. A smooth, rosy Pear Cranberry Butter is an excellent alternative to traditional apple butter. And the firm's Sparkling Strawberry-Lime Preserves are slightly more expensive ($4.95 for an 8-ounce jar), due to the ingredients used, but well worth it.

It is best to write for a catalog or call for information about seasonal specials. Savory pecans, a roasted herbed pecan ideal for snacking, are available over the Christmas holidays. Cookies may be ordered in tins or boxes, and most items can be included in lavish holiday or special occasion baskets.

Takoma Kitchens participates in a number of local farmers markets and has a stand at the Montgomery County Farm Women's Cooperative Market, on Wisconsin Avenue in downtown Bethesda, Maryland. Farm families and modern entrepreneurs sell produce, baked goods, meats, flowers, and prepared foods in a Depression-era market set among modern skyscrapers.

ORDERING ADDRESS
Takoma Kitchens
1812 East-West Highway
Hyattsville, MD 20783
301/422-0097
FAX: 301/422-0098
e-mail: takomakit@dclink.com
No credit cards

TONY PACKO PICKLES

"Tony Packo's is Toledo!" was the headline of the Sunday magazine cover story in the *Toledo Blade* some years ago. And, indeed, the 67-year-old restaurant has been voted Toledo's favorite ethnic restaurant. Never mind that it has only one recognizably ethnic dish (Hungarian stuffed cabbage) on the menu. It is the home of Tony Packo's Hungarian hot dog, a spicy smoked sausage covered with a chili beef sauce, called by the *Blade* writer "an adult hot dog. You glow for hours afterward, with heat lingering in the midsection and gentle gastric vulcanism. Mauna Loa must feel a great deal like the man who just had lunch at Tony Packo's."

The hot dog had always been a local favorite, but it gained national prominence thanks to an ad lib by actor Jamie Farr, a Toledo native, who played Corporal Max Klinger on the TV show *M*A*S*H.* Klinger, in the episode broadcast February 24, 1976, was being interviewed about his hometown: "Hey, incidentally," Klinger said, "if you're ever in Toledo, Ohio, on the Hungarian side of town, Tony Packo's got the greatest Hungarian hot dogs. Thirty-five cents. . . ." The show's writers, who liked the Packo name, wrote in additional mentions in five more episodes, including the farewell show.

The exposure was the start of Packo's tourist business. Since then, visiting celebrities invariably wind up at Packo's and are obliged to sign their names on a hot dog bun—a tradition started by Burt Reynolds and continuing to this day. Enshrined on Packo's walls are scores of celebrity "buns," including those of presidential candidates, musicians, and notable stars.

A big part of the Packo hot dog experience has always been the pickles. In 1980, the family business (now run by Tony and Rose Packo's children, Tony, Jr., his sister, Nancy, and her son, Robin) decided to package the pickles for retail sale. There is now a full line of pickles and relishes, and they are well-spiced, excellent products. Tony Packo's ships its pickles—one of the few companies that will.

The colorful labels, with cartoon depictions of anthropornorphic pickles and peppers, tell the story of how the line developed. First there was Pickles & Peppers, thickly sliced cucumbers and Hungarian banana peppers in a sour dill brine. The label shows a pickle and pepper on their wedding night. The two are at the beach on their honeymoon on the next product, a handy combination of prepared mustard and relish. A sweet mixture of pickle relish and red peppers has a label with the two on a picnic. The chunky hot pepper is shown on her own in the pepper-only jar. It was the answer to fans' pleas for more peppers in the Pickle & Peppers.

Another Packo pickle product (say that quickly three times!) is Sweet Hot Pickles & Peppers, which are the banana peppers and sliced cucumbers in a sweet brine. They are crunchy and assertive, with a jolt of garlic.

All the pickles and relishes plus 16 other gourmet food products ranging from Hungarian salsa to spicy ketsup can be ordered on their web site. Gift packs are available that offer an assortment of Packo's most popular items. Prices range from $14.95 to $44.95, excluding shipping and handling. Customized gift services are provided by the company to satisfy every need or wish. In 1999, the Cool'Hot pickle joined the Packo line up. This addition is a crispy, cold-packed pickle available in three varieties—Spicy Jalapeño, Kosher Dill, and Natural Green Sours. Prices average about $3.49 per jar. All Tony Packo products have the signature Packo "Zing"!

If you are in the Toledo area, a visit to any of the four Tony Packo locations is a memorable experience. The original location, at 1902 Front Street, has wonderful weekend entertainment ranging from magicians during the day to a hot Dixieland band in the evenings.

ORDERING ADDRESS
The Tony Packo Food Company
1902 Front Street
Toledo, OH 43605
419/691-1953
800/366-4218
FAX: 419/691-4865
www.tonypackos.com
Credit cards accepted

VISITS: Tony Packo's restaurants have four locations in the Toledo area. The Original at 1902 Front Street, Sylvania at 5827 Monroe Street, and two express shops inside of the Anderson's (one at 530 Illinois Avenue, the other at 3401 Talmadge Road).

Monday–Thursday, 11 A.M.–10 P.M. Friday–Saturday, 11 A.M. –midnight. Sunday, Noon–9 P.M.

TOPOR'S PICKLES

The Topor Pickle Company of Detroit has a priceless collection of love letters. When the ladies' auxiliary of Orchard Lake Seminary Chapter Three used the company's pickles as door prizes at its ice cream social, it prompted the woman in charge to write: "All the ladies were hoping to win Topor's pickles instead of a sheet, towel set, etc. One lady approached me and asked me to sell her a quart, but I couldn't and didn't."

A mother wrote in to tell the company she serves the pickles with almost every meal: "As far as my little two-year-old daughter is concerned, there just isn't enough of your pickles to go around. She would eat them with her morning cereal if she could. I wouldn't be surprised if one day I had a pickle with two legs in a dress rather than a little girl."

Another fan wrote to say she uses a quart of Topor's pickles every week and thinks they are the closest on the market to homemade. She proceeded to tell what happened one day when she invited seven couples to her home for a pinochle game. The seven women guests were in the kitchen with her, chatting about the game, when one spied the jar of pickles on the sink. "Well, that was the beginning," the woman wrote. "Before the men returned to the kitchen there we were, all eight of us, eating pickles. We must have looked funny." She added, "if you wish to have this verified, I can furnish you the telephone numbers of the women."

Topor's pickles are a Detroit phenomenon. The company has been in business 40 years, having started in the basement of Harry Topor's deli, where he made pickles to serve upstairs; their popularity spawned the second business.

Topor's pickles are kosher dills, but they part company with the rest of the pack in that they are made with no preservatives, using natural fermentation. They must be refrigerated even before opening. Company president Larry Topor, son of founder Harry Topor, explains that his pickles are ones like grandmothers used to make. "That's why the brine is a little bit cloudy," he told the *Detroit News,* who picked his pickles as tops in a blind tasting in September 1999. Said Topor: "We use all fresh ingredients—fresh garlic, dill weed, natural pickling spice and no vinegar, sugar, or additives. It's like a fine wine because the taste comes from the natural fermentation."

Just taking the lid off a jar releases memories of the best old-fashioned Jewish deli that ever existed. The pickles are crunchy, garlicky, but do not have the sharp, acid taste of vinegar-cured pickles. They are pickles you can eat without wincing, and Detroit residents rightly prize them. A column in the *Detroit Free Press* listed Topor's pickles as one thing residents would willingly pay twice the price for without complaining.

The company also makes dill green tomatoes, hot pickles with red peppers, Sweet Julie red peppers and Hungarian hot banana peppers. The company's products are available at Farmer Jack's, Kroger's, shopping center markets and other fine supermarkets, and at restaurants and bars throughout the metropolitan area. For large accounts, Topor's delivers in bulk quantities from 5-gallon pails to 45-gallon drums.

You used to have to travel to their home turf to enjoy Topor's pickles, but the company now will ship its pickles by next day air.

The price is a bargain, like so many of the very best foods. A case (12 quart jars) of Natural Barrel Dill Pickles, New Dills, or Golden Dills is $22. Hot dill pickles are $18 a case for 12 pint jars. And the red peppers and hot banana peppers are $25 a case for a dozen quart jars. Overnight shipping charges are added to these prices.

ORDERING ADDRESS

Topor's Pickle Company, Inc.
2850 Standish
Detroit, MI 48216
313/237-0288
FAX: 248/681-7845
No credit cards

WIDOW'S MITE SALAD DRESSING MIX

Widow's Mite Vinegar (or Salad Dressing Mix, as it is called on the label) is a product that refuses to die. It has been rescued from culinary oblivion at least four times, and possibly more. The reason is a loyal cadre of Widow's Mite users, who make up a mail-order customer list that has been passed from manufacturer to manufacturer.

The name comes from the New Testament (Mark 12:42), where Christ declares that the meager contribution or mite of a poor widow is more valuable than large amounts from the rich, for the widow's gift represents everything she had. The mixture of vinegar and spices was first produced commercially by Katherine Lindsay Franciscus, known as "Oma," in the 1940s. She chose the name Widow's Mite as the result of her pledge to contribute some of the profits to charity.

This pledge was in keeping with her family history. Her great grandfather founded Traveler's Aid when he left one-third of his estate to "stranded wagon trains." Oma gave a portion of the profits of her business to unwed mothers.

After Oma's death in the 1950s, there was such loyalty and demand from those who knew of Widow's Mite that Mr. John Jay of St. Louis and later the Clark family, of Carthage, Illinois, continued to bottle the fine vinegar, paying royalties to the Franciscus family through the 1970s. In 1983, Janet Truitt of Peoria, Illinois, who had depended on Widow's Mite to make her tomato dressing, wrote the Clarks when she could no longer find it on supermarket shelves. Truitt, whose father had started a successful canning company from scratch, knew something about food production. She soon contracted with the Franciscus family to produce the vinegar. Truitt made it herself, by hand, in her kitchen selling only a few hundred cases a year. In the late 1980s Sandy Kriess and Norman Van Auken moved Widow's Mite Vinegar into the hands of a professional contract bottler.

But the full tale is not yet told. When a sudden illness hit the Kriess-Van Auken owners and they announced they might consider selling the secret Widow's Mite formula, grandson John Allen Franciscus realized one of his boyhood dreams: to return Widow's Mite Vinegar to the Franciscus family and offer the product nationwide. And so it is that John Franciscus and his family now continue to donate to charity part of the proceeds through the

Franciscus Family Foundation. Two of its projects are donating movies and italic pens to schools and museums.

Amazingly, Oma Franciscus's original customers and those who had been introduced to Widow's Mite Vinegar through three different bottlers remained faithful and followed Widow's Mite wherever it went.

These loyal adherents substitute it for vinegar in recipes, and pass around a half-dozen time-honored Widow's Mite recipes. These include a pickled beet recipe (basically adding sugar and Widow's Mite to hot sliced beets and refrigerating), an excellent mustard sauce, and an old-fashioned sweet-sour sauce for green beans.

Recipes are printed on the bottle's colorful label, which describes the vinegar as "Creole spiced," but Widow's Mite reminds us of the smells of our grandmother's kitchen at pickling time. We have had roaring success with all of the recipes, and can understand why longtime users are so delighted to have the tradition continue.

Widow's Mite is available in various specialty and retail stores, and can be ordered on a per bottle basis via the company's website.

ORDERING ADDRESS
Widow's Mite Vinegar Company
1309 P Street NW, Suite 6
Washington, D.C. 20005
787/728-3444
www.widowsmitevinegar.com
e-mail: jimdc@worldnet.att.net
No credit cards

WOEBER MUSTARDS

Talk about low profile. In its 95 years of existence, there has been almost no national publicity about the Woeber Mustard Manufacturing Company in Springfield, Ohio. Third-generation mustard makers Dick Woeber (pronounced Whoa-ber), age 41, and his brother Ray, 44, say they prefer it that way.

We'd prefer to spread the word, because the Woeber brothers are responsible for some pretty terrific products at unbeatable prices. (And we are partial to their labels, which feature a smiling man in a chef's hat, one of our favorite food graphics. His motto is "Makes Good Food Taste Better," which is appropriately modest.)

The company's Superior Mustard is a smooth, light brown mixture that is unlike any mustard we've tasted. It is spicy and sweet and moderately hot. It has much more character than yellow prepared mustard, but shares its consistency.

Woeber's®

A separate version with horseradish is also unusual and makes a wonderful topping for grilled fish or meat. Sweet and Spicy Mustard is excellent on crackers and cheese, and comes in a 16-ounce squeeze bottle, as does the Hot and Spicy Mustard, which really packs a wallop, and the sweet-hot Horseradish Sauce, which has a mayonnaise base and a recognizable ingredient list. Woeber's makes a full line of fine mustards and seafood and tartar sauces available in 4- to 16-ounce sizes in many stores throughout the United States and Canada.

All the companies products are very reasonably priced. Why are the prices so low? "Well, basically, mustard is an inexpensive condiment," said Dick Woeber. You can call or write the company with your order and of course, check out its website for more product and pricing information.

ORDERING ADDRESS

Woeber Mustard Company
1966 Commerce Circle
Springfield, OH 45504
937/323-6281
800/548-2929
FAX: 937/323-1679
www.woebermustard.com
e-mail: dickwoeber@woebermustard.com
No credit cards

VISITS: **It is possible to buy mustard at the front office of the plant. Springfield is in southwestern Ohio, near Dayton. From I-70, take exit 52 north to the first Springfield exit. Drive to the first traffic light and turn left onto Bechtle Avenue. Go to the second traffic light and turn left on Commerce Road. The plant is the last building at the end.**
Monday–Friday, 8:30 A.M.–5 P.M.

WOS-WIT BACON DRESSING

It can be as difficult to preserve culinary heritage as it is to preserve a business after the founder exits. Wos-Wit Foods has managed to stay true to its Pennsylvania Dutch roots and survive the change in ownership when its founder died after 34 years at the helm.

Current owner Paul Zukovich has named the company Grouse Hunt Farms, but the Wos-Wit label still adorns its foods. Wos-Wit is Pennsylvania Dutch for "What do you want?" It is an unusual company in that virtually all the ingredients for its large line of jellies, relishes, and dressings are grown on the farm where the products are canned or on a farm in the surrounding area. One neighbor has been growing the firm's peppers for three decades. Another supplies Detroit Red beets, which have an especially deep purple-red color.

The Pennsylvania Dutch influence is seen in its wide variety of sweet-and-sour relishes, like chow chow, corn relish, pickled beets, Dutch sweet, sweet peppers, and sauerkraut. Out-of-the-ordinary jellies include quince, crab apple, and elderberry. In addition to the expected strawberry and peach preserves are sour cherry, pineapple, and tomato. Apple butter is made with sassafras—a standard Pennsylvania Dutch ingredient—and comes with sugar and without. Peach and an unusual lemon butter also are available.

Far and away the most popular Wos-Wit item is the bacon dressing. It accounts for about half of the company's business and eats up a good chunk of the work time of 12 employees. On a day when bacon dressing is made, employees hand-crack more than 4,000 eggs, fry bacon in 75-gallon vats, and add a special flour ground at a small Milford, Pennsylvania, mill that gives the dressing its creamy consistency.

The other ingredients in the dressing are water, sugar, vinegar, whole milk, mustard flour, cornstarch, and salt and pepper. It is a light-colored, thick dressing designed to be heated and poured over salads. It can be used in wilted green salads or as a base for potato or pasta salads. A recipe on the bottle for Pennsylvania Dutch potato salad results in a soothing, "comfort-food" version, with chunks of eggs and grated carrot for color. We like to pour the warm dressing over cold vegetables.

An 18-ounce jar is $2. It is also sold in 12-ounce and 32-ounce sizes. UPS shipping is additional. It's easiest to write or call Grouse Hunt Farms and ask to be sent the retail price list for all the products.

Gift packs of four 14-ounce relishes and two 10-ounce jellies are $13, plus shipping.

New products include brandied peaches and spiced peaches and pears, hot pepper relish, and a line of 5½-ounce preserves and jellies under the Grouse Farm Label.

ORDERING ADDRESS
Grouse Hunt Farms, Inc.
R.D. #4, Box 408-A
Tamaqua, PA 18252
507/467-2850 (also good for fax transmissions)
No credit cards

VISITS: **Tamaqua is in eastern Pennsylvania's Mahoning Valley, west of Allentown. The farm is about 3 miles north of Hometown, which is north of Tamaqua on Highway 309. From Tamaqua, going north on 309, turn left at the third stoplight, which will be at Walt's Drive-in. The cannery is 1.2 miles down the blacktop road, on the left. There is a Wos-Wit sign at the road.**
Monday–Friday, 7 A.M.–4 P.M. Saturday, 8 A.M.–noon

Dessert Sauces

C.C. BROWN'S OF HOLLYWOOD DESSERT TOPPINGS

Four years ago, C.C. Brown's closed its doors on its historic ice cream parlor at 7007 Hollywood Boulevard, and an era came to a close. C.C. Brown's, which began as a candy shop in downtown Los Angeles in 1906, had been a fixture on Hollywood Boulevard since 1929—even before Grauman's Chinese Theatre.

Many believe it was where the hot fudge sundae was born. Company lore holds that owner Clarence Clifton Brown fiddled with the blend of sugars and flavorings on his hot fudge sauce every day for 20 years until he got it exactly right.

Whether it was the first hot fudge sauce in America or not, C.C. Brown's in Hollywood was *the* place to get a hot fudge sundae in Los Angeles for decades and decades. The ice cream parlor attracted celebrities, celebrity watchers, and all those who appreciated the care and attention lavished on its ice cream treats. Here is how a hot fudge sundae was presented at C.C. Brown's: French vanilla ice cream was scooped into a silver goblet, then topped with real whipped cream (made in the store) and chopped roasted almonds. A brown ceramic pitcher of warm hot fudge sauce was served on the side.

The same ceramic pitchers were used for the ice cream parlor's hot caramel sauce and hot mocha sauce. All three sauces were superlative, but the company was best known for its hot fudge sauce. However, the hot mocha sauce—a caramel sauce with a pleasing trace of coffee—is an absolute original. We are not aware of another sauce like it in the country.

When we heard that C.C. Brown's was closing for good, we mourned the loss of all three sauces, and the sad fact that another of America's unique high-quality ice cream parlors was no more. But we were especially crushed to realize that there would be no place to find hot mocha sauce.

This story has a happy ending. The owners of C.C. Brown's, the Schumacher family, who bought the business in 1958 from Clarence Clifton Brown, Jr., the son of the founder, resurrected the company as a mail-order-only enterprise, and now sell the three beloved sauces by phone, fax, mail, and over the Internet. We have ordered the sauces from its website (www.ccbrowns.com), and can report that they are just as we remember them from the Hollywood Boulevard location.

Here is what we love about C.C. Brown's sauces. They are flavorful and substantial. When warmed and poured on cold ice cream, they get chewy, but never grainy. If you are going to have a hot fudge or hot caramel sundae, why waste the calories on inferior substitutes? Go for the first-class versions. And don't overlook the hot mocha. We keep it in our pantry at all times. Nothing can take its place.

The website includes C.C. Brown history, and a page of its sundae recipes. Call it up and learn what goes into a Cinderella (sliced peach, vanilla ice cream, sliced strawberries, lemon sherbet, chopped pineapple, roasted almonds and whipped cream) or a Buster Brown (fresh banana, vanilla and chocolate ice cream, chopped roasted almonds, whipped cream, and a pitcher of hot fudge).

The sauces come in 10-ounce glass jars and are a bargain at $5 each, plus shipping. Shipping costs are reasonable, too. In the continental United States, add $7 for up to five jars and $9 for up to 10 jars.

Thank you, Schumacher family, for rescuing a legend. C.C. Brown's lives on, and we are all the better for it.

ORDERING ADDRESS
C.C. Brown's of Hollywood
26560 Agoura Road, Suite 113
Calabasas, CA 91302
818/878-0032
FAX: 818/880-4592
www.ccbrowns.com
Credit cards accepted

CHERRY HUT SUNDAE SAUCE

The smiling red face of Cherry Jerry welcomes you to the Beulah, Michigan, Cherry Hut, which is a culinary temple to the Montmorency cherry. The Cherry Hut has every right to be unabashedly commercial about its pies, jams, and preserves because they are superb examples of homemade cooking at its best.

Once you taste the Hut's cherry sundae sauce, you'll swear off maraschino cherries for good. This sweet, whole cherry sauce is the perfect item to keep in the refrigerator for impromptu ice-cream sundaes. It would even do well as a garnish for hams and that cafeteria standard, cottage cheese on a pineapple slice. The fresh, tart taste of a naturally colored, unadulterated cherry could win back an entire generation of cooks who have given up on processed cherries.

The Cherry Hut was begun in 1922 by James and Dorothy Kraker, local orchard owners who wanted an outlet for their produce. They cut the first Cherry Jerry smiley face into the crust of their pies, and a landmark restaurant was born. The Krakers ran the Hut, which persistently outgrew its quarters, until 1959. At that time, Leonard Case, who began with the Hut as a high school sophomore in 1946, took over. Case has owned the Hut with his wife, Brenda, ever since: a total of 54 years of cooking the jellies, sauces, and pies that have made Beulah famous to cherry lovers. Their son, Andrew, a recent graduate of Michigan State, has decided to come back to the business and is the manager.

Although cherries put the Hut on the map, it also is a full-service family restaurant featuring fresh turkey dinners every day. It has a wonderful menu, both in the graphics department and in the foods listed within. This is the place to find meat loaf sandwiches and egg salad sandwiches, a baked lake trout special, homemade vegetable soup made with turkey broth, and homemade cinnamon rolls. In a nice touch, the red cherry-shaped menu lists all of Cherry Jerry's helpers, and tells where they are going to school.

Cherry items on the menu include a cherry chicken salad plate, (made with dried cherries), black cherry frozen yogurt, frosted cherry ade, cherry muffins, cherry sundaes, and cherry pie. Most mornings, visitors standing on a sidewalk promenade may watch the Hut's cherry pies being made.

Aside from their quality, freshness, and good taste, the Hut's products are a bargain. A 10-ounce jar of the sundae sauce, cherry jam, jelly or conserve is $3.25. The Hut will ship a minimum of three, plus $7 for postage and handling. Other cherry products that can be ordered are tart cherry preserves, jam, and jelly, and sweet cherry conserves, preserves, jelly or cherry butter.

For visitors, a cherry pie to take out is a bargain $4.75, or three for $13.50. A few years ago, one of us happened to be near Beulah during a family reunion and dashed over to the Cherry Hut late in the afternoon, hoping to find some pies still available. Pies were just being taken out of the oven, and we were able to make a triumphant entry at the reunion, with warm cherry pies that were the hit of the weekend.

ORDERING ADDRESS
The Cherry Hut
P.O. Box 305
Beulah, MI 49617
231/882-4431
888/882-4431
FAX: 231/882-9203
Credit cards accepted

(Although the restaurant is not open year-round, cherry products can be ordered all year.)

VISITS: The Hut is 30 miles southwest of Traverse City, Michigan, on U.S. 31. You can't miss the red-and-white-striped umbrellas and Cherry Jerry sign.

Memorial Day weekend—third weekend in October: Every day, 10 A.M.–9 P.M.

ELMER'S GOLD BRICK TOPPING

About a decade ago, several large food companies introduced chocolate sauces that harden when they are poured on ice cream, creating what many believed was a new wrinkle in the dessert business. Don't be fooled. There's a Louisiana company, Elmer's, that has been making its patented Gold Brick Chocolate Pecan Topping since the 1930s.

Gold Brick began in 1936 as a candy bar, a rectangle of chocolate and nuts wrapped in gold foil. When other candy bars of the era were selling for a nickel, a Gold Brick sold for a dime. "People who remember it said that buying one made them feel rich," says Rob Nelson, Elmer's chief operating officer.

Shortly after the bar was introduced, Elmer's created Gold Brick Topping. The Gold Brick formula is, naturally, a secret, but Elmer's uses no paraffin or other wax to form its shell and blends three different kinds of chocolate. Small pieces of pecans also are in the sauce, which must be heated before using. It is a light-colored topping, with a fleeting, melt-in-your-mouth quality. It hardens quickly on cold ice cream, and makes for a special sundae that is much fun to serve, especially to children.

Gold Brick is sold nationwide for about $4 for a 7½-ounce jar, but it sometimes can be hard to find outside the South and Southeast. So it is comforting to know that it can be ordered directly from the company's website.

The Gold Brick candy bar is no more, but the company makes tiny Gold Brick eggs, sold only at Easter, and Gold Brick snowmen, available at Christmas. The topping also is sold to restaurants and country clubs, so it's possible to see Gold Brick Sundaes on menus.

Elmer's dates to 1855, and always has been a family-run business. It is now owned by the Nelson family of New Orleans, who bought it from the Elmer family. The company was founded in New Orleans and still calls itself "Elmer's New Orleans Chocolates" although the plant now is located in Ponchatoula, 35 miles north.

Gold Brick is not the company's only long-time product. Elmer's has the patent on the name and recipe for the original heavenly hash, the combination of milk chocolate, marshmallow, and pecan that originated in a tiny

New Orleans confectionery shop at the turn of the last century. Elmer's has owned the name and the recipe since 1923. It manufactures heavenly hash eggs at Easter, and other heavenly hash items at other holidays. The name is a legal trademark, and protecting that trademark keeps Nelson busy, as ice cream and candy makers regularly "borrow" the title for their products.

Elmer's also is known as the nation's second-largest manufacturer of boxed Valentine chocolates, and for printed candy Valentine hearts. It will also sell custom-printed hearts, and has supplied them for political campaigns, product launches, and the like. We can think of dozens of times a pithy saying on a heart-shaped candy would come in handy. The company will print a minimum of 10 pounds for $100, plus shipping. Custom colors and shapes are extra.

Sadly, two of Elmer's other early distinctive treats—Mint Bublets, "the original aerated mint," circa 1935, and its Chee-Wees, the original cheese-covered puffed corn snack, are no longer made.

ADDRESS
Elmer Candy Corporation
401 North Fifth Street
Ponchatoula, LA 70454
504/386-6166
800/843-9537
FAX: 504/386-6245

ORDERING ADDRESS
www.elmercandy.com
www.customhearts.com
e-mail: info@elmercandy.com
Credit cards accepted

LARDER OF LADY BUSTLE TANGERINE SAUCE

Boy, were our first impressions of this company wrong! When we heard the name, we thought it too clever by half. "Probably some new outfit trying to sound Olde English," we sniffed.

But the English pedigree of this company, begun nearly 20 years ago, is real. Joan Moore is British and she and her husband, Donald, used to run a tearoom and antique shop in England called Bustle. When she and Donald, an expert in 18th-century English porcelain, settled in Atlanta a decade ago, Joan began making lemon curd, using her grandmother's recipe. They chose the company's name because "larder" refers to a pantry, and because they thought "Lady Bustle" sounded very Victorian.

Lemon curd, a sweet and thick lemon sauce, is not well known in America, but the English devour it by the jar, slathering it on biscuits and pound cake and using it for fillings. The Moores called their curd "lemon sauce," which proved more palatable to Americans, and their top-notch version spawned a business. Donald has since cut back on his antique dealing to devote most of his time to food. "Food is hard work. There is lots of hand labor involved," he said. "But our business has become too big not to stay in it full time."

What makes the Larder of Lady Bustle lemon sauce extraordinary is that it contains only real lemons, not lemon oil, for its flavor. "Lemon oil leaves a strange taste behind," said Donald. We adore it, but are even more partial to the Moores' tangerine sauce, which is an original. The tangy, bright-yellow sauce has only eggs, butter, sugar, and tangerine juice for ingredients. It is superb between cake layers, on top of sliced fruit or layered, parfait-like, with a vanilla or tapioca pudding.

The Moores also make an excellent butterscotch sauce. It tastes exactly like the foil-wrapped Callard & Bowser's hard butterscotch candies. If you are a fan of those (and millions have been for eons) you'll take to this sauce, guaranteed. There is also an unusual minted butterscotch sauce, which is a combination rarely seen in this country. It is a more sophisticated taste.

Rounding out the product line is a raisin sauce with mustard, a reddish-brown mixture with a pronounced sharp mustard taste, and a sweet and hot barbecue sauce. The raisin sauce is ideal for brushing on baked ham or serving with cream cheese and crackers.

The unique barbecue sauce gets its heat from vinegar, mustard, and a mélange of spices, and its sweetness from molasses. It can be used to make molded aspic or spaghetti sauce, as well as for the more traditional uses of barbecue sauce. It comes in both a hot and mild version.

The company ships a minimum of four jars of sauce. All the sauces are $6.75 each for 8-ounce jars, except the hot or mild barbecue sauce, which is $8 for a 16-ounce jar. UPS costs are added to these prices.

ORDERING ADDRESS

The Larder of Lady Bustle, Ltd.
P.O. Box 53393
Atlanta, GA 30355
404/365-9679
FAX: 404/266-1405
No credit cards; checks OK

NARSAI'S DESSERT SAUCES

It has been years since Narsai David closed his extraordinary restaurant and market north of Berkeley, California, to concentrate on catering, food writing, and consulting. But for a long time afterward, he received wistful calls from former customers wanting to make reservations. Eaters missed his informative bi-monthly newsletters and the well-edited selection of wines, cheeses, and take-out foods in his market.

Now Narsai's son is doing the catering in the family and Narsai is busy with his own radio show, writing, and his line of food products. Luckily for us, he still will send his superlative mustards, dessert sauces, dressings, and marinades to individuals who write or call. If you can't persuade stores near you to carry his products (and you should insist they do), it's a relief to know you won't be denied the pleasures of tasting his Chocolate Caramel Decadence, say, or his Nectarine Chutney.

There are six Narsai mustards ($3.50 each for 8-ounce jars) and five dessert sauces in his Decadence line ($9 per 1-pound jar). The best loved is the original Chocolate Decadence, an aptly named extremely thick, dark, not-too-sweet mixture that can be heated and spooned on ice cream or chilled and rolled in cocoa to quickly create truffles. Other Decadence flavors include Orange Chocolate, Butter Caramel, Raspberry Chocolate, and Chocolate Caramel, which is simply a fifty-fifty blend of the original Chocolate Decadence and the Butter Caramel. It makes the quintessential black and tan sundae.

Narsai develops the recipes and packaging, and does the testing, concentrating on unusual items, such as Assyrian marinade or cranberry conserve, which reflect his original and inventive ways. He then hunts for a co-packer willing to make items his way without preservatives, artificial colors, and flavors, and using quality ingredients. His choice for the Chocolate Decadence is the only manufacturer willing to work with the temperature tolerances his sauce demands. "We could get a better price going with a larger firm," he says, "but we are staying with the smaller one for quality."

Prices listed do not include shipping costs.

ORDERING ADDRESS
Narsai's
350 Berkeley Park Boulevard
Berkeley, CA 94707
510/527-7900
Credit cards accepted

R & R HOMESTEAD HOT FUDGE TOPPING

Ruth Roffers remembers the day in her DePere, Wisconsin, kitchen years ago when she said, "I've got it!"

"I had been working on a recipe for hot fudge topping because I was dissatisfied with the grainy and syrupy chocolate sauces on the market," she said. "I wanted a thick hot fudge sauce without using thickenings.

"I think it took me a year of working to come up with the solution. All of a sudden one day the ingredients and proportions were right and I said, 'This is it."

She named the sauce R & R (for Ruth and Richard, her husband) Homestead Hot Fudge Topping, and began producing it in her home, in a state-approved basement kitchen. It is an unusually smooth topping with a pronounced cocoa taste. Some fans insist it tastes like a rich chocolate pudding. It is not a dark, bittersweet fudge that is favored by many hot-fudge sundae connoisseurs, but it is a satisfying, chocolaty, extremely smooth sauce. It can be used as a fondue for dipping fruit, as a flavoring for milk shakes, and as a topping for custards. Children particularly like it spread on graham crackers or toast.

Imported cocoa is used, and no preservatives, but vanillin is used instead of pure vanilla. It still is made in small batches. After Ruth outgrew her basement, she hired four employees and moved to a small factory on Main Street in DePere, which is in the northeastern part of the state, south of Green Bay. The couple now lives in nearby Wrightstown, and production has moved to the town of Kaukauna, about seven miles away. The operation is overseen by Richard Roffers and the couple's daughter, Susan Peters. Ruth has retired from the day-to-day heavy lifting of the sauce making, but still is actively involved, baking amazing pound cakes using her late mother's recipe, Katie's Golden Pound Cake, that is now part of the company's line.

Ruth, who was the first woman to open up a licensed bed and breakfast in Brown County, when they lived in DePere, is getting ready to open another at their house in Wrightstown. Lucky travelers will get to taste Ruth's cooking at the source.

In addition to the best-selling Hot Fudge Topping, the company has two other dessert sauce flavors: Carmelscotch and Bittersweet Mint. All three toppings come in 13.5-ounce jars and 7-ounce jars, sold for $7 and $6, respectively, plus shipping charges. A gift box of the three toppings, in the 7-ounce size, is $17, plus shipping charges.

Other items sold by R & R are the pound cake (weighing in at more than 3 pounds), and Richard's homemade fudge, as well as Wisconsin specialties such as maple syrup, cherry jam, summer sausage, and cheddar cheese. Gift boxes can be made containing any assortment of items.

ORDERING ADDRESS
R & R Homestead Kitchen
P.O. Box 332
Wrightstown, WI 54180
920/532-0253
800/201-3879
FAX: 920/532-0293
www.rnrfudge.com
Credit cards accepted

SANDERS CHOCOLATE TOPPINGS

When updating this book, we were distressed to learn that Bailey's Butterscotch Sauce, which debuted in Boston in 1873, and was sold along with hot fudge sauce at Bailey's own candy stores in the Boston area, is no more. The last two Bailey's stores, in Belmont and Wellesley, closed several years ago, and there isn't even a mail-order operation.

In Detroit, there was a scare 15 years ago for Sanders, makers of incomparable ice cream toppings and candy, when the firm went through bankruptcy proceedings. Thanks are in order to Country Home Bakers of Shelton, CT, who bought Sanders and is continuing to make its fine products available to wholesale and mail-order customers. This year, the company celebrates its 125th anniversary. There's no better way to mark the occasion than to e-mail, write, or call for a catalog, and order some ice cream toppings!

The company was founded by Fred Sanders, a German immigrant who is given credit in Detroit for inventing the ice cream soda in the mid-1870s. (In Philadelphia, the honor is claimed by someone else.) Sanders also became known for his elaborate storefronts and fixtures. In 1891, he built a Baroque "Pavilion of Sweets" with a mosque-like roof. At another Detroit location, he designed an interior that mimicked the throne room of Ludwig II, the Mad King of Bavaria.

Over the years, the company became known for its hot-fudge sundaes and its three chocolate toppings—milk chocolate, Swiss chocolate, and bittersweet. The milk chocolate, light-colored and light-flavored, is the most popular. About the consistency of corn syrup, it is smooth and pourable. The bittersweet is chewier and thick, and the Swiss chocolate neatly takes the middle ground. The company sells a four-pack of 10-ounce jars of each chocolate topping, plus its caramel topping, and sells it by mail for $14.59, plus shipping.

Diane Lynch, division director of Sanders Candy, says the secret to the unique taste of the toppings is the use of heavy cream. "You're never going to get that rich taste without it," she says. "Also, the temperature we take the sauces to brings out a hint of a caramel taste. There's nothing like them anywhere."

Other unique Sanders offerings are two candies that have been made relatively the same way since before the turn of the century: Mint Smoothies-chocolate squares made with fresh Michigan-grown mint, and Honeycomb Molasses Chips covered with dark or milk chocolate. The chips are airy rectangles less than ¼ inch thick that, when broken open, reveal a brittle honeycomb of tiny molasses taffy cells. It's an old-fashioned candy, rarely made today because it involves time and skill to hand-pull the taffy. Almost as much fun as eating the candy is biting off either end and blowing through them.

The smoothies are a "meltaway" mint, in the same family as a Bavarian mint, and are covered with milk chocolate. The chips, in both dark and milk chocolate, come in a 10-ounce box for $7.99, plus shipping. The smoothies are $6.99 for 7 ounces.

All are available through the catalog. One long-time Sanders treat that can't be mailed, but is still available at selected retail outlets in the Detroit area, is Sanders' devil's food buttercream "bumpy" cakes, which have been requested as the "no-substitutes" birthday cake for generations of Detroit residents.

ORDERING ADDRESS
Sanders Inc.
41212 Bridge Street
Novi, MI 48375
800/651-7263
FAX: 248/348-1499
www.sanders-hotfudge.com
e-mail: sanders@globalbiz.net
Credit cards accepted

FISH

BAY VIEW HERRING

Milwaukee is a city with serious ethnic roots. That translates to many small food makers working to please residents who emigrated from Germany, Hungary, Poland, and most recently, Mexico.

One such company is the Bay View Packing Company, located in a small white frame building in the Menomonee Valley area of the city. The hand labor that this company provides makes many traditional German suppers possible, as it supplies the herring that accompanies boiled red potatoes. This family-run firm prides itself on its hand-packed, hand-trimmed fish and meats. It relies on word of mouth, rather than advertising.

Its products—herring, rollmops (herring wrapped around a pickle), smoked ham hocks, pickled eggs, and turkey gizzards—also are popular with hunters, snowmobilers, and campers, a large subset of the Northwest population who like portable food that doesn't require refrigeration. There are four full-time employees. Frank Lehmann is the sole part-time worker. He comes in at night after a day job of "pushing papers," and feels great satisfaction working a table of Nova Scotia herring. "You get to see a finished product at the end of the day!" he enthuses.

The herring is mixed with large Bermuda onions and real sour cream. Unlike large commercial canners, they don't stir the herring in the cream, as the motion releases fish oils, which turns the cream gray. Instead, the herring is placed in jars by hand. The cream stays white without chemical brighteners and each herring piece gets coated. The firm's other herring variety is packed in a wine sauce.

Similarly, the ham hocks are boned by hand before being cured for five days in 100-gallon tubs for brining. Once packed, the jars are checked for eye appeal. This is hands-on work, and president Reiny Liebner says demand is causing the company to acquire bigger tubs.

The herring is far superior to mushy varieties often found in supermarkets. The brine has bite and the skin remains firm.

A 12-ounce jar of herring in wine or cream sauce is $2.60, plus shipping. The fish also comes in 22-, 32-, 65-ounce sizes, or for serious eaters, an 8-pound pail.

Visitors may call ahead for an appointment to see the plant. Products are available locally and by mail order. The company also sells horseradish, hot German mustard, hot Polish sausage, dilled brussels sprouts, pickled asparagus, and spicy mushrooms.

ORDERING ADDRESS
Bay View Packing Company
1906 West Saint Paul Avenue
Milwaukee, WI 53233
414/344-3050
800/645-7976
FAX: 414/344-3051

TELEPHONE ORDERS
Monday–Friday, 7 A.M.–4:30 P.M. Central time.
No credit cards; checks okay. Call first so they can tell you the correct amount to pay for shipping.

VISITS: **As you approach Milwaukee from Chicago (going north), drive west on I-94. Exit at Clybourn and drive west to 25th Street. Take a left on 25th Street to St. Paul Avenue. Drive left on St. Paul to 1906. If you're driving south to Milwaukee, there is an exit off I-94 for St. Paul Avenue.**

DUCKTRAP RIVER SMOKED FISH

Sending fine fish around the country is not cheap, granted. One reason is that it needs to be well packed. That lesson was firmly imprinted after we received some highly touted (and quite expensive) fish from California that arrived by regular mail, in a battered reused box with a "blue-ice" packet that had completely melted. The fish was no longer even cool, and we were afraid to taste it.

That company could take some instruction from Ducktrap River Fish Farm on the Maine coast. Its wonderful smoked fish not only comes by overnight delivery, but its carefully designed package imparts a real sense of place. Open the thick cardboard box that is insulated with a foam liner and there is an unfinished wooden box, with Ducktrap River's brand burned into the wood. When you pry open the box (no tools or heft required—we did it with a fork), you first smell the sprig of balsam that was added just before sealing. The next olfactory sensation is the smoked trout or salmon lying inside. The branded wood box, the greenery sprig, the smoky aroma—all combine to let you know that this isn't fish from the neighbor's pond.

Ducktrap River's fish does its packaging proud. The trout, which are raised at the farm, are flaky and moist. They come whole but gutted, and can easily be skinned. We heated some for a quick entree, and used others cold on a lunch plate. Warm trout also makes a delicate accompaniment to any egg dish for breakfast. Try some on a fish hater!

The farm uses no chemical preservatives or additives in preparing any of its fish, and all its products have clean, simple tastes. The tiny smoked scallops and Maine mussels are especially appealing. The mussels are shucked, then hot-smoked and packed in a small amount of vegetable oil. The southern bay scallops are blanched and then cold-smoked over apple wood. Both can be added to pastas or salads, served on an appetizer tray, or consumed straight from the container.

Ducktrap offers a sampler of 8 ounces of very thinly sliced cold smoked Eastern Atlantic salmon, 8 ounces of smoked trout fillets, and 6 ounces of mussels for $38. Arranged on a plate, the sampler is an instant hors d'oeuvres tray. A half dozen trout are $32. A full dozen costs $42, so it's more economical to buy 12 and freeze any extra. Shipping is extra.

Fish farm president Des (for Desmond) FitzGerald turned a lifelong appreciation for fish into a business a decade ago. He grew up buying exotic fish for home aquariums and then majored in biology at Harvard, primarily so he could study and draw fish. After college, he spent time on a salmon-catching crew in Alaska and then, after visiting a trout farm in California, studied aquaculture at the University of Washington's School of Fisheries.

He picked a site in Maine, a state he knew from family summer vacations, and hired a dowser to search for water to augment a small stream on the property. Geologists and hydrologists thought he was crazy, but at 150 feet below where the dowser had indicated, a gusher was struck and his trout raising began. The smoking took trips to England and Scotland and experiments with vine clippings and different woods before he found satisfactory mixtures to fit each fish.

In addition to Eastern Atlantic salmon, the company smokes peppered mackerel, tuna, sturgeon, bluefish, and shrimp. The firm also sells very good smoked seafood pâtés and seafood sauces. With several of the fish, customers have a choice between whole or sliced pieces.

ORDERING ADDRESS
Ducktrap River Fish Farm
57 Little River Drive
Belfast, ME 04915
207/338-9019
800/828-3825
FAX: 207/338-6288
www.ducktrap.com
e-mail: smoked@ducktrap.com
Credit cards accepted

EKONE SMOKED OYSTERS

Nick Jambor has been farming for 22 years, and now has 200 acres under cultivation. Not much by Midwestern standards, but then again he isn't planting corn or soybeans. He is an oyster farmer, growing mollusks from seed to harvest to market. He also owns a cannery that produces smoked oysters, both vacuum packed and canned, using his own oysters and those from other growers in Willapa Bay in southwestern Washington. These days, West Coast oysters are farmed, since the naturally occurring oysters were depleted long ago. Oysters from Willapa Bay have long been prized because the bay is believed to be one of the cleanest in the nation, as there is no industry nearby and the water is too shallow to permit navigation by large ships.

In the recent past, most oyster seed was purchased from Japan. Now Puget Sound and Willapa Bay farmers have their own hatcheries, where they buy their larvae. Larvae are placed in tanks of heated seawater that contain clean, empty oyster shells, scavenged from previous harvests. The larvae attach themselves to the old shells and grow their own shells. These new shells, called seeds, are strung 6 inches apart on plastic line and then taken out on boats to the tide flats to grow. This is known as the "long-line" method of aquaculture, literally stringing the oyster seeds on lines that are staked in the mud flats. By keeping the oysters off the ground, they can use more marginal acreage than those who use the traditional method of seeding oysters on the floor of the bay, transplanting them later to fattening grounds and harvesting them with a dredge. The "off-bottom" culture, as the line method also is known, makes the oyster seed less susceptible to bad weather, since the lines stay about 18 inches above the often-shifting ground. When the oysters are harvested, the ones to be smoked are steamed, shucked, and put in a brine of salt, brown sugar, and small amounts of garlic and onion. Then they are painstakingly arranged on trays and put in a smokehouse over hardwood for five hours.

"Most places smoke oyster pieces or seconds," said Joanne Jambor, a wildlife artist who started Ekone Oyster Company with her husband. "We smoke our best oysters." They are plump, firm oysters and will surprise eaters whose only association with the mollusk has been the wet, raw variety. They are infinitely better than the smoked oysters packed in oil we've seen from Korea. If you have shunned oysters in the past, Ekone (the name is Chinook Indian for "Good Spirit") will win you over.

Nick became interested in oyster farming while at a marine biology station near Coos Bay, Oregon, where the couple met. He learned the business from Stan Gillies, a longtime oyster farmer whose family history has been intertwined with shellfish harvesting back to the 1850s. Nick worked with Stan until Stan's death in 1994. "I could not have gotten to where I am without his knowledge and guidance," Nick states.

The couple began Ekone Oyster Company as a small venture, doing much of the work themselves. A decade ago, they had 5 employees. Now, there are 30 full-time employees working year-round, including plant manager Kevin Funkhouser, one of the original 5 employees.

Joanne Jambor now spends most of her time teaching art and math in the local school. A series of her wildlife sculptures are prominently displayed along Highway 101 through the town of Raymond, Washington.

The company's oysters are primarily sold wholesale to distributors and then to businesses with seafood retail outlets, but restaurants and individuals across the country also are regular customers via mail order. There are four flavors of smoked oysters: the original version, teriyaki, lemon pepper and habanero hots, named after the ultra-hot habanero pepper. The company also will send fresh shucked oysters by second-day or overnight delivery. The fresh smoked oysters are $32 for the first pound, and $21 for each additional pound per address. Shipping costs are included in those prices. They come in half-pound packages, and customers can mix flavors in their orders. The packages must be refrigerated upon arrival.

The smoked oysters in 3-ounce cans come in the original flavor only. No refrigeration is needed until the cans are opened. The cost is $24 for 6 cans, which includes shipping costs. Additional cans are $3.75 each. Fresh shucked oysters are available by the half-gallon, in four sizes of oyster. Prices and shipping costs are quoted upon request.

ORDERING ADDRESS
Ekone Oyster Company
29 Holtz Road
South Bend, WA 98586
360/875-5494
888/875-5494
FAX: 360/875-6058
Credit cards accepted

VISITS: Ekone is located in Bay Center, on the east side of Willapa Bay, in the southwestern part of Washington. From Highway 101, drive north toward Bay Center. At the KOA Campground, turn left and drive 2½ miles on a winding road until you reach the corner of Rhodesia Beach Road and Bay Center Road. The plant is the brown building on the left side of the road. The address is 378 Bay Center Road.

Monday–Friday, 7 A.M.–4 P.M.

JOSEPHSON'S SMOKED FISH

Josephson's has all the attributes you seek in quality food producer: an illustrious history, continued family ownership, an old-fashioned processing method unique to the company, a wonderfully preserved building, and extraordinary products. It's no wonder that its reputation has grown far beyond northwest Oregon.

Since 1920, Josephson's has cured salmon, then smoked it over a low alderwood fire for up to two days. Since the temperature reaches only 80 degrees, the process is known as cold smoking. Hot smoking, which is a more recent addition to the company's production capabilities, involves heating fish to 180 degrees for shorter periods of time.

Josephson's offers a staggering selection of salmon choices. The company does about everything to the fish but have it swim up your driveway. It can be ordered cold smoked, hot smoked, nova style (lightly salt cured), canned, pickled (tart or sweet-and-sour), or as jerky. You have a choice of chinook, coho, or sockeye salmon, depending on the smoking method you prefer. The company packages the nova style whole or thinly sliced in half-pound packages (ideal for lox and bagels) and will also send fresh center-cut chinook steaks or jars of salmon caviar. The fish is packed in styrofoam chests with plastic ice inside and sent UPS second-day air.

Josephson's also offers its own clam chowder, Dungeness crabmeat, Pacific razor clams, and halibut fillets. The newest attraction of Josephson's, however, is its hot smoked seafood, which can be ordered by the half-pound. Fourteen different kinds of fish are offered, and they arrive moist in vacuum-packed plastic. We tried chinook salmon, albacore tuna, scallops, prawns, and boneless Oregon trout, and were delighted by the firm, fresh appearance and rich taste. The tuna was particularly noteworthy.

The hot-smoked fish ranges in price per half pound from $7.50 to $14. One pound of cold-smoked salmon in a Styrofoam box is $32, the same price as one pound of chinook lox. One pound of hot-smoked salmon is $24 or more, depending on the variety. Four or 5-pound sides of cold smoked chinook salmon can be ordered ($125 and $145). For an additional $4 per pound, the lox will be sliced. Shipping charges are in addition to the prices given.

Linda Josephson, who runs the business with her husband, Mike, says that the traditional cold-smoked salmon, lox, smoked oysters, and scallops are the company's biggest sellers, along with the wine maple salmon and salmon jerkies. "We are unique in that we have the retail, mail order, wholesale, and processing all under the same roof in a historic building." It is one busy building. In recent years, the company's retail mailing list alone has topped ten thousand names.

ORDERING ADDRESS
Josephson's Smokehouse & Dock
P.O. Box 412
Astoria, OR 97103
503/325-2190
800/772-3474 (outside Oregon)

TELEPHONE ORDERS:
Monday–Saturday
8 A.M.–6 P.M. PST
Credit cards accepted

VISITS
106 Marine Drive
Astoria, OR 97103
Astoria is in extreme northwest Oregon. Josephson's is located in a historic building on the Columbia River in downtown Astoria.
Monday–Friday, 8 A.M.–6 P.M. Saturday–Sunday, 9 A.M.–5:30 P.M.

KARLA'S SMOKEHOUSE

It is some measure of the wide reputation of the smoked fish shop in northern Oregon run by Karla Steinhauser that we heard about it from a friend in Georgia. Burt Bralliar was even more exuberant than usual in describing the shop's fish: "A must," he said firmly. When we stopped at the shop on Highway 101 in Rockaway, we heard another unsolicited testimonial from a fisherman who walked in carrying a large fish. "Are you Karla?" he asked the short-haired woman in the sweatshirt behind the counter, who nodded. "Good. Then I'm at the right place. My friend tells me you do the best salmon smoking in the whole country."

Karla was demure about the compliment, but we wouldn't argue with his friend's assessment. Karla uses only fresh, brilliantly colored chinook salmon ("no spawned-out stuff"), first curing it briefly in sugar and salt, and then smoking it over alderwood in the back of the shop for six or seven hours. Prices vary from season to season, and most recently were $16.95 per pound for the chinook and $17.95 per pound for boneless salmon.

Firm, smoked tuna, still warm from the smoker and as memorable a piece of fish as we've had, sells for $16.95 a pound. Smoked black cod, halibut, trout, and Willapa Bay oysters also are available smoked. "My motto is, if it swims, we can smoke it!" Karla said.

She has one of the last old-fashioned homemade smokers that the FDA allows. Larger concerns use computerized smoking equipment, but with Karla, the process is highly controlled and an art form. We applaud the Oregon Historical Society, which considers Karla a folk artist. We think it's high time culinary craftsmen were recognized for their talents and are grateful that Karla is writing a book about fish smoking and cooking.

Karla opened the shop 36 years ago after studying marine geology, marine biology, music, and art. It was originally famed for boiled crabs, but over the years Karla learned the fine points of smoking from a German butcher, Orin Marque, who was known for his kippered fish. She does all the fish smoking, using only fresh fish, some of it flown in from California, Tennessee, and Alaska. She ships via FedEx second-day service, using two to three jell packs (blue ice) for cool climates and four to five for humid or hot areas. She will ship overnight if you desire. Shipping charges are based on weight and zone and range from $9.70 to $17.80 for 2 pounds of fish in the continental United States.

If you buy at the store, prices are about $4 per pound less.

ORDERING ADDRESS
Karla's Smokehouse
P.O. Box 537
Rockaway Beach, OR 97136
503/355-2362
Credit cards accepted

VISITS: **Rockaway is 17 miles north of Tillamook on the Oregon coast. Karla's Smokehouse is at 2010 Highway 101 North, on the north end of Rockaway, on the east side of Highway 101.**
Thursday–Tuesday, 10 A.M.–5 P.M.

LEGAL SEA FOODS LOBSTER

Thyroid specialists say they can tell whether someone is from the Midwest because their lack of consumption of iodine-rich seafood changes the contour of his or her thyroid. Indeed, fresh fish was a rarity if you grew up in the Midwest in the 1950s. Thankfully, our father was raised in Atlantic City, so he took the extra steps to find seafood whenever possible, in addition to the obligatory annual lobster dinners at Hackney's restaurant in Atlantic City during vacations.

Today, efficient operations like Legal Sea Foods, combined with speedy delivery services, have extended the reach of fresh seafood. We still prefer to mail-order seafood rather than buy the dried-out or ammoniated varieties displayed at the new fish counters in many supermarkets. Sadly, supermarkets still don't put a premium on acquiring fish fast enough, and it's the rare inland supermarket that sells genuinely fresh fish.

The Legal Sea Foods business has grown mightily from its origins in 1904 as the Legal Cash Market Grocery, owned by Harry Berkowitz. The name came from Legal Cash Stamps, which were an older version of Green Stamps. Harry's son, George, opened the first Legal Sea Food Market in 1948 and added a restaurant in 1967. The expansion in Boston has continued, with 12outlets today.

The commissary will ship you everything from a lobster, littleneck steamers, four kinds of clam and fish chowder, clambake dinner for two ($124.99, including overnight delivery), and shrimp cocktail. You can order two lobsters, at a cost of $89.99 delivered, or you can add an enameled 19-quart pot for another $20. Bibs and claw crackers are included.

A nice touch is the company's light white clam chowder, with no butter or cream. There's also Rhode Island red clam chowder, a tomato-based soup with sweet sausage. The company also sends gift certificates for lobsters, so that the recipient can choose the timing.

ORDERING ADDRESS

Legal Sea Foods
Mail Order Department
33 Everett Street
Allston, MA 02134
617/254-7000
800/343-5804
FAX: 617/254-5809
www.legalseafoods.com

TELEPHONE ORDERS

Monday–Friday, 8 A.M.–6 P.M.– EST
Credit cards accepted

PICKWICK SMOKED CATFISH

Three days after Quentin and Betty Knussmann received our order, our smoked catfish arrived—a perfectly intact whole catfish lying in a plastic bag in its own catfish-size box, looking not at all as if it had just made a journey of hundreds of miles from its home in Counce, Tennessee. With its peppery coating and light smoking, the fish flaked into moist, cream-colored chunks that resembled smoked trout, but milder.

Our prior acquaintance with catfish was similar to that of many Americans who had not tasted farm-raised catfish. We had been to fried-catfish dinners at roadhouses along the Mississippi and usually had come away thinking the catfish deserved its reputation as a bottom feeder, where man's pollutants have turned a good fish sour.

Fortunately, farm-raised catfish are a different kettle of fish. In fact, manmade ponds are now one of the cleanest, purest sources of seafood you can eat. With tank-raised fish, you can eat all the low-cholesterol, low-fat protein food the nutritionists advise without worrying about unwanted extras. And there's another bonus in getting to like catfish—its bones are easy to remove, usually in one lift of the spine. We liked the smoked catfish cold, as an appetizer (just score the whole fish and put it in a plate), but it also works well served hot, with an onion sauce.

The Knussmanns have been culturing catfish since 1974 on a fish farm they bought as government surplus when federal plans for a catfish co-op proved too ambitious. They have used another surplus to their advantage as well. The hickory for smoking their catfish—the sawdust produced by an ax-handle maker in Savannah—comes free.

The Knussmanns opened a modest restaurant (Eat Them Where They Grow Them) to sell some of the 40,000 pounds of fish on the farm. With their four children grown, they have cut back on the restaurant's schedule, so that their homegrown fish, tomatoes, and watermelon are served only Friday through Sunday. It's a wonderful feed, especially the all-you-can-eat fresh catfish special. "Some people will drive 100 miles just to come to eat," said Betty Knussmann.

Quentin, who ended his career in the glass industry to start the catfish farm, still keeps his hand in business by teaching management classes at the nearby university in Florence, Alabama. But he handles most of the smoking, too, marinating the 1-pound fish overnight in a mildly salty brine before hanging them in the smoker he devised.

Because the smoked fish keeps for about four days at room temperature, it can be shipped. It will keep for about a month when refrigerated and can be frozen. A box of two catfish is $25, including priority shipping, to U.S. addresses. Shipping by next day air is extra. Fish is not shipped June through August.

ORDERING ADDRESS
Pickwick Catfish Farm
Route I
Counce, TN 38326
901/689-3805
www.pickwickcatfishfarm.com
e-mail: KnussK@msn.com
No credit cards; checks OK

VISITS: Counce is located where the boundaries of Tennessee, Alabama, and Mississippi meet. The catfish farm is on Highway 57, 4 miles west of Pickwick, Tennessee. You'll notice the 10 catfish ponds along the left side of the road, then the Knussmanns' white, green, and maroon sign.

Restaurant: Friday–Saturday, 5 A.M.–10 P.M. Sunday, Noon–8 P.M. The Knussmanns, who live up the hill from the farm, will sell catfish to travelers at other reasonable hours.

RUSS & DAUGHTERS SMOKED FISH

What kind of fish emporium inspires such customer loyalty that a patron would pay $67 in shipping costs for one order? Regulars at Russ & Daughters, the venerated fish store on New York's Lower East Side, understand this. The 86-year-old firm, long known for its large selection of caviars, salmon, and sturgeon (its slogan is "The Queens of Lake Sturgeon") has a worldwide following. We also like its other slogan, "Lox et Veritas."

The shop offers personal service for eaters who are well familiar with the company's top-notch smoked fish. "We sell mostly to people who know us and who have moved to gastronomic wastelands," said managing partner Mark Russ Federman, of the third generation of the Russ family to run the firm. "For them, the fish is not only wonderful, it's nostalgic."

The selection is impressive. Salmon comes from Scotland, Ireland, Norway, Denmark, the Gaspé Peninsula, and from U.S. waters. The two the company likes best are the Gaspé, at $26 a pound, and the American chinook (or nova) at $26 a pound. Both are firm-fleshed, nongreasy, and impeccably smoked. The presentation is lovely, with the salmon sliced and replaced on its skin. The lake sturgeon, which is $38 a pound, is moist and memorable.

Given the prices, it is not difficult to understand why the company has a $100 minimum for individual, one-time mail orders. Federman says he is most often asked to ship sides of salmon, sturgeon, and fresh caviar.

ORDERING ADDRESS
Russ & Daughters
179 East Houston Street
New York, NY 10002
212/475-4880
800/RUSS 229 (787-7229)
www.russanddaughters.com
Credit cards accepted

VISITS: **Russ & Daughters is on the Lower East Side. Take First Avenue south to Houston Street, then turn east.**
Monday–Friday, 9 A.M.–6:30 P.M. Saturday, 9 A.M.–7 P.M. Sunday, 8 A.M.–6 P.M.

SLATHER'S SMOKEHOUSE SALMON

Our culinary soul mates Jane and Michael Stern alerted us to Slather's, an unpretentious, small smokehouse and restaurant on Washington's Olympic Peninsula. The founder, Stephen Torgesen, did all the fish smoking himself, and took great pride in it: "We smoke fish slowly using alderwood, much the same as the Indians have done for centuries," he told us. His longtime employee and manager, Allison LaGambina, now owns the business and is carrying on his recipes and techniques.

The smokehouse's mail-order business is blessedly simple. Just fresh smoked salmon is offered. Torgesen used to can the salmon, but he sold the cannery. The salmon we sampled had appealing color, a firm texture, and a rich salmon taste that wasn't overpowered with smoke. It arrived in a vacuum-sealed foil package, via second-day air, and was extraordinarily fresh.

A 1½-pound side of salmon is $33.95, including UPS or FedEx priority shipping.

ORDERING ADDRESS
Slather's Smokehouse
193161 Highway 101
Forks, WA 98331
360/374-6258
Credit cards accepted

VISITS: Slather's has a restaurant in front of its smokehouse where its products are sold. The Smokehouse Restaurant is 1 mile north of Forks, which is on Highway 101 in northwestern Washington on the Olympic Peninsula. Smokehouse hours may vary; check with the restaurant.

October–May: Monday–Friday, 11 A.M.–9 P.M. Saturday–Sunday, 4 P.M.–9 P.M.

Summer: Sunday–Thursday, 11 a.m.-10 P.M. Friday–Saturday, 11 A.M.–11 P.M.

UGASHIK WILD SALMON

For eaters who are sensitive to chemicals and for the rest of us who love fresh food, the Briggs family has been a godsend. Started in 1966, this family-run firm is continuing to send exquisite red and medium red salmon that employees catch, skin, bone, fillet, and hand-pack in glass jars.

Their business is proof that any obstacle can be overcome if you sell a superior product. When the company began, their tiny town of Ugashik, Alaska (winter population, three families), had no telephone service. The business has thrived despite its remote location on the Alaska Peninsula.

The packers use nonchlorinated water to wash the fish, which are steamed. The meat is checked for bruises and imperfections before being put in 5.5-ounce jars. (As anyone with a half-used can of salmon drying in the refrigerator recognizes, the size is sensible.) "The time from sea to icing the fish is minutes, as we catch our fish in front of our cannery," notes Roland Briggs, who took over operations when his parents retired in 1993.

The Briggs and their four children first moved to the Alaskan wilderness from Anchorage in 1956. Realizing that they needed to develop a business to make a living, in 1962 they moved to Ugashik and started the cannery. Roger and Emorene educated all their children via correspondence courses from the Calvert School in Baltimore. All finished eight or more grades at home, went to Anchorage for high school, and then went to college.

Their particular method of canning the fish in glass jars came about when founder Emorene Briggs's older brother, a well-known Chicago allergist, requested a "less chemically contaminated" seafood for his chemically sensitive patients.

The company estimates that the time from sea to glass is well under 12 hours, as compared to 48 for most commercial fishing operations. "In the meantime," Emorene wrote us, "the fish may come in contact with hydraulic oils, diesel oils, and other type of engine fuels." The Briggses sterilize with live steam, eliminating possible contamination. Packing in glass avoids problems with the colored linings common in metal cans.

The salmon is brilliant red and has a clean, fresh taste. Salmon comes either lightly salted or without salt. Six jars are $18.50, plus $11.30 for shipping and handling; 12 jars are $37.20, plus $20.40 for shipping. Twenty-four jars are $82.80, plus $29.05 for shipping. A sample pack of one jar each of red salmon, medium red salmon, and smoked salmon, and one 1.5-ounce jar of caviar pâte is $12.50, plus $9.50 for shipping. All orders are shipped UPS and should arrive in four to nine days.

ORDERING ADDRESS
Ugashik Wild Salmon Company
Ugashik
King Salmon, AK 99613
907/797-2232
FAX: 907/797-2232
www.briggsway.com
e-mail: uwsco@aol.com
Credit cards accepted

FROZEN ITEMS

BASSETT'S ICE CREAM

How much of a sin is it to have ice cream for breakfast? We've all seen commuters drinking colas before 9 A.M., so it isn't surprising that visitors to Philadelphia's Reading Terminal Market find themselves holding ice cream cones way before lunch.

If you need an excuse, Bassett's, the oldest commercial ice cream maker in America, is edible history. Quaker schoolteacher Louis DeBois Bassett started the enterprise in 1861 in his Salem, New Jersey, home, using a mule to turn the churn. His first flavor? Tomato. The business moved to the venerable center city Philadelphia market when it opened in 1893. You can belly up to the same marble counters your grandfather did and order the perennial favorite, vanilla.

This is a dense, super-premium ice cream. If your cardiologist must know, that means nearly 17 percent butterfat. It is best eaten at the counter, on vintage stools, while watching the business of the market.

Every generation has made its mark. The founder's grandson, Louis Lafayette Bassett, Jr., bought spices and flavorings from his market neighbors, turning out varieties in the mid-1900s as current as today's chic dessert menus—guava, kiwi, papaya, and yellow tomato. He even created a borscht sherbet for Nikita Khrushchev's visit to the United States.

The current company president, Michael Strange, is the fifth generation, the great-great-grandson of Louis Bassett. Among other improvements, he and his mother, Ann Bassett, have introduced full-flavored yogurts. Production, which for decades was in the terminal market's basement, is now accomplished at the Galliker Dairy Company in Johnstown, Pennsylvania.

There are now three flavors of vanilla—French, butterscotch, and cherry—and about 42 other flavors of ice cream, yogurt, and sorbet. The champagne sorbet contains the real thing—eight bottles of Great Western Champagne are used for every 50 gallons produced.

Cones are $2.10 each; pints $3.55 and quarts $5.85. It's not unusual to see patrons at the market order a pint and a spoon and sit contentedly, eating the entire carton.

Nearly every Philadelphian has his or her favorite flavor. Supermarkets in eight states carry the brand, but the firm remains small, under 15 employees. The best news is that Bassett's is cautiously getting into the business of shipping its ice cream to individuals. FedEx charges aren't cheap, but for serious fans, they're a necessary expense.

ORDERING ADDRESS
1211 Chestnut Street
Philadelphia, PA 19107
215/864-2771
888/999-6314
FAX: 215/864-2766
Credit cards accepted

VISITS
Reading Terminal Market
N. 12th and Market Streets
Philadelphia, PA
215/925-4315
No credit cards
Monday–Friday, 9 A.M.–6 P.M. Saturday, 8 A.M.–6 P.M.

TED DREWES' CUSTARD

Summer nights in St. Louis are not complete without a visit to one of Ted Drewes's two roadside stands for a "concrete," a thick shake made of Drewes's incomparable vanilla custard.

In 1929, when Ted Drewes, Sr., began his company, it would have been odd to inform customers he used only real vanilla and whole eggs. At that time, ersatz ingredients weren't the industry standards. Now Drewes's son is virtually alone in the true French custard field. The thick white custard—which has a trace of honey—is hand-scooped, not forced into cones by machines.

The Chippewa Avenue stand is open year-round, with the exception of the four weeks customers are least likely to want something cold—mid-January to mid-February. The stand dates to 1941 and is on old Route 66. The red-and-white neon trimmed stand on Grand Avenue has a shorter season, from Memorial Day to Labor Day. We know why this stand isn't open longer—his employees can't take the constant crush for a full year.

Drewes, Sr., knew he had a sure thing, for even in the midst of the Depression there were always many waiting in lines for this product. The founder began experimenting with custard flavors when he ran away with a carnival and first started dispensing custard in Florida from a mobile machine hooked to the back of a Cadillac truck.

Speedy delivery service has brought one happy improvement. Ted Drewes will now ship its custard by FedEx. Fans may order 6 quarts, 9 regular concretes, or 18 mini-concretes (the 9-ounce size).

Prices are reasonable—a concrete is $1.60 for 9 ounces and $3.40 for 16 ounces. Cones are 40¢ (kiddie size), 80¢ for one scoop, $1.20 for two scoops, $1.60 for three scoops, and $2 for a towering four scoops. Pints are $1.99 and quarts are $2.99. There are dozens of flavor possibilities, depending on toppings. Strawberry and chocolate have joined the basic vanilla custard, which are sold in quarts and pints. The stands also sell malts, shakes, sodas, and floats. Special concoctions have clever names, like Fox Treat, after the city's famed Fox Theater, and Terramizzou, a play on the state university's nickname.

The company has another unusual product—Christmas trees. Every December, Ted Drewes, Jr., travels to Nova Scotia, where he selects Balsam fir trees to sell for the holidays. As he explained, "We have people buy their trees from us year after year, and they don't even know we sell ice cream!"

VISITS
6726 Chippewa Avenue
St. Louis, MO 63109
314/481-2652
Credit cards accepted
From downtown, take I-44 west. Take the Arsenal exit right. Turn left onto Jamieson. Travel 1½ miles and take a left on Chippewa for half a block.

4224 South Grand Avenue
St. Louis, MO 63111
314/352-7376
FAX: 314/481-4241
Credit cards accepted
From downtown, take I-44 West. Take the Grand Avenue exit. Travel south for 3 miles and the stand is on your left.
Chippewa Avenue Stand open mid-February–mid-January; Grant Avenue Stand open mid-May–August: Every day, 11 A.M.–11 P.M.

IT'S-IT ICE CREAM BARS

Talk about loyalty. Just asking the directory assistance operator for the It's-It Company's number drew unsolicited raves: "Oh, they're great. They're my favorite kind of ice cream!"

We've yet to find anyone who isn't wild about this ice cream treat, which is as intimately tied to San Francisco cuisine as sourdough. Two large oatmeal cookies with a slice of vanilla ice cream between them were hand-dipped in chocolate and sold frozen at San Francisco's sorely missed amusement park, Playland-at-the-Beach, which used to be just below the Cliff House at Seal Rocks. This meal-in-itself was a staple at Playland from 1928 until the early 1970s, when the amusement park was torn down. Then, for three years, the city had no It's-It bars. Times were grim.

But Charles Shamieh, a San Francisco resident who had been in the restaurant business, missed It's-It bars. So did his friends and family. So in 1974, the Shamieh family bought the name and rights to It's-It and started making them again in San Francisco. It wasn't that existing ice-cream companies, knowing the devoted following It's-It bars had, didn't want to make them, Shamieh said, "but when they looked at the amount of hand labor involved, they shied away." The name, by the way, was coined by the bar's inventor as he experimented with ice-cream novelties. "It's It!" he was quoted as exclaiming when he hit upon the oatmeal cookie and chocolate combination.

Although the company has automated the dipping, there still is a lot of work done by hand. The cookies and ice cream are made by the company, not purchased. Placing the cookies, covering the ice cream, and packaging involves chiefly hand work. In 1978, the company expanded to a larger facility in Burlingame, a southern suburb adjacent to the airport, and lately the distribution of It's-It has gone beyond northern California into 15 western states, as well as New York, Chicago, Milwaukee, and Boston. All the bars, however, still are made in Burlingame. "We will not let anyone else make it," said Shamieh. "With a franchise, you will always have people skimping."

Large, chewy, homemade-style cookies, It's-It are habit-forming. One of our most enduring memories of Stanford University is the speed at which students and staff would empty a huge chest-type freezer in the student union filled with nothing but It's-It bars.

It's-It bars sell for 85¢ and now come in mint, strawberry, chocolate, and cappuccino ice cream, as well as the traditional vanilla. Three new delights have been introduced with great success. The Super Sundae is a chunk of ice cream dipped in milk chocolate and rolled in peanuts. It comes on a stick in your choice of vanilla, chocolate, and strawberry ice cream. The North Pole is a block of vanilla ice cream dipped in chocolate. The Big Daddy is a chunk of ice cream between dark chocolate wafers. All retail for 85¢ to 89¢, depending on the store.

Although it is very costly to send their products, the company will ship by next-day FedEx if customers genuinely wish to pay the freight charge of $75 per case. Each case contains 24 bars. The ice cream bill would be $15, a fraction of the shipping. Two shipped cases are $105. If you're interested, contact Alex McDow at the plant.

There is no retail outlet at the plant, but they are sold throughout the San Francisco area and should be an essential experience on any tourist's itinerary.

ORDERING ADDRESS
It's-it Ice Cream Company
865 Burlway Road
Burlingame, CA 94010
650/347-2122
FAX: 650/347-2703
e-mail: it'siticecream@aol.com
No credit cards; checks OK

KOPP'S FROZEN CUSTARD

When we were growing up, there was an ice-cream shop in our village center called Custard's Last Stand. It had a cutesy picture of General Custer, but we thought the name a sad announcement of the rarity of true frozen custard. (The shop didn't serve the real stuff, either.)

Only a few places in America are fortunate enough to have genuine custard made from high-butterfat milk, not from a mixture of synthetic sweeteners, thickeners, and stabilizers. One such place is Milwaukee, where Elsie Kopp has been serving vanilla and chocolate custard since 1950. A German immigrant who came to the United States in 1930 and started life as a maid, she turned to custard after her husband, Karl, a tool and die maker, became ill with Parkinson's disease. Hard work and high quality allowed the firm to prosper.

There are now three Kopp's Frozen Custard stands and the company keeps its menu simple: only Swiss chocolate or vanilla custard, plus one additional flavor that changes every day. Pray that you're there on days it's caramel cashew, the only custard we've found with huge, whole nutmeats. Talk about chock-full-o-nuts! The shops promote Magic Mondays, where an unannounced flavor is produced, with free samples for all. The shops' telephone recordings will give customers a three-day flavor forecast for short-term planning.

There's more to Kopp's than custard. Its hamburgers, with a pat of butter melted on each one, are memorable. There's limited seating in all but the newer Brookfield store.

Karl Kopp, Jr., the son of the founder, runs the operations day to day, ensuring that the local dairy that produces the custard according to the Kopp recipe keeps the butterfat at 14 percent and the formula according to tradition. The rich custard, which is smoother and more long-lasting on the tongue than its ersatz cousins, is sold in pints ($2.35), quarts ($4.70), and half gallons ($7.50), as well as in cones and sundaes ($1.28 and up). And we do mean up—you can get a six-scoop dish for $3.85.

This company is a good neighbor. It sponsors the "I Remember Milwaukee" television show, where local notables talk about the past, and donates 5 percent of its sales on Thursdays to the Greater Milwaukee Committee for UNICEF.

It is worth it to stay friendly with people who live in Milwaukee and who travel, because Kopp's does not ship its custard. We are fortunate to have a brother-in-law whose mother was an inventive shopper and gift giver. Before her recent death, she managed to bring several quarts east every year in her carry-on luggage to grateful relatives who savored every bit. Before leaving Milwaukee, true Kopp fanatics stop at the Hometown Filling Station and Convenience store, one mile north of the Greenfield store, on 76th Street, and buy dry ice. Step two is wrapping the custard quarts and ice in newsprint, then stuffing it into your luggage, where it stays in good shape throughout an airline flight. That's our idea of a souvenir!

VISITS
Kopp's Frozen Custard
7631 West Layton Avenue
Greenfield, WI 53220
414/282-4312
Flavor line: 414/282-4080
www.kopps.com
No credit cards
Take I-94 to the 895 bypass. Exit on 76th Street and drive south to Layton Avenue.

5373 North Port Washington Road
Glendale, WI 53217
414/961-3288
Flavor line: 414/961-2006
No credit cards
Take I-43 north to the Silver Spring exit. Drive south on Silver Spring.

18880 West Bluemound Road
Brookfield, WI 53045
262/789-9490
Flavor line: 262/789-1393
No credit cards
Head west from Milwaukee on Bluemound Road. The store is 2 miles past Brookfield Square on the north side of the road.

Sunday–Thursday, 10:30 A.M.–11 P.M. Friday–Saturday, 10:30 A.M.–11:30 P.M.

THE PIEROGI PLACE PIEROGIS

Call them piroshki, pirojki, pirogen, pirogi, or pierogi. They are small pastry turnovers stuffed with sweet or savory fillings. They are of East European origin and are a staple in Russian, Polish, and Ukrainian cooking, but, as pierogi expert Marilyn Marciniak points out, "almost every culture has a noodlelike dough stuffed with something."

Marilyn makes and sells pierogis based on her husband's grandmother's 100-year-old recipe. His grandmother ran a large household in Detroit, plus taking in boarders. "It took her all day to prepare the evening meal. Pierogis were her way of feeding everyone economical, good-quality, filling food," said Marilyn.

Pierogis came to the Marciniaks' rescue in 1984 when the couple, unemployed and with two children, were looking for a food item they could sell in the resort area where they lived in western Michigan. Marilyn took pierogi-making lessons from her mother-in-law, who had carried on the family tradition. She began selling pierogis filled with a potato Cheddar cheese mixture or fresh sautéed cabbage to area mom-and-pop grocery stores, butcher shops, and health-food outlets. Growth was steady, with customers telling the couple that, at last, they had found pierogis like their mothers, or grandmothers, used to make.

Making them is becoming a lost art, it seems. It is not that they are terribly difficult to prepare, says Marilyn. "But I tell people you've got to be willing to use every pan in the kitchen." Marilyn makes her pierogis in a state-approved kitchen, and now sends them, frozen, by overnight delivery. The cabbage and potato-cheese, still the best sellers, have been joined by potato-cottage cheese and chive pierogis and a sweet, dessert pierogi filled with farmer's cheese.

They can be prepared two ways. Either boil the frozen pierogis in water, then remove with a slotted spoon, or fry them over low heat in a little oil or butter, browning each side. We recommend frying the pierogis in order to impart an appetizing toasted color. We particularly like the potato fillings (appreciating cooked cabbage must be an inherited trait). The potatoes are mashed, creating smooth, well-flavored fillings. The ingredient list is wholesome, reflecting Marilyn's first choice for a company name, "Naturally Good Foods."

Her pierogis are large—the crescents are a good 3 inches long and 2 inches wide—and one would be hard-pressed to eat more than two or three at a sitting. With soup or a salad, they make a complete meal. The dessert pierogis are delightful served with cinnamon sugar or sour cream (or both).

The pierogis are $6 per dozen and any quantity can be shipped. She will ship two dozen pierogis of your choice for $37, which includes packing materials and overnight shipping charge. Prices differ for larger shipments.

ORDERING ADDRESS
The Pierogi Place
8197 W. Harrison Road
Mears, MI 49436
231/873-5313
No credit cards; checks OK

ST. CLAIR ICE CREAM FRUITS

We are constantly surprised at how well food ships. Fragile cookies, breads, cheesecakes—no problem with today's packing materials and speedy service. "But what about ice cream?" is often the cynic's question.

It's true that you wouldn't want to mail-order most of your ice-cream purchases. Not because they wouldn't arrive in great shape—we've successfully tested home purchases from across the country in 100-degree-plus August heat—but because of the cost. There are, however, some instances when it makes sense to order far-flung ice-cream delicacies. For a special occasion like a wedding, the ice-cream fruits of the St. Clair Ice Cream Company in South Norwalk, Connecticut, simply can't be duplicated.

The company was founded by two Toronto natives, Gillian Kerr and Barbara Zernike, who were astounded to discover that the beloved ice-cream fruits of their childhood weren't widely available in this country. They arranged a licensing agreement with the St. Clair Ice Cream Company in Toronto, using copies of the molds and recipes that firm has used since 1932.

The company turns out ice cream and sorbet versions of the colorful marzipan candies you still can find in old-time confectioneries. Strawberries, peaches, pears, and walnuts are duplicated in the corresponding flavor of rich ice cream or sorbet. Tiny green paper stems are added to the fruits to further enhance their elegant presentation. There are ginger pears, apple ice cream glazed in red, and walnuts of chocolate chocolate chip ice cream. The four shapes are also molded in other flavors, including passionfruit, lemon, mango, blackberry cassis, and black raspberry. All the sorbets are certified as kosher.

Caterers throughout the country order the fruits and add one or two on plates serving pieces of wedding cake. The fruits also can be served in champagne glasses with creme anglaise or placed between fanned slices of real fruit. The company advises you to avoid serving the fruits directly on silver or stainless steel, as they will begin melting faster than the normal 10 minutes once out of the freezer.

Each fruit is about 1½ inches by 1 inch. They are packed by the dozen in thick plastic bags. We're most partial to the walnuts and strawberries. The ice-cream fruits and sorbets are $14 per dozen. Shipping is by FedEx and ranges from $30 to $100, depending on quantity. The firm does not have a retail operation, but will accept orders by phone and pack items for pickup for those within driving distance.

Gillian Kerr has moved back to Toronto. Her replacements, Bunny Wayt and Ines Rivera, work with Barbara Zernike at a new South Norwalk location. The women also create hand-molded, hand-glazed items, like day lilies, hearts, Christmas trees, corn-on-the-cob, roses, turkeys, swans, and bunnies. These creations are a far cry from what you see in franchise scoop shops. In their case, they marry ice cream artistry with sophisticated, delicate flavors. These are special occasion, show-stopping desserts.

ORDERING ADDRESS
St. Clair Ice Cream Company
140 Water Street
South Norwalk, CT 06854
203/853-4774
FAX: 203/852-9192
www.stclairicecream.com
e-mail: stclairice@aol.com
No credit cards; checks OK
Retail sales at the company by appointment only

FRUITS & NUTS

BYRD'S HOOT OWL PECAN RANCH PECANS

Bigger isn't always better, at least when it comes to pecans. Missouri pecans are generally smaller and slimmer than their more southern counterparts, but their fans believe they are sweeter and more intense in flavor than the giant, jumbo, mega-pecans that photograph so well.

What better gift could there be for a cook than a bag of shelled Missouri pecans? It's a food gift that doesn't have to be consumed immediately, since nuts keep beautifully in the freezer. In fact, if you want to grind nuts without losing their oils, freeze them first and grind them while frozen. They'll be light, dry, and fluffy.

That little hint comes from Missouri pecan growers Loyle (L. V.) and Mary Byrd. The couple has been selling pecans for 30 years, but have been growing them since the early 1950s. (It takes patience to be a pecan grower, since it takes 15 years for a tree to produce.)

The couple began raising pecans because they couldn't bear to see the native pecan and black walnut trees being bulldozed—a common practice as land was cleared in the early 1950s. Over the years, they have added acreage to their original tract of timber ground, and now have two pecan farms, a 160-acre grove and processing plant near Butler, and a 219-acre grove farther south, near Nevada, Missouri. They have helped others get into the business, hosting field days for growers, and have helped establish nut growers associations in Missouri and Kansas. Now, the region harvests more than 3 million pounds of nuts each year. It's a bona fide industry, as opposed to neglected native groves.

After the first killing frost in the fall, the Byrds and their three children move into high gear. They harvest, wash, and crack pecans virtually nonstop until the end of the year. The mail-order business continues year-round.

In addition to shelled pecans, the Byrds sell cracked pecans, which are partially shelled. Loose pieces of shells are removed, and the nuts can be removed from the cracked shells using only your fingers. It's a bit of work to shell a 3-pound bag, but it's a good task to occupy children—especially those who think all nuts come in cellophane packages. These are straight-off-the-farm pecans, and they'll appreciate every nut. Hoot Owl Pecan Ranch's prices are low. Prices are adjusted according to the growing season, so call first for prices. The nuts are sold in 1-pound bags (shelled) and 3-pound bags (cracked). The Byrds also offer Missouri black walnut kernels, in 1 -pound bags.

ORDERING ADDRESS
Byrd's Pecans
Route 3, Box 205
Butler, MO 64730
660/925-3253 (ranch)
660/679-5583 (business)
e-mail: goodbye1@ckt.net
No credit cards; checks OK

VISITS: Butler is 68 miles south of Kansas City. From Butler, drive 9 miles west on Highway 52 to the pecan store.
November–January: Every day, 9 A.M.–5 P.M.

CUSHMAN'S CITRUS

This listing is given in self-defense for the moment when your doorbell rings and a high schooler says: "Our booster club is taking orders for Florida oranges and grapefruit." How many times we have purchased boxes of citrus, only to be delivered pithy, half-frozen specimens that largely went out in the trash. The problem is that there are 145 or so gift-fruit shippers in Florida. All sound good, and look good—at least in the four-color brochures.

At the risk of offending the many other reputable, longtime fruit shippers, we'd like to pass on the name of a favorite. Cushman Fruit Company, which started in business in 1947, has seen the mail-order side of its operation grow from a side line to more than half of its income. Its customers are loyal and patient. The patient part comes from having to wait all year until January, when Cushman sells HoneyBells, a cross between the Duncan grapefruit and the Dancy tangerine known in the citrus industry as the Mineola tangelo. Created in 1931 by government fruit researchers, it was a relatively obscure hybrid until the late Ed Cushman found a few bushels in a harvest of grapefruit from a grower who supplied his retail fruit shop. He trademarked the name HoneyBells, which refers to the bell shape, and promoted it with gusto.

HoneyBells are a deep orange, extremely sweet, and extremely juicy. The Cushman family, ever alert to marketing possibilities, play up the juiciness by including plastic bibs with each order. (The little ditty on the bibs reads: "Insurance can cover your losses, Reporters can cover the news. HoneyBell lovers who don't wear bibs can quickly be covered in juice.") They are available during January only, but you need to reserve yours early. One year we waited until January 8 and found them all sold out.

If you miss the HoneyBells, there is still a good selection of citrus varieties the rest of the winter and spring (navel oranges from November on, red grapefruit through the winter until May, temple oranges in February, tangerines in March, Valencia oranges in the spring). Cushman's only ships fruit at its peak. With a toll-free number, it's easy to deal with Cushman Fruit. If you aren't happy with what arrives on your doorstep, there is a money-back guarantee—a feature that booster clubs, no matter how well intentioned, can't match.

Cushman's also will send you boxes of ripe, beefsteak tomatoes and comice pears.

A 9-pound box of HoneyBells is $25.99. An 18-pound box is $34.99. Ten pounds of giant navel oranges are $26.99, and 20 pounds of jumbo red grapefruit are $34.99. Ten tomatoes, shipped year-round, are $21.99. Delivery is $4.95 per package. Since fruit prices vary with the success of the growing season, it's wise to call and confirm. Cushman's will ship citrus to Canada and Europe, but cannot send fruit to Arizona, Hawaii, and Puerto Rico.

ORDERING ADDRESS
Cushman Fruit Company
3325 Forest Hill Boulevard
West Palm Beach, FL 33406
561/965-3535
800/776-7575
FAX: 800/776-4329
e-mail: info@honeybell.com
www.honeybell.com
Credit cards accepted

VISITS: There are three Cushman stores in the Palm Beaches, at 3325 Forest Hill Boulevard in West Palm; 227 S. Ocean Boulevard, Manalapan; and 204 US Highway 1 in North Palm Beach.
Monday–Saturday, 9 A.M.–5:30 P.M.

HADLEY ORCHARDS TRAIL MIX

Paul and Peggy Hadley, founders of California's premier dried-fruit and nut empire, regret to this day that they didn't copyright the name "trail mix." At least 30 years ago (they aren't sure of the date), one of their longtime employees at their wildly successful, homey farmstand on Interstate 10, west of Palm Springs, developed a mixture of fat, dark raisins, sunflower and pumpkin seeds, large pieces of cashew nuts, and whole peanuts and almonds. The snack was designed to be used by hikers on nearby Mt. San Jacinto, and the employee, Howard Doebereiner, coined the name "trail mix." Hadley's Fruit Orchards did not register the name, and today "there are a hundred different kinds, made by every Tom, Dick, and Harry," said Paul Hadley, now retired. "You ask someone if they like trail mix and it all depends on who made it."

At one time, Hadley's sold more trail mix than any other item in its crowded store, which is quite a statement, given the immense popularity of Hadley's unsulfured dried fruits, honeys, fruit wines, vitamins, and health foods. The Hadleys literally sold tons of the snack, which comes roasted and salted, raw, or roasted only. It still is one of the company's best-sellers, and any of the three styles is a far cry from the skimpy cellophane packets containing mostly peanuts, coconut, and stale clumps of crystallized dates that are fixtures at checkout stands. The roasted-only seems the best choice because salt tends to detract from the taste of the raisins, and the raw variety lacks the rich flavor that roasting imparts. An 18-ounce bag of roasted-only mix is $4.59, and a 40-ounce plastic tub is only $8.49.

You may also buy a mix with dried cranberries added to each of the basic trail mix varieties. Shipping is extra and the mix may be shipped worldwide.

Visiting the store is an experience. It is open every day of the year and is thronged with customers enjoying the atmosphere and the free samples that are a Hadley Fruit Orchard trademark.

The company does an especially nice job with gift orders, offering tastefully decorated tins for Medjhool dates, for example, and gift packs of dried fruits.

ORDERING ADDRESS
Hadley Fruit Orchards
P.O. Box 495
Cabazon, CA 92230
909/849-5255
800/854-5655
e-mail: hadleys@hadleyfruitorchards.com
www.hadleys.com
Credit cards accepted

VISITS: **The original store is 16 miles west of Palm Springs on I-10. Take the Apache Trail off-ramp. There is another store about an hour north of San Diego in Carlsbad, California, at 6115 Paseo del Norte (telephone: 760/438-1260). The newest store is in downtown Palm Springs, at 122 La Plaza on Palm Canyon Drive between Arenas and Tahquitz Canyon Way (telephone: 760/325-2160).**

Every day, including Christmas. Cabazon store: 8 A.M.–8 P.M.
Carlsbad store: 8 A.M.–8 P.M. Palm Springs store: 10 A.M.–5 P.M.

HAMMONS PANTRY BLACK WALNUTS

Black walnut trees grow wild throughout the central and eastern United States and in many areas are a neglected resource. One potent reason is that the nuts are a nuisance to shell. The shell is tough—it is used by explosives manufacturers as a filler in dynamite—and it'll stain your hands brown.

We remember our Illinois neighbor, Eunice Flaig, wearing gloves and pounding her black walnuts with a hammer. This was done after she dried the nuts on the roof of her chicken house for several months. Our Missouri neighbor, Bittsy Lindgren, put the nuts in her driveway and ran over them with her car.

If such convolutions don't appeal to you, but the earthy taste of black walnuts does, call, write, or visit Hammons Pantry in the southwest part of the state. The pantry's parent company, Hammons Product Company, has been in business 54 years and is the world's largest processor of American black walnuts. Chances are the black walnuts in the ice cream or baked goods you find in your supermarkets come from Hammons.

The pantry has been in business 17 years and was originally run by Donna Hammons, daughter-in-law of the founder, Ralph Hammons. He was a grocery-store owner who recognized the wealth of "black gold" nuts in Missouri and set out to create a market for them.

The pantry handles other nut varieties, including native Missouri pecans and has a goodly number of fancy gift packs that combine nuts with candy. The candy, including black walnut fudge, taffy, brittle, milk chocolate bark, and a black walnut version of a turtle, is made by a local candy maker using nuts supplied by Hammons. It is shipped only October through May.

Since walnut meats will keep for six months in your refrigerator, and up to two years in your freezer, it makes sense to buy in bulk. Don't fall under the tyranny of the absurdly high prices for the small cellophane packets hanging at the grocery. A 5-pound "home box" of large black walnut pieces, in no-frills packaging, is $40.25, plus the $6.25 shipping charge imposed on all orders. The same size box of "recipe ready" smaller nuts that are about the size of unpopped corn kernels is $40. A 2-pound, 12-ounce gift tin of the nuts is $25.95.

A brochure of black-walnut recipes is included.

ORDERING ADDRESS
Hammons Pantry
414 North Street
Stockton, MO 65785
417/276-5151
800/872-6879
e-mail: hammonspantry@u-n-i.net
www.marketplaza.com/walnuts
Credit cards accepted

VISITS: **Stockton is on the edge of the Ozarks, approximately 50 miles northwest of Springfield, Missouri.**
Every day, 8 A.M.–5 P.M.

KOINONIA PARTNERS SPICED PECANS AND HONEY-NUT PEACH CAKE

Koinonia Partners is a 55-year-old successful example of Christian living and outreach. Koinonia residents and volunteers, black and white, live at the farm in Americus, Georgia, following a life of worship, work, and fellowship. They run a day-care center for area children and operate a mail-order food business using pecans and peanuts from their farming activities. Visitors—some of whom return to Americus as volunteers for Koinonia (pronounced coy-nó-nee-ah)—are continually amazed at the concrete achievements the partnership has made in housing and education.

On a smaller level, we admire Koinonia's handmade foods, in particular its unique and delectable spiced pecans and its peach cake. The cinnamon-dusted nut meats are coated with a vanilla, sugar, and shortening concoction that imparts a sweet, creamy taste. The pecans are grown on 3,500 of the Koinonia trees and are supplemented by purchases from local growers. An 8-ounce box is $6.45, plus shipping.

The honey-nut peach cake, made with peaches, dates, raisins, pecans, and honey, is moist and delicious. A 1-pound, 5-ounce cake is $10.40, plus shipping. The kitchen also makes an oat-nut granola (sold for $6.45 per pound), chocolate peanut crunch, and spiced peanuts. We feel particularly good about the fact that all profits from the food sales are used to support the partners' projects for the poor of surrounding Sumter County. We know that Clarence Jordan, the Baptist preacher and Greek scholar who founded the experiment in 1942, would be pleased at how well the partnership is faring.

ORDERING ADDRESS
Koinonia Partners, Inc.
1324 Georgia Highway 49 South
Americus, GA 31709
912/924-0391
877/738-1741 (toll-free)
Credit cards accepted

VISITS: The farm is 8 miles south of Americus, which is in southwest Georgia near former President Jimmy Carter's hometown of Plains, on Route 49 south. A small, white roadside sign directs you to the Koinonia office. The store offers a 10 percent discount on all food items.
Monday–Friday, 8 A.M.–5 P.M.

LEE SEED COMPANY SOYNUTS

We have an inherent conflict of interest here. One of us is married to a man who used to raise soybeans and has been selling soybean and other seeds for 20 years. That said, we will point out that we aren't the only ones touting soybeans. Nutritionists like them because they are protein dense, easily digested, and high in fiber.

Although soybeans were brought to this country from China to be used as human food, for years most of our soybean crop has been enjoyed by livestock. Tofu and soybean oil have changed the picture, but soybeans generally weren't something you ate out of hand—until soynuts.

Soynuts are roasted soybeans. They have been available in some health-food stores for years, but haven't been widely known. Now, Iowa soybean farmers Paul and Joyce Lee and their children are doing their best to change that picture.

It was decades ago that Paul and Joyce tasted some soynuts and thought they could be packaged and marketed as gift items. Fifteen years ago, a business was born.

Paul already had a seed business of his own, custom-cleaning soybean seed, so Lee Seed Company simply expanded to include the marketing of soynuts. The Lees praise soynuts as a healthy snack, pointing out that they have 30 percent less fat than other nuts. One-third cup of the seasoned soynuts contains about 60 calories, 6 grams of protein, and 3 grams of fat.

The Lees offer soynuts in sweet versions—cherry, chocolate, yogurt, and chocolate with a candy shell. There are savory varieties, such as honey mustard, jalapeño and Cheddar, ranch, barbecue, and onion-garlic. Lightly salted, and unsalted soynuts are also available, as well as mixtures, such as unsalted soynuts, raisins, and dried cranberries.

The soynuts are not at all greasy, and a small amount is filling. We particularly liked the lightly salted varieties.

A plastic sampler tray of seven flavors is $6, plus shipping, and various pretty tins, stenciled fabric bags, and gift boxes are available to be filled with your choice of soynuts. Shipping is free for five or more 1-pound bags. One pound of soynuts is $8, 3 pounds $15, and 5 pounds is $20.

The Lees' farm is 1,200 acres and Paul uses his own soybeans for the soynuts. A confectioner adds the flavors, but the roasting, packaging, and shipping are done at the farm. As a result, the Lees control the variety of soynuts and the roasting technique. Since the farm operation also includes cattle and hogs, it is a busy place year-round.

The soybean cleaning and bagging end of the business is geared toward edible soybeans, and Paul says that lots of the beans are sent to California and end up in tofu and miso. "It's a niche market," he said of food beans, "and it's a way for a farmer to make a living out here."

Both of the Lees' sons, Scott and Mark, grew up working on the farm, promoting Super Soynuts at shows. After both graduating from college in agriculture-related fields, they joined the company full-time.

ORDERING ADDRESS
Lee Seed Company, Inc.
2242 Highway 182
Inwood, IA 51240
712/753-4403
800/736-6530
FAX: 712/753-4403
e-mail: scottlee@soynuts.com
www.soynuts.com
Credit cards accepted

VISITS: **Inwood is in the northwest corner of Iowa, almost to the South Dakota line. The Lees' farm is 1 mile north of Inwood at 2242 Highway 182. There is a large sign on the road.**
Monday–Friday, 8 A.M.–4 P.M.

SHADY GROVE ORCHARDS CHESTNUTS

Chestnuts are a terrific health food that chefs are now discovering. They're low in fat and high in carbohydrates, protein, and Vitamin C. With less than 2 percent fat (most nuts are more than 50 percent fat), they're the only nut approved by the Pritikin System. Plus that, they taste wonderful and can be used widely throughout one's cooking repertoire.

If you want testimonials to chestnuts' good qualities, ask your grandparents. Chestnuts used to be a common food in America, until Asian chestnut trees infected American strains with blight, a form of fungus. By the late 1930s, several billion American trees had died or were cut down. "Under the spreading chestnut tree" had become just a phrase in a poetry book, as the American chestnut industry essentially disappeared.

The chestnuts you buy at holiday times, at ultra-high prices, and from vendors on New York City streets, are imports, mostly from Italy. But in the last 25 years, progressive botanists and foresters in America have been working on hybrids to begin the long process of reviving the American chestnut.

Among these food pioneers is a company that is shipping chestnut food products to individuals and restaurants across the country.

Shady Grove Orchards, run by Omroa and Annie Bhagwandin, sells fresh chesnuts, sweet chestnut flour, dried chestnut kernels, marron glacé (which uses the larger Italian chestnuts), a chestnut roasting pan, seedlings, and a chestnut cookbook. Except for the marron glacé, the chestnuts used are U.S. grown, from European-variety chestnut trees. No pesticides are used. Omroa, a botanist, sets up chestnut orchards for others, promising to buy all of their crops because he realizes the pent-up demand for the nuts.

Their chestnut flour, which comes in a 1-pound container for $14, plus shipping, is used in cakes and sauces, and can replace up to one-third of the flour in pasta for a rich, unusual taste. The company starts shipping fresh chestnuts in late October, but there is a limited supply.

"Chestnuts are so nostalgic," said Annie. "People bring out their family stories when they taste them."

The dried chestnuts are peeled and sell for $7 for 8 ounces, which rehydrate to 1 pound. Annie's *Chestnut Cookbook* is sold for $9.95, plus shipping.

ORDERING ADDRESS

Shady Grove Orchards
183 Shady Grove Road
Onalaska, WA 98570
360/985-7033
e-mail: shadygrove@myhome.net
www.chestnutsource.com
No credit cards; check OK

SHAWNEE SPRINGS CANNED PEACHES

Most commercially canned peaches belong in the Agricultural Hall of Shame, right next to the rock-hard tasteless commercial tomato. Store-bought canned peaches are beautiful to behold, but they are as firm as apples. That shouldn't happen to a tender fruit.

We know of only two commercial canneries in this country that are holdouts for the time-consuming, old-fashioned methods that produce tender, flavorful peaches. These companies still peel their peaches by hand, with steam instead of a lye solution. There is Walnut Acres, the natural foods source in Pennsylvania, and Shawnee Canning Company in northern Virginia.

"Canned the way Grandma did," Shawnee's brochure states. Its peaches—Red Havens, Glow Havens, and Lorings—are grown by the cannery owners and hand-packed as well. The end product is infinitely better than any other commercially canned peach we've tried. They look and taste like home-canned.

Even better, Shawnee, located in Frederick County, Virginia, packs unsweetened peach halves, as well as halves in heavy sugar syrup. And the company will send its peaches in gift packs, with other top-quality fresh and canned fruit products the family-run operation makes. What a find!

George and Damaris Whitacre began raising apples and peaches in northern Virginia in the 1930s, selling their fruits to the Brathwaite brothers' cannery at Cross Junction. In 1966, when the cannery owners wanted to retire, George, a distant relative, bought it. Actually, it was a survival tactic. There are very few peach processors left in the area, and the Whitacres wanted to make sure they would have a place to take their fruit.

Now the operation is run by their son, William Whitacre. His daughter, Lisa, is general manager. The family begins each season canning peaches, then moves on to apple juice and cider (including a cider flavored with cherries), with apple butter processed after the fall harvest. The family raises several kinds of apples, and tries to have three different varieties blended in its apple butter and cider. "We figure it gives you a better flavor and the color of the juice is better, too," said William.

Apple butter, which is very thick, comes in sweetened and unsweetened styles. Of the preserves we sampled, we can enthusiastically recommend the blueberry and the seedless black raspberry. Both were simply berries, sugar, pectin, and citric acid. The blackberry preserves had a jellylike consistency and were very flavorful. The blueberry had small berries that tasted wild, although they were not.

The products are well priced. A 10-ounce jar of most of the preserves and jams is $3.39. Jellies are 30 cents cheaper. Fruit spreads, which use white grape juice instead of sugar, are $5.95 for a 20-ounce jar. The company will individually create a wide variety of gift packs, so we recommend writing for its brochure and price list. It also will send case lots of its canned peaches. A case of 24 of its 29-ounce cans of peaches is $54 for sweetened, $50 unsweetened, plus shipping. Cans of irregular pieces in heavy syrup, perfect for slicing into pies, are $50 per case, plus shipping.

The company also sells unusual pint jars of vegetable products, like hot Brussels sprouts, pepper hash, pineapple pepper salad, and corn salsa, at $5.99. Virginia honey and fresh apples are also shipped.

ORDERING ADDRESS
Shawnee Canning Company, Inc.
P.O. Box 657
Cross Junction, VA 22625
800/713-1414
FAX: 540/888-7963
e-mail: shawcan@crosslink.net
www.shawneespring.com
Credit cards accepted

VISITS
Shawnee Springs Market
Route 522 North
Cross Junction, VA 22625
Cross Junction is in northern Virginia, northwest of Winchester and almost at the West Virginia border. The market is 10 miles north of Winchester. There are signs to direct you.
Every day, 6 A.M.–9 P.M.

SHIELDS DATE GARDENS
DATE CRYSTALS AND DATES

There's a sprawling roadside stand south of Palm Springs in Indio, California, that has been devoted to fruits since 1924. Even as commercial development eats away at the date groves in Indio, Shields Date Gardens looks much as it did 75 years ago.

The decor of Shields Date Gardens—a date, fig, citrus, and date-product shop—has longevity and our loyalty. Signs are in old-fashioned typefaces, displays are simple, and the products are as we remember them from years past. Along one wall is a vintage soda counter where Shields employees dispense 55,000 date milkshakes a year.

The store sells vintage postcards of the desert and has tools like a pruning ax, pollinating knife, and a dusting puffer on display. Visitors may still see that hit movie, "The Romance and Sex Life of the Date" and learn such nifty facts such as one palm tree can bear 150 pounds of dates, the trees originally came from Algeria, and it takes 20 years for dates to yield.

The key ingredient that sets Shields apart from other date shops in the area is date crystals—crisp nuggets of chopped, dried dates. The crystals, which can be used in recipes calling for dates, are unique to Shields. A 3-pound bucket is $22.75, including shipping. Date bits, coated in oats, also are good for baking. Two pounds are $11.90, delivered.

The shop was opened in 1924 by Floyd and Bess Shields. Floyd, a mining engineer by trade, owned an apartment house in Long Beach that was going broke. He met a rancher from Indio who owned a date garden that was going broke. They traded properties and "always argued about who got the best end of the deal," said Frank Wilson, who was the longtime general manager of Shields. His son, Dick, now runs the business.

Selling directly to the public turned out to be the only thing the Shields could do, since the rancher had planted 119 palm trees, each bearing a different variety of date, and date-packing houses were interested in only a few commercial varieties. Now, the palms that surround the store represent just a handful of varieties: Bread Dates, Blond and Brunet Dates, Deglet Noors, Medjhools, and Shields's own variety. All are unpasteurized and must be refrigerated, but they have much richer, distinctive flavors than the sticky blocks of fruit sold in supermarkets.

A 1-pound box of super jumbo Medjhool, Deglet Noor, Blond and Brunet Dates, and dates rolled in coconut is $14.95, delivered. Walnut-stuffed Medjhools are $17.50 per pound, delivered. Chocolate-covered dates, in dark and milk chocolate, are $21.50 per pound, delivered.

A chewy dessert date cake, with more dates and walnuts than cake, is $17.95, including shipping, and weighs 2 pounds. Dense and rich, the cake is at best 2 inches high and can easily be sliced into bars. It is made for Shields by a local bakery, and the ingredients are simply dates, nuts, eggs, sugar, flour, vanilla, salt, and baking powder.

The date industry has been pushed out of the area around Palm Springs as land prices have soared. Now it is moving from the Indio area toward Coachella. Aside from a few date palms remaining amid the golf courses and luxury homes, a visitor whizzing by on Interstate 10 or staying in Palm Springs could miss any evidence of the area's most famous product. It's worth a trip of a few miles to Shields to remind yourself what dates should look and taste like.

ORDERING ADDRESS
Shields Date Garden
80225 Highway 111
Indio, CA 92201
760/347-0996
800/414-2555
e-mail: shieldate@aol.com
www.shieldsdates.com
Credit cards accepted

VISITS: The salesroom should not be missed. It would be hard to avoid it, since there are plenty of billboards in the area pointing the way to Shields. From Palm Springs, drive 20 miles south on Highway 111 and you'll see the palms towering over even the billboards.
Every day, 8 A.M.–6 P.M.

SUNRAY ORCHARDS PRUNES

There's a new strategy by the California Prune Board to bring more eaters to its maligned, and delicious fruit. Henceforth, they are to be referred to as dried plums.

Forgive us, but we'll stay with the old name.

We know that even in the produce business, there are fads. The latest in prunes is a very soft pitted prune, preserved with sorbic acid and sealed in an airtight sack. They are so sticky and moist that you put your fingers in the sack with trepidation.

At Sunray Orchards in southwest Oregon, different kinds of prunes are sold. They haven't changed much since the business was founded in 1923, and the present owners, John and Peggy Black, don't see any reason to change direction.

Sunray's prunes are not pitted. The long processing required to pit adversely affects flavor, texture, and nutrients, the Blacks say. Preservatives are needed for pitted prunes, so keeping them unpitted allows Sunray to avoid any additives. "Our prunes are not overprocessed like our competitors," said Peggy. "That gives them more food value and flavor." The orchard processes prunes throughout the year and only packages enough to ship out within a week or two, so the prunes are extraordinarily fresh.

And you get a choice of prunes. There are Oregon Tarts, which are Italian prunes, with a tart, dark-orange flesh. Eating them reminded us of prunes we had eaten as children at roadside fruit stands. The orchard's most popular prune, and the one that was developed in its home county, is the Moyer prune. A good 2 inches long, these prunes are very sweet and chewy, but not sticky. There is an abundance of meat on each fruit. One or two make a satisfying dessert.

The prunes are packed in 1-pound cellophane sacks. A box of 12 sacks of Oregon Tart Italian prunes is $16.80, plus shipping. The Moyers are $18 for 12 one-pound sacks. A $21 gift box contains 4 pounds Moyer Colossal prunes, 4 pounds Oregon Tart large prunes, 1 pound Umpqua Blackberry Honey, and 1 pound Oregon hazelnuts. Shipping for the cheery mustard-yellow box varies from $7 to $13.30, depending on UPS zone.

During the summer and early fall, the Blacks run a farmstand, which also sells vegetables and fruit from its 1,600 peach, cherry, and nectarine trees.

ORDERING ADDRESS
Sunray Orchards
P.O. Box 2138
Myrtle Creek, OR 97457
541/863-3770
www.sunrayorchards.com
No credit cards

VISITS
1229 N. Old Pacific Highway
Myrtle Creek, OR
Myrtle Creek is in southwest Oregon, along I-5, south of Roseburg. There are no set hours, so call ahead. The farmstand operates during daylight hours from mid-July to September.

TIMBER CREST FARMS DRIED FRUIT AND TOMATOES

Nothing ruins the flavor of dried fruit and vegetables faster than a heavy sulphur taste that brings to mind not orchards but chemistry labs. Unsulfured fruits are darker and not as pretty to gaze upon as treated fruits, but the flavors are true and acid-free. Timber Crest Farms, near the northern California town of Healdsburg, is known for high-quality fruits and tomatoes that are picked when ripe, dried, kept in cold storage, and packaged without preservatives or additives.

Ron Waltenspiel runs the business with his wife, Ruthie. Ron began selling fruit to consumers 43 years ago when his father suggested that he try marketing his produce directly, instead of to cooperatives or large packers. "It's so much more satisfying than seeing your fruit go off to Del Monte or Sunsweet," observes Ruthie Waltenspiel. "You are ultimately responsible to the people who eat it, which colors your whole attitude toward growing."

Much of the company's produce is grown on their Sonoma County ranch, such as the plum tomatoes, pistachios, almonds, peaches, apples, apricots, pears, cherries, and prunes. Most are grown organically under the strict regulations of the California Health and Safety Code. Those that aren't grown at Timber Crest, such as pineapple and papaya, are chosen carefully to fit the farm's philosophy.

The pineapple rings and spears are good examples. Most dried pineapple actually is glacéed, and is produced by soaking fresh pineapple in sugar water and then evaporating the water. Since sugar usually is cheaper than fruit, it is to the producer's advantage to use as much sugar as possible, and some dried pineapples are as much as 85 percent sugar. When the Waltenspiels' longtime sugar-free pineapple supplier in Ecuador went bankrupt, their search for a dependable source led to Taiwan, where a supplier uses pineapple concentrate instead of sugared water to process the dried fruit. The result is plenty sweet, and we would have bet money that sugar or honey had been added if the Waltenspiels had not insisted otherwise.

The company offers the usual dried fruits, as well as Calimyrna and Mission figs, tropical starfruit, Monukka raisins, red cherries, and Roma tomatoes, all in 5-pound bags or small, less-than-a-pound bags. No sugar, salt, or sulfur compounds are added. It is a shock to see, say, brown wrinkled peaches and pears instead of the Technicolor versions we have become accustomed to, but the Timber Crest catalog includes realistic color photos so even those ordering by mail need not be surprised.

Fruit and tomatoes are packed at Timber Crest five days a week, and it is possible to stop at the farm's retail store and packing plant and see fruit harvested, washed, cut, dried, and packaged in one visit. The farm uses warm-air drying, rather than sun drying, which robs fruit of needed moisture. Ruthie Waltenspiel is particularly proud of the cleanliness and uniformity of the farm's fruit, and said a supervisor of state inspectors made a special trip to Timber Crest because he couldn't understand why his inspectors had never rejected a batch of fruit from the farm.

A fruit basket containing dates, white and Mission figs, prunes, walnuts, and almonds is $9.95, plus shipping, for the 1-pound basket and $12.95 for a 2-pound basket. A 3-pound redwood fruit tray containing pineapple rings, dates, figs, pitted prunes, almonds, and walnuts is $18.95, plus shipping. Timber Crest also will send its dried tomato products. The company also produces a tomato chutney and salsa. The tomato bits are particularly useful in adding color and taste to salads, sandwiches, omelets, and baked potatoes. A 1-pound, 3-ounce gift pack containing marinated tomatoes, pasta sauce, and tomato bits is $12.95, plus shipping. The dried tomato halves are $2 for a 3-ounce package. A case of 12 assorted packages is $29.95, plus shipping.

ORDERING ADDRESS
Timber Crest Farms
4791 Dry Creek Road
Healdsburg, CA 95448
707/433-8251
FAX: 707/433-8255
e-mail: ruth@timbercrest.com
www.timbercrest.com
Credit cards accepted

VISITS: Healdsburg is in Sonoma County, north of San Francisco. From Highway 101 going north, take the Dry Creek Road turnoff at the north end of Healdsburg. Go west 5 miles on Dry Creek Road to 4791 and you will see the Timber Crest store.
Monday–Friday, 8 A.M.–5 P.M. Saturday, 10 A.M.–4 P.M.

VIRGINIA DINER PEANUTS

We're fond of the old-fashioned style in which growers named their crop varieties, as in the Big Boy, Better Boy, Best Boy trilogy of tomatoes, so we knew we had a friend when Bill Galloway, president of Virginia Diner Peanuts, rattled off the names of the legumes used in his Wakefield, Virginia, company: the Virginia Fancy and the Virginia Jumbo.

The peanuts, first boiled in water and then roasted in a special vegetable oil, are sold from Galloway's 165-seat diner. The boiling process causes the peanuts to blister, which gives them extra crunch, although Galloway invariably gets questions from first-timers about whether the different-looking nuts are supposed to be bumpy. The company, whose motto is "a legend in a nutshell since 1929," is happy to explain the process to eaters.

The peanut is much lighter and sweeter than the standard Spanish peanut, which has much more oil. Diner peanuts are available salted, unsalted, or butter roasted, in bags or tins. A 1-pound cellophane bag is $4.95 and a 2½-pound tin is $12.50, both plus shipping.

The diner also makes very good candy that uses peanuts, particularly its extra-thick crunch. It is $8.75 for a 20-ounce tin. Its chocolate-covered peanut brittle is $13.95 for a 24-ounce can. All are available in Victorian and other attractive tins. A peanut pie and tarts can be ordered, along with peanuts flavored with Old Bay Seasoning. Combination baskets, and baskets containing Virginia hams and biscuits, also are sold.

The diner has been popular ever since it opened in 1929. It originally was a railroad car that recently has been rebuilt and enlarged. As the diner states openly on its letters, Wakefield cannot claim to be the home of George Washington, but it consoles itself by being "the home of good food."

ORDERING ADDRESS
Virginia Diner
P.O. Box 1030
Wakefield, VA 23888-1030
757/899-3106
800/868-NUTS (6887)
FAX: 757/899-2281
e-mail: vadiner@vadiner.com
www.vadiner.com
Credit cards accepted

VISITS: Wakefield is 60 miles south of Richmond and 60 miles north of Norfolk, halfway between Petersburg and Suffolk, Virginia, on U.S. Route 460. The Virginia Diner is in the middle of town, right past the huge blue and white sign proclaiming Wakefield "Peanut Capital of the World."

Every day, 6 A.M.–8 P.M. Summer hours: Until 9 P.M.

Honeys, Syrups, & Preserves

ALASKA WILD BERRY LINGONBERRY JELLY

In a fortunate mix of government and commerce, Hazel Heath, the former mayor of tiny Homer, Alaska, founded this firm six decades ago. It makes one-of-a-kind jams and sauces from local wild berries, most of which grow in the towns of Soldotna and Kenai, about 70 miles northeast of Homer.

The company is on the Homer Spit—a narrow tongue of land on the end of the Kenai Peninsula, about 220 miles southwest of Anchorage. It's worth visiting the shop, as you can view the kitchen, as well as a small museum of company, animal, and Eskimo artifacts. Its headquarters are now in its Anchorage store, which means more walk-in customers.

The midnight sun ripens these lingonberries, which must account for their deep flavor, far duskier than the mountain varieties of Colorado. Since 1946, these wild berries—also known as low-bush cranberries—have been turned into a garnet-colored jelly with a delicate hint of cranberry. The same high-quality production methods are used to turn elderberries and raspberries into notable jellies. (Two of the more obscure berries, the salmonberry and mossberry, are not such successes as jelly flavors.)

The company advertises on the radio and in the newspaper for pickers and sets up buying stations in the two berry towns. If there are excessively dry or wet growing seasons, the company will make appropriate substitutions for berries that are unavailable.

Transportation costs make it unwise to send small quantities, so the Alaska Wild Berry folks ship mostly assortments of many of their products, packed in boxes that begin at $25. (That assortment includes a Polish sausage, a tin of salmon, and a jar of sourdough sauce that can be exchanged for any of the jellies or jams.) Its Wildberry Jelly Festival box includes four small jars of jelly and one large of lingonberry jelly for $25.

At the shops in Homer and Anchorage, the lingonberry and other jellies are $3.50 per 5¼-ounce jar and $5.50 for 10-ounce jars.

ORDERING ADDRESS
Alaska Wild Berry Products
5225 Juno Street
Anchorage, AK 99518
907/562-8858
800/280-2927
FAX: 907/562-5467
www.alaskawildberryproduct.com
Credit cards accepted

VISITS

Anchorage store, same address.

Winter: Every day, 10 A.M.–5 P.M. Summer: 10 A.M.–11 P.M.

Homer store: 528 East Pioneer Avenue, Homer, AK 99603, tel.: 907/235-8858. The plant is on the main street of Homer, in the middle of town.

Winter: Every day, 10 A.M.–5 P.M. Summer: Every day, 9 A.M.–9 P.M.

AMERICAN SPOON PRESERVES

With some food companies, you must pick and choose carefully from among the offerings. At American Spoon Foods, throw caution to the wind. Open any of its handsome catalogs and jab a finger on any page. Whether it is dried red tart cherries, native wild nut meats, any of its preserves, or its no-oil salad dazzlers, all of American Spoon Foods products are the very best you can find.

Since 1981, American Spoon has been reintroducing Americans to some of the vast wild bounty once common in this country. Dried morel mushrooms, tasty salmon-colored wild thimbleberries, butternut meats, and tiny pungent wild blueberries are some of the foraged foods the company makes available to eaters everywhere. Located in northwestern Michigan's fruit belt, American Spoon was founded by Justin Rashid and his wife, Kate Marshall, native Michigan residents who returned after several years as actors in New York City, and the well-known chef of An American Place restaurant in New York City, Larry Forgione. Two decades ago, Rashid was Forgione's guide when the chef was visiting a buffalo farm in Michigan.

Surrounded by the incredible cornucopia of produce, both wild and cultivated, along Lake Michigan, Forgione asked the couple to send him foods for his restaurant. That led to preserving fruits to the chef's specifications. The offerings have grown to fruit butters, grilling and roasting sauces, native nut meats, and dozens of sweet and savory sauces.

The jellies are childhood tastes brought to life. There is wild elderberry for $7.50 and an intense grape for $4.95.

The preserves and marmalades are made with little or no pectin, and with whole fruits or chunks. They are intensely flavored, not overly sweet and soft. There are wonderful combinations like blueberry lime and gooseberry with cherries and oranges, and old favorites like sour cherry, strawberry-rhubarb, and damson plum. The strawberry preserves were judged the best in America in the book *Tastings: The Best from Ketchup to Caviar* by Jennifer Harvey

Lang. Preserves come in 9.5 and 10-ounce jars and vary in price from $4.95 to $7.95. A preserve made from the dwindling supply of wild scarlet thimbleberries is $14.95 and worth it.

American Spoon's no-sugar fruit preserves are called spoon fruits, and they are sweetened with concentrated fruit juices. The description in the catalog is apt: "like fruit spooned from inside a freshly baked pie." They come in 9-ounce jars in the following flavors: apricot, black cherry, black raspberry, blackberry, blueberry, boysenberry, peach, pineapple-orange, red raspberry, and sour cherry. The price is $4.75 to 5.95 per jar.

Mother Nature and simple human effort dictate the availability of the company's offerings. Drought, forest fires, early frosts, and the like can swell or deplete pickings. There are so many extraordinary items to select from that disappointment over a soldout item is fleeting. What wonderful gifts American Spoon items make! The graphics on the labels and the folk-art gift boxes are terrific. (A Fruitlands Box, for example, contains two preserves, a spoon fruit, a fruit butter, and three kinds of dried fruit for $39, plus shipping.) Or, order items packed in birch bark baskets made by an Upper Peninsula fisherman, Jim Tinker, and his sons, furthering the sense of place that American Spoon products impart.

We appreciate the unusual items, such as dried wild blueberries and cranberries (to use in place of raisins in baking), hickory nuts, smoked buffalo and pork sausage, and the salad dazzlers, designed to replace dressings or marinades. (They come in herb mustard, raspberry, chili, ginger, and curry flavors.)

And, American Spoon generously shares credit with other top-notch food producers across the United States, offering their wares in the catalog as well. There are so many choices, we recommend calling for a catalog, if for no other reason than to enjoy artist Kristin Hurlin's covers.

In short, American Spoon is an innovator, using food memories for inspiration.

ORDERING ADDRESS

American Spoon Foods, Inc.
1668 Clarion Avenue
P.O. Box 566
Petoskey, MI 49770
616/347-9030
800/222-5886
FAX: 800/647-2512
e-mail: information@spoon.com
www.spoon.com
Credit cards accepted

TELEPHONE ORDERS
Monday–Friday, 9 A.M.–5 P.M. (until 9 P.M. October 20–December 20)
Saturday, 10 A.M.–5 P.M.

VISITS
411 Lake Street
Petoskey, Michigan
Petoskey is about 40 miles northeast of Traverse City. Petoskey is a tourist town, and the store is in the restored gaslight district. The preserves are now made in a kitchen on the outskirts of town, the business having outgrown the Lake Street shop.
Monday–Saturday, 10 A.M.–5 P.M. Sunday (July 4–Labor Day only): 10 A.M.–5 P.M.

Other stores are at: 309 Bridge Street, Charlevoix, MI, tel.: 231/547-5222; 230 East Front Street, Traverse City, MI, tel.: 231/935-4480; Grand Traverse Resort, Traverse City, MI, tel.: 231/938-5358; 245 East Main Street, Harbor Springs, MI, tel.: 231/526-8628; and 308 Butler Street, Saugatuck, MI, tel.: 616/857-3084.

BAINBRIDGE'S APPLE PIE AND PARSLEY JELLIES

It's a firm, reddish brown jelly, so clear you can see the suspended flecks of cinnamon and other spices. The taste? The most patriotic imaginable—apple pie. It was created by Tom Bainbridge, who plied an unlikely combination of companies—insurance in Nashville and jelly in nearby White Bluff.

Twenty-one years ago, Bainbridge introduced a line of Southern-style jellies, none of them run-of-the-mill. The company is now owned by Bobbie Hood. It relocated to Tunica, Mississippi, where it produces Bainbridge's recipes, along with many new varieties. There are red and green pepper jellies, a garlic with parsley jelly, and a fig-strawberry preserve. Blackberry jelly and peach and strawberry preserves are a bit more conventional.

A black walnut topping stands out as one of a kind. Caramel colored, with a wealth of chopped nut meats inside, it is a pourable gel that is tart and sweet and presents an interesting combination of textures: both crunchy and slippery. Given that black walnut is a taste much in demand, this topping has numerous uses both on breads and ice cream.

The company now makes 13 different items, including pickles, preserves, spice tea mix, and a parsley mustard sauce, as well as jellies.

The company sends its unusual products by mail and allows customers to make their own selections. You may call or write for a brochure detailing all the possibilities. The products are between $5 and $6 per 8 to 10 ounce jar, plus shipping.

ORDERING ADDRESS
Bainbridge Festive Foods, Inc.
P.O. Box 305
Tunica, MS 38676
662/363-9891
800/545-9205
FAX: 662/363-9895
e-mail: bainbridge@tecinfo.com
Credit cards accepted

VISITS
1211 U.S. Highway 61 South
Tunica, MS
Tunica is south of Memphis, Tennessee, just east of the Mississippi River.
Monday–Friday, 8 A.M.–5 P.M.

C. S. STEEN PURE RIBBON CANE SYRUP

The sweet aroma of bubbling cane syrup announces your proximity to the factory in Abbeville, Louisiana, that Charles Sidney Steen, Sr., founded in 1910. Inside the tin building, employees use paddles to stir the sugarcane juice as it cooks in seven brass kettles. The process takes eight hours and nets a golden-brown syrup with a decided hint of blackstrap molasses. The thick syrup is a staple in cooking pecan pie, candied yams, and other Southern treasures.

The company president is Albert C. Steen, grandson of the owner, and the operations are run by Charlie Steen, his son. The firm's distinctive yellow-and-black cans are sold throughout the southern states. (The label states "Nothing added -nothing extracted.")

The company will ship a case of 4 of its 25-fluid ounce cans for $22.25, which includes shipping. A 4-pack of the 12-ounce cans is a bargain at $16, including shipping.

A recent addition is a cane vinegar, made from sugarcane juice. It's slightly sweet and used in marinades or in oil and vinegar salad dressings. Three 12-ounce bottles are $13, including shipping.

Those buying at the plant pay $2.25 for 12 ounces of syrup, $3.50 for 25 ounces of syrup, and $1.35 for a bottle of vinegar.

ORDERING ADDRESS
C. S. Steen Syrup Mill, Inc.
P.O. Box 339
Abbeville, LA 70510
337/893-1654
800/725-1654
FAX: 337/893-2478
e-mail: steens@tlxnet.net
www.steensyrup.com
Credit cards accepted

VISITS: Abbeville, a city of 12,000 people, is 50 miles north of the Gulf Coast in the middle of Louisiana. From the east, take I-10 west to I-67 south. Abbeville is the last city on I-67, and the road dead-ends there. Take a left and drive one block. Cross a bridge. At the first light, turn left onto Main Street. The syrup mill is at 119 North Main.
Monday–Friday, 7 a.m.–noon, 1 P.M.–4 p.m.

CALLAWAY GARDENS MUSCADINE SAUCE AND SPECKLED HEART GRITS

The muscadine grape was just a tough-skinned fruit Cason Callaway overproduced as part of his work with the Georgia Better Farms Program in the 1940s. Serendipitously, he substituted it for plums in his mother-in-law's spiced sauce recipe. The result was a tart mixture, fragrant with cloves, that has been bottled since 1952.

Callaway's farm is now a huge resort enterprise featuring an 800-room inn, vacation homes, three golf courses, and a man-made beach. It is operated by the Ida Cason Callaway Foundation, named after his mother, which was set up to encourage horticulture education.

Our interest is fixated on the sauce, which has remained unaltered by the commercial growth of Callaway Gardens. The Gardens also bottles a muscadine jelly and muscadine preserves, neither of which have the arresting flavor of the sauce. However, by mail order, they come as a trio: three 20-ounce jars for $16.95, plus shipping. At the Gardens store, the muscadine sauce is $5.45 for 20 ounces and $3.95 for a 10-ounce jar.

We're also grateful to the Callaway family for devoting attention to hominy grits, which most corn processors ignore because of the limited market. Their Speckled Heart Grits contain bits of the corn "heart" and are stoneground for the Gardens at the Adams Mill in Dothan, Alabama.

New York food writer Barbara Kafka, who once ran a food shop devoted to America's finest, counts the speckled grits among her personal favorites: "It's one of those products that's totally taken for granted in its area, and isn't known elsewhere," she said.

By mail, the Gardens sells three 2-pound bags of grits for $10.95, plus shipping. A bag also is sold in combination with a 2- to 3-pound slab of an excellent peppery bacon for $18.95, plus shipping. At the Gardens store, a 2-pound bag is $2.99.

ORDERING ADDRESS
Callaway Gardens Country Store
P.O. Box 2000
Pine Mountain, GA 31822-2000
800/280-7574
FAX: 706/663-5058
www.callawaygardens.com
Credit cards accepted

VISITS: The store and gardens are 35 miles north of Columbus, Georgia, on Highway 27. Watch for the green-and-white sign. If driving from Atlanta, it's a 75-mile trip. Take I-85 south and then a left onto Highway 27 to Pine Mountain.
Every day, 9 A.M.–6 P.M. (later hours during summer)

CENTENNIAL FARMS APPLE BUTTERS.

For most farmers these days, diversification means raising both livestock and crops. One hundred years ago, it meant growing just about everything that would thrive on your land. Centennial Farms embraces the historic view of diversification. Growing grapes, vegetables, and apples; running a pumpkin patch; pressing cider; raising mums; operating a U-pick fruit business; and giving school tours of the farm at harvest take up most of the growing season. The winter is spent putting up apple butter and preserves, which are sold by mail and at the farm's market.

Centennial Farms has been in the Knoernschild family for nearly 150 years. Bob Knoernschild, the great-grandson of the Bavarian immigrant who began the operation, has used his love of plants to expand from selling strawberries on the side while working full time as a biology teacher to running a year-round farming venture. His wife, Ellen, makes apple butter and preserves, and handles sales.

Knoernschild, who has a bachelor's and a master's degree in horticulture, grows Jonathans, Golden Delicious, Rome Beauties, and 22 other apple varieties in his orchard, and uses all of them in his apple butters. A mechanical stirring gadget allows the hot mixture to be kept moving continually for 12 hours in a 50-gallon copper kettle. "You cannot hurry apple butter," said Bob. "We use fresh apples, and no artificial coloring or flavoring."

There are four varieties: old-fashioned (sugar and cinnamon added), sugarless, anise-flavored, and honey. All four are worthy of attention. The anise is a pleasant twist, with apple, not licorice, kept as the dominant flavor. The honey and old-fashioned have lovely flavor, but the real standout is the sugarless. You could fool almost anyone into believing it had sugar added.

A case of 12 pints of the old-fashioned, anise, and no sugar butters is $32. A case of half-pints is $19.45. The honey variety is $34 per case of pints; $ 20.45 for half-pints. Shipping is extra. A case of 12 pints is about 25 pounds. The half-pints weight about 15 pounds. There's a $2 handling and packing charge per case. Missouri residents need to add sales tax. The farm's preserves are sold only at the market.

ORDERING ADDRESS
Centennial Farms
199 Jackson Street
Augusta, MO 63332
636/228-4338
Credit cards accepted

VISITS: Augusta is in eastern Missouri, about 30 miles west of St. Louis. From Highway 94, take the west Augusta exit. The farm, and its seasonal market, is on the same road right in the town of Augusta.
July–October: Monday–Saturday, 10 A.M.–5 P.M. Sunday, Noon–5 P.M.

CORTI BROTHERS CAPITAL VINTAGE MARMALADE AND MINCEMEAT

In the 1930s and 1940s, well-established Sacramento families planted Seville orange trees along city streets near the state capitol because they thought the blossoms would be aromatic. If Washington could have its cherry blossoms, why not orange blossoms in Sacramento?

Their well-intentioned plan went awry when fruit replaced the blossoms. The Seville orange, studded with seeds and quite bitter, makes for terrible eating. Considered useless, the oranges would drop on the ground, where they would rot, smell, and generally litter the streets of Sacramento.

Darrell Corti, one of the owners of the city's Corti Brothers market, famed for its wide selection of wines and high-quality produce, hated to see the oranges go to waste and so, nine years ago, made a marmalade using the oranges. The recipe, adapted from one in Isabella Beeton's historic cookbook, calls for equal parts of sugar to oranges and, instead of pectin, uses the boiled seeds as a thickening agent. "A Capital Vintage Marmalade" Corti called it, and Sacramento artist Laura Jane Coats designed a full-color label that depicts the California capitol peeking between two Seville orange trees.

Actually, oranges are not picked from the capitol grounds. State law forbids that. But Corti has permission from the city's parks department to pick nearby oranges, despite an early warning from the parks superintendent that the oranges "are so astringent that nobody will want to bother with them." The oranges are picked each winter in a five- or six-block area near the capitol, and the resulting marmalade is aged a minimum of one year, and often up to three years. Marmalade improves as the pulp and peel mellow. A 10-ounce jar is $4.99, not including shipping. A case of 12 is $59. Fans are so enamored of the marmalade some even write limericks to its makers.

CORTI BROTHERS

It is tangy, but definitely not astringent, and makes a fine glaze for fatty meats such as ham or duck. Mixed with bouillon and sherry, the marmalade becomes an orange sauce. It is available at the Corti Brothers store in Sacramento, and, like most of the special items sold there, it can be obtained by mail order.

Another of Corti's superlative products cannot be shipped, but if you are in Sacramento, you shouldn't miss buying it. That item is mincemeat, which is aged one year before it is sold. Corti discovered a mincemeat recipe in an 1825 English cookbook and began producing it in bulk for sale at the markets. Steeped in sherry, brandy, and hard cider, the mixture includes beef suet, oranges, lemons, citron, raisins, and currants.

Always innovating, the Corti market carries unusual olive oils, pastas, jams, pickles, relishes, Greek wines, and salts.

Perhaps the most endearing contribution Corti Brothers makes to the well-being of wine drinkers and eaters everywhere is its quarterly newsletter. Simply printed, usually four pages, it is like a short course in interesting wines, olive oils, and other foodstuffs, many of them unique to Corti Brothers. Darrell Corti gives his observations about the wine or oil and tells a bit about its history, its producer, or maybe something about the way it is made. The descriptions are so intriguing that a reader wants to order everything.

Happily, he or she can. Corti Brothers will send wines and olive oils by the bottle or case, giving all of us access to the special vintages it offers. One issue of the newsletter, for example, offered Tuscan olive oil from Barone Ricasoli, black olive paste and dried-tomato paste from a producer on the Riviera, pasta from eastern Italy that had not before been imported to the United States, a dark black-red Italian wine that was available only from Corti, and three California Chardonnays from small producers. More treasures include French chocolates, oil and olives from Galilee, canned tuna, premium dried mushrooms, and old Spanish sherries.

We recommend that anyone interested in such treats ask to be put on the mailing list.

ORDERING ADDRESS
Corti Brothers
P.O. Box 191358
Sacramento, CA 95819
916/736-3800
800/509-FOOD (3663)
FAX: 916/736-3807
Credit cards accepted

VISITS
5810 Folsom Boulevard
Sacramento, CA
This business is near the junction of I-80 and Highway 50.
Monday–Saturday, 9 A.M.–7 P.M. Sunday, 10 A.M.–6 P.M.

ESPER PRODUCTS DELUXE JELLIES AND PRESERVES

Maybe it's the long history of tourism. Maybe it's the flights of fancy that gave rise to such stylish excesses as Opa Locka or alligator wrestling. For whatever reason, Florida has often been synonymous with bad food souvenirs. While there are dozens of reputable companies selling good fresh citrus, experienced travelers avoid the processed edibles—the ubiquitous coconut patties and the petrified sugared orange slices.

But there are a few companies that turn Florida's extraordinary tropical fruits into worthy processed items. One is Esper Products Deluxe, which has been making jellies, preserves, marmalades, and conserves in Kissimmee, which is in central Florida, just south of Orlando, since 1937. The McFarlane family—Susanne, her son, Andy, and his wife, Colleen—have been running the business for the last 50 years.

When the late Duncan McFarlane and his wife, Susanne, bought the company, it had a repertoire of about 40 flavors. Now, the jelly factory makes about 63 flavors, many not produced anywhere else in the country. There are jellies (made with just the juice of a fruit), preserves (made with the whole fruit), conserves (a combination of whole fruit with nuts), and marmalade (a citrus-fruit spread that includes peel).

There's an unusual ambrosia, with oranges, grapefruit, cherries, coconut, and dried bananas. There's guava jelly, mango chutney, and calamondin marmalade. The calamondin is a tart fruit grown in Florida that makes a deep-orange marmalade. A bright-red pineapple-cinnamon conserve, which owes its color to a bottle, not nature, tastes exactly like liquid red-hots. A thin layer of Esper's pina-colada conserve would be a wonderful filling for a tart or sponge cake.

Our only quibble is that the spreads are on the sweet side. The tangerine butter we sampled was simply sweet, not fruity. The problem might be one encountered by several longstanding companies. By adhering strictly to recipes developed decades ago, the amount of sugar hasn't kept pace with Americans' more recent preference for less sweet sweets. For proof, try any pre-1960 recipe. The sugar can usually be cut down substantially, and many cookbooks are being revised to reflect that.

However, the Esper spreads win our approval for quality, originality, and an honest reflection of Florida's treasures. The jellies and preserves come in homey pot-bellied 8-ounce glass jars. Gift packs range from $9.95 to $20.55, postpaid. Jellies average about $2.50 a jar, and range in price from 75¢ to $4.50. Jelly gift packs are sold from $9.95, including shipping, to $42.75. Visitors to the Orlando area often like to buy the jellies directly at the factory, where they can watch the employees at work through a window.

ORDERING ADDRESS
Esper Products DeLuxe, Inc.
2793 North Orange Blossom Trail
Kissimmee, FL 32741
407/847-3726
800/268-0892
e-mail: colleen1014@webtv.com
Credit cards accepted

VISITS: Kissimmee is about 17 miles south of Orlando and about 10 miles east of Disney World. Go east on Highway 192 to Highway 1792, which is also known as Highway 441 and the South Orange Blossom Trail. Go north on 1792 about 2 miles, and the store will be on the right side.
Monday–Friday, 9 A.M.–4:30 P.M.

EVA GATES PRESERVES

Cary Siess runs the company started by her great-grandmother, Eva Gates, an inspired Northwest cook whose recipes are made daily by a fourth generation of family jam makers.

Cary's mother, Pamela Gates Siess, first sent us newspaper clippings about the company that date back to 1955, six years after Eva began making preserves on a wood range in a log cabin. The first article shows Eva, in apron, filling jars five pints at a time. Incredibly, the business still makes its products in batches of the same size. The recipe is well over 100 years old—it belonged to Eva's grandmother—and the preserves and syrups are still made in five-pint batches. The article in the July 1958 issue of the *Kalispell News-Farm Journal* had another great photograph. This showed Eva's husband, George, leaning out the window of a 1956 Ford station wagon with "Eva Gates Home Made Preserves" written on the door of the driver's side.

Until 1979, the cookhouse was the two-room log cabin next to the Gates's home. Then it was moved to Bigfork, a town so small that some customers simply write "downtown Bigfork" on letters. Visitors are welcome to watch and visit with the cooks daily.

The company's first product, strawberry preserves, is still a favorite. If you like whole berries in your preserves and a sweet strawberry flavor, this is for you.

The company's most popular product is its wild huckleberry preserves, and they are superior. We tasted it with a jar from Oregon, and were amazed at how different two huckleberry preserves could be. The Oregon berries were dry, with many stems attached, and simply swam in a sweet syrup. Eva Gates preserves, however, feature soft, but intact, berries that are suspended in a thick preserve. One reason might be the addition of butter to

the recipe. Butter is also an ingredient in the black cap preserves, a similar preserve with a chewier berry. Both are a rich deep purple, and are a welcome change on a morning bagel.

Eva turned the business over to her daughter-in-law, Maxine, who retired, passing the stewardship on to Pamela. At her death, Cary took over, producing a daily legacy to the talented women cooks in her family.

Like the size of its batches, the company keeps its product list down to a manageable size. In addition to the aforementioned preserves, there are cherry, raspberry, and spiced-apple varieties. There are three fruit syrups—wild huckleberry, wild chokecherry, and black cap.

A sampler of all six preserve varieties is $29.90 for 6-ounce jars or $43 for 10-ounce jars. Six 16-ounce jars are available for $56.60. Three 12-ounce bottles of syrup are $32.90. Numerous combination packages are available. All prices include shipping within the United States. The company regularly sends its preserves overseas, so an order to Madagascar won't send it into a panic.

ORDERING ADDRESS
Eva Gates Homemade Preserves
P.O. Box 696
Bigfork, MT 59911
406/837-4356
800/682-4283
FAX: 406/837-4376
e-mail: evagates@digisys.net
Credit cards accepted

VISITS
456 Electric Avenue
Bigfork, MT
The village of Bigfork, a very small town in western Montana, is near Kalispell, in the Flathead region. Turn off Highway 35 toward Bigfork and look for the shop in the small downtown.
Daily: 9 A.M.–5 P.M. Also evening hours daily mid-June–August.

GLORIA SAMPLE PRESERVES

The last thing we need in this book, one of us growled to the other over the phone, is yet another jam and preserve company. Yet we had to include Gloria Sample's preserves. Her combinations are so well balanced; the products are unusual and delicious, and the packaging is dainty and pretty. If there are any preserves that are tailored for gift-giving, they are hers.

Take the Mt. Hood marionberry preserves. They are flavored with apricot brandy, a fortuitous meeting. Apricot marmalade (called Oregon Gold) includes oranges and pineapple but has not a hint of bitterness. Her blueberry marmalade (Oregon Blue) is equally as toothsome. One of her secrets, said Gloria, is that she and her employees hand-slice the fruit for the marmalades. "We don't get any bitter parts in there." The preserves and marmalades come in 8-ounce jars and are $5 each.

No-sugar fruit spreads, sweetened with white grape juice, include raspberry, blueberry, marionberry, tart cherry, rhubarb, gooseberry/apricot, and strawberry. Intense and brilliantly colored, they come in 10- to 12-ounce jars at $5 to $6 each.

Cranberry-walnut conserve, with oranges, raisins, and brandy, doesn't hit you over the head with the alcohol—a common mistake. "Add a bit to nonfat yogurt, and it makes you feel wonderful!" exclaimed Gloria.

She makes three multi-ingredient "catsups" designed to be basted on meats, spread on sandwiches, and used in egg dishes. She also makes a no-oil catsup, salad dressings, and salsas.

There's a traditional brandy-soaked fruitcake that is notable for its sumptuous packaging. A 1-pound cake is beautifully packaged in a gold-foil box with green tissue inside and green ribbon outside, for $14.50.

Gloria, who started in business 14 years ago, gets our vote as a one-woman marketing dynamo. She has placed her products in any number of high-end stores and catalogs and has been in the forefront of getting her items shown to global buyers. Thanks to help from WUSATA, the Western United States Agricultural Trade Association, her products are being shipped to Australia now.

Closer to home, mail-order customers in the United States should add shipping and handling costs to their orders. There are several gift pack combinations.

ORDERING ADDRESS
Gloria Sample & Company
425 2nd Street Alley
Lake Oswego, OR 97034
503/636-3520
800/782-5881
FAX: 503/636-8582
e-mail: glosample@teleport.com
www.gloriasgourmet.com
Credit cards accepted

GREEN BRIAR'S SUN-COOKED PLUM JAM

It seems fitting that mischievous Peter Rabbit, and his nemesis, Old Farmer Brown, have been immortalized by a jam kitchen in Sandwich, Massachusetts, that converts good things from the garden into even better treats. This happy mix of literature and food occurs because the kitchen is owned by the Thornton Burgess Society, a nonprofit environmental education association named after the nature writer and author of the American version of Peter Rabbit. The kitchen also is notable for having preserved the decades-old process of sun-cooking jams.

Burgess was born in the Cape Cod town of Sandwich and grew to know the woods well as a messenger boy for a mail-order pond-lily business. He later used the settings for animal characters in his son's bedtime stories. Publication of these tales made famous such places as the Old Briar Patch, Smiling Pool, and Crooked Little Path. Burgess patronized the jam kitchen in later years, taking great pleasure in its wares.

Now in its 97th year, the kitchen's recipes and equipment are the same as when Ida Putnam, its founder, installed a 20-foot sun cooker along its south wall. As the *New England Farm Bulletin* claims, the kitchen uses one of the oldest commercial solar food-preparation devices in the nation.

To sun-cook the jams (plum, blueberry, strawberry, peach, and apricot), the fruits are heated lightly in a sugar syrup on the stove, then spooned into wide enamel pans that sit on wooden slats underneath a sloped glass cover. The sun cooking, which can be done only in June, July, and August, takes two to three days. The result is a perfectly preserved whole fruit in a thick syrup. The exterior of the fruit is slightly tough, but the interior remains plump and flavorful. The jars are beautiful, with their perfectly formed fruits nestled together. "Jam" is a misnomer: The sun-cooked berries are best used as toppings for cheesecake, ice cream, or cakes because of the syrup base.

The kitchen also uses conventional, old-fashioned cooking methods (with no preservatives) to produce cranberry conserves, quince jelly, other spreads, pickles, and relishes. Its marmalade offerings are varied—carrot, grapefruit with cherries, and lemon-lime, among others. All are $3.95 per 8-ounce jar. All proceeds from the kitchen are used to maintain its adjacent nature center, which sponsors walks, lectures, and excursions. The kitchen also offers jam-making classes, but only for the conventionally cooked varieties.

The sun-cooked fruits are $4.95 per 8-ounce jar, plus shipping.

ORDERING ADDRESS
Green Briar Jam Kitchen
6 Discovery Hill Road
East Sandwich, MA 02537
508/888-6870
e-mail: tburgess@capecod.net
www.thorntonburgess.org
Credit cards accepted

VISITS: East Sandwich is 59 miles south of Boston, on Cape Cod. From Boston take the Southeast Expressway, which becomes Route 3. Cross the Sagamore Bridge to Cape Cod and take the first exit, which takes you to Route 6A. The kitchen is about 5 miles east on Route 6A. Watch for its small green sign at Discovery Hill Road. Take a right at that point and look for the farm kitchen, which is the first building on the right at the end of a long driveway.

Mid-April–December 24: Monday–Saturday, 10 A.M.–4 P.M. Sunday, 1 P.M.–4 P.M.

HALLAM'S NATURAL PEANUT BUTTER

Scan the fine print of the ingredients list on most jars of peanut butter and you'll be in for a rude shock. In addition to peanuts, you'll find that salt, sugar, and dextrose (another sugar) have been added, as well as partially hydrogenated vegetable oil, a stabilizer. Compare that to the label of Hallam's Peanut Butter, a Missouri favorite for nearly 70 years. The label states: "Ingredient: Peanuts."

Unlike some all-natural peanut butters we've tried at health-food stores, Hallam's has an excellent, nongrainy texture and is not visibly oily. Bob Zoppelt, the company president, says that any natural peanut butter will separate if it sits for several months, but Hallam's doesn't seem to require a daily stirring, as some health-food-store versions seem to. The peanut butter is also softer than the national brands, due to the absence of stabilizers, which makes it possible to spread it effortlessly right after taking it from the refrigerator. The taste is pure peanuts and is excellent.

Hallam's was begun in Springfield, Missouri, and stayed in the Hallam family until 1978, when it was run by the founder's grandson. The firm, which was called Sesame Snacks, Inc. (to reflect its other produce line), was experiencing financial difficulties then, and was purchased from a bank by Zoppelt, who moved it to Missouri and changed the company's name back to Hallam's. The company now sells raw honey, pure sorghum, and a green tomato relish.

The peanut butter recipe and methods have remained the same, and today it is being enjoyed by growing numbers of people outside the state. In addition to Missouri, it is now available in the Denver, Omaha, Memphis, and Oklahoma City areas. If you live elsewhere, the company will ship cases of the peanut butter, which comes in smooth or crunchy. A case of twelve 16-ounce jars is a bargain $22.80, plus shipping. Individual jars are $1.90. The honey is $3.20 for 22-ounces and a metal can of the sorghum is $2.67 per pint.

ORDERING ADDRESS
Hallam's Inc.
1207 North 9th Avenue
Ozark, MO 65721
417/581-3786
FAX: 417/581-3786
e-mail: RZKZozark@cs.com
No credit cards

HOMEMADE BY DOROTHY'S WILD BERRY JELLIES

We encountered Dorothy's Wild Berry Jellies on a trip to Boise and were intrigued by the unusual fruits she used for her jellies and syrups. We bought wild Saskatoon jelly, wild elderberry syrup, wild chokecherry syrup, huckleberry-apple jelly, and wild currant jelly, and felt bad about passing up the other possibilities.

So we wrote Dorothy Baumhoff and asked her about her company. She wrote back: "Using my knowledge of wild edible plants has helped me create unusual types of jellies, syrups, and now a new line of ice-cream toppings." And she included a product list, with no fewer than 42 out-of-the-ordinary offerings. Have you been longing for the taste of wild crab apple? Saskatoon berry? Wild red plum? Chokecherry? Quince? Dorothy's Wild Berry Jellies is the source for them all.

She founded a bona fide family business that is continuing to grow in the years following her death. Her daughters, Anna and Cini, work full time at the concern, with help from their father, Oscar, their uncle Wally, and sister Ginger Williston. The firm is now in its 16th year, with four to six employees, depending on season.

They've kept all of Dorothy's recipes in production and have added pumpkin butter (made only in September and sold through Christmas), sourdough pancake mix, scone mix, an Idaho potato pancake mix, gingerbread cake mix, and a corn muffin mix. They sell their very good huckleberry syrup with the sourdough mix, for an unusual breakfast gift package.

The jellies, preserves, and syrups are put up in clear glass jars that show off their jewel-colored tones. One of the most popular kinds—and one of our favorites—is huckleberry-apple. Huckleberries are hard to find, but the search is worthwhile. The deep-red jelly is flecked with bits of berry, and the addition of apple juice cuts its sweetness. It tastes a bit like a sweet cranberry.

Another big seller is wild black raspberry. Without the seeds or fruit to distract you, it's possible to experience the full flavor of the purple-black berry. (They also offers wild blackberry jelly, which is lighter in color and flavor.) Chokecherry, with its full perfume and a taste of sweetened pie cherries, is another favorite with customers.

The lessons learned in growing this business have been passed on to other small producers, as Anna served as an officer with the Idaho Specialty Foods Association for four years and Cini is now in her second year as its treasurer. Anna has been able to combine parenting with the family business, and now she and her husband and sons Grant and Spencer live next door to the kitchen, which is in her mother's old house. "I just walk next door to work each morning," she told us. "It's wonderful."

The company's mint-apple jelly is much preferred over the toothpaste-flavored versions found in supermarkets. It has a much more subtle mint flavor, although it too is colored bright green. The mint comes from nearby growers in Boise's Treasure Valley.

We remember our mother and grandmother making jelly, squeezing cheesecloth bags that hung from upper kitchen cabinets (and dying their hands purple in the process!). Many older people have memories of these jelly treats, and we bet that a sampler pack from Dorothy's would make a most welcome gift.

A small jar of huckleberry jam or jelly is $3.75 for 4 ounces. Thirteen varieties of fruit syrups are $4.75 for 8.5-ounce bottles. There are no-sugar fruit spreads and syrups from $3.50 to $6.50. Shipping is extra.

The fruit butters and jellies are a bargain at $2.75 for 4 ounces. The gift boxes also are a good deal at $19.99, plus shipping. The Huckleberry Breakfast box, for example, includes jam, syrup, sourdough mix, and Idaho coffee mug and your choice of coffee, tea, or cocoa mix.

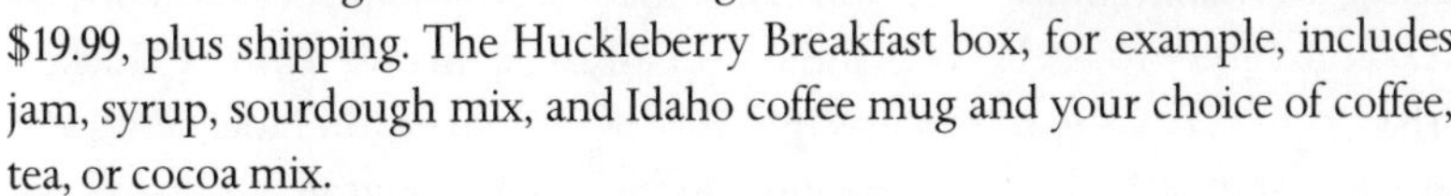

Idaho is a state with an active group of small food entrepreneurs, and they receive more than token platitudes from the state's department of agriculture. (Other states, take note.) Kelly Olson, a marketing specialist with the state, speedily sent us a master list of the state's specialty food makers, a brochure from a state-sponsored marketing conference, and other details of state help for small food companies.

Dorothy's products are available in a cooperative gift shop, the Boise Co-op, 888 W. Fort Street, as well as the Swiss Village Cheese Factory in Nampa, and the Made in Idaho stores in Boise, Twin Falls, and Idaho Falls.

ORDERING ADDRESS
Homemade by Dorothy
5150 Montecito Place
Boise, ID 83704
208/375-3720
800/657-7449
FAX: 208/322-7645
e-mail: dorothys@micron.net
www.dorothys.cc
Credit cards accepted

VISITS
Monday–Friday. Call ahead for hours.

HUCKLEBERRY PATCH WILD BERRY JELLIES

Hungry Horse, Montana, is surrounded by approximately 4 million acres of land in the public domain: Great Bear Wilderness, Bob Marshall Wilderness, Glacier National Park, and others. Wild berries proliferate on these acres and if humans can get to them before the bears do, they are free to pick them.

The Huckleberry Patch is the reincarnation of the four-decades-old Willows Honeyberry Farm, whose owner, Jim Willows, retired in 1987 and moved to California. The operation is now run by John Petrone and Jackie Watkins, who still use most The Huckleberry Patch of the Willows' recipes and follow the practice of buying berries from pickers and turning them into jellies, syrups, fruit butters, pie fillings, and jams.

The business bought thousands of gallons of berries last year, which means there is no shortage of huckleberries for the fruitcakes, bread, hotcakes, ice cream, milkshakes, and candy made from them at the restaurant. Naturally, the huckleberry is the star of all the fruits used at the Huckleberry Patch. The small, deep-purple berries look like wild blueberries and are similar in taste. They make a soft and spoonable preserve. The firm's no-sugar huckleberry preserves, as well as a variety made with honey, are the latest popular uses of the berry.

A restaurant near the west entrance to Glacier Park is part of the Huckleberry Patch. A tasting bar inside allows customers to sample the collection of jellies and preserves, some of which may be unfamiliar. (Not everyone has grown up with rose-hip butter, chokecherry jelly, wild buffalo-berry jam, wild blackcap preserves, or wild Saskatoon-berry jelly.)

There is also a notable crabapple butter, a very thick, spicy brown puree that brings to mind tart apple butter. Rose-hip butter is similar, but darker and thinner. Blackcap preserves, one of the rarer varieties, has seeds and a taste a bit like elderberry. It makes a very thick preserve.

The company is happy to send by mail. There are a variety of different berries (huckleberry, chokecherry, elderberry, buffalo berry, and blackcap), fruits, and huckleberry and Montana-made honey. You can create your own arrangement by choosing any four 8-ounce jars of jelly, syrup, jam, or preserves for $22, plus shipping. The honeys are $5.50 each for two 8-ounce jar, of $9.95 for a 16-ounce bottle, including shipping.

ORDERING ADDRESS
The Huckleberry Patch
Highway 2
Hungry Horse, MT 59919
406/387-5000 or -5670
800/527-7340
FAX: 406/387-4444
e-mail: huckpatch@cyberport.net
Credit cards accepted

VISITS: The Huckleberry Patch is 10 miles west of West Glacier Park, in northwest Montana, right on Highway 2.
Every day, 9 A.M.–5 P.M.

TELEPHONE ORDERS: Every day, 7 A.M.–9 P.M.

KOZLOWSKI FARMS NO-SUGAR JAMS

Kozlowski Farms is an American success story. It is a post–World War II venture that drew on the hard work of Tony Kozlowski, fresh from military service, and that of his bride, Carmen Lorenzo, and her parents, Florencio and Julia Lorenzo, Spanish immigrants from the Costa del Sol. With the help of her parents, Tony and Carmen began growing cherries, apples, and berries in 1947 in the loam soils of west Sonoma County. An overproduction of apples and consumer demand for red raspberries prompted Tony to plant 15 acres of raspberries in 1968, which in turn encouraged Carmen and her mother to create jams, jellies, and fruit butters for their farm store.

The close-knit family overcame the 1982 tragedy of Tony's death in a plane crash while on a blueberry-buying trip. The Kozlowski children, Carol, Perry, and Cindy, all work in the business. "Dad kept us all here when we were growing up," explained Carol Kozlowski Every. "He wanted his business to expand with his family. Now, whenever something good happens in the business, we realize it is because of him and we thank him."

The farm, located in wine-producing Sonoma County, includes 50 acres of apples and 15 acres of berries (raspberries, strawberries, blackberries, boysenberries, blueberries, loganberries, and olallieberries), all overseen by son Perry Kozlowski. The produce is sold at a colorful stand that is open year-round and features homemade juices (apple-blackberry, apple-raspberry), berry vinegars, raspberry ice cream, wine jellies (made from real wine, not grape juice), condiments, and a most appealing line of regular and no-sugar jams and 100 percent fruit spreads.

It took Carmen Kozlowski years to perfect the family's no-sugar varieties, and she experimented with honey before developing a mixture of dried apples, cider, fruit, pectin, and citric acid that successfully mimicked a sugar-sweetened jam. The jams are remarkably good—sweet, thick, and fruity. The no-sugar apple butter is more flavorful than most made with sugar.

All of the farm's jams are made without artificial colors, flavors, or preservatives and are made one batch at a time. Health concerns are relected in the offerings—there are also fat and oil-free salad dressings and no-salt mustards.

No-sugar conserves include black raspberry, blackberry, blueberry, boysenberry, red raspberry, strawberry, apricot, Bing cherry, peach, and kiwi. Sugared jams include all of those flavors, plus a sweet cider jelly and seedless blackberry and seedless red raspberry jam. No-sugar-added butters include apple, plum, and pear. They also sell no-sugar added apple, peach, and tomato chutneys.

Surprisngly for a company so closely identified with fruit, one of Kozlowski Farms' best-selling items of the 60 different products it makes is tangy mustard, called Old Uncle Cal's. A red raspberry vinegar and the fruit-sweetened apple butter also are big sellers. For sugar fans, there's also a wonderful raspberry dark fudge sauce.

The products are shipped in a minimum package of four 10-ounce jars. Four jars of all the products are $20.75, except for the fudge sauce, which is $24.75. Shipping is extra.

At the farm, there is a tasting table where customers may try all their products. There's also a deli, espresso bar, and fresh baked goods for sale.

ORDERING ADDRESS
Kozlowski Farms
5566 Gravenstein Highway North
Forestville, CA 95436
707/887-1587
800/4-R-FARMS (473-2767)
FAX: 707/887-9650
e-mail: koz@kozlowskifarms.com
www.kozlowskifarms.com
Credit cards accepted

VISITS: Forestville is slightly west of Santa Rosa and is about an hour and a half north of San Francisco. The fruit stand is 1 mile south of Forestville on Highway 116. There are signs on the highway to direct you.
Every day, 9 A.M.–5 P.M.

LANEY FAMILY NUTS AND HONEY

Most honey sold today is blended honey, an amalgamation of many honeys that is heated to high temperatures to extend the shelf life. It is first and foremost a standardized product, lacking the nuances and evocative flavors of "source-flavored" honey—that is, honey made from nectar collected from particular wildflowers or tree blossoms.

It's a lot more work for beekeepers to locate bee colonies in particular areas to capture certain blooms and flavors. More work, but well worth it to eaters.

Dave and Kay Laney and their daughter, Linda, have spent nearly two decades pleasing honey-lovers with their "source-flavored" honeys from their 32-acre farm in North Liberty, Indiana, not far from the Michigan border. The Laneys keep about 100 bee colonies on nearby wildflower fields and pastures, and buy honey from other beekeepers who pay attention to what their bees eat.

In their manufacturing plant on the farm, the family bottles several Midwestern honeys, including cranberry blossom (from Wisconsin cranberry bogs), basswood (from the blossom of linden trees), blueberry blossom, clover, buckwheat, Michigan star thistle, spring blossom, wildflower, and autumn wildflower. The company also sells orange blossom honey, which it buys from Michigan beekeepers who take their hives to Florida orange groves for the winter. The Laneys are always experimenting with new habitats and flavors, and recently bottled small amounts of a honey from bees that fed on native plants in a prairie restoration project.

There is a real difference in taste among the honeys. Autumn wildflower and buckwheat are dark and strong-flavored; blueberry blossom has spicy overtones, and clover is light and mild. The Laneys make it easy to buy an assortment of flavors, so you can experience the range of blossom-flavored honeys in their line.

The family's most unique products, however, are its half-pint jars of honey and whole nutmeats. These toppings are made for ice cream, pancakes, hot cereals, toast, or pound cake—or eaten right from the jar. There is honey with Georgia pecans, honey with Indiana black walnuts, and honey mixed with cinnamon poured over whole almonds. The Laneys report that some customers spread the nut toppings over coffeecake batter to produce a glazed nut topping.

The jars themselves are pretty, with the nutmeats suspended in the amber honey. And the taste is something to buzz about. The preserved nuts maintain their crunch, and the combination of crunchy and smooth textures is an inspired one.

Any combination of three 9-ounce jars of nuts and honey is $18, plus $6.50 shipping to any one address in the continental United States. Small plastic squeeze jars of the varietal honeys, 6.5 ounces each and perfect for table use, sell for 6 flavors for $14.50, plus shipping. What a sweet and charming gift that makes, allowing you to present an array of honeys at the breakfast table.

The Laneys also sell comb honey, shaped in rings about 5 inches in diameter. Unlike honeycomb squares that drip where the edges have been cut, the edges of the rings are sealed with wax by the bees in the hive, making for a neat package. They sell for $5 each, plus shipping. Comb honey freezes well, so it makes sense to buy enough to make the shipping charge worthwhile.

ORDERING ADDRESS
Laney Family Honey Company, Inc.
25725 New Road
North Liberty, IN 46554
219/656-8701
FAX: 219/656-8603
www. laneyhoney.com
Credit cards accepted

MANZANITA RANCH OLALLIEBERRY PRESERVES

The olallieberry, a cross between the red and the black raspberry, is grown on the fruit farms of California and rarely is seen outside the state. Dark purple in color, the berry grows on a small, scrubby bush and is slightly sour.

Although best known for its apples and apple cider, the Manzanita ("Little Apple") Ranch offers such regional specialties as a delicious blood-orange marmalade, pomegranate jelly, and olallieberry preserves. More than 50 varieties are produced.

The tart, whole-berry preserve was devised by the late Franklin Barnes and his wife, Alice, founders of the ranch. The business is now run by their son, Woody, and his daughter, Jo.

The ranch will send you a list of its preserves prices; handling and shipping charges are extra.

ORDERING ADDRESS
Manzanita Ranch
P.O. Box 250
Julian, CA 92036
769/765-0102
FAX: 769-765-2085
Credit cards accepted

VISITS
4470 Highway 78
Julian, CA 92036
The town is 60 miles east of San Diego. The ranch is 4 miles west of Julian on Route 78. Watch for the green-and-white sign on the right.
Every day, 10 A.M.–5 P.M. (Closed December 25)

MAURY ISLAND FARM RED CURRANT JELLY

For 18 years, Pete and Jude Shepherd have been farming on Maury Island, Washington, raising sheep and cattle. To protect their grazing land, they bought several acres of red currant berries and then began cooking the juicy native berries into a jelly. The jelly found favor with a chef in Seattle, a 20-minute boat ride away, and a cottage industry was born.

Lieutenant William Maury was an American naval officer in the Wilkes Expedition, a 19th-century exploration that charted the islands in Puget

Sound. To honor him, the Shepherds gave their jelly his name, an apt designation since the wild red currants have been a part of the island's agriculture from its beginning.

"The berries like our clay soil," said Pete Shepherd. He and his wife have kept the tangy taste of the currant intact by using less sugar than conventional recipes for the jelly. It has a tart flavor that is pure currant; the berry juice is used undiluted. The couple and their three children also bottle and ship pure red currant juice for use by home cooks in preparing sherbets or ices, as well as many other flavors of jam, jelly, and marmalade.

The company is a terrific source for unusual flavors, such marionberry. All its products are cooked open-kettle in small batches. Six whole-fruit toppings—raspberry, blackberry, apricot, marionberry, tart cherry, and boysenberry—are winning new converts to the farm's quality.

The Shepherds ship two 11-ounce jars of the dark red jelly for $13.95, plus shipping. For those who take the car ferry to their store, the price is $4.85 per jar. Three jars of the fruit toppings are $17.95, plus shipping. In the store they are $4.25 each. Customers are encouraged to call for a free catalog.

ORDERING ADDRESS

The Maury Island Farming Company
Box L
Vashon Island, WA 98070
800/356-5880
FAX: 206/463-6868
www.goodjam.com
Credit cards accepted

VISITS

20317 Vashon Highway SW
Vashon Island, WA
Vashon Island is a 20-minute boat ride from the west ferry terminal in Seattle. After disembarking, drive for 15 minutes south on Vashon Island Highway to Valley Center. The shop is at the intersection of Vashon Island Highway and S.W. 204th Avenue, across the street from the Sound Food Company restaurant. The farm itself is on Maury Island, which is connected to Vashon Island.
Monday–Saturday, 10 A.M.–5 P.M. Sunday, 11 A.M.–5 P.M.

THE MAYHAW TREE MAYHAW JELLY

Chances are, unless you hail from Georgia, you've never tasted mayhaw jelly. Even if you do hail from Georgia, chances are you've never tasted it. The wild mayhaw (pronounced *ma*-hau) is a tart red berry that grows in the swamps and bogs of southwest Georgia and in parts of Louisiana, Mississippi, Texas, and South Carolina. It's actually a member of the rose family, along with hawthornes and apples, and not technically a berry, but it resembles a cranberry. It has a fleeting season for a few weeks in May and is difficult to pick. The fruit itself is extremely tart and not very meaty, so you didn't exactly have people lining up to gather mayhaws. Until 16 years ago, if you didn't know a home cook from the area who had put some up, you couldn't find mayhaw jelly or syrup.

Then, four women in Colquitt, concerned about the area's declining economy, decided to capitalize on Miller County's unique and underappreciated wild resource. They started The Mayhaw Tree, a jelly and condiment business, to provide a few jobs and bring attention to the area. The business is now part of Hillside Orchard Farms in Tiger, Georgia. It has its own small plant, provides paychecks for full-time employees, and pays cash to a small army of local mayhaw pickers each spring.

The object of berry pickers' attention is a berry with beautiful white flowers that blooms along riverbanks, ponds, and bogs. Pickers often use boats for the harvest. The resulting jelly is a pretty, coral-colored mixture that has a very delicate taste. It has such a subtle flavor that it is best eaten on neutral ground, like hot baking-powder biscuits or coiled in a jelly-roll cake.

The company sells mayhaw syrup and wine jelly, as well as a variety of other jellies, salad dressings, and Vidalia onion mustard, relish, and vinegar. Best among those we sampled was the Deep South Dressing, a tomato-based salad dressing made with Vidalia onions and mayhaw jelly. It is particularly suited to citrus salads.

Three 9.5-ounce jars of mayhaw jelly, Vidalia onion jelly, and peach preserves are $23, postpaid. Six jars, any variety, are $39, shipping included.

ORDERING ADDRESS
The Mayhaw Tree, Inc.
105 Mitcham Circle
Tiger, GA 30576
706/782-4995
800/2MAYHAW (262-9429)
FAX: 706/782-7848
www.mayhawtree.com
Credit cards accepted

PALMER'S MAPLE SYRUP

There are two thousand maple-syrup producers in Vermont alone, an astounding increase of 50 percent in the past 25 years, reports the State Department of Agriculture. Consumption, happily, also has increased, with more Americans turning from the caramel-flavored syrups that have corrupted our idea of genuine maple taste.

The purest maple flavor is found in the syrup known as fancy grade, or light amber. Lighter than the others, it is made early in the season and has to be handled carefully and quickly. The sap is boiled down immediately after collection, because letting it sit even overnight could result in medium-amber syrup. As the sugaring season progresses, the sap gets stronger in flavor, with more caramel tones. Although it lacks the fine flavor of the fancy grade, dark amber syrup is better for cooking, since it retains its flavor better when heated.

With two thousand sugarhouses in Vermont and hundreds more in the other eastern states and the upper Midwest, there is a small army of Americans working to give true maple its due. Many of the places are small and family-run, and are willing to let visitors watch the proceedings. In Vermont the state publishes a list of sugarhouses open to the public. The list also describes what maple products they sell, whether they send by mail, and whether they gather sap by pipeline or with buckets. Some places collect their buckets using oxen or teams of horses, and a few let visitors take a turn. For a free copy of the list, write: Vermont Department of Agriculture, Development Division, 116 State Street, Montpelier, VT 05602.

Although it is nearly impossible to select one favorite maple producer, we are partial to the syrup from the Palmer Family of Waitsfield, Vermont. The business is now in the fourth generation, tapping trees on the same 32 acres where they live. Delbert Palmer, son of Kathryn and the late Everett Palmer, now runs the company. His mother still takes part in the enterprise.

The Palmers sell the 800 or 900 gallons of syrup they make yearly directly from their frame sugarhouse to visitors who come to watch the syrup made from mid-March to mid-April and from their home to locals, skiers, and "leaf peepers" (tourists who come to view fall foliage). During sugaring, visitors are treated to a small dish of fresh syrup. For years, Kathryn has been making maple cream—a spread for toast, waffles, and muffins—and maple candies. The collecting, sugaring, canning, and selling is nearly a round-the-clock effort, but Kathryn discounts the hard work. "Sugaring season is a wonderful time of the year for us," she says.

The season extends nearly year-round. The months between sugaring are spent chopping and stacking the endless cords of wood needed to keep the fire under the sap evaporator roaring.

The Palmers will send their syrup, maple cream, and candies by mail. The syrup is in three varieties. Their fancy light amber syrup is a lovely tawny gold and is as delicate a syrup as we've tasted. Fancy and medium amber are available in five sizes, ranging from a gallon to a half-pint can. Dark amber comes in gallons, half-gallons, and quarts. Prices vary every year, depending on weather conditions and supply, so write or call first.

ORDERING ADDRESS
Palmer's Maple Products
Route 1, Box 246
Waitsfield, VT 05673-9711
802/496-3696
FAX: 802/496-3696
Credit cards accepted

VISITS
72 Maple Lane
Waitsfield, VT
Waitsfield is in central Vermont, west of Montpelier. From Route 100, take Warren Road east and cross the covered bridge. Drive 1 mile farther and you will see the Palmer's sign on your right. No set hours.

ROCKY TOP CHERRY BUTTER

Tom Cooper had a brainstorm. To keep freshness front and center, he put his jam kitchen in the middle of an orchard.

Cooper carries color photographs of his 300-acre farm in northwest quadrant of Michigan as if it were his child. He'll show you bushels of luscious peaches, cherries, and raspberries from harvests past, just so customers understand that Rocky Top controls the main ingredients in its unusual line of preserves, fruit toppings, and fruit butters.

To describe the cherry butter, you need to imagine what cherry pie filling might taste like if it were exquisitely made, with a silky Montmorency cherry base. The most plentiful ingredients are sweet cherries and tart cherries, and the real cherry fragrance hits you after you open the jar. The fruit has not been overcooked, so it still has a satisfying crunch. The mixture is thick with fruit and can be used on toast or pound cake, spread with cream cheese on miniature bagels, or, most likely, devoured as is.

Cooper, 55, began his business 22 years ago after careers as a schoolteacher and salesman. "I grew up in an evergreen nursery and just missed being out of doors," he said. "It was a total gamble."

He developed his recipes from old Dutch cookbooks and by continual tastings with the elder cooks in Ellsworth, the town nearest his farm. His hilltop acreage gets plenty of sun, allowing him to grow his own peaches, blackberries, strawberries, raspberries, and cherries. Another Michigan orchard provides the apricots for his apricot butter. A neighbor, George "Geppetto" Muto, uses Michigan white cedar to build finished gift boxes that are filled with Rocky Top products.

Many of the berries are hand picked. All of the products—his rhubarb chutney, blackberry preserve, and 22 others —are cooked in a 40-gallon copper kettle, in batches of about 8 gallons.

Detroit department stores were the first outsiders to discover the superlative quality of Rocky Top's products. Cooper and his wife, Ruth Ann, will ship boxes of 3, 4, 6, or 12 jars, all 10 ounces each. A 3-jar redwood gift crate is $14.50, plus postage. A dozen of any assortment is $36.50, plus shipping. A sliding lid gift box with a seagull, pheasant, or Shay train engine silk-screened on it is offered with 3 jars of Rocky Top products for $17.50, plus shipping.

The Coopers ask that you send or call for a catalog before ordering.

ORDERING ADDRESS

Rocky Top Farms
R.R. 1, Box 163-A
Ellsworth, MI 49729
231/599-2251
800/862-9303
FAX: 231/599-2352

VISITS

11486 Essex Road
Ellsworth, MI 49729
The farm welcomes visitors and has a sales area in one section of the main barn. Rocky Top is 6 miles west of Ellsworth on Essex Road, about ¼ mile east of the intersection of Essex Road and Route 31.
Monday–Friday, 10 A.M.–4 P.M.

WACKY MOUNTAIN WILD FRUITS AND JELLIES

Halfway between the taste of a quince and a currant is the wild buffalo berry of the Montana woods. Although Indians and settlers used the berries for puddings and pies, the formidable thorns protecting the small clusters of berries have discouraged modern-day harvesters. The bushes are up to 15 feet high. Only after the first frost does the scarlet fruit loosen and can be shaken to the ground.

Until Glada Abel and her late son, Herb, began their jelly business 25 years ago, they weren't collected in any substantial volume around their Miles

City home. Now Glada's son, Bill, buys berries from family and friends. In addition to the buffalo berry, the Abel harvests and processes tart chokecherries and wild plums from the hillsides and creek bottoms in the Yellowstone Valley.

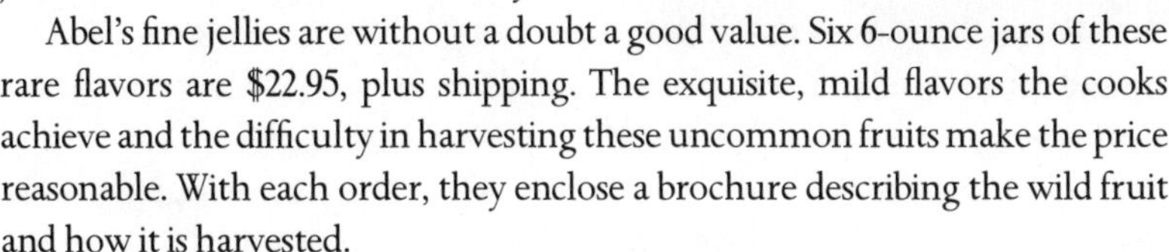

The firm also sells 6- and 10-ounce jars of Montana wildflower honey.

Abel's fine jellies are without a doubt a good value. Six 6-ounce jars of these rare flavors are $22.95, plus shipping. The exquisite, mild flavors the cooks achieve and the difficulty in harvesting these uncommon fruits make the price reasonable. With each order, they enclose a brochure describing the wild fruit and how it is harvested.

ORDERING ADDRESS
Wacky Mountain Enterprises
Route 2, Box 3150
Miles City, MT 59301
406/232-0151
877-687-7591 (toll-free)
FAX: 406/259-2633
e-mail: abe@mcn.net
www.wackymountain.com
Credit cards accepted

WAX ORCHARDS FUDGE SWEET TOPPINGS AND FRUIT PRESERVES

The Wax family has found a way to make food sweet without sugar or artificial sweeteners. Using nothing but fruit and a blend of concentrated fruit juices from their 40 acres of orchards in western Washington, the family has created preserves, a minced fruit "mincemeat," fruit butters, fruit syrups, chutneys, and dark fudge topping with an unbelievably low calorie count.

Betsy Wax Sestrap, whose father, August Wax, founded the family orchards in 1920, has developed an impressive array of fruit condiments, many of them low calorie. The fruit berry spreads, 10-ounce jars of peach, raspberry, strawberry, blueberry, orange-pineapple, and pineapple-berry, have only 7 calories per teaspoon. They have exceptional flavor and have no additives, including pectin. They make a good addition to plain yogurt, waffles, and pancakes and are $5 a jar for 10 ounces.

What has garnered the most attention is the orchard's fudge toppings, made of imported Dutch-process cocoa and concentrated fruit juices. They weigh in at a mere 16 calories per teaspoon and taste very much like the topping that the Baskin Robbins ice-cream stores pipe around the sides of their sinful ice-cream pies. Yet they have no fat and can be enjoyed nearly guilt-free. There are four chocolate variations: plain, amaretto, orange, and peppermint.

The American Diabetes Association has included the fudge toppings in its catalog, and diabetics are delighted to find good-tasting fudge sauces, reports Betsy Wax Sestrap. The fudge toppings are $6 each for a 10-ounce jar.

The newest flavors are peanut butter fudge and orange passion fudge. Another useful item is the orchards' all fruit "mincemeat." It contains no fat and can be used exactly as conventional mincemeats. The price is $5 for 15 ounces.

The company also sells a lot of fruit sweet, pear sweet, and grape sweet to home cooks as sugar substitutes. These jars of concentrated fruit sweeteners have 280 calories per cup versus 385 calories per cup of sugar. The fruit sweets are $5 for 12-ounce glass jar or $10 for a 32-ounce plastic container. Shipping is extra for all products and there is a 15 percent discount for any 12-jar case (any combination).

It is worth writing for a catalog to learn about all of the firm's unusual offerings. Betsy and her husband, Robert, also welcome visitors to the Vashon Island farm on weekdays.

ORDERING ADDRESS

Wax Orchards
22744 Wax Orchard Road, S.W.
Vashon Island, WA 98070
206/463-9735
800/634-6132
FAX: 206/463-9731
e-mail: waxorchards@earthlink.net
www.waxorachards.com
Credit cards accepted

VISITS

Vashon Island is a 20-minute ferry ride from the west Seattle ferry dock. After one lands, the orchards are 11½ miles away. Take the main highway, Route 99, to 204th Street. Turn right and drive 3½ miles to Wax Orchard Road, S.W. Turn left and drive ½ mile. The orchard is on the left. There is a sign at the blacktop driveway. (If you take the Vashon Island ferry from Point Defiance in Tacoma, the orchards are a 4½ mile drive north.)

Monday–Friday, 9 A.M.–4 P.M.

WILLIS WOOD'S APPLE-CIDER JELLY

When you think of pancakes and waffles, think of Willis and Tina Wood, who make some of the purest products to enliven a breakfast. We're partial to products with short ingredients lists, and apple-cider jelly, the original offering of this 120-year-old company, has just about the shortest. There's just one ingredient: apple cider.

Willis Wood's family began pressing apples into cider and boiling the liquid into jelly in 1882, shortly after converting its water-powered sawmill in Springfield, Vermont, into a cider mill. Willis and Tina make three pressings of cider a day on the original screw press throughout the apple season—every day from mid-October through early December. "We hire help so that we don't live at the mill, although some days it feels as though we do," said Tina.

The cider is boiled into jelly in a 4x14-foot evaporator until it is one-ninth of its original volume. As it cools, the concentrated cider jells without the benefit of pectin, sugar, or preservatives. The result is a tart, clear, dark-amber jelly that is a welcome substitute for sweet jams. We've used it with success as a meat glaze and in beef stew, and we especially like it on toast and cooked cereals. Because it is concentrated, only a mere smear is needed.

This remarkable jelly needs no refrigeration and keeps indefinitely. A box of four 8-ounce jars is $14.85, including shipping. Orders going west of Mississippi are $1 more. The Woods will ship their larger sizes (10 ounces, 20 ounces, 2½ pounds, etc.), but again, only in units of 4 or 12.

A boiled cider, which is concentrated to about seven parts cider to one of water, is sold in pint and quarts, for $5.50 and $9.25 respectively. It's used as a drink, in meat recipes, to top pancakes, and over ice cream.

They also make a cider syrup, a blend of boiled cider and maple syrup, that is sold in half-pints, pints, and quarts. A new flavor has been added, a cinnamon cider syrup that is half maple syrup and half boiled cider with a stick of cinnamon added. They also produce their own maple syrup, in light, medium, or dark amber grades. It is available in half-pints to gallons. Write first to get the shipping details on the quantity you desire.

ORDERING ADDRESS

Willis Wood Cider Jelly
1482 Weathersfield Center Road
Springfield, VT 05156
802/263-5547
FAX: 802/263-9674
e-mail: wwcider@sovern.net
Credit cards accepted

VISITS

Fall, spring: every day, 9 A.M.–5 P.M. Call ahead other times of year.

INGREDIENTS

BAKEWELL CREAM

In many Maine households there is only one biscuit recipe—the Bakewell Cream "No Fail" recipe printed on every bright-yellow tin of this unique leavening agent. Developed during World War II by chemist Byron H. Smith because of a shortage of cream of tartar, the powder is a mixture of sodium pyrophosphate and redried starch. It is used instead of baking powder or cream of tartar (but not for beating egg whites). It works by reacting with the baking soda in recipes. The reaction is stronger, making biscuits higher and lighter, and Bakewell Cream leaves no trace of taste, as some baking powders do. There also is no aluminum or dye added.

We've found its claim of producing a superior biscuit to be true, even, as the company notes, "for a heavy handed amateur cook." Because it does not contain bicarbonate of soda, the powder doesn't lose its high-rising ability over time.

Smith's granddaughter, Linda Buckley, sold the company to Lolly Sevigny and her pharmacist husband, Paul, in November 1987. Lolly has been a Bakewell Cream baker all her life and was looking for a small business to run.

The Sevignys are the sole full-time employees, turning out the tins New Englanders depend on for their strawberry shortcakes, biscuits, and pastries. "The people in the hunting camps love it for their biscuits and pancakes," Lolly noted.

The only change the Sevignys were forced to make was to change the oblong tin for a round one, as the price doubled on the original tins. But the homey label and, most important, the contents have stayed the same. Because it does not contain soda, Bakewell cream has almost an indefinite shelf life. The Sevignys will ship as little as one can (8 ounces) for $2.25, plus $3.50 shipping. If you want to give all your transplanted New England friends a present they will remember fondly, you can order a case of Bakewell Cream (12 tins) for $24, plus $6.50 shipping. There also is a cookbook with recipes for Grape Nut bread, blueberry buckle, molasses doughnuts, and other New England favorites. It's $2.25 plus 75¢ shipping.

Bakewell Cream is available throughout Maine, in northern Massachusetts, and eastern New Hampshire in mom-and-pop stores, as well as in Shop N' Save, Shaw's, and IGA's.

Visits to the plant are by appointment only.

ORDERING AND VISITING ADDRESS
The Apple Ledge Company
170 South Road
Holden, ME 04429
207/989-5576
e-mail: appleledge@aol.com

TELEPHONE ORDERS: **Monday–Friday, 9 A.M.–1 P.M. No credit cards; checks OK**

BELL'S POULTRY SEASONING

We are grateful to Brady Enterprises for continuing to manufacture one of New England's time-honored seasonings, the pungent blend created between 1861 and 1867 by inventor William G. Bell and cited by Fannie Farmer in the *Original Boston Cooking School Cook Book* in 1897. A pinch of this seasoning goes a long way, so do not be surprised at the diminutive size of the 1-ounce yellow package, festooned with a Technicolor blue turkey on its label. This wonderful vintage label is so good, we'd like to see it on wrapping paper, or on postcards, so we wouldn't have to keep dragging friends to our spice cabinet for a look.

Many New England cooks swear by Bell's Poultry Seasoning, and there exists the semblance of an underground network to help Bell's cooks outside the region discover where to acquire more. It is available throughout New England and in parts of Pennsylvania and Florida, usually in grocery stores that have carried it for years.

The seasoning is used in marinades, in poultry stuffing and bastes, in tuna, egg salad, and other sandwich fillings, and in coating for fried or baked chicken. It is salt-free, and contains rosemary, oregano, sage, ginger, marjoram, thyme, and pepper. Its most pungent ingredient is its special sage, which makes it particularly good in soups. We followed the company's suggestions and like it with fried apples and sprinkled on canned peach halves before broiling.

The seasoning imparts a wonderfully aromatic flavor that is altogether unique. Do be careful to keep the box tightly closed or seal it in a plastic bag. The fragrance of the seasoning is so strong that, unless you take these measures, the smell will drift throughout your spice cupboard.

It is very reasonably priced. You can find it in stores for about $1.19. The company will send a 4-pack of the seasoning for $6, including delivery costs.

Visits are by appointment only.

ORDERING ADDRESS

Brady Enterprises, Inc.
P.O. Box 99
East Weymouth, MA 02189
781/337-5000
www.brady-ent.com
No credit cards; checks OK

VISITS

167 Moore Road
East Weymouth, MA
Weymouth is 20 miles south of Boston, heading toward Cape Cod. From Boston, take the Southeast Expressway to Route 3 south. The plant is in the Weymouth Industrial Park, off Route 53, just a few miles from Route 3. By appointment only.

BICKFORD'S FLAVORINGS

The stories of how small companies manage to survive from owner to owner are often tales of luck and timing. The story of Bickford Flavors is true to this formula, as Lionel Anderson, the aged proprietor of the once-prosperous Akron, Ohio, company, simply closed the doors when his health deteriorated in 1975. Fortunately, Steve Sofer, the owner of a health food store that had become Bickford's last customer, arranged to have Anderson driven in three hours a day to teach him how to make the 72-year-old recipes, writing out the chemical formulas and demonstrating the processes. Anderson agreed to pass on his recipes and his factory, all for a donation to the Masonic Home where he lived.

The company sells nonalcoholic, no-sugar flavorings just as Anderson made them, minus the flowery Victorian label, which did not meet FDA standards. In 1990, Sofer moved the operations to Cleveland, where he has lived for 41 years. "I got tired of the commute," he said.

The company's best-seller remains its superior white vanilla. It is made by cooking the vanilla beans in corn oil rather than extracting the essence with alcohol. Other white vanillas on the market—used in wedding cakes and other light-colored baked goods—are made with synthetic powders. The Bickford's process results in a vanilla that is slightly more than single strength. "Don't use a heaping teaspoon with ours," warns Sofer. "Just pour it level or even convex."

Because the company eschews alcohol, it has built up a following with bakeries. Those searching out rarely produced flavors, such as nutmeg, hazelnut, raisin, blackberry, black currant, and guava seem to find Bickford's, too. Lately, its peanut-butter flavor has zoomed in popularity, due in some part to the millions of Americans drinking powdered diet drinks that are improved mightily by a jolt of peanut-butter flavor.

The company will mail-order any of its 100 flavors for $2.39 for a 1-ounce bottle. There's a flat rate of $6.50 for shipping. Larger sizes are available, from 16 ounces to 5 gallons. Its oils (banana, black walnut, clove, mango, and 46 others) are sold in ½-ounce, 1-ounce, and 4-ounce sizes. The dark and light vanillas are sold in 1-ounce to 5-gallon sizes.

ORDERING ADDRESS

Bickford Flavors
19007 St. Clair Avenue
Cleveland, OH 44117
216/531-6006
FAX: 216/531-2006
800/283-8322
e-mail: bickfordflavors@aol.com
Credit cards accepted

CHUGWATER CHILI

The name Chugwater Chili is so appropriate it sounds made up. But there really is a town called Chugwater in southeastern Wyoming, and it is home to a chili-seasoning business. The business is a cooperative effort of five Chugwater-area ranch families who are trying to help the local economy. In the process, they've come up with a hearty, low-salt chili seasoning that quickly turns 2 pounds of ground meat and a can of tomato sauce into a complex chili that tastes like it's been fussed over for hours.

They've been in business for 13 years, and have a stack of fan letters from across the country: "I have tried all the 'gourmet' chili mixes available here [Massachusetts] and have found them all quite inferior!" stated one letter. "We will not eat any other chili," wrote a woman who found the product while on vacation in Colorado. "Wonderful stuff—best I've ever had! Need more pronto!" penned a Denver man.

The object of their affection is a blend of 10 spices, masa harina (corn flour), and brown sugar. It contains about 20 percent salt, versus as much as 80 percent in other chili mixes. It is an assertively spiced, although not overwhelming, product. If you want it so hot you have to chug water, simply add more of the mix than the recipe requires. We made the Quick & Easy Chili recipe printed on the packets and apothecary jars, and had great success. We also tried it using ground venison from the Texas Wild Game Cooperative, and found it equally tasty.

The company grew out of the concerns of several Chugwater families about declining school enrollments and ailing businesses they feared would doom their children's chances of staying on the family farms. First came brainstorming for business ideas at community rejuvenation forums. Then a relationship was developed with a marketing specialist from the State Department of Agriculture. He suggested the chili company get in touch with a Cheyenne man, Dave Cameron, who had won chili cook-offs using a recipe he had trademarked as Chugwater Chili.

An agreement was reached with Cameron to purchase the name and recipe, and five families formed a corporation. In 1988, one of the couples was replaced with another area family, but the remaining founders have continued packing, shipping, and promoting the product. Every June the small town holds an annual chili cook-off drawing teams from Colorado, Nebraska, and Wyoming.

Many states have small-business promotion efforts, but few can match the official enthusiasm shown for Chugwater Chili. The enterprise has been aided by the University of Wyoming's Small Business Institute, which has conducted three feasibility and marketing studies. The governor, state travel commission, and other agencies all have pitched in to push "The Gourmet Spice of Western Life." When Al Simpson was in the U.S. Senate, he and his wife gave bottles of the chili spice to his congressional colleagues for Christmas.

Taking advantage of another trend that is creeping up in more and more colorfully named food businesses, Chugwater Chili sells T-shirts, caps, and aprons with its logo on it. One 2.67-ounce jar of the chili mix, which flavors 6 quarts (or 27 servings) of chili, is $5.25, plus shipping. A case of 12 is $58.20, plus shipping. Individual 1-ounce packets are available at $2.15 each or $48 for a case of 24, plus shipping. The mix is also available in bulk, in 1- and 3-pound sizes.

The company also has a Chugwater dip and dressing mix, designed to be added to sour cream and mayonnaise. It is $4.85 for a 2.5-ounce jar, plus shipping. There's also a red pepper jelly and jars of chili nuts.

ORDERING ADDRESS
Chugwater Chili Corporation
P.O. Box 92
Chugwater, WY 82210
307/422-3345
800/97CHILI (972-4454)
FAX: 307/422-3357
e-mail: chugchili@coffey.com
www.chugwaterchili.com
Credit cards accepted

VISITS
Chugwater Chili Corporation
210 First Street
Chugwater, WY 82210
Chugwater is in southeastern Wyoming, north of Cheyenne on 1-25.
Monday–Friday, 9 A.M.–5 P.M.

DEMI-GLACE GOLD

Making stock is like flossing. We know we should take the time, but we don't. It's just too much effort to spend the hours simmering and straining.

So we're very grateful to a stock reduction company, More Than Gourmet, that produces highly concentrated veal and chicken glaces and stocks, as well as a vegetable glace.

It's comic that something so elegant resembles a hockey puck. These concentrated reductions are packaged in small plastic ovals and have an 18-month shelf life. After opening the foil lid, the glace can stay fresh for weeks in the refrigerator. A teaspoon-size chunk is all that's needed for most sauces. To use, add 3 parts hot water and whisk for about 3 minutes. You vary the dilution according to your taste.

Founded in 1994 in Akron, Ohio, the company has outgrown its downtown home on the grounds of B.F. Goodrich's former headquarters. Its warehouse is now located on the city's outskirts. The most popular of its reductions remains its classic French demi-glace, but there are new duck and fish demi-glaces and stocks. Brothers Bernie and Harvey Leff devised the products, keeping batches small and chemical-free.

The demi-glace takes 30 hours to produce, over low heat. The veal stock has a small bit of flour added as a binding. You can use it as is a meat glaze, reconstituted as a sauce, or diluted as a stock.

The chicken and veal stocks also come in a concentrated liquid form— Jus de Poulet Lié Gold and Glace de Poulet Gold. For vegetarians, its Veggie-Glace Gold is a meatless demi-glace substitute.

All of the products work well in seasoning grains as well as meat. For those nights when you're exhausted, trying to get dinner on the table, the demi-glace is a lifesaver for sauteéd chicken breasts.

The products come in 1.5-ounce cups, 16-ounce containers, and 1 pound containers for the home cook, and up to 50-pound buckets for foodservice use.

The company does not sell its product by mail, but asks that you call, toll-free, to find a store near you. If in its Akron birthplace, it's well worth a stop at the West Point Market, one of America's oldest and most innovative gourmet groceries. Owner Russ Verdon was an early supporter of Demi-Glace Gold and carries its full line.

Shopping at West Point is a sensory experience, with a dozen free food stations, traveling minstrels, food demonstrations, and other excitement. There's also a restaurant, Beside the Point, on site. The market will ship Demi-Glace products. In the store, Demi-Glace Gold is $4.99 for a 1.5-ounce tub and $35.99 for a 16-ounce container.

ORDERING INFORMATION:
More Than Gourmet
115 W. Bartges Street
Akron, OH 44311
330/762-6652
800/860-9385
FAX: 330/762-4832
e-mail: info@morethangourmet.com

VISITS
West Point Market
1711 West Market Street
Akron, OH 44303
330/864-2151
800/838-2156
FAX: 330/869-8666
e-mail: gdtaste@westpointmarket.com
www.westpointmarket.com
Credit cards accepted
The market is 2.5 miles west of downtown Akron on Market Street.
Monday–Friday, 8 A.M.–8 P.M. Saturday, 8 A.M.–7 P.M.

ECLIPSE AND AUTOCRAT COFFEE SYRUPS

There's one sure-fire conversation starter with any Rhode Islander. Ask him or her about coffee milk. Though ice-cream manufacturers have known for years that the Northeast is the strongest market for coffee ice cream, it's one of life's charming mysteries why the coffee-milk tradition took hold in Rhode Island. Rhode Islanders drink so much cold coffee-flavored milk that dairies carry it in 2 percent, skim, and yogurt varieties.

The granddaddies of the sweetened coffee syrups are the Eclipse and Autocrat brands. The syrups are made of hard, harsh African coffees—a blend too strong to drink straight. The familiar pint bottles, with the Eclipse red-and-yellow labels and Autocrat's chirping red bird, are part of table-time customs in the state. Candy makers use the syrup for cordials, ice cream parlors use it for shakes, and some Rhode Island restaurants—particularly those with Portuguese clientele—keep bottles on the table for their customers' use.

"As soon as babies are old enough to hold a glass of milk, they get coffee milk," said Carl Romano, a sales manager for Eclipse, who noted that the caffeine in the syrup—less than 1 percent—is diluted in the milk to a negligible level. The syrup also is used in puddings, cakes, gingerbread, frostings, and custards by home cooks.

One of our favorite ways to use it is in a coffee egg nog or in mocha pudding, replacing 1 cup of milk with coffee syrup when making packaged chocolate pudding. One friend from Rhode Island adds coffee syrup to marshmallow cream and spreads it on graham crackers for her children. A popular ice cream frappé, called a coffee cabinet in Rhode Island, combines coffee syrup, ice cream and milk, beaten until the ice cream dissolves.

The Autocrat Company, of Lincoln, Rhode Island, bought Eclipse, and now sells it, along with the Café Frio and Coffeetime syrups and cappuccino mixes. The Autocrat brand, founded by Frank O. Field, was first established in 1895. Elipse came later, in 1914.

Six plastic pint bottles of either brand of coffee syrup are $16.95, shipping included. There also are vanilla and strawberry syrups sold at the same price, as well as a low-calorie coffee version. Stores throughout Rhode Island and in scattered areas of Massachusetts, New York, and New Jersey carry the pint bottles of coffee syrup at prices ranging from $1.80 to $2.50.

ORDERING ADDRESS
Autocrat Coffee Syrup
10 Blackstone Valley Place
Lincoln, RI 08265
401/333-3300
800/288-6272
FAX: 401/333-3719
e-mail: sales@autocrat.com
www.autocrat.com
Credit cards accepted

VISITS
Same address.
Monday–Friday, 8 A.M.–4:30 P.M.

FOX'S U-BET CHOCOLATE SYRUP

Every Jewish male comedian in America seems to have grown up drinking egg creams made with Fox's U-Bet Chocolate Syrup: Woody Allen, Mel Brooks, Jerry Lewis, Alan King—all have sung the praises of this specialty syrup. For the uninitiated, an egg cream is a soda-fountain drink that became popular in New York in the 1920s and 1930s. It's one of the great mysteries of delicatessen lore why an egg cream has neither egg nor cream in it. "Honest to God, I don't know," said David Fox, whose great-grandfather started the family syrup business in Brooklyn 91 years ago. "It probably started out with both and became too costly with the cream, and no one wants the slimy egg in there." John Mariani, author of the exhaustive *Dictionary of American Food and Drink,* has another explanation. "There is no egg in an egg cream, but if the ingredients are mixed properly, a foamy, egg-white-like head tops off the drink."

The ingredients in a true egg cream are an inch of Fox's syrup, 2 tablespoons of milk, and a glassful of seltzer water. There are divided camps on the best way to make a perfect egg cream, and Fox braces himself for the mail from opposing viewpoints every time he offers the company line. It seems strange that such a simple concoction could stir such loyalty, but for New Yorkers, Philadelphians, and New Jerseyites, egg creams are associated with the complex memories of family, childhood, and growing up.

The company is respectful of these emotions and has never considered changing the syrup's antiquated label. The syrup's name came from grandfather, who took a sabbatical from his father's business to drill oil wells in Texas. He picked up the slang of the derrick tenders. "You bet" was the "Have a nice day" of the moment. When he returned to New York, Fox's Chocolate Syrup was renamed. "He said, 'I came back broke, but with a good name for the syrup,'" his grandson related.

The syrup, which comes in a 33-ounce glass jar, sells for $2.19 in stores throughout New York and is available in specialty stores and delicatessens in several of the country's major cities. Write to the company to find the nearest distributor.

If there is no distributor in your area, the company will ship the syrup direct. The company is sticking with glass bottles for its supermarket sales. "We're loath to come out with plastic, because glass is recyclable," said David Fox. "In fact, we might put a label on our jars pointing that out."

ORDERING ADDRESS
H. Fox & Company
417 Thatford Avenue
Brooklyn, NY 11212
718/385-4600
No credit cards; checks OK

G. B. RATTO OLIVE OILS AND SPICES

Our spice cabinets haven't smelled the same since we discovered G. B. Ratto & Company, and for that we thank Bob and Ann Reckert of Rock Rapids, Iowa, who wrote us: "We have found their spices and herbs to be not only fresh and flavorful, but also quite inexpensive," they wrote.

Ratto's has been in business for 102 years in Oakland, California, and from the day it was opened by Italian immigrant Giovanni Battista Ratto, it has been an international grocery. Its shelves feature items from Tahiti to Taiwan and they're a godsend for serious cooks. Need pomegranate concentrate for Persian cooking? Annatto seeds to color Indian food? Aspic jelly powder from Switzerland? Italian truffle puree? Ground sumac? Dried powdered tomatoes? And that's just scratching the surface.

Ratto's most celebrated offerings are its California olive oil and vinegars, made to order for the store. John Thorne, the *Simple Cooking* newsletter author who dishes out equal helpings of strong opinions and common sense, hailed Ratto's olive oil as one of the best—and inexpensive. Ratto's calls its rich, cold-pressed oil "the olive oil lover's olive oil," and says it can be diluted with vegetable oil for more delicate palates. We prefer it straight from the plastic bottle. Try using it for popping corn. Terrific.

The company's red and white vinegars use "robust" California wines, aged in oak. They compare well with vinegars at three times the price. A 1-quart plastic bottle of either white or red vinegar is $3.50.

Other Ratto exclusives are its spice blends. Use them as introductions to a foreign cuisine. Instead of investing in an array of unfamiliar individual spices for Ethiopian food, we tried one unfamiliar "house blend" of Ethiopian spices—berbere, a hot mixture used in soups or stews. Ratto's assertive taco seasoning will liberate you from the tyranny of buying those overpriced packets at the grocery every time you make tostadas. A 4-ounce bag, good for at least half a dozen dinners, is $2.25.

Try the Italian herbs strewn over pizza, and the Greek seasoning on salads. Zather was described as a mixture of ground sumac and ground thyme that Middle Easterners mix with olive oil and spread on toasted bread. We tried it and became converts. The curry powder, which comes in mild or hot versions, is a superior, complex blend that tasted amazingly different from the curry we had in our cupboard.

The company was owned and run for years by Martin Durante, a descendant of founder Giovanni. Durante's daughter, Elena Voiron, is taking over ownership. The store remains a family-run enterprise, well positioned to serve the increasingly global tastes of American eaters.

Ratto's is no longer in the mail-order business, but will ship for repeat customers who know exactly what products they're ordering and purchase at least $40 of goods.

VISITS

G. B. Ratto & Company International Grocers
821 Washington Street
Oakland, CA 94607
510/832-6503
Credit cards accepted

The store is on Victorian Row in Old Oakland, 1 block from the Convention Center and steps from the newly renovated Historic Housewives Market, which has produce sellers, meat stalls, a fishmonger, cafés, and the Museum of Children's Art. Take I-80 from San Francisco and cross the Bay Bridge to 580, following the signs for Oakland/Hayward. Go to 980 toward downtown Oakland. Exit at the 11th and 12th Streets exit, then follow Brush Street to Seventh Street. Turn left on Seventh and go through several stoplights to Washington Street. Turn left again and drive 2 blocks. Ratto's is on the left.

Monday–Friday, 9 A.M.–6 P.M. Saturday, 9:30 A.M.–5:30 P.M.

HOO-MEE CHOW MEIN MIX

If the Oriental Chow Mein Company had a public relations department or a consumer affairs department (it has neither), we would lay odds that the copy on its charming yellow, blue, and red box would receive a severe edit. "Hoo-Mee Brand Chow Mein Mix is the original chow-mein mix, packaged since 1926, for home preparation by the housewife" is how the side label begins. The P.R. person would wince and delete "housewife." "The ingredients contained in this package will make a delicious meal of chow mein, of the type generally served in the better Chinese restaurants of southeastern Massachusetts," the label continues. The person wielding the blue pencil would change the ending to read "around the country" or, if feeling particularly grandiose, "around the world." He or she probably would replace Barbara Wong's Kitchen-Tested Recipes on the back with something that didn't mention canned peas.

Let us hope that such a scenario never comes to life. We think, and the Society for Commercial Archeology agrees, that there are too few examples of early commercial packaging that have successfully resisted updating. In this case, the contents of the box also have resisted updating—a fortunate turn of events.

A bona fide regional favorite made by a small company, the mix is a true original that's been passed down from father to son since the 1920s. The crispy noodles are not like the ones we all learned to eat from the Chung King cans. These are flatter, darker in color, and much tastier. The mix consists of 7 ounces of noodles and a 1-ounce packet of gravy mix. You add the packet contents to warm water, then to 3 cups of boiling stock that has celery, onion, and bean sprouts in it. The mixture thickens as it boils, and then is poured over the noodles for nearly instant chow mein. Shredded chicken, shrimp, ground meat, or any manner of vegetables can be added for variety.

It does taste like the chow mein you've been served in better Chinese restaurants. We were tempted to spoon the leftovers into white cardboard containers! The noodles soften after the first serving, of course, but it is still good eating the next day.

We would never have known about Hoo-Mee Chow Mein Mix had it not been for a reader, Arlene Chouinard, of North Bend, Washington, who wrote us a wonderful letter. "The noodles are unique," she wrote. "They have a flavor and texture all their own. I have lived many places on both East and West coasts, also in the Far East, but I have never been able to find this type of noodle except in the northeastern part of the States." She orders it often, she wrote, noting that the company is very prompt and sends via UPS. "I believe you have found in researching your book that once you have become addicted to a particular food item, nothing can replace it."

She is not the only Hoo-Mee addict, but the company says its mail-order business is strictly a sideline. "We cater to the restaurant trade, and are in some supermarkets in the Fall River area," said Alfred Wong, one of the owners. "But people move around and remember the taste of it. It's something like when you go to your roots, you remember chow mein."

The company sends a case of 12 boxes of mix for $12, plus a $4 handling fee and the UPS charge to your address. As a charming touch, the boxes are wrapped in thin brown paper before being placed in the shipping container.

Hoo-Mee bills itself as "authentic New England Chow Mein." For those who never knew such an animal existed, we recommend that you get acquainted.

ORDERING ADDRESS
Oriental Chow Mein Company
42 Eighth Street
Fall River, MA 02720
508/675-7711
No credit cards; checks OK

VISITS: **Fall River is between New Bedford, Massachusetts, and Providence, Rhode Island, just north of I-195.**
Monday–Saturday, 9:30 A.M.–4:30 P.M.

KARY'S GUMBO ROUX

When Archange Le Fleur ran the Pig Stand restaurant in Ville Platte, Louisiana, his roux—the base for his crawfish bisque and chicken gumbo—was as well known as his barbecue sauce. Customers would beg him for containers of the chocolate-brown roux, and he began bottling it in 1975. When he died in 1980, his wife, Annie, and their son, Kary, closed the restaurant but carried on his roux-making tradition. Kary now runs the operation and his mother has retired.

The roux, a mixture of flour and salt that has been browned in vegetable oil over very low heat, makes superlative gravies and soups. It is much easier to add a teaspoon of roux to thicken a sauce than to worry about lumps from cornstarch, arrowroot, or plain flour.

Five employees turn out the roux in 1-pound, 32-ounce, 1-gallon, and 36-pound bucket sizes. The smaller bottles have a faded blue label depicting a chef stirring a furiously boiling caldron. It is sold in grocery stores in Louisiana and in parts of Texas for about $1.59 for the 1-pound jar. Gazin's, a mail-order house specializing in Cajun foods, sells 3 of the 1-pound jars for $8.99, plus $4.95 shipping, or a case of 12 for $32.50, plus $6.95 shipping. Gazin's 32-page catalog is $1, refunded with your first order.

Kary has added a dry roux, for a fat and cholesterol-free gravy or gumbo. It's sold in a 16-ounce bottle for the same prices as the original dark roux.

ORDERING ADDRESS
Gazin's
P.O. Box 19221
New Orleans, LA 70179
504/482-0302
800/262-6410
FAX: 504/488-6239
e-mail: gazins@aol.com
www.gazins.com
Credit cards accepted

LIVINGSTON FARMS PEPPERMINT AND SPEARMINT OILS

Buying mint oils from Doris Livingston, 89, is what's known as going to the source. She and her late husband, Alden, began raising mint on a diversified farm in central Michigan in the 1920s. For almost as long she has been selling spearmint and peppermint oil by the ounce from their farmhouse. These oils, freshly extracted by steaming mint leaves, are extremely concentrated and pungent. They should be used sparingly in recipes, in amounts much smaller than those calling for mint flavorings.

But what flavors they are! Without even uncapping the lids, you can smell the clear, fresh mint. The spearmint has a sweeter smell than the peppermint, but a whiff of either will send a bracing chill all the way down your lungs. The peppermint is first-rate for homemade candy, but Mrs. Livingston says that many people use it in vaporizers to chase off colds, or even rub it on themselves to help arthritis or soothe a cut or burn.

The Livingstons' mint, most of which goes to candy and chewing-gum manufacturers, is processed right on their farm. Mint, which requires much moisture and must be irrigated, is cut like hay, chopped, and put in huge vats in a mint "still," characterized by a tall smokestack. Steam pressure is used to extract the oil.

Mrs. Livingston and her daughter-in-law, Carole, will put up oils (at $4 an ounce) in any size bottle a customer desires, and will send it by mail (shipping is extra). "We will mail it first and then ask for payment," said Mrs. Livingston. "We're quite trusting."

The farm is a place where corn, wheat, oats, barley, hay, and carrots also are grown, and a herd of Jerseys are milked. Since Alden's death in 1992, nearly all the work is done by the couple's son, Eugene. If that wasn't enough, the Livingstons also have been boiling down and bottling their own maple syrup since 1906. Prices for the syrup, like the mint, are more than fair: $4 a half-pint, $6 a pint, $10 a quart, $18 a half-gallon, and $33 a gallon. The Livingstons will mail it, and shipping is extra.

ORDERING ADDRESS

Livingston Farms
2224 Livingston Road
St. John's, MI 48879
517/224-3616
No credit cards; checks OK

VISITS

St. John's is halfway between Grand Rapids and Flint at the junction of U.S. 27 and Highway 21. The Livingston farm is 3 miles north of St. John's on U.S. 27. Turn west on Livingston Road, drive ¼ mile, and it is the second house on the north side of the road. Call ahead for hours.

LOS CHILEROS DE NUEVO MÉXICO FOODS

"Our focus is introducing New Mexico's ancient foods to the public," says Tandy M. Lucero, the owner of Los Chileros de Neuvo México in Santa Fe. He and his wife, Terrie, carry products that are difficult to find even in New Mexico and nearly impossible to find elsewhere.

Among the many items they offer are chicos (dried yellow corn), which add texture and flavor to cooked pinto beans or pork. Atole (roasted blue cornmeal) is cooked with hot water, then mixed with heated milk and sugar for a traditional warm breakfast drink. Or, it can be made into a hot cereal. Panocha (a sprouted whole-wheat flour) is the base for a pudding that has been served during Lent for generations. Posole, or hominy, can be ordered in white- or blue-corn versions. It makes a nutritious, filling dish with cubed meat and chiles.

New Mexico-grown piñon nuts can be had roasted, in the shell. It's a lot of work to crack the small nuts for their sweet meat, so if you plan to make brittle, you might want to order them shelled. The Luceros can't guarantee that the shelled piñons are local, however.

The couple sells 11 kinds of Mexican chiles and several New Mexican varieties. Green chiles are already roasted, peeled, and dried—a real time-saver. You simply let them stand in hot water for 5 minutes and use them in recipes. Another time-saver is the salsa mix. One packet, mixed with tomatoes, is enough to make 4 quarts of salsa. It contains both coarsely ground red chile and japonés chile—and tastes it. It is highly spiced. There also are meat rubs, marinades, and fajitia mixes.

The company carries excellent blue-corn popcorn and blue-corn tortilla chips. If you want to make your own blue-corn tortillas, the Luceros will sell you harinilla, or blue-corn flour. For Santa Fe corn bread, they have blue cornmeal.

Tandy Lucero began the business 19 years ago in the midst of a backpacking trip around the world. A native New Mexican, he returned home midtrip and got sidelined selling chiles with a friend. A year later, the friend had left the business and Tandy had met his future wife, also a New Mexico native.

The bulk of their customers are out of state, divided evenly between individuals and wholesale accounts. The couple contracts a local company to prepare frozen prepared foods using their products, such as green chile rellenos, blue-corn tamales and tortillas, and frozen chiles, and send them to restaurants and stores around the country. It will also send those items to individuals.

If you are visiting Santa Fe, the Luceros suggest buying their products at one of the area stores that sells them. Los Chileros products can be found at The Market Place on Alameda Street, at Woolworth's, and at Gift and Gourmet on the plaza. You may also visit their store.

To order by mail, it is easiest to write, call, or visit their website for their retail price list and product descriptions. Blue cornmeal, panocha, or atole, for example, is $2.19 for a 12-ounce package. A 3-ounce packet of salsa mix is $4.49. There is a $5 minimum order and a $5.50 shipping charge.

ORDERING ADDRESS
Los Chileros de Nuevo México
P.O. Box 6215
Santa Fe, NM 87502
505/471-6967
FAX: 505/473-7306
e-mail: chileros@uswest.net
www.hotchilepepper.com
Credit cards accepted

VISITS
197-J East Frontage Road
Santa Fe, NM 87505
Monday–Friday, 10 A.M.–5 P.M.

MEYENBERG GOAT MILK

Cow's milk is protein-filled, but causes digestibility problems for many stomachs. The Jackson-Mitchell Company has made its mark selling goat milk—in cans of evaporated milk, shelf-stable boxes, and dried powder.

Goat milk has only traces of cow milk's strongest protein. Also, its fats are smaller and more dispersed than in cow milk, allowing sensitive stomachs to handle it. Chefs and home cooks have discovered its creamy uses in soups, ice cream, candy, and baked goods.

We're convinced, because goat milk was the basis of our fondest food memory from childhood—goat milk fudge. When we would take car trips in the late 1950s and early 1960s through Ohio, Pennsylvania, and New York, yard signs advertising homemade goat milk fudge were common along country roads. Our father would turn the 1957 red and white Chevrolet station wagon down the lane to a farmhouse and we'd usually have our choice of creamy chocolate or vanilla fudge.

The signs disappeared over the years, but we thought the resurgence of interest in goat milk would have meant new life for the fudge. After all, there now are goat milk dairies producing nearly every form of cheese imaginable. But try as we might, contacting goat milk producers, state agriculture departments, produce stands, and the like, the only fudge we found was through a resourceful friend, Joyce Gemperlein. She tracked one down in Philadelphia, but sadly, it was a too-sweet version with several artificial ingredients.

Finally, while grocery shopping nearly Pawley's Island, South Carolina, we were drawn to a beautiful can of Meyenberg goat milk. We wrote to the distributor, the Jackson-Mitchell Company, in Santa Barbara, California, on the chance it could supply a fudge producer. In fact, the company was selling a microwave goat milk's fudge! That product didn't last (not enough people with our travel memories, we guess), but we've used the canned milk successfully to replicate our childhood fudge. We went overboard the first year and even entered the county fair's competition and won. Yes, we've got the ribbons to prove it!

It may all be psychological and tied up with a wonderful childhood, but we are very grateful to the Jackson-Mitchell Company, which, of course, is an old family-run firm. Vice president Carol Jackson explains that most of its mail orders are from people requesting the milk for digestibility problems, but that home cooks are warming to its wider possibilities. The milk comes in whole and 1 percent low-fat versions.

ORDERING ADDRESS
Jackson-Mitchell, Inc.
P.O. Box 5425
Santa Barbara, CA 93150
800/565-1538
800/342-1185
e-mail: info@meyenberg.com
www.goatmilk.com
No credit cards; checks OK

NIELSEN-MASSEY VANILLA

Vanilla beans are not unlike coffee beans, or even wine grapes, in that they vary immensely from region to region and variety to variety, resulting in a great number of possible extract strengths, qualities, and flavors. Add to that the several permutations of artificial vanilla extracts and blends of artificial and pure, and you have a product with its own descriptions and flavors as complex as any wine.

The company to best sort out the complexities is Nielsen-Massey Vanillas of Lake Forest, Illinois, the largest independent family-run vanilla firm in the nation. Nielsen-Massey has been selling its different vanillas primarily to ice-cream manufacturers and professional bakers for 90 years, and it is only in the last 17 that its vanilla has been made available to the retail market.

Home cooks got lucky when, as a favor, the company hand-filled a few bottles of its pure, single-strength vanilla for a local cookware store. An alert employee at Williams-Sonoma, the cook's catalog that originated in northern California, bought a bottle and put it in the catalog, selling more than 17,000 bottles the first year.

Nielsen-Massey is the largest pure-vanilla specialist in the world, producing pure vanilla in 25 different strengths and blends. (It discontinued selling imitation vanillas in 1985.) "Liquid gold," is how one professional Chicago cheesecake baker refers to Nielsen-Massey vanilla, and she isn't referring only to the price. The pure vanilla that's available retail has a full-throated flavor that carries through to finished products, particularly delicately flavored items such as custards and ice creams.

The company uses Madagascar beans from the Bourbon Islands and shuns the quicker heat process to extract the flavor from the beans, unlike most other vanilla processors. Heat is detrimental to the flavoring essences of the vanilla bean, so Nielsen-Massey extracts the flavor by circulating a series of cold solutions of alcohol and water through the beans.

Individual 8-ounce bottles of extract are available through Williams-Sonoma for $11, plus shipping.

ORDERING ADDRESS
The Williams-Sonoma Catalog
P.O. Box 379900
Las Vegas, NV 89137
800/541-2233
FAX: 702/363-2541
www.williams-sonoma.com
Credit cards accepted

NORTHWESTERN COFFEE MILLS SALT-FREE SEASONINGS

In its 125 years of doing business, Wisconsin's Northwestern Coffee Mills has pretty much figured out what works and what doesn't. In its very complete catalog, the owner, Harry Demorest, explains: "We work for substance before appearance. . . . We also know that our earnings must include satisfaction as well as dollars for us to stay at our work in the long run."

Blending is serious business at Northwestern, where coffees, teas, and seasonings are all approached by careful mixing. Northwestern has customers all across the country that depend on it for its slow-roasted coffees, which include Islander's Blend ($8.25 a pound), the mellow coffee that the business was built upon in 1875. The company is also a good source for reasonably priced filters (including obscure sizes) and extracts for flavoring coffee, if you are of that persuasion.

Northwestern tells customers that the proper way to flavor coffee is to add an extract after or while it is being brewed, not to buy flavored beans. Flavored beans taint grinders and tend to be so perfumy that the coffee taste gets smothered, they explain.

The items that really caught our attention were the salt-free seasonings, many unique to the company, that Northwestern offers. Seasonings, like prepared foods, often are hidden sources of salt. Salt is inexpensive, and can be used to extend spices. Northwestern has an all-purpose salt-free seasoning that is wonderful on fish or eggs. There are Italian and French herb blends, and two varieties each of chili or curry powders. Pickling spice mix, no-salt cream of tartar, filé powder, Chinese five-spice, and lemon pepper are other offerings. There are eight varieties of peppercorns. Dried fruits and vegetables include lemon peel granule, horseradish powder, and juniper berries. None costs more than $1.75 per ounce, and you can select exactly how much you wish to try.

NORTHWESTERN COFFEE MILLS

In its lineup of seasonings with salt, Northwestern has a terrific Dixie chicken spice that makes a savory addition to any poultry dish.

In keeping with its low-key philosophy, Northwestern Coffee Mills products are packaged simply, in reclosable paper sacks (for the coffee substitutes) and zip-top plastic bags for the spices. The discounts increase with larger orders, so the company recommends combining orders with family or friends for additional savings.

After more than a century in downtown Milwaukee, the store is now on Madeline Island, at the very northern tip of Wisconsin. This island has fewer than 200 year-round residents, but thousands of summer visitors. There are ferries between Bayfield and La Pointe daily from April to early December, running every half-hour during mid-June through October. In the winter, travel is accomplished by motorized windsleds. When the lake freezes, cars use Lake Superior as an ice highway.

The company offers coffee roasting and tea blending seminars and training as well as casual visitors during the weekdays. Please call first.

ORDERING ADDRESS
Northwestern Coffee Mills
P.O. Box 370
LaPointe, WI 54850
715/747-5555
800/243-5283
FAX: 715/747-5405
e-mail: nwcoftsp@win.bright.net
www.nwcoffeemills.com
Credit cards accepted

VISITS
1370 Middle Road
La Pointe, WI 54850
La Pointe is on Madeline Island, one of Wisconsin's Apostle Islands in Lake Superior. Ferries run every half-hour during the summer from Bayfield, Wisconsin. Please call ahead before visiting.
Monday–Friday, 10 A.M.–4 P.M.

PENZEYS SPICES

We love the Penzeys Spices catalog. Where else do you see cover lines such as "New Expanded Pepper Coverage," or read fascinating accounts of how political upheavals in Sri Lanka are affecting the supplies of Ceylon cinnamon? This quarterly free publication is more than a catalog. It is an encyclopedia of spice information. Reading it, and looking at the color pictures, you understand for the first time how nutmeg is harvested from trees in Indonesia, and see how honey-colored tentacles of mace cover the outer shell of the nutmeg seed kernel. You can discover that there are three kinds of cardamom—white, green, and black—and that each is particular to different world cuisines. (Black cardamom has a smoky flavor and is a staple of African cooking. Scandinavian countries favor white cardamom for flavoring cakes, cookies, and yeast doughs. In the Middle East, both green and black cardamom are used in meat and vegetable dishes, and are sometimes mixed with green coffee beans before brewing.) And you can expand your culinary knowledge by learning about (and ordering) spices that are unfamiliar to you, such as ajwain seed (a key ingredient in Indian and Pakistani lentil and bean dishes), or Indian charnuska (known as black caraway seeds), or mahlab (the pit of the sour cherry used in Turkish and Syrian baked goods). To top it off, the Penzeys Spices catalog includes great recipes using its spices, with step by step instructions.

A brother and sister, Bill and Pamela Penzey, are the driving forces behind this company. Their parents had a coffee and spice business, so they grew up in the spice trade. Sixteen years ago, they began their business with one clear mission: to seek out high-quality spice growers around the world and persuade them to ship their rarest and finest to America. It has taken some persuading, because the perception among spice growers is that Americans, represented by huge spice companies, buy large amounts of run-of-the-mill spices and won't pay for top quality.

So the Penzeys travel to remote locations, forging relationships with individual growers and shippers, to bring the best of the world's harvests to their company in Wisconsin. Their second mission is freshness. Spices are ground and mixed according to demand, and don't sit around for months exposed to the air and losing potency. Bill Penzey explains that supermarket spices may be several years old even prior to packaging. The stock in their quickly expanding chain of retail stores in Wisconsin, Minnesota, Illinois, and Connecticut might look spare, but that's because Penzeys doesn't keep barrels of spices and herbs on display, getting stale. Penzeys sells most of its spices in a thoughtful assortment of sizes. You can order 1-ounce or 4-ounce bags of an unfamiliar spice for a taste, or order 8-ounce bulk bags. The firm sells glass and plastic spice jars in several sizes, and your selection can be packed in those, if you desire. Prices are extremely reasonable. Check out Penzeys taco seasoning, which can be purchased in a 1-pound bag for $8.40. Much more flavorable and less expensive than those single packets in the grocery store.

One of the great things the company offers is gift boxes. There's a Spice Replacement Set for those who are starting afresh in life, or simply tired of a cupboard-full of stale spices. There's a Pepper Crate, with two peppermills and jars of black, green, and white peppercorns, and a 4-peppercorn blend that includes pink peppercorns, as well as a jar of Mignonette pepper, a mix of coarse cracked black pepper, white pepper, and coriander. There are Grill and Broil boxes for flavoring meats and fish. There's a Taste of Mexico box, including epazote, ancho chili peppers, freshly ground cumin, cilantro, chipotle peppers, adobo seasoning, cinnamon, and oregano. And there are our favorites, Spicy Wedding gift boxes in various sizes. We've given them several times for wedding and shower presents, and they are memorable gifts. Tucked in the boxes are a few spices for good luck charms—rosemary leaves (the herb of lovers), star anise (given in China to bridal couples to signify unity and tenaciousness to stay whole), and whole nutmeg (to satisfy the old European belief that as long as there is a whole nutmeg in the kitchen, the marriage will be sound).

We can't recommend Penzeys too highly. The company's selection is unparalleled (we drool over the cinnamon and vanilla choices), and it does an amazing job of demystifying spices and herbs to make global dishes accessible to anyone. Add to that the company's social consciousness, and its support of high-quality growers worldwide, and you have one of the most innovative and respected small food companies in America.

ORDERING ADDRESS
Penzeys Spices
P.O. Box 933
W19362 Apollo Drive
Muskego, WI 53150
800/741-7787
FAX: 414/679-7878
www.penzeys.com
Credit cards accepted

VISITS
There are six retail stores:
18900 West Bluemond Road
Brookfield, WI (on the west side of Milwaukee, right behind Kopp's Frozen Custard)
262/641-0999
3234 University Avenue
Madison, WI (in the Shorewood Shopping Center west of the University of Wisconsin campus)
608/238-5776
674 Grand Avenue
St. Paul, MN (Dale Street, Highway 94, take exit 240)
651/224-8448
3028 Hennepin Avenue
Minneapolis, MN (across from Calhoun Square Shopping Center, take Hennepin Avenue South exit from I-94)
612/824-9777
1138 West Lake Street
Oak Park, IL (off Harlem, exit 21B from 290)
708/848-7772
197 Westport Avenue
Norwalk, CT (on Route 1, exit 16 off I-95)
203/849-9085
All stores: Monday–Friday, 9:30 A.M.–5:30 A.M. Saturday, 9:30 A.M.–5 P.M.

SABBATHDAY LAKE SHAKER HERBS

When an item, such as herbs, becomes trendy, the market is flooded with dozens of brands, many suffering from gingham-bow disease. Thus it is a relief to deal with Maine's Sabbathday Lake Shakers, a small, well-respected religious group whose history has been intertwined with herb growing for more than 160 years. The Shakers, whose herb business revived in the 1960s after decades of relative inaction, grow or forage nearly everything they sell on the 1,700 acres of heavily wooded land they own in Poland Spring, Maine, in the southwest part of the state.

An exhaustive line of herbal teas and culinary herbs is available at the community's store or through the mail. No fewer than 17 herbal teas are offered, including camomile, catnip, dandelion (leaf or root), lavender, horehound, rose hips, and wintergreen. The expected culinary herbs are sold, as well as marigold, anise seed, fennel, coriander seed, and chervil.

The herbs, packed to overflowing in round metal tins with tight-fitting lids, are dried but aromatic. They also are available in smaller amounts in plastic bags, which is an aid to occasional cooks and to those wishing to refill the tins. The Shakers have introduced four useful herb mixes—a dill dip, poultry seasoning, Italian seasoning, and salad seasoning.

The tea blends are rich mixtures of identifiable flowers and leaves, not pulverized, anonymous stews. Also available is a fragrant potpourri, in tin or jar, that faithfully follows an 1858 "receipt" of Eldress Hester Ann Adams. A true bargain for cooks accustomed to the steep price of imported rose waters is the Shaker rose water, which is $2.75 for a 4-ounce plastic bottle. Made from the Shakers' own roses, it adds a lovely taste to custard and other delicate desserts. It also can be used in making hand creams at home. A new mint water, good in chocolate recipes and jellies, also is offered at the same size and price.

But all the prices are reasonable. Teas range from $4.75 per tin and herbs from $1 to $4.25. The weights of the herbs vary, although the size of the tin does not.

There are five Shaker Sisters and four Shaker Brothers who live at the community. The nine, known as The United Society of Shakers, are descended from a settlement founded in 1794. The community, with a community herb house built as early as 1824, was known for its medicines made from herbs. However, when the Pure Food and Drug Act of 1906 ended the patent-medicine industry, the Shakers stopped selling herbs for healing purposes, and over the years the herb operation waned. Now, with a market receptive to their unusual quality offerings, the Shakers have begun selling an Alfred fruitcake at Christmas, named for a former Shaker community in Alfred, Maine. Also sold by mail are dates stuffed with pecans and rolled in sugar, long made by Sister Mildred.

A museum depicting Shaker life is open at the community in the summer and the Shaker store is open from May until early December. The museum shop is an important source for books on herbs, as well as for Shaker publications on topics such as spinning wheels and Shaker spirituals. Virgin wool yarn, spun from the fleece of the community's flock, is sold in 25 colors and shades.

The society's herb catalog is free. Tours of the herb department and herb garden are available by appointment.

ORDERING ADDRESS
United Society of Shakers
707 Shaker Road
New Gloucester, ME 04260
207/926-4597
www.shaker.lib.me.us
No credit cards; checks OK

VISITS: **Sabbathday Lake is on Highway 26 in the town of New Gloucester. The six-story brick main dwelling house, one of 17 buildings in the settlement, is an area landmark, as is the 1794 Shaker meetinghouse.**
Shaker Store: Memorial Day–first Saturday in December. Monday–Saturday, 10 A.M.–4:30 P.M.
Shaker Museum: Memorial Day–Columbus Day. Monday–Saturday, 10 A.M.–4:30 P.M.

SHAHARAZAD HANDMADE FILO

Several mornings a week, a ballet is performed at the Shaharazad Bakery in San Francisco. As he has done for 40 years here and for many years in his native Istanbul, Mihran Sagatelyan, 70, faces his partner across a large table covered with canvas and performs a delicate pas de deux that begins with round circles of dough and ends with immense paper-thin sheets of filo. The Shaharazad Bakery is the last in San Francisco to make filo dough by hand and one of the few places in the country where the dough—the critical ingredient in strudels, baklava, bastilla, and other dishes—isn't made by machine.

Mihran, dressed in white, works quickly in the back of his family's small storefront in the Sunset District, a residential part of the city. He starts by keeping one hand steady and stretching and pulling at the dough with his other hand, in a motion not unlike a knitter making a skein, until it is large enough to pass to his partner waiting across the table. Then the two, while stretching the edges, toss the dough in the air like a blanket, much like firefighters waiting for someone to jump. They stop to sprinkle on cornstarch, and smooth the finished sheet taut and perfect, without a hole or tear. They dust it with cornstarch, using wood-handled brushes, and go on to the next circle of dough. When finished, the sheets are folded, wrapped in plastic and white paper, and sold for the humble sum of $6 a pound.

The difference from filo that is machine made and shipped to supermarkets is readily apparent. Shaharazad's has no preservatives, for one, containing only flour, cornstarch, water, and salt. The dough, because it is sold freshly made, does not stick together and is a lighter product, resulting in flakier pastries. Mihran used to stretch with his brother, Migirdich, until he retired. Migirdich told us: "Machines push on the dough, making it very heavy. Ours is very, very light. But no one wants to make it by hand anymore. I make fifty pounds, and in the same amount of time, the machine makes ten thousand pounds."

Currently, about 120 pounds of week of filo are produced here, usually on Tuesday, Wednesday, and Thursdays. It takes from 11 A.M. to 3 P.M. to complete the process, which is why large numbers of downtown San Francisco chefs buy their filo here. Mihran's daughter, Ani Burke, helps out with stretching, as does his wife, Rose.

On display in the bakery are pastries that the Sagatelyans make using their dough, including baklava, kadaiff (a treat that resembles a haystack filled with pistachios, walnuts, and cinnamon), bird's nest (a square pastry with a filo topknot surrounded by bright-green chipped pistachios), and cherry-filled turnovers. All are excellent and not cloyingly sweet, as filo-dough pastries are inclined to be. Again, the prices are bargains—$1 per piece of baklava and $1.75 for a bird's nest.

The shop is tiny, but visitors linger, buying a cup of coffee for 50¢ and sitting at a few tables, eating fresh pastry. They're actually eating culinary art. The skill required to produce this dough keeps us in awe.

We vote that this neighborhood bakery should be designated a national treasure. Why shouldn't baking skills to be esteemed in the manner of all other arts?

VISITS
Shaharazad Bakery
1586 Noriega Street
San Francisco, CA 94122
415/661-1155
No credit cards
From Golden Gate Park, go south on 19th Avenue (Park Presidio) 6 blocks to Noriega. Turn right. Drive to 23rd Street. The bakery is on the right.
Monday–Saturday, 9 A.M.–5 P.M.

SPICELAND HERBS AND SPICE BLENDS

Thank you, Mike Optie of Harwood Heights, Illinois, for writing us about Spiceland. While there are any number of mail-order spice and herb shops around the country, we have come to appreciate this small husband-and-wife operation for its high quality, low prices, and willingness to seek out unusual items for customers.

Doris and Jim Stockwell are former academics (in philosophy and history, respectively) who have turned their research skills to seasonings. Not all spice information comes from books, however, Doris has learned. "It comes from schmoozing with spice people."

The couple also schmoozes with customers, who represent a League of Nations of ethnic groups. If someone requests a particular spice, the Stockwells often inquire about the intended use, often acquiring a new recipe to share with other customers.

The couple began their business in a circuitous way when Doris inherited a house filled with antiques in 1974. She and Jim sold the furniture at a weekend flea market and enjoyed the experience so much that after the antiques ran out, they began selling spices. Their inventory grew to the point that they opened a tiny storefront in a Polish Chicago neighborhood in 1984. Many Poles purchase large quantities of caraway, white pepper, allspice, marjoram, and bay leaves to send to relatives overseas.

The company packages spices under its Spicelords label, named after the science fiction spice men in Frank Herbert's novel *Dune.* "We don't offer many blends since most of our customers create their own combinations," Doris wrote us. "We do blend an all-purpose salt-free spice. We invented it in response to requests for a product that's salt-free, all-purpose like Mrs. Dash but doesn't contain lemon flavor. People who are on a sodium-restricted diet and have never experimented with the use of spices and don't know where to begin to find this product useful. They can throw it into stews, soups, on meats, lasagnas, etc." Another winner is the couple's pizza seasoning. Simply mix the dried spices and vegetables in tomato sauce and pour over pizza dough.

Spiceland is a good source for dried soup bases—chicken, beef, onion, ham, or seafood. "People augment their own soup stocks, since chicken broth is often bland, using the new less-flavorful chickens," said Doris. "They also use it wherever some broth may be needed, as in stir frying." The beef and chicken flavors come in low-salt versions—a welcome alternative to highly salted bouillon cubes.

Spiceland is a source for exotic flavorings, such as rose water, pineapple extract, spinach powder, and it is an economical source for staples such as cinnamon sticks, which cost a small fortune on the supermarket shelves. A pound of 4-inch sticks (about 64 sticks) is $8. We've seen a measly 6 sticks sell for $2 in gourmet shops.

"We figured out that at our price for whole cloves, $7.35 a pound, an equivalent amount at grocery-store prices would be $170," said Jim. "That gives you an idea of how much you are paying for spices in the little containers at the supermarket."

Another bargain is whole black peppercorns. Premium Tellicherry peppers, grown in southwest India, are known as the finest of all peppers. The usual varieties sold in supermarkets are the harsher Malabar or Lampong peppers. Spiceland sells a pound of pungent Tellicherry peppercorns for $7.75, about half the price we saw advertised in a catalog from a large mail-order concern.

All shipping is extra, but the top shipping cost in the continental United States is $4.95, no matter how large the order. It's worth it to study the lengthy order form carefully for hidden gems. We found six kinds of dried mushrooms, an interesting saffron substitute called Bijol, from Florida ("sold in the world markets for over thirty-five years"), inexpensive sesame and poppy seeds, and sweet and hot Korean chili spice.

The company also sells related kitchen items, such as peppermills, spice infusers, graters, and garlic presses. It supplies many of Chicago's gourmet restaurants with spices and blends. Orders may be picked up at its warehouse, but items are not sold there.

ORDERING ADDRESS
Spiceland, Inc.
P.O. Box 34378
Chicago, IL 60634
773/736-1000
800/FLAVOR1 (352-8671)
Credit cards accepted

TO PICK UP ORDERS
6604 W. Irving Park
Chicago, IL 60634
Monday–Friday, 10 A.M.–4:30 P.M.

VIVANDE PORTA VIA ITALIAN SPECIALTIES

There is plenty in San Francisco to beckon visitors, but some of its most charming places will never make a Grey Line bus tour. We'd hate to see busloads of tourists pour into Vivande Porta Via, a café-deli-specialty food shop in Pacific Heights, but we also hate to think that serious eaters might visit the city without stopping there. Vivande Porta Via has been compared favorably with Fauchon of Paris, Peck's of Milan, and Dallmayr of Munich in the world-class deli category. Run by Carlo Middione, author of the 1987 cookbook *The Food of Southern Italy,* and his wife, Elizabeth (Lisa), this food shop is a national treasure.

The Middiones import and sell critical Italian ingredients (cheeses, flours, arborio rice, etc.) and create authentic fresh items, such as pâtés, pasta, sausages, antipasti, biscotti, and various sweets.

Happily for those of us who can't visit San Francisco every time the urge for superlative Italian food strikes, Vivande Porta Via (the name translates literally as "Food to Take Away") will mail its nonperishable products. For a self-improvement course in Italian cuisine, you can't do better than to order a copy of Carlo's book (winner of a Tastemaker Award for the best international cookbook of the year and correctly described as "aimed . . . at the kind of eater who is sophisticated enough to enjoy simple food") and to ask for the store's Notizie! publication, which lists the many foods it will ship. Try the excellent anchovies, roasted peppers, balsamic vinegars, dried porcini mushrooms, and Parmesano-Reggiano cheese for starters. The cookbook (autographed) is $25.

VIVANDE
Porta Via

If pasta alone piques your interest, there's an impressive assortment of air-dried Italian pasta, buckwheat pasta, and durum and semolina flours.

The pantry items can be ordered individually, as can many of Vivande's specialties, such as Pasta Via Appia, an assertively seasoned trail mix of variously shaped dried pasta and cheese. We've seen imitations of this product all over the country, but none have the appeal—and jolt of garlic—that Vivande's does. It is $11.50 per pound.

Handmade Italian cookies are other often-ordered treats. Almond-poppyseed bars are distinctive, buttery rectangles with an abundance of toasted slivered almonds inside and a paving coat of poppyseeds. Crunchy, nut-studded biscotti di prato, chocolate pepper cookies, almond balls covered in confectioners' sugar, and 1-inch round, full-flavored amaretti cookies also are available. The cookies are $12 to $16 a pound and can be ordered individually or as a mixed pack. All are superbly suited for dipping in coffee or wine. A savory cheese wafer, made at Vivande, can be ordered for $16 a pound.

Vivande, open since 1981, looks small from the outside. The narrow storefront is quite deep, however. And its influence on the food industry greatly exceeds its four walls. When well-known food writers come to San Francisco to promote their books, they head to Vivande. A small amount of shelf space is allotted to books, perhaps thirty titles, "but you'd be surprised at the number of books we sell," said Lisa.

The front part of the store is a wonderful place to browse, either before or after you've had a bite at the café. "Basically, we provide the public the ingredients that we use in our own fresh items," said Carlo.

Even Vivande's carefully selected Italian wines can be shipped, state law permitting.

It is rare to find this level of passion about good food without a hint of pretense. We urge you to experience Vivande, either in person or long-distance.

ORDERING ADDRESS
Vivande Porte Via
2125 Fillmore Street
San Francisco, CA 95115
415/346-4430
Credit cards accepted

VISITS: *Deli: Daily, 10 A.M.–7 P.M. Restaurant: Daily, 11:30 A.M.–10 P.M.*

THE WHIPPLE COMPANY MINCEMEAT

It seems a contradiction in terms, but there exists an excellent packaged mincemeat that omits a critical ingredient—meat. Grandmother's brand mincemeat, made since 1899 by the Whipple Company of Natick, Massachusetts, is an exceedingly tasty mix of apples in small dice, currants, raisins, citrus peel, vinegar, sugar, spices, and vegetable shortening. In fact, we ate three spoonfuls straight from the jar before we realized there was no meat.

Company president Dight Crain, great-grandson of Harrison L. Whipple, the founder of the firm, said the original recipe did have corned beef in it, but that the firm slowly phased out meat nearly four decades ago. The reason, he said, was in large part because the firm was not using kosher beef, making its product unacceptable to the large Jewish population in Whipple's main distribution area, the Northeast. After a period of substituting beef suet, the company switched to vegetable oil. "it is the spice variation that differs from brand to brand and makes the real difference," says Crain, "and the rest of our secret recipe has remained intact. The only way people notice [the absence of meat] is by reading the label. We have not had one iota of complaint."

Not having the opportunity to taste Grandmother's mincemeat years ago, we can't offer an opinion. But we can vouch for the spice-filled, lively flavor that avoids the acrid taste that mars many packaged mincemeats.

Twenty-five years ago, the company introduced a rum mincemeat flavored with the genuine article. A brandy mincemeat has been added to the line, but the flavoring is imitation. Made without preservatives, all the mincemeats will keep indefinitely in the refrigerator after opening. Aged mincemeat, says Crain, a year or so old, is even better than fresh. The product already is cooked, so pies need only be cooked until the crust browns.

Grandmother's™
FINE FOODS SINCE 1899

The mincemeat is packed in 28-ounce jars that contain enough filling for a 9-inch pie. A jar sells for $5 and can be ordered from outside the New England area all year long. A case of 12 jars of the plain version is $51, plus UPS charges. During the holiday season, New England residents are asked to look for the product on their grocery shelves. At other times of the year, however, the company will send mincemeat to New Englanders.

The mincemeat is made only in the fall in a large former shoe factory in downtown Natick, a town due west of Boston. During the rest of the year, the company makes pie fillings, fruit syrups, preserves, ice-cream toppings, and relishes, mostly for institutions and for sale under other labels.

Crain's son, Andrew, helps run the company into the start of its second hundred years.

ORDERING ADDRESS
The Whipple Company
P.O. Box 275
Natick, MA 01760-0275
508/653-2660
800/345-2925
FAX: 508/653-2662
No credit cards; checks OK

VISITS
The Whipple Company
58 North Main Street
Natick, MA 01760
Natick is a far western suburb of Boston, on Route 135.
Monday–Friday, 9 A.M.–5 P.M.

WALNUT ACRES NATURAL FOODS

Walnut Acres has earned the right to say "We told you so." In 1946, Paul and the late Betty Keene began farming organically and offering healthy food by mail. Now, the company they began is the largest mail-order natural foods company in the United States and boasts its own grain mill, cannery, bakery, freezing plant, and retail shop, located on the 600-acre farm where cattle, chickens, and crops used in the hundreds of Walnut Acres products are raised. Another 400-acre organic farm in Washington, Virginia, owned by major investor David Cole, contributes livestock, fruits, and vegetables.

Cole now owns a majority stake in the enterprise, bu the Keene family still is involved in day-to-day production, with Keene's son-in-law, Bob Anderson, as president, and his daughter, Ruth (called Chip) in charge of catalogs.

These days, with chemical-tainted food serving as cover stories for news magazines, the interest in organically raised food has turned into a stampede. Paul Keene, 89, and the thousands of customers who have been with him for decades, has every reason to be smug. But he's not. He's retired and still living on the farm. In one of his "Greetings from the Farm" essays, he wrote passionately about controlling our own destinies, starting with the foods we eat. "Unless we rise above our present situation in which we are fed docilely by unseen and unknowable hands, we can see the end by simply looking at the direction in which we are moving."

Since the Keenes began farming before the days of modern insecticides and herbicides, which they have always shunned, Walnut Acres can justifiably say their land is untainted. "Had we decided suddenly, just yesterday or a year ago, to become 'organic' because it seemed the thing to do, we would . . . feel a little hesitant at declaiming our naturalness," Keene noted.

Walnut Acres is user-friendly. There's a 24-hour ordering number, computerized billing, and quick service. The catalogs are helpful, with items marked as certified organically grown, or grown at Walnut Acres, or grown without chemical sprays. Recipes are sprinkled throughout the copy, and there are color pictures of almost everything. More recipes and instructions come with your order—even directions on what to do should a can arrive dented. The company's best-sellers are peanut butter, nuts, soups, canned vegetables and fruits, granolas, and dried fruits.

The peanut butter comes smooth or chunky, with salt and without, and uses the entire red skin of the nut, giving it a reddish color, with small flecks of skin. We tried the lightly salted chunky peanut butter and were hooked. It has a much more concentrated peanut taste than supermarket varieties and infinitely better flavor. For those concerned about contaminants, the label states that it is aflatoxin tested and that no chemical fertilizers, no ED13, no preservatives, and no fumigants were used. A 1-pound jar is $4.49.

The soups are made at Walnut Acres, using ingredients produced there, and are canned in heavy lined tin cans with no lead in the seams. Some are available unsalted, but the regular versions have very little salt added. They may be a little on the bland side, but it's easy enough to add some herbs or curry powder if you desire more zip.

We especially liked a New England clam chowder, sweet potato chowder, and organic vegetable beef soup. There are more than two dozen canned soup varieties to choose from, as well as an array of dried soups. Then there are the quick canned suppers, such as braised beef hash, beef or chicken stew, and chili con carne. After years of shunning these time-savers because the commercial versions are loaded with sodium, it is such a joy to have these on the shelf. The canned soups cost from $1.99 to $2.49 per 16-ounce can. The canned entrees, also in 16-ounce cans, range from $2.79 to $3.99 for the hash.

Chef Nora Pouillon, who runs two natural foods gourmet restaurants in Washington, D.C., has developed very good organic soup, risotto, and mashed potato mixes for Walnut Acres. The Moroccan 7-vegetable soup with couscous is a standout, as are the mashed potatoes with spinach and double mustard.

We were also taken with the company's mayonnaise. Its ingredient list has but seven entries: canola oil, fresh eggs, cider vinegar, honey, salt, mustard, and white pepper. Compare that to 21 ingredients in the jar from Kraft! The Walnut Acres mayonnaise has a tangy, pleasant taste and spreads more easily than the gelatinous supermarket mayonnaise. One pint is $3.99.

Walnut Acres, with its housewares and cookbooks, its spices and dried fruits and nuts, its flours, juices, vitamins, and meats, is like having a well-stocked natural food store on the other end of the phone. It's a good source for learning about hitherto unfamiliar products, like anasazi beans (palomino-colored beans that are a combination of pinto and kidney beans) or wehani rice, which turns slightly lavender when cooked.

There's also an expanded selection of organic meats, including hot dogs, hamburgers, chicken breasts, turkey burgers, and steaks.

The company has long been a steward of the larger community, too. It set up a foundation in 1961 to support a family village farm in India and a community center in Penns Creek. It also is a sponsor of Penn Releaf, a tree-planting program run with the Pennsylvania Forestry Association. We like that it replants three trees for every tree used to print its catalogs.

ORDERING ADDRESS
Walnut Acres
Penns Creek, PA 17862
570/837-0601
800/433-3998
FAX: 570/837-1146
www.walnutacres.com
Credit cards accepted

VISITS: Penns Creek is in central Pennsylvania, between Williamsport and Harrisburg. If driving north from Harrisburg on Route 11 and 15, turn onto Route 104 about 5 miles north of Liverpool. Route 104 takes you into Penns Creek, where you will see signs for Walnut Acres.
Monday–Wednesday, Friday–Saturday, 9 A.M.–5 P.M. Thursday, 9 A.M.–8 P.M. Sunday, Noon–5 P.M.

TOURS: *Monday–Friday, 9:30 A.M., 11 A.M., and 1 P.M.*

LUNCH BAR: *Monday–Saturday 11 A.M.–2 P.M.*

WILBUR BUDS AND DUTCH COCOA

Before there were chocolate chips and before Mrs. Wakefield cut up semisweet chocolate bars to make her immortal Toll House cookies, there were Wilbur Buds, made in Lititz, Pennsylvania, by the Wilbur Chocolate Company. Wilbur Buds, buttonlike drops of chocolate nearly an inch in diameter with the word "Wilbur" stamped on the underside, have been made continually since 1884 but suffered a decline after World War II, when financial difficulties in the company caused a serious lapse in marketing.

It is now owned by Cargill, a giant in agricultural grains, and Wilbur Buds have been returning to the shelves of candy and gourmet shops. They come in two flavors—the original European dark chocolate, and milk chocolate. Since the company's primary business is supplying chocolate to other candy and food makers, it knows chocolate. Wilbur Buds are solid and smooth, not overly sweet, and rich enough so only a few will satisfy.

Another Wilbur product that hails back to its founding days is Dutch-process cocoa, packaged in a tin that is very close to the original design used in the late 1880s. Although it represents a fraction of the company's business, Wilbur feels an obligation to continue making the cocoa. The Amish in particular use the cocoa because it is critical to the rich, dark, red-brown cake that is standard in their households. It is the process of "Dutching," or making the cocoa less acid by treating it with alkaline substance (in this case, potash), that makes the color darker and brings out the red-brown cast. The name has nothing to do with the Netherlands, although most consumers think otherwise.

Both Wilbur Buds and the Dutch-process cocoa are available by mail from the company. The buds (any flavor) are $5.30 for a 1-pound bag, plus shipping, and a 14-ounce tin of the cocoa is $7, plus shipping. Better yet would be a visit to the factory and chocolate museum itself, located smack in the center of town and easy to find by the telltale aroma of chocolate. Prices are less at the store; $3.75 for Wilbur Buds and $4.95 for the cocoa. There are free samples of buds at the candy museum.

ORDERING ADDRESS
The Wilbur Chocolate Company, Inc.
Lititz, PA 17543
717/626-3226
888/2WILBUR (294-5287)
FAX: 717/626-3256
www.wilburbuds.com
Credit cards accepted

VISITS
Wilbur's Candy Americana Museum
46 North Broad Street
Lititz, PA 17543
Lititz, a town of 7,000 in Pennsylvania Dutch country, is in the south-central part of the state, about 8 miles north of Lancaster. It is at State Routes 501 and 772, south of the Pennsylvania Turnpike (exit 20).
Monday–Saturday, 10 A.M.–5 P.M.

MEATS

AMANA SMOKED MEATS

The Amana name that is known for food freezers and refrigerators got its start in 1855, when a religious group with German, Swiss, and Alsatian origins moved to east-central Iowa from the state of New York, where they had lived communally since 1842. The Amana Colony they founded was made up of seven villages located on 26,000 acres and became known for superb craftsmanship in looming wool, making furniture, smoking meat, and making wine and breads. These industries continue today. Restaurants located in the Amana Colonies rightly are known for their table-groaning family-style meals, reminiscent of communal meals served in the large kitchen houses in early Amana.

Originally, each of the seven villages had its own meat shop where meats were processed for the people in that village. Meats were smoked in large towers at each of the shops. Today, two meat shops remain: one in the village of Homestead and one in the village of Amana. Both shops serve the local trade and visitors. Hundreds of thousands of people come from all over to tour the unique colony each year.

The Amana Meat Shop sells its products by mail and through the Internet. Specialties include smoked hams, bacon, and sausages made with time-tested recipes. The catalog includes gift assortments of smoked meats and cheeses as well as the finest Midwest-grown steaks and pork. The markets make several traditional specialties, like *schwartenmagen,* a mixture of pork heart, pork tongue, jowls, and skin, that do not appear in the catalog but can be ordered.

ORDERING ADDRESS
Amana Society Meat Shop & Smokehouse
P.O. Box 158
Amana, IA 52203
319/622-7595
800/373-6328
www.amanameatshop.com
Credit cards accepted

VISITS: The shop in Amana is a block north of Highway 220 that runs through the village of Amana. In Homestead, the shop is just south of the intersection of Highways 151 and 6. The colonies are 18 miles west of Iowa City on Highway 6 or 5 miles north of I-80, exit 225.
Both stores: Spring–Summer Hours: Monday–Saturday, 9 A.M.–5 P.M. Sunday, 10 A.M.–4 P.M. In winter, the shops usually close earlier.

BROKEN ARROW RANCH WILD GAME

When it comes to wild game, there is a definite imbalance in supply and demand. If you are a hunter, your freezer is invariably stuffed with pheasants or venison sausage from the past three seasons and your friends no longer welcome you with outstretched hands. If you aren't a hunter or don't know someone who is, you usually don't have a clue how to obtain exotic meats.

In 1983 Mike Hughes formed the Texas Wild Game Cooperative, a group of 80 ranches, to make antelope, wild boar, and especially venison available to restaurants and individuals. The ranches originally looked upon the venture as a useful way to deal with overpopulation but have realized that there is a market potential for the game beyond the narrow gourmet niche. Venison's low-fat and low-calorie qualities, particularly the tender venison from axis deer, are attracting health-conscious eaters. The cooperative's Broken Arrow Ranch brand venison has been tested by Texas A & M University as having nearly one-eighth the fat content of beef and significantly less than chicken.

Hughes takes pains to point out that no native species, like the whitetail deer, are hunted, so it is legal for the cooperative to hunt year-round. Whitetail venison, which is the variety most Americans are familiar with, is known for its pronounced gamey taste, resulting, Hughes says, from its diet of leaves and weeds. Axis deer, which hail from India, eat mostly grass, which results in a milder flavor.

The cooperative also hunts sika deer, originally from China, and fallow deer, from Europe. These exotic species were brought to the Texas Hill Country in the 1930s as surplus zoo animals and have been multiplying since.

"Our company was the first to develop and implement a procedure for harvesting truly wild game animals under inspection by a government agency," Hughes wrote us. Employees of the cooperative use a mobile slaughterhouse that is driven to member ranches within a 100-mile radius of the operation's base in Ingram, Texas. A state meat inspector travels with the unit to inspect live animals and carcasses.

Fancy restaurant chefs favor wild boar (which are trapped, not hunted), and saddles and legs of venison, but individual consumers like the easier-to-use products, such as ground venison, venison stew meat chunks, and smoked venison or wild boar sausage. We tried venison cubes and used a recipe for stew from the cooperative's recipe booklet with good results. Ditto for the chili we made with ground venison and scaloppine using venison strips. (The scaloppine was not cut in thin slices, like veal. We had to pound it, and it was more the thickness of medallions or a pork chop. Braising it, however, made it a tender entree that even a picky 4-year-old ate.)

Broken Arrow Ranch products can be found in the frozen meat section of some grocery stores around the country, or they can be sent directly to individuals. There is no minimum order. Shipping is free on orders over 10 pounds. A $25 fee is added to orders under 10 pounds.

Ground venison or chili meat is $6.50 per pound; venison and wild boar stew cubes are $7.50 per pound. Boneless leg fillet is $16.50 per pound. Six varieties of well-spiced sausage links range in price from $8.50 to $9.50 per pound. Specially grouped packages are available and make exceptionally good choices for gifts. Prices range from $79.95 to $109.95, shipping included.

ORDERING ADDRESS
Broken Arrow Ranch, Inc.
104 Highway 27W
Ingram, TX 78025
830/367-5875
800/962-GAME (4263)
www.brokenarrowranch.com
e-mail: sales@brokenarrowranch.com
Credit cards accepted

TELEPHONE ORDERS: **Monday–Friday, 8 A.M.–5 P.M. CST**

VISITS: **Ingram is 60 miles northwest of San Antonio off I-10. From I-10 take exit 505 (Ingram and Harper exit) to the right. Cross over the interstate, and you will be on Harper Road. Drive 2 miles to Highway 27, and turn right. Downtown Ingram is about 5 miles away. At the traffic signal where the highway reduces to 2 lanes, take a right and turn immediately right into the parking lot in front of the Ingram Grocery and Market. The office has "104" on the door.**
Monday–Friday, 8 A.M.–5 P.M.

COUNTRY CLUB BAKERY PEPPERONI ROLLS

Pepperoni rolls are a simple concept, but there is nothing simple about pepperoni rolls. It is a product that has done battle with the USDA's Food Safety and Inspection Service (and won), and has been responsible for expanding the slogan of Fairmont, West Virginia, from "The Friendly City" to "The Pepperoni Roll Capital of the World."

According to Frank "Cheech" Argiro, the spicy sausage and bread rolls were invented in Fairmont in 1937 by his father, Joseph Argiro. The elder Argiro, an Italian coal miner turned baker, created the rolls after noticing that the favorite lunch of many miners was a piece of pepperoni washed down with a piece of bread. The Argiro version, and those of most of the other 20-odd bakeries in West Virginia that make the roll, uses three thin rods of pepperoni baked inside a long, thick yeast bun. The rolls are 10 inches long and are hand-twisted in the center to form a natural place to break the rolls into manageable pieces.

The Argiro family owned Country Club Bakery in Fairmont until three years ago, when Frank retired and sold to Chris Pallotta and his son, Chris II. The Pallottas have continued the pepperoni roll tradition, going through more than 2 tons of pepperoni each month. And the Pallottas have continued to produce a full line of Italian breads, fruit breads, and 15 varieties of cookies.

More than a decade ago, the government's food safety service tried to force Argiro and other pepperoni-roll bakers to conform to health regulations required for meat processing plants. "They wanted us to have cement floors and the ability to hose down the walls and everything else required of a meat packer," said Argiro, who called the requests ridiculous. "I'm running a bakery shop, not a slaughterhouse."

After intervention from West Virginia representatives and senators (who count themselves as pepperoni-roll fans), the USDA backed off.

The bakeries are not allowed to send their rolls across state lines, however, so you must visit in person, or get a friend to mail you a box. They freeze well. The Country Club Bakery charges 55 cents per roll or $5.65 per dozen, plus tax, at its shop.

VISITS

Country Club Bakery
1211 Country Club Road
Fairmont, WV 26554
304/363-5690
Fairmont is in northern West Virginia. From Clarksburg, take I-79 north to the Fairmont South exit and go to Country Club Road. Turn left, and it is 1 mile to the bakery.
Monday, Tuesday, Thursday, and Friday, 6 A.M.–6 P.M. Saturday, 6 A.M.–3 P.M.

DRIER'S BOLOGNA AND LIVER SAUSAGE

At few places is it as satisfying to make a purchase as at Drier's Meat Market in Three Oaks, Michigan, a small town just over the Indiana border about 70 miles from Chicago. To begin with, the well-preserved building has been used as a meat market since 1875 and is on the National Register of Historic Places. With its rounded clapboard false front, tidy scalloped wood trim, and vintage lettering signs, it comes by the description "quaint" honestly. The potbelly cast-iron stove, the sawdust on the floor, and the antiques on the walls all have a reason and a history with meaning to the store.

Owner Ed Drier died in February 1994, but his daughter, Carolyn, who worked with him for several years, took over the business. With the help of her nephew, who is the fourth generation, she has been able to carry on the tradition that was taught to her by her father.

Carolyn continues to concentrate on a few products and is scrupulous about making them well. All-beef ring bologna (Drier's prefers to spell it "baloney") is the 125-year-old-firm's best-selling item, but the other smoked meats—bacon, hams, and hot dogs—also are noteworthy.

Drier's bologna is a marvel, a complex blend of flavors with no bitter aftertaste. We were stunned to learn that the seasoning consists of only salt and pepper. It is the smoking, over cherry wood cut from 80 acres of land Drier's owns, that supplies the unusual flavor. Also, good cuts of meat are ground for the bologna, rather than the common meat-market practice of using trimmings and leftovers.

But the product that has us, literally, dreaming about Drier's after our visit is the homemade liver sausage. Creamy, rich, stuffed tightly in a plump natural casing and tied with string, this liverwurst has a superior texture and an addictive, mellow flavor. It is simply the best we've ever eaten. It used to be made only in the winter, but customer demand has prompted Drier's to make it available year-round.

Carolyn retains features learned from her father, who was a clever marketer: a "Used-Knife Department," chairs for customers waiting in line, free samples, and humorous signs scattered about. "No Dancing" reads one. "Make it a double-ring ceremony—one of liver and one of baloney," says another. At the satellite store outside town, located in an old milkhouse, a sign reads: "Bare Feet Accompanied with Money Are Most Welcome." Famous patrons have frequented the store, but as Ed Drier once said, the family continues to "make our money from the guy who carries a lunch bucket—he's the one who makes the world go round."

Three Oaks has long had men and women who carry lunch buckets. The spotless village of 1,800 ("home of the nation's largest Flag Day parade") was once home of the Warren Featherbone Company, a manufacturer of buggy whips and corset stays that used turkey bones to do the job that whalebone once did. By the 1880s, the company had 75 employees, many of whom bought sausage for their lunch from the Union Meat Market (the name referred to Civil War allegiances) that had been established in 1875 by an Englishman, Alec Watson. A delivery boy who worked at the store was Edward Drier, Sr., who later took over and changed the store's name to his.

Drier's will send the cured meats by mail, and at Christmas this is a big part of the business, which now includes a website, brochure, and e-mail address.

ORDERING ADDRESS
Drier's Meats
14 S. Elm Street
Three Oaks, MI 49128
888/521-3999
www.driers.com
e-mail: info@driers.com
Credit cards accepted

VISITS: **From I-94 just over the Michigan-Indiana line, take Exit 4A east. Drive 5 miles and turn left on Elm Street, Three Oak's main street. The store is on the left. To reach the satellite store, do not turn left on Elm. Drive through the light, and you will be on Highway 12. Drive a little over 1 mile, and you will see the store on the left.**

Downtown store: Monday–Saturday, 9 A.M.–5:30 P.M. Closed January 1–two weeks prior to Easter. Satellite store: 616/756-9087, Sunday, 11 A.M.–5:30 P.M. May–November 1

GASPAR'S PORTUGUESE SMOKED SAUSAGE

Within the Portuguese communities of Massachusetts and Rhode Island, *linguica* and *chourico* sausages have been widely available. But until the Gaspar family began shipping these brilliant orange sausages, few people outside the region had a source of supply.

The Gaspar family has been making the *linguica* (mild) and *chourico* (spicy) links since 1912, when Manuel Gaspar emigrated from Lisbon to the United States. First established in New Bedford, Massachusetts, the business now is run by Gaspar's grandsons from a plant in North Dartmouth that employs 55 workers.

The striking color of the smoked sausages has a tendency to frighten away would-be eaters, who assume the meats are too spicy. Although the *chourico* does have some bite and comes in mild, hot, and extra-hot varieties, the strongest flavor of the popular *linguica* is that of pure ham. The color is imparted by a large dose of paprika.

Commonly eaten grilled or in bean soups, the *linguica* is seasoned with a hint of vinegar and garlic. But it's a far milder sausage than its Italian cousins. The *linguica* also is formulated into luncheon slices, which are used by several schools in Portuguese neighborhoods. There also are bite-size *linguica* cocktail franks and regular-size *linguica* and *chourico* franks, as well as beef and pork Polska kielbasa rings.

The sausages are $3.50 per pound plus shipping. Other Portuguese favorites, such as coffee syrup (16 ounces of the Autocrat brand), Portuguese sweet bread, and *salpicao,* a gourmet lean pork sausage that is similar to Canadian bacon, are also available at $3.50 per pound plus shipping. There is a minimum order of 3 pounds. Shipping charges range from $9 for 3 to 5 pounds to $24 for 26 to 99 pounds.

ORDERING ADDRESS

Gaspar's Sausage Company, Inc.
384 Faunce Corner Road
North Dartmouth, MA 02747
508/998-2012
800/542-2038
www.linguica.com
e-mail: GLinguica@aol.com
Credit cards accepted

VISITS: **From Boston, take I-95 east toward Cape Cod. When you reach North Dartmouth, take the Faunce Corner Road exit. Turn left, and the factory outlet store is 1 mile farther on the left.**

Monday–Friday, 8 A.M.–4 P.M. Saturday, 8 A.M.–noon

GREENBERG SMOKED TURKEY

When the smoked turkeys are ready at Greenberg, the company takes out a small notice in its hometown paper in Tyler, Texas. It reads: "Greenberg Smoked Turkey—now through Christmas." That's the only advertising the 60-year-old company has ever done. Demand is so great, the owners wouldn't mind dropping even the annual notice, except that it's a service to loyal local customers. "We just don't solicit business," said Joyce Greenberg. "If you buy, it's because you heard of us."

GREENBERG
Smoked Turkeys, inc.
THE HOLIDAY ARISTOCRAT

We're grateful that Marc Rosenbaum, a regional-foods maven and friend, told us about Greenberg. He recalls with fondness the yearly turkey his father orders, always confident that the bird will be as special this year as the last.

Since 1940, the Greenberg family has been smoking turkeys for a growing circle of fans. They season the trimmed birds according to an old family recipe and then hang them over hickory smoke until the slightly salty Greenberg taste is achieved. From raw bird to boxed bird, the process takes about four days.

These turkeys are not cured with nitrites or vacuum packed, as so many are today. Greenberg turkeys are frozen before shipping, and can be thawed and eaten immediately, or kept in the freezer for later.

First-timers may wonder why the skin is so dark (it's a deep, deep brown), but it's part of what makes this turkey special. Although the skin is burnished, the meat inside is always moist and has the succulent taste of a well-smoked salmon.

The skin is recommended for use in soups, and even the carcass is treasured. Many customers use it in a rich base for split-pea soup. Writer Calvin Trillin declared that his wife's lentil soup, with a stock based on a Greenberg carcass, has achieved a place in his "pantheon" of soups.

Part of the success of the Greenberg product is due to the devotion to quality of the family members and longtime associates who work there. Greenberg customers stay loyal for decades. Ditto for its employees. The workforce swells to more than a hundred at holiday time, with a year-round crew of about 10.

Sam Greenberg, grandson of the founder, runs the company today, with his mother, Joyce.

The turkey is a bargain $3.30 per pound, plus shipping and a handling fee of 25 cents per turkey. The turkeys arrive speedily in an insulated cardboard box, and the image of one on your doorstep is one of life's most welcoming sights.

ORDERING ADDRESS
Greenberg Smoked Turkeys, Inc.
P.O. Box 4818
Tyler, TX 75712
903/595-0725
No credit cards

HOFF'S SMOKED SAUSAGES AND MEATS

In Japan, it is possible for individuals to be named national monuments. Artists of various sorts are considered so important to the country that they are given special protection and awarded the utmost deference. We think it's a splendid idea, and would even expand the program to include a few favorite foods. Hoff's smoked sausages and meats of Brownsville, Wisconsin, would be up there on our list for consideration as a national monument. Owner Wayne Hoff, who died in 1997, perfected a summer sausage that was named national grand champion summer sausage by the American Association of Meat Processors in 1977 and 1978, and won six awards in subsequent years.

The smoked sausage, which sells for the modest price of $3.29 a pound, draws people from beyond the state to the tiny town in eastern Wisconsin. In the combination grocery store and meat plant, Wayne's wife, Dorothy, and son, Tim Hoff, dispense the sausage along with a crew of sausage makers. Tim's marinated meats, along with his Buffalo chicken wings, have skyrocketed in sales recently. Following in his father's footsteps, Tim entered meats in a contest in Springfield, Illinois, in 1999, and took the national award.

Writes his proud mother, "Tim has done a beautiful job" with the business.

The company doesn't confuse customers with several variations on the same sausage theme. There is but one summer sausage made. It is a mellow and not overly spicy mixture of beef and spices, with no trace of bitterness. The smoke flavor is unobtrusive and is attributed by the family to not cleaning out the smokehouse too regularly. The Hoffs also sell a lean bacon taken from the Boston butt, rather than the fatty belly. It is very meaty and sells for $3.29 per pound. The Hoffs will mail to individuals and add shipping charges to the prices given.

ORDERING ADDRESS
Hoff's United Foods
P.O. Box 145
Brownsville, WI 53006
920/583-3734
Credit cards accepted

VISITS
617 Main Street
Brownsville, WI 53006
Brownsville is south of Fond du Lac. Take Route 41 South until you reach Highway 49. Turn right and drive 2 miles to Brownsville. Hoff's is at 617 Main Street. From Milwaukee, take 41 North. Turn left at Highway 49 and proceed to Brownsville.
Open daily, 8 A.M.–4 P.M.

J & E PROCESSING SWEDISH POTATO SAUSAGE

We were worried when we learned that Jack and Chantee Dooley had left Lindsborg, Kansas, where they had turned out incomparable potato sausage at the Farmer's Union Locker plant for the last decade. Fortunately, the hardworking couple had just moved to a larger facility, in Salina, Kansas. With three times the space, production is easier and more Kansans and travelers are able to acquire their special meats.

The Swedish sausage, made up of raw ground potato, pork, and beef, is a meal-in-a-casing. The links are irregular in size, but the taste is consistently good. It is a mild, lean sausage that is our favorite with sauerkraut. The recipe was developed by a Swedish farmer in Lindsborg, who gave the formula to the farmers' cooperative. Like the now-closed locker plant, the Dooleys' new operation is state-inspected. Most small producers cannot afford to hire federal meat inspectors and, thus, their products cannot be shipped.

VISITS
J & E Processing
236 Smither Street
Salina, KS 67401
785/827-6607
No credit cards
From I-35, take Route 92 (Crawford Street) and turn north at the second light onto Broadway. At the next stoplight, turn right and travel for a half-block. The meat plant is on the west side of the street.
Monday–Friday, 8 A.M.–5 P.M. Saturday, 8 A.M.–noon

KRAMARCZUK HAM SAUSAGE (KRAKOWSKA)

In most metropolitan areas of any size, there exists a handful of meat markets founded by European immigrants on a shoestring that have prospered due to long hours, hard work, and the dedication of family members. In Minneapolis, a particularly successful example is the Kramarczuk Sausage Company, founded by Wasyl and Anna Kramarczuk 46 years ago. The company specializes in Ukrainian meats, and 21 years ago expanded the shop to encompass a restaurant and deli featuring breads, dumplings, tortes, cabbage rolls, borscht, and other Eastern European fare. On selected Saturdays there's live accordion music. The interior decor leans heavily on murals of the Statue of Liberty standing over a sunlit New York Harbor because, as son Orest Kramarczuk explains, "It was the first thing my parents saw when they came to this country."

The company makes dozens of kinds of sausages, from plump, old-fashioned wieners to spicy Polish sausage to head cheese to smoked liver sausage. But it is particularly known for its *krakowska,* or ham sausage. Made in continuous long cylinders, *krakowska* tastes like hearty smoked ham. It is lighter in color than a summer sausage and not as finely ground as Polish sausage. Thinly sliced, it makes a remarkable sandwich. It sells for $4.99 a pound.

At Kramarczuk's, natural casings are used, and the ends of some wursts are tied with string, giving them a hand-crafted look. All seven products we tried were excellent, including an unusual Russian-Ukrainian sausage called *poltazska,* which is notable for the large squares of creamy white fat that stud the sausage. Meats at Kramarczuk's are moderately priced, with most sausages costing between $2.99 and $4.99 a pound. The company sells its meats retail and wholesale, but not by mail.

VISITS
Kramarczuk Sausage Company
215 East Hennepin Avenue
Minneapolis, MN 55414
612/379-3018
Credit cards accepted
The sausage company is located a block east of the river, on Hennepin Avenue, one of Minneapolis's main east-west thoroughfares.
Store hours: Monday, 8 A.M.–6 P.M. Tuesday–Saturday, 8 A.M.–8 P.M.
Restaurant hours: Monday, 8 A.M.–4 P.M. Tuesday–Saturday, 8 A.M.–8 P.M.

LAWRY'S PASTIES

Many parts of Michigan's Upper Peninsula revolve around iron ore and copper operations, and the needs of the miners who work them. The pasty, a Cornish meat and potato pastry, was created as a simple, filling lunch for workingmen. Home cooks still make them, but what is surprising is that there exists an excellent commercial version that is essentially homemade.

In the town of Ishpeming, Nancy Lawry Cope and her son, Peter Lawry, bake up to 700 pasties a day. They also produce a local specialty, the *cudighi* sandwich (Italian sausage on a homemade bun with pizza sauce and cheese).

You can watch them making their pasties at the roadside shop. Nancy insists that everything be homemade and handmade. Their pasties are covered with a flaky, hand-crimped crust that encases slender oblongs of potato and rutabaga, as well as beef chunks and onion. They are made in batches of 50, the dough being rolled by hand the day before baking. The hefty pockets are baked for an hour, as all the ingredients are raw, and then sold over the counter or to patrons at tables in their small shop.

A small pasty sells for $2.09, the large, for $2.69. The *cudighi* sandwiches are $3.59. They are individually wrapped in insulated white bags, and travelers frequently take a box home to freeze. Visitors might also want to try the shop's oversize chocolate-chip cookies, the Moose Chip Cookie, for $1.59 each.

Lawry's has opened a shop in Marquette in Jilbert Center at 2166 U.S. 41 South (telephone: 906/226-5040).

ORDERING ADDRESS
Lawry's Pasty Shop
2381 U.S. 41 West
Ishpeming, MI 49849
906/485-5589
888/485-5589
FAX: 906/485-1420
www.upsell.com/lawry/pasties.html
e-mail: nlawrycope@aol.com
Credit cards accepted

VISITS: Ishpeming is 20 miles west of Marquette. The shop is on the left side of Highway 41, 4 miles west of Ishpeming.
Winter: Every day, 7 A.M.–9 P.M. Summer: 7 A.M.–11 P.M.

LOVELESS MOTELS HAMS AND JAMS

One look at the vintage neon sign outside the Loveless Motel near Nashville and you know you're in for a treat. The Art Moderne sign advertises "Hot Biscuits" and "Country Ham," and diners get the best of both. The biscuits are so memorable that we would invent a trip to Nashville just to taste them one more time. But there's also a great fried chicken, homemade salad dressings, grits, sausage and gravy, and delectable peach and blackberry preserves.

It's a small, informal place, with Formica tables and a beat-up linoleum floor. The waitresses are real pros, carrying armfuls of filled plates with ease. Eating there is so popular with families, tourists, locals, and everybody else that waiting is usually part of the Loveless Motel experience. Reservations are accepted, however, and the night we visited, with a toddler along, we were glad we had called ahead.

The motel part of the operation is no longer going, but may emerge again, what with the completion of the Natchez Trace Parkway less than a half mile away. The 13 rustic white cottage-style cabins are arranged in a "U" around the freestanding white building that used to be a house before it became a restaurant in the 1940s.

Where did the name come from? It sounds like Elvis coined it, but the truth is less romantic. The original owners were named Loveless.

So many customers began asking to buy the motel's preserves and country ham and sausage that eight years ago, Loveless began offering them by mail. The Loveless "Hams and Jams" catalog offers some of the same foods served at the restaurant, although it should be pointed out that only the preserves are actually made at the restaurant.

The sorghum comes from west Tennessee, and the country ham comes from the restaurant's longtime supplier. The sausage comes from a local company but it is not identical to that served in the restaurant because Donna McCabe and her son, George, who run the business, can't find a source to supply enough sausage they like for both.

We ordered the "teaser" package and received the following: 20-ounce jars of peach and blackberry preserves; 16-ounce jars of sorghum and honey; a pound each of country ham and bacon; and a 2-pound muslin bag of smoked sausage. The charge was $44.95, plus a $27.50 shipping charge since the meats must be sent via second-day air.

Everything was first rate, but the sausage was extra special. It is very smoky and spicy, and has the traditional edible rind not found in the plastic chubs sold in supermarkets. We made a heavily peppered white sauce, added crumbled sausage we had fried, and served the mixture over fresh biscuits. The result was as close to Southern biscuits and gravy as we've been able to muster.

"I know that some customers would like the spicy sausage better than what we serve," said Donna McCabe, "but then again, we get compliments on the kind we serve everyday. They are both excellent." A 2-pound bag of sausage alone is $9.95, plus shipping.

The preserves contain only fruit and sugar, and both are fine examples of home canning. (They come in glass canning jars.) The 20-ounce jars of peach, blackberry, or strawberry preserves are $6.95 each. They are sent via regular UPS.

The Loveless Motel also will cater nationwide, with George McCabe flying in with fried chicken, pancakes, country ham and biscuits, and other specialties. The McCabes don't send the food unaccompanied, so the service is most practical for large events.

The cafe also has a cookbook, *Meet Me at the Loveless,* that includes Southern recipes such as sweet potato casserole, shoe peg corn salad, and chocolate chess pie. It is $19.95, plus shipping.

ORDERING ADDRESS
Loveless Hams and Jams
8400 Highway 100
Nashville, TN 37221
615/646-0067 (ordering number)
615/646-9700 (restaurant number)
800/889-2432
FAX: 615/646-1056
www.lovelesscafe.com
Credit cards accepted

VISITS: The restaurant is about 18 miles southwest of downtown Nashville. From I-40 west take exit 192 (McCrory Lane). Turn left and go 4 miles and you will run into Highway 100. Turn left and look for the Loveless sign.

Tuesday–Saturday, 8 A.M.–2 P.M. and 5 P.M.–9 P.M. Sunday, 8 A.M.–9 P.M.

MOLINARI SALAME

A curious thing happens to dry salami made in San Francisco: it molds. The nontoxic, helpful mold develops because humidity and temperature in the city (or The City, as residents prefer to write it) remain constant all year. The mold is a critical ingredient, enhancing the surface color, retarding moisture loss, extending the shelf life, and enhancing the flavor and aroma of the salame.

Along with sourdough bread, Dungeness crab, and cioppino, dry salame is a legendary San Francisco food.

There are several salame manufacturers in the city that turn out the long cylinders of sausage with chalky white mold on the casing, and most local meat markets and delicatessens have a string of salame hanging behind the counter. However, one firm, P. G. Molinari & Sons, stands out not only because it is the oldest—established in 1896—and still family-run, but also because it is renowned for its top quality. "This is a salame family," says Frank Giorgi proudly. He is the great-grandson of Pasquale Giuseppe Molinari, the founder. Frank Molinari, P. G.'s son, was still active in the business until his death 12 years ago at age 90. His son-in-law, Peter Giorgi, was chairman of the board. "Young Frank," of the fourth generation, is Peter's son and president.

The company makes approximately 20 kinds of sausage and slicing meats, including mortadella, head cheese, cooked salame, and coppa Veneziana (pork butt with salame stuffed around it), and you can see pictures of several of them on the company's website. Its dry salame is the best known product. Pungent and spicy, it peels easily and makes an eminently satisfying snack with cheese or crackers.

Corti Brothers, the famed Sacramento food purvayor, calls Molinari's salame a Milano-style salame with a distinguishing *grana di riso* or grain of rice interior that shows small flecks of fat in the lean meat. "Truly a California original, Molinari San Francisco Dry Salame is as good as this dry-cured sausage gets," writes Darrell Corti in his Spring, 2000 newsletter.

We learned about the firm's history several years ago from P. G.'s daughter, Irene Bacigalupi. Her father, who was born in Italy, first spent time in Mexico living with a family who owned a restaurant before coming to San Francisco to work for a sausage maker. He opened his own shop and began importing delicacies from Italy, only to see everything destroyed in the Great San Francisco Earthquake and fire of 1906. He started anew at another location in North Beach, an Italian community, where the business remained until 1962, when federal meat-inspection laws forced a choice: stop making sausage or relocate in larger quarters acceptable to the government. The Molinaris moved to a factory on Yosemite Avenue and sold the North Beach delicatessen to a man who uses the name and sells Molinari meat products, but is not part of the family.

The red, white, and blue label featuring P. G. Molinari's flowing signature across the center is found in stores across the state and in quality-conscious stores elsewhere, such as Zingerman's in Ann Arbor, Larry's Markets in Seattle, and Dean and DeLuca in New York City. The company will send salame to individuals if they request, shipping it C.O.D. Molinari Salame comes in ¾-pound, 1¼-pound, 2-pound, and 3-pound sizes, and costs about $4.50 a pound, without shipping charges. It's possible to order from the website, if you don't live in the San Francisco area.

Or, if you want to order with a credit card and not C.O.D., you can order it from Corti Brothers, P.O. Box 191358, Sacramento, CA 95819; tel.: 916/736-3800.

ORDERING ADDRESS
P.G. Molinari & Sons, Inc.
1401 Yosemite Avenue
San Francisco, CA 94124
415/822-5555
FAX: 415/822-5834
www.molinarisalame.com
e-mail: Sales@MolinariSalame.com
No credit cards

NETO PORTUGUESE SAUSAGE

Neto Sausage might have been the genesis for *Food Finds*. In February 1978, in the first month as a reporter for the *San Jose Mercury*, one of us, casting about for feature stories, wondered about the many small businesses that dotted The Alameda, a formerly grand street that links downtown Santa Clara and San Jose. They seemed like interesting, tucked-away places, welcome counterpoints to Silicon Valley's burgeoning shopping malls. A series of picture pages resulted, several of them featuring small, family-run food businesses. It became apparent that these companies operated on a different wavelength from most of corporate America. In these tight-knit clans, it was hard to tell the difference between employees, relatives, customers, and friends. Quality was all, and the businesses grew primarily by word of mouth.

Years later, when we were casting about for a book idea, we remembered Neto's and theorized—correctly—that many cities and towns had out-of-the-way storefronts where superlative food was quietly made.

Neto's is now in its 52nd year and third generation of family ownership. Portuguese immigrant Arthur Goncalves came to America and started the business with $6,000 in used equipment and a 200-year-old recipe for the Portuguese sausage known as *linguica.* Now his grandchildren Edward Costa, Sue Romano, and Mary Harp have bought the business from their parents. Said Costa: "We continue to manufacture quality sausage with spices we blend ourselves, using quality cuts of meat, no fillers, and only preservatives required by the USDA."

In the beginning, all employees were Portuguese or related to someone who was. "We'd get them right off the boat," recalled Costa. "Whenever someone had relatives come from Portugal, they'd bring them around here first." Later, when some employees of Italian descent were hired, the company began making Italian sausage as well. By dint of its location in an area with a large Mexican population, spicy chorizo sausage was added. The company also makes both Mexican beef and pork chorizo (Zorro brand!) and a Spanish Basque chorizo. The Basque version contains wine vinegar. The Mexican chorizo has cereal and pork fat and no vinegar. Both are used in egg dishes, in casseroles, and braised.

Neto's popular *linguica* comes in sticks, links, or bulk, and can be ordered in the regular or picante style. *Linguica* is a sweet, reddish sausage that is unsurpassed for grilling or adding to bean dishes. It is a fairly fatty sausage, but you don't need much to make a notable impact.

Other Neto varieties include a pork sausage with apples and cinnamon that has won several state meat awards, Polish sausage, a Spanish pork sausage known as *longaniza, morcelas* (blood sausage), and *torresmos* (marinated pork). Neto's has added chicken and turkey sausages, snack sticks, and gourmet jerky as well. Product brochures are available; check their website or call for specials. Items are sent UPS.

ORDERING ADDRESS
Neto Sausage Company, Inc.
3499 The Alameda
Santa Clara, CA 95050
408/296-0818
888/482-NETO (6386)
FAX: 408/296-0538
www.netosausage.com
e-mail: netosausage@msn.com
Credit cards accepted

VISITS: Santa Clara is in the southern part of the San Francisco Bay Area, adjacent to San Jose. Neto Sausage is 3 blocks north of the University of Santa Clara campus on The Alameda, the school's main street.

Monday–Thursday, 8 A.M.–5 P.M. Friday, 8 A.M.–6 P.M.

NEW BRAUNFELS SMOKEHOUSE SMOKED MEATS

New Braunfels Smokehouse is truly a regional food source, offering Texas-style meats that are difficult to find anywhere else. It's a longtime family-run business that handles orders promptly, sending a separate written verification, and including two notes of thanks, one with the letter and one with the delivery. You get the idea your business is appreciated.

We appreciate the variety of meats the smokehouse has. Most places can turn out acceptable ham, bacon, and smoked poultry, but very few smokehouses offer smoked beef brisket. It is a cut favored for Texas-style barbecue, but it comes here fully cooked, ready to slice for sandwiches or to warm up for an entree. Like many of New Braunfels Smokehouse meats, it has a cracked pepper coating.

In fact, we started wondering about the pepper bill at the smokehouse. There is peppered beef jerky, which is addictive and one of the smokehouse's best-selling items, peppered dried beef, peppered smoked turkey, peppered smoked pork chops, and wonderfully peppered smoked pork tenderloin. The tenderloin, which we rarely see in mail-order catalogs, is fully cooked and very versatile. Simply slice in thin rounds and use for sandwiches or hors d'oeuvres. Heat briefly and add a glaze or sauce, and you've got medallions of pork. The dried beef, peppered or plain, also can be ordered by the chunk (there's a 2-pound minimum) and used in the same manner. A 2- to 2½-pound pork tenderloin is $34. Plain dried beef in a chunk is $14.00 a pound, and peppered dry beef is $19 a pound. A 4- to 6-pound cooked brisket is $41. What handy items to have in your freezer!

A good introduction to the range of items available at the smokehouse is one of its combination boxes, from the simple Tastin' Box at $26 to the elaborate Anniversary Wunderbar box, which contains ample portions of 9 cuts of meat for $138. Shipping is by UPS for $7 to $19, or 12 percent of the order.

New Braunfels was settled by German immigrants, and the sausage recipes date back to the smokehouse's founding in 1946. Since 1952, the company has operated an adjacent restaurant. It's a popular place that has expanded several times, and is known for its desserts as well as its smoked meats.

ORDERING ADDRESS
New Braunfels Smokehouse
P.O. Box 311159
New Braunfels, TX 78131
800/537-6932
www.nbsmokehouse.com
e-mail: meats@nbsmokehouse.com
Credit cards accepted

VISITS: New Braunfels is in the Texas Hill Country, northeast of San Antonio. The smokehouse has a restaurant and store right off I-35 at the Highway 46 exit. There is also a sandwich shop and store in San Antonio at 6450 North New Braunfels Avenue (tel.: 512/658-6226).
New Braunfels location: Every day, 7:30 A.M.–9 P.M.

NODINE'S SMOKED BEEF JERKY

America's smokehouses range from backyard operations to those applying the most advanced technology that food science has to offer. Ronald Nodine is a former mechanical engineer who used to work on computer projects. Almost 30 years ago, he left engineering to establish a custom smokehouse, drawing on his knowledge of raising hogs on his small farm in Goshen, Connecticut.

Nodine knew there was a need for a custom smokehouse to service area locker plants and farmers. The one man who did custom smoking was elderly and ran his smokehouse in his garage, contrary to state health regulations. The man knew meat smoking, however, and promised to teach Nodine everything. Just when Nodine finished building his smokehouse, the man died. Nodine hurriedly sought out the advice of meat science professors, spice salesmen, meat locker owners, and anyone else who would give him information, and he learned on the job.

The results are impressive. He has expanded to retail and wholesale meat sales. One of the first smokehouses in the country to make nonnitrated bacon, he got a lucky break one week after he had first sold his bacon to Balducci's, a New York City gourmet store. Food writer Mimi Sheraton, then of the *New York Times,* tried his bacon, liked it, and wrote about it, spurring dozens of orders. Now, Nodine's bacon and other meat products are found in several fancy food shops and top-notch restaurants. The nonnitrate line includes the bacon, a skinless hot dog, hot or sweet Italian sausage, a fresh sausage, and a fresh kielbasa during the Easter season. Another big seller is the boned, delicately smoked chicken breast. "We try not to overpower it with smoke," says Nodine. He uses hickory and maple chips for smoking, as well as juniper berries.

The smoked product we consider the best at Nodine's is one that is less well known than the bacon or chicken—smoked beef jerky. This much-maligned meat is usually just cured and dried, but at Nodine's the beef is smoked as well, and the outside of the beef is spiced quite heavily before slicing. Even with the generous seasoning, the good, beefy flavor of the meat is maintained. Not too salty, it is flavorfully peppery. It is $31 per pound, and comes packed in a cloth bag.

The nonnitrite bacon is $5.25 per pound. Nodine's also has gift packages and a variety of deli selections. There is a $25 minimum order for all shipments, and shipping charges are based on geographical location.

ORDERING ADDRESS
Nodine's Smokehouse
P.O. Box 1787
Torrington, CT 06790
860/489-3213
800/222-2059, ext. 99
www.nodinesmokehouse.com
e-mail: nodines.smokhouse@snet.net
Credit cards accepted

VISITS
Nodine's Smokehouse Store
North Street, Route 63
Goshen, CT 06756
860/491-4009
The smokehouse store is on Route 63 in Goshen, directly across the street from the town hall. Products are not sold to the public at the smokehouse in Torrington, but informal tours are given there for groups larger than 10 if a week's notice is given. The Torrington smokehouse is at 65 Fowler Avenue. *Goshen store: Monday–Saturday, 9 A.M.–5 P.M. Sunday, 10 A.M.–4 P.M.*

NOLECHEK'S MEATS

One of the many charms of Wisconsin is the status to which it elevates sausage. A sausage shop in this state can't get by with mediocrity. Unfortunately, many of the small sausage shops can't ship out of state, hostage to the federal meat-inspection laws that don't consider inspections in some states adequate for interstate shipments. Most shops can arrange for informal shipments sent by a third party. Even though we think the federal law is enforced chiefly to provide employment for the strong federal inspectors union, we are uneasy about the clandestine nature of the transactions.

So when there is a first-rate small Wisconsin sausage company that pays the premium for federal inspection, it is worth spreading the word. Nolechek's Meats, in operation 48 years in the small town of Thorp off Highway 29 in central Wisconsin, is worth checking out. The Nolecheks are in their second generation of ownership, with brothers Bill and Kelly Nolechek running the company along with sisters Jennifer and Tracy, and mom (and secretary) Dee Nolechek. They have the help of three other dedicated employees: Robin, Kathy, and Leo.

Nolechek's sliced bacon, fully cooked hams, and what could well be the state's official sausage—fresh brats—are just a few of their award-winning products. The makers use hardwood chips for smoking, not Liquid Smoke, and offer natural casings for wieners and other sausages. Their bacon is among their most popular items and can be ordered sliced or slab, from pork butt or belly, from beef or Canadian style. The regular sliced bacon has a straightforward, tantalizing smoked flavor, with a minimum of fat. Supermarket bacon is limp and fatty in comparison.

Smoked Polish sausage, plain or with garlic, is another standout, and can be ordered in a coarse or fine grind. It comes cooked, and is useful in quick skillet dinners. For many fans, the only way to serve it is grilled, with mustard.

Our favorite offering at Nolechek's is the summer sausage with garlic, a thick, finely ground chub of sausage that needs no embellishing condiments. There's no bitter aftertaste, or chemical flavors, that mar so many inferior summer sausages found in gift packs everywhere. The company also offers smoked pork spare ribs and smoked beef ribs, which is unusual, as well as ring bologna. The family encourages customers to visit their website and discover all they have to offer.

ORDERING ADDRESS

Nolechek's Meats, Inc.
P.O. Box 599
Thorp, WI 54771
715/669-5580
800/454-5580
www.nolechekmeats.com
e-mail: nolechek@nolechekmeats.com
Credit cards accepted

VISITS

104 North Washington Street
Thorp, WI 54771
Thorp is in northern Wisconsin, northeast of Eau Claire. From Highway 29 take the Thorp exit north on Highway 73. It will go right through Thorp's downtown, where Nolechek's is located.
Monday–Thursday, 8 A.M.–5 P.M. Friday, 8 A.M.–7 P.M. Saturday, 8 A.M.–3 P.M.

NUESKE SMOKED HAMS AND BACON

Splashed across the front of food section of the *New York Times* on February 16, 2000, was a 29-paragraph love letter, with abundant photographs, to the great bacon produced at Nueske's Hillcrest Farm. Legendary political journalist and gourmand R. W. Apple, Jr., wrote the piece, and he made his feelings clear. "The sweet, thick slices held their shape as they cracked on the stove," he wrote. "They tasted pure, porky and intensely smoky, in the Midwestern style. . . . Nueske's struck me as the beluga of bacon, the Rolls-Royce of rashers."

Apple detailed what makes the bacon and ham so special at this northern Wisconsin firm. The family-run business doesn't raise its own hogs or have a particularly special curing recipe. What it does have is 16 concrete-block smokehouses, where applewood logs burn in open fires.

In a smokehouse, the wood used to build the fire is as critical to the recipe as the quality of meat or seasoning, and reputations are cemented on the basis of using hickory smoke, fruitwood smoke, or even corncob smoke. At Nueske's, most meats are smoked 20 to 24 hours over glowing applewood embers.

Local apple wood is purchased by the cord, manager Jeff Bushman says, "and then covered with a special blend of hardwood chips to impart the unique flavor this company is famous for." Workers tend the fire each night until midnight to keep the smoldering wood from turning into flames, and then the smokehouses are on their own until 6 A.M. "But there are several fire alarms should anything kick up," he added.

The long smoking time and high temperatures mean that fat renders out of the bacon while it's smoking, and not in your frying pan at home. That means that a pound of Nueske bacon will reward you with more meat—about three times more than ordinary supermarket brands.

Nueske's (pronounced *noo*-skis) also is famed for its hams, and it takes the company several days to complete the curing and smoking process. Wisconsin maple syrup, brown sugar, and honey are used to cure the hams. They spend their last day over smoldering applewood.

Robert C. Nueske, a Wisconsin native, launched the business in 1933 by driving a display truck with meats, eggs, and fresh vegetables to the resort areas of northern Wisconsin. For years, the company operated from a small plant next to the Nueske farmhouse, and the business grew primarily by word-of-mouth. The annual advertising budget was $5 for ads in the local newspaper at Christmas and Easter.

Since 1980, however, Robert's sons, James and Robert, Jr., have presided over a larger plant and retail store about a mile from the original site. A talking myna bird, Sambo, lived there for nine years, uttering phrases such as "Good morning" and "How are you?" While customers were shopping, it helped by squawking "Oh, so reasonable!" Sambo died in 1990, and Rico, an African gray parrot, is now learning the ropes.

The ham is a deep, moist deep pink color with a smoky crust. It is fully cooked and ready to eat. If desired, it can be warmed in an oven or microwave. It has a full flavor, with no gristle or fat, and makes most canned hams look sickly indeed.

Nueske's will send its hams, bacon, many sausages, and smoked poultry nationwide, and they arrive in excellent condition. A 3- to 4-pound ham is $36.45, including shipping, and a 6- to 7-pound ham is $61.45, including shipping. Bacon can be ordered by the pound, sliced in 1-pound packages. A 2-pound order is $26.45, and 5 pounds is $48.90, including shipping. For a dollar more, you can order bacon coated with cracked black pepper.

The company's retail store is in a reconstructed barn. There are other historic buildings on the property, including Wittenberg's first schoolhouse (now an antique store), and Robert C. Nueske's first meat shop and stone smokehouse.

ORDERING ADDRESS
Nueske's Meat Products
R.R. 2, P.O. Box D
Wittenberg, WI 54499
715/253-2226
800/392-2266
FAX: 800/962-2266
www.nueske.com
e-mail: nueske@nueske.com
Credit cards accepted

VISITS: Wittenberg is 1 hour west of Green Bay on Highway 29. Exit "Business 29" and you will see the meat plant on Highway 29, east of town.
Monday–Thursday, 8 A.M.–5:30 P.M. Friday, 8 A.M.–9 P.M. Saturday, 8 A.M.–4 P.M.

OSCAR'S SMOKED CANADIAN BACON

The scenic area of Glens Falls, New York, is always worth a stop. Not just for its beauty but also because there is Oscar's in nearby Warrensburg.

A famous smokehouse in the area since 1946, Oscar's is located at the base of Hackinsack Mountain in the Adirondacks. In town, you can follow your nose to the store, because Oscar's insists on using natural smoke from hickory logs and apple wood to flavor its hams, chickens, and cheeses. In a showcase crowded with superlative goods, this third-generation firm's lean

Canadian bacon is a standout. Thick, fat-free, and flavorful, this Canadian bacon is not at all salty and has a subtle taste of hickory.

But don't stop at a single nationality of bacon. Oscar's has Irish bacon, English bacon, and beef bacon (from the brisket) to try. Its regular bacon, which has no chemicals in it, sells by the ton per week.

There are 159 smoked products to choose from, including fish. The Canadian bacon is $5.69 per pound. Shipping charges (by UPS) are added for mail-order purchases.

ORDERING ADDRESS
Oscar's Smokehouse
22 Raymond Lane
Warrensburg, NY 12885
518/623-3431
800/627-3431
FAX: 518/623-3982
www.oscarssmokedmeats.com
Credit cards accepted

VISITS: From Glens Falls, travel north on Route 87. Take Exit 23 (Warrensburg) onto Route 9, which turns into Main Street. Look for the Oscar's sign on Raymond Lane at the second right after the third traffic light in town.
Open daily, 8 A.M.–6 P.M.

OZARK MOUNTAIN SMOKEHOUSE MEATS

The only place to get Arkansas bacon, a round, just-in-front-of-the-loin cut of cured pork, is from this family-run smokehouse that began business in 1946. It looks like a cross between Canadian bacon and familiar strip bacon, and makes an unparalleled BLT. No crumbled ends will fall out of your sandwich with Arkansas bacon. For family appetites, the Ozark Mountain Smokehouse sends ten ½-pound packages of the bacon for $44.95 postpaid, and will send the bacon year-round. Five packages are $25.75.

The late Roy Sharp began his food career smoking turkeys, and today his son, Frank, and his wife, Sara, do a big business in whole birds, turkey breasts, and smoked Rock Cornish Cross chickens. The poultry is dark-skinned and the smoked meat delicate pink. Both have a deep, hickory-wood flavor. No Liquid Smoke shortcuts employed here.

The boneless turkey breasts, which average 3½ to 4½ pounds, are particularly convenient. They are $45.95 postpaid. The chickens, which serve 3 to

4, are $29.95 for 2 and $49.95 for 4. Whole turkeys are available in sizes from 7 to 11 pounds.

The family enterprise in Fayetteville has grown to include a bakery, a commercial kitchen where jams and jellies are produced, and a print shop where type still is set by hand. There are 70 employees.

"I started when I was eight, cleaning floors and fetching boxes," recalled Frank. He left the business to get a degree in chemical engineering and even took a job with an oil company. "After three months, I decided I was a hillbilly and came back!"

The smokehouse is a good source for Arkansas-grown basmati-type rice—the nutty-flavored long-grain rice often specified in Indian cooking. A 2-pound bag is sold with 2 smoked chickens for $35.95.

The Sharps have our appreciation for offering half a country ham—a policy we wish more smokehouses would adopt. Fifteen or more pounds of country ham is a lot for any household to digest, no matter how well it keeps. Ozark Mountain hams, which are well-flavored and not as salty as others we sampled, can be purchased whole, of course (between 17 and 19 pounds), or as an 8-pound half-ham.

Country ham is uncooked, but fully cooked hams are available, either spiral sliced or scored, studded with whole cloves, and glazed. Either variety can be ordered as half a ham. The spiral-cut half-hams are about 7 pounds for $53.95, and the half scored and clove-studded hams weigh about 7½ pounds and sell for $59.50.

All prices include shipping. However, poultry and hams shipped between April 15 and September 15 are sent only by air, at an additional charge.

ORDERING ADDRESS
Ozark Mountain Smokehouse
P.O. Box 37
Farmington, AR 72730
501/267-3330
800/643-3437
www.ozarkfamily.com
e-mail: smokehouse@ozarkfamily.com
Credit cards accepted

VISITS
U.S. Highway 62
West Fayetteville, AR 72701
501/267-3567
There are 10 retail stores in Arkansas. The smokehouse, plant, and office are at the Mount Kessler store, just west of Fayetteville, in northwest Arkansas.
Fayetteville location: Monday–Saturday, 9 A.M.–4 P.M.

RADD DEW'S BARBECUE

Each state south of the Mason-Dixon line (and a few above) has barbecue wars between the various practitioners of the backwoods art. South Carolina is no exception, but we know of no barbecue king other than the late Radd Dew who successfully packaged barbecue for sale in supermarkets. His wife, Betty, and son, Jim Dew, are carrying on his tradition of supplying restaurants, grocery stores, and huge political and company feeds with his vinegar-laced barbecue. The meat base is sliced pork, with a sharp, tangy sauce of red pepper, Worcestershire sauce, mustard, and lemon juice.

They run a roadside restaurant on the weekends in front of their federally inspected processing plant in Conway, a few feet from the family home. For the catered feeds, often for employees of local wool and cotton plants, the Dews cook the barbecue over wood coals, but for the home market they use electric ovens.

A 1-pound carton is $5, and a 10-pound bucket is $38. If you arrive in Conway during the week, the barbecue is sold in the local Piggly-Wiggly and IGA supermarkets. At the restaurant on the weekends, a buffet is $8.

ORDERING ADDRESS
Radd Dew's Bar-B-Q
3430 Highway 701 South
Conway, SC 29527
843/397-3453
No credit cards

VISITS: From Myrtle Beach, take Route 501 to Highway 701 South (toward Georgetown). The plant and restaurant are 2 miles south of the Route 501/701 intersection, on the right side.

Restaurant hours: Friday–Saturday, 5 P.M.–9 P.M.

ROY L. HOFFMAN AND SONS SMOKED BACON AND COUNTRY HAM

When we eat the Hoffmans' bacon, we are shocked anew at what most of the country must settle for from supermarkets. The 77-year-old Hagerstown, Maryland, company doesn't engage in any silly peek-a-boo games with customers, grudgingly exposing a tiny package flap so you can examine what you're buying. Hoffman bacon is packaged in clear plastic so that its meatiness is on full display. Dry-cured and smoked, you'll be impressed by the minimum cooking shrinkage.

Its country ham is dry-cured and smoked over white hickory. No Liquid Smoke here! The taste is very meaty, very basic, with no aftertaste of chemicals because none are used. Both products have won seven years of awards in the American Cured Meat Championships in the excellence-of-quality division.

At the farm and country market, these meats and other fresh, frozen and cured beef, pork, veal, and lamb can be bought. Modern packaging and shipping has meant that many meats, from filet mignon to porterhouse steaks, can be shipped quickly.

A sampler package of one pound each of the bacon, country ham slices, and breakfast sausage links, is $21.95, plus shipping and handling. The bacon also comes in 3- and 5-pound quantities. Country hams are 14 to 16 pounds and cost $49.95, plus shipping.

ORDERING ADDRESS
Hoffman's Quality Meats
13225 Cearfoss Pike
Hagerstown, MD 21740
301/739-2332
800/356-3193
www.info@hoffmanmeats.com
Credit cards accepted

VISITS: **Hagerstown is in western Maryland. From Washington, D.C., take I-270 north to Frederick, where it becomes I-70. At the intersection of I-81, just below Hagerstown, drive north to Exit 7B (Route 58, Cearfoss Pike) and continue 1 mile west. You'll see the barn and the Country Market on the right hand side of the road.**
Monday–Wednesday, 8:30 A.M.–5 P.M. Thursday–Friday, 8:30 A.M.–5:30 P.M. Saturday, 8 A.M.–3:30 P.M.

RUEF'S SMOKED MEATS

One step inside the door at Ruef's Meat Market in New Glarus, Wisconsin, reveals the secret of this homemade sausage. Forget all the claims that Liquid Smoke or sawdust chips are just as good as real wood for smoking meat. At Ruef's the products are smoked over real hickory and oak, producing the Old World flavor that fills the entire shop with an incomparable aroma.

This is the place to find wonderful homemade sausages, including several hard-to-find Swiss specialties.

Willy Ruef came to this country in 1951 from Switzerland and worked for the meat market as a young boy, purchasing the business in 1966 from the family who had established it in the 1920s. His son, Bill, has worked there since high school (close to 20 years) and about a year ago bought the business from his parents. Willy and Annette have helped Bill with the transition, and so little has changed that many customers don't realize yet that the store is in new hands.

Everything we sampled from Ruef's was outstanding. The shop is known especially for its Swiss veal sausage, or *kalberwurst,* which includes crackers and whole milk, and its *landjaeger,* a dried jerky-like beef and pork strip that is often served at bars in Wisconsin and elsewhere, to be washed down with beer. *Landjaeger,* which is cured, smoked, and then dried, has been carried by Swiss hunters and hikers as a quick source of energy for centuries. Ruef's *landjaeger,* with its excellent smoky flavor, puts the rock-hard, over-salted, plastic-wrapped jerky sticks to shame.

Other special Ruef products include pork bratwurst, Swiss *mettwurst,* beef summer sausage, a fine ring bologna, smoked pork chops, wieners, and *cervelas,* which is a delicate garlic sausage. They've also added specialty brats, including apple, Swiss cheese, potato sausage, and an extra-spicy version. The meats are so good it would be worthwhile to go out of your way to visit the shop. Luckily it's on one of the main streets of a charmingly restored Swiss village with many attractive stores.

ORDERING ADDRESS
Ruef's Meat Market
538 First Street
New Glarus, WI 53574
608/527-2554
e-mail: bruef@mail.tds.met
Credit cards accepted

VISITS: New Glarus is about 22 miles southwest of Madison, Wisconsin. From Highway 69 into New Glarus, turn west at the stoplight onto Sixth Avenue (Highway 39) and then right on First Street.
Monday–Friday, 8 A.M.–5:30 P.M. Saturday, 9 A.M.–5 P.M.
Sunday (June–September), 10 A.M.–4 P.M.

Open special hours during town festivals, of which there are several: a Heidi Festival during the last weekend in June; Volksfest (Swiss Independence Day) on the first Sunday in August; and a William Tell Festival over Labor Day weekend.

SMOKEHOUSE INC. SAUSAGES

Dave Nosiglia made a brilliant move when it came time to learn a trade. He went to Europe and spent three years as an apprentice to a German butcher and then another year working for a butcher in Austria. When he came home to Massachusetts, at the age of 25, he knew sausage making inside and out. As he told the trade publication *Meat Industry* not long after his return: "Without a doubt, it's the best training you can get anywhere in the world."

Nosiglia's mission is to bring fine European sausage to Americans. His customers are European-born residents who miss native specialties, travelers who have been to Europe and tasted good sausage, and eaters everywhere who appreciate well-seasoned links.

Smokehouse's offerings are a veritable United Nations of sausage: Swedish *kor koru* (a sweet ring sausage made with barley), English bangers, Irish pork sausage, Italian sweet sausage with fennel, spicy Cajun andouille, Bavarian weisswurst, German bratwurst, and more. "We make a range of ethnic sausages, and each has its own group of customers," said Victor Nosiglia, Dave's father, who sold his interest in a meat-processing machinery sales company to work full time in his son's business.

It was Victor who took Dave, fresh from high school, to Milwaukee to visit Usinger's, one of his customers, to see if his son would like the sausage business. Victor's involvement has turned out to be a seven-day-a-week one. His wife helps with the books, and Dave's wife, Kate, works in one of the retail shops.

We hope that eaters will recognize that not all sausages are created equal. The range of Smokehouse offerings, all made with quality ingredients and great attention to texture and seasoning, is one rarely seen in this country. If you are concerned about fat, it is a comfort to know that all Smokehouse fresh sausage is made from 80 percent lean pork. USDA minimums require only 65 percent lean, the company's product information sheet states, which is what is commercially available in most supermarkets.

Smokehouse also uses only whole spices, freshly ground, and does not use preservatives in any of the fresh sausages and some of the cooked ones. All of the uncooked sausages are made without nitrite, and many of the cooked meats, including bacon, bologna, and liverwurst, are also available without nitrite.

We ordered the cooked bratwurst and grilled it. Even harsh critics raised on Wisconsin brats were won over. The andouille we chose after reading how Nosiglia spent time in Beaux Bridge, Louisiana (near Lafayette), to learn how to properly make Cajun sausage. His time was well spent. If you want a spicy sausage to wake up a bean dish or to lift a cookout from the ho-hum category, this is it. Another variety we tried, the jalapeño fresh sausage, is just the ticket for confirmed jalapeño guzzlers, but might be too fiery for novices and children.

Slab bacon had a wealth of flavor—even the nonnitrite version. In addition to dozens of sausages and luncheon meats, Smokehouse has a wide selection of smoked meats and fish, including finnan haddie, eels, and suckling pigs. The company has a 20-pound minimum order. The company recommends writing for its current retail price list; a website—www.smokehouseinc.com—is coming soon.

ORDERING ADDRESS
Smokehouse Inc.
15 Coventry Street
Roxbury, MA 02119
617/442-6840
www.smokehouseinc.com
No credit cards

VISITS: *Monday–Friday, 8 A.M.–4 P.M.*

SUMMERFIELD FREE-ROAMING VEAL

The Humane Farming Association, a San Francisco organization that campaigns against abusive livestock-raising methods, urges consumers, in heart-rending advertisements that show mistreated calves, not to buy veal. The association, however, does endorse one veal producer, Summerfield Farm, in northern Virginia, using it as an example to show that calves do not need to be confined and made anemic to produce tasty meat.

Consumers are a big part of the problem. We have come to believe that white veal is the most desirable, and restaurants and meat markets supply what is demanded. However, white veal is almost always anemic, formula-fed veal. Exposés on television have shown the cruel treatment of veal calves, causing many eaters to be uncomfortable about ordering or buying veal.

Sixteen years ago, Jamie and Rachel Nicoll began a veal and lamb farm that had as its premise a humane, free-range existence for its animals. "We take the attitude that we're going to keep those calves as comfortable and happy as we can for the fourteen weeks they're alive," Rachel said not long after they began business. The calves are fed whole milk from the mother cow, resulting in a pinkish, not white, meat.

Summerfield Farm hit a responsive chord. Although success was due in large part to Jamie's dogged "cold" calls to fine restaurants and even door-to-door calls in likely neighborhoods, the operation has been helped by some mighty enthusiastic press. "Puts white veal products to shame," wrote the *New York Times.* "Superb veal . . . so flavorful and tender that it is found in many leading restaurants around the country," stated *Food and Wine.* "Even a good smell when cooking," commented the *Philadelphia Inquirer.*

We ordered veal scaloppine, loin chops, shanks for osso buco, and two small tubs of the farm's glace de veau, a reduced veal stock that is a magical substance to have on hand in your freezer. Add a few tablespoons to a pan after sautéing, say, chicken breasts, swirl in a little wine and some herbs, and you've suddenly got a presentation.

The veal itself was simply the best we've ever had, in our own kitchen or elsewhere. One serving crystallized the maxim that it does make a difference to use the very best raw ingredients. The scaloppine was paper-thin and cooked in a flash. We used an osso buco recipe that we'd tried before with other veal, and noticed a world of difference in taste and tenderness.

The veal is beautifully cut, clearly marked, and can be ordered fresh or frozen. Yes, it is expensive to have it sent by air, in a special Styrofoam box. But for those who want to be assured that their veal is raised humanely, and who want a singular dining sensation, it is well worth it. Summerfield's list of restaurants and hotels it supplies reads like a "Who's Who" of fine dining.

Summerfield also offers spring lamb, veal sweetbreads and liver, venison, poultry, and gamebirds, and its own sausages and smoked products. We ordered a dry aged leg of lamb (you have a choice of whole, bone removed, or Frenched, with the meat pulled down from the end of the bone), and discovered how simple it was to make a knockout entree. Sausages include veal with sun-dried blueberries or sun-dried tomatoes, venison with cranberries, and pheasant Boudin with orange zest. Smoked products include an applewood smoked salmon.

ORDERING ADDRESS
Summerfield Farm Products, Ltd.
10044 James Monroe Highway
Culpeper, VA 22701
540/547-9600
800/898-3276
FAX: 540/547-9628
www.summerfieldfarm.com
e-mail: sfp@mnsinc.com
Credit cards accepted

VISITING ADDRESS: Culpeper is in northern Virginia, about 45 miles north of Charlottsville. The plant, where meat can be purchased, is 3 miles south of Culpeper on Highway 29. The building is on the east side of the road.

Monday–Friday, 9 A.M.–4 P.M.

WHISTLING WINGS DUCKS

Contrast a visit to Whistling Wings, a unique 36-year-old firm that raises and sells mallard ducks, to picking up a frozen bird out of the supermarket bin. This business is in a setting of incomparable beauty, especially in the morning, when a mist hangs over the pines. At each lake there is a sight that isn't easily forgotten: thousands of young mallard ducks swimming, preening, flapping, and flying. Founder Leo Whalen, who died in June 1989, preserved this land, turning a cornfield into lush acres covered with 70,000 pine trees and five spring-fed lakes of 5 acres, 18 acres, and 22 acres in size. Whalen planted the trees and built the lakes on this rolling land near the Mississippi River in northwest Illinois.

The ducks are sold live (for restocking lakes, medical research, etc.) and dressed. The firm has put tiny Hanover, Illinois (population 1,243), on the map as the Mallard Capital of the World.

Whalen knew nothing about the business when he began ("The only eggs I ever had were for breakfast"), but he started small and learned by trial and error. "If the bank could have found a way to use ducks, I would have been out of business," he observed of the early days. But the bank trusted him to stick with it, and Whalen, with the help of his wife and five children, built the business to the point where it sells ducks across the nation and beyond.

His daughter, Marianne Whalen Murphy, is now president of the company, running it along with her husband, Bill, and her brother, Bill Whalen. "Everything runs the same as before, because we all worked with Dad so long," Marianne said.

Ducks mate at a farm south of town, and their eggs are collected and taken to the Whistling Wings hatchery in town, where they are kept warm and moving in an incubator for 26 days. Two days later, chicks hatch. The company sells some of the chicks then, but raises others to sell as fledglings or breeders.

Ten years ago, the company started selling frozen dressed birds, either smoked or plain, and shipping them by air around the country. The smoked ducks, which are hung over hickory wood at Weber's, a smokehouse right over the state line in Cuba City, Wisconsin, are the most popular. The meaty birds slice easily and have a rich flavor. One duck will serve two to four people as an appetizer, which can be either hot or cold. Although it is a different bird than the pressed duck used in Chinese dishes, we substitute smoked mallard with excellent results.

Ducks are sent two at a time in a reusable Styrofoam cooler. Frozen unsmoked ducks are $32 for 2, and smoked ducks $39.95 a pair. Add $8.50 for shipping and packaging per order. The company also sends pheasant (smoked and plain), wild turkey, partridge, and quail. The quail, for example, are 8 for $29.95. The wild turkey, which averages about 10 pounds, sells for $36.95.

Frozen ducks also can be purchased at the hatchery, which allows you to experience Whistling Wing's office, complete with duck paintings, old wooden desks, a vintage freestanding safe, deer antlers, turtle shells, snakeskins, and a huge intact wasps' nest as decoration.

ORDERING ADDRESS
Whistling Wings, Inc.
113 Washington Street
Hanover, IL 61041
815/591-3512

VISITS: **Hanover is in northwest Illinois, south of Galena, on Highway 84. The hatchery and office are in a freestanding building on the downtown strip. Coming from the south, Highway 84 makes a right turn in downtown Hanover. Shortly after the turn, you will see Whistling Wings on the left.**
Monday–Friday, 8 A.M.–5 P.M. Saturday, 8 A.M.–noon

WILLIAMS OF VERMONT MEATS

For more than 60 years, Williams of Vermont (originally William's Smoke House) has been using whole corncobs, along with apple wood, for smoking meats—and no Liquid Smoke. The smoking processes and recipes have been handed down through the generations.

Smoked meats are enjoying a renaissance, and restaurant menus are filled with items such as smoked trout mousse, smoked turkey salad, smoked duck breast, and stir-fried smoked chicken. Quality-conscious restaurant chefs around the country order from RoseMary's, the mail-order and retail shop for the products, run by founder Rose and Mike Williams' niece, RoseMary Valentine. Mere mortals get the same personal service, whether they want a whole smoked ham ($62.95 for 8- to 9-pound size) or a smoked or raspberry-honey turkey breast ($62.95 for 9-pound size or $56 for 8-pound size, respectively). Shipping is extra.

We recommend everything we sampled, which includes the smoked ham and smoked turkey, and the smoked sliced bacon, which comes in 2-pound packages for $13.95. The bacon was memorable, with a very pleasing smoked flavor. If you are limiting your bacon intake for health reasons, don't waste your infrequent chances to eat some on fatty, chemically smoked supermarket brands. Try Williams of Vermont's. A little will remind you what a wonderful treat bacon can be.

RoseMary's also offers 100 percent Vermont maple products, the finest Grafton Cheddars, and a variety of specialty foods.

ORDERING ADDRESS

RoseMary's
1802 West Road
Bennington, VT 05201
802/447-0373 (call collect)
FAX: 802/447-0054
www.sover.net/~rosemary/
e-mail: rosemary@sover.net
Credit cards accepted

Pastas, Grains, & Flours

BROWNVILLE MILLS MULTIPLE-GRAIN CEREAL

"Mail-order business certainly helps out when you're sitting in a little town of 148 people a little out of the mainstream," says Harold Davis, the owner of Brownville Mills in tiny Brownville, Nebraska. The town is a stone's throw from the Missouri border and just a few miles from the southwest corner of Iowa. But residents in states all over the country do their grain and flour shopping in Brownville, via UPS. The mill's catalog lists 25 varieties of flours and meals (stoneground electrically, not with water power), as well as 22 kinds of grains, seeds, and cereals, and an impressive array of nuts, seasonings, dried fruits, oils, honeys, and syrups. How often do you encounter artichoke flour, potato flour, amaranth flour, rice flour, and gluten flour?

The mill's home is a large, 140-year-old building that started out as the Lone Tree Saloon in 1860 and was transformed into a grocery store, an opera house, and finally a fish restaurant before lying vacant for several years. In the 1950s, it was turned into a mill.

Davis, a former hog farmer who has owned the mill for 19 years, pledges: "You are assured absolutely fresh merchandise that has not gone stale lying on retailers' shelves for many months."

Probably the best-known product at the mill is its 12-grain hot breakfast cereal, originated by the mill's owner, the late Courtney Miner. The dozen grains (corn, wheat, oats, rye, barley, buckwheat, millet, brown rice, flaxseed, sesame seed, sunflower seed, and toasted soybean grits) sounded like something that perhaps would feel more at home in the bird feeder, but we were surprised at its texture (like coarse cornmeal) and its character. This keeps your interest, retaining some crunch even after being cooked for half an hour, as recommended. A 2½-pound sack is $2.95, plus shipping. There is $1 packing charge for orders under $20.

ORDERING ADDRESS

Brownville Mills
P.O. Box 145
Brownville, NE 68321
402/825-4131
FAX: 402/825-6581
http://skyport.com/brownvillemills/
e-mail: Jm62006@havix.net
No credit cards

VISITS: **Brownville is on Highway 136 just before you cross the Missouri River. The mill is on the main street.**

Monday–Saturday, 9 A.M.–5 P.M. Sunday (May–November): 1 P.M.–5 P.M.

CARBON'S GOLDEN MALTED WAFFLE AND PANCAKE FLOUR

In 1937, Fred S. Carbon was a flour salesman with a brilliant idea. He gave free waffle irons to hotels and restaurants if they would use the special waffle flour he had developed.

He had hand-mixed his waffle flour formula in an oak barrel, and tested it on neighborhood kids in his town, Buchanan, Michigan.

The kids liked the waffles, and the hotels and restaurants liked the free appliance. If you eat breakfast in downtown hotels or fancy restaurants across the country, look for the menu tip about their "special malted waffles." That's usually the clue that the establishment uses Carbon's patented recipe. And the company still uses the same time-honored sales lure. If a restaurant or university or theme park agrees to purchase only Malted Pancake and Waffle flour, it is given a free waffle iron. The company now sells worldwide and manufactures its own waffle irons in various sizes and configurations.

We've eaten these flavorful waffles dozens of times and never knew the Carbon connection. Happily, Williams-Sonoma now sells tins of the flour, as do some Costco stores. It's also possible to mail-order the flour directly from the factory.

The malted waffle flour, which contains cornmeal, malt, salt, sugar, baking powder, milk, and flavorings, is a terrific, never-fail mix. The malt lightens the batter, so that the waffles are crisp, light, and have a distinctive taste. If you start making these waffles, be prepared to stay on your feet in the kitchen, because eaters will demand seconds and thirds. They are that good. The mix also can be used for pancakes, and recipes are provided on the handsome tins that feature a picture of a boy wearing a red bow tie and holding a waffle. Other vintage company pictures can be seen on its website, including a great photo of a Malted Pancakes & Waffles truck that used to deliver the mix to eating establishments across the country.

The waffle flour is produced in South Bend, Indiana. Local customers and visitors may buy tins directly from the plant. For mail orders, the company will ship a minimum of two 33-ounce tins, for $15 plus shipping costs.

ORDERING ADDRESS
Carbon's Golden Malted Company
4101 William Richardson Drive
South Bend, IN 46628
219/247-2270
800/253-0590
FAX: 219/247-2280
www.goldenmalted.com
e-mail: newcrabon@qtm.net
Credit cards accepted

VISITS: Driving south on U.S. 31, turn left on Cleveland Road. Go past Portage and Bendix Drives, and head toward the by-pass. At Meghan Beeler Street, take a right. Carbon's is the third office on the right.
Monday–Friday, 8 A.M.–4:30 P.M.

CHRISTINE & ROB'S OLD FASHIONED OATMEAL

Oatmeal is the ultimate comfort food, quick to make, inexpensive, and good for you. It seemed immune from tampering, but if you've tasted the microwave varieties, you'll agree that it has been sweetened, flavored, and softened in texture like never before.

If you long for substantial, thick-cut oatmeal, try a box of Old Fashioned Oatmeal from Christine & Rob's, a small family firm south of Salem, Oregon. It is distinct, chewy oatmeal with a pronounced toasted flavor. It has such character that customers get hooked. "Our oatmeal is something that people will eat every day," said Christine. "We have a customer in Florida who called to ask us to hurry with his order because he gets grumpy if his wife makes any other kind," she said. Another regular customer is actor Arnold Schwarzenegger. *He* became grumpy when he couldn't find good oatmeal while on location in Mexico, and had his production assistant order a four-month supply to be sent via overnight express. Now, the oatmeal is always present on his movie sets, and several of his actor friends also have become customers.

Christine and Rob Bartell married 16 years ago, merging two families, and the couple imparts a real family sense to their business. Early on, the company published a journal called "Food Talk," to which family members and customers contributed recipes, short articles, kitchen hints, and family pictures. There was always a "Kids' News and Views" column written by one of their four sons, and frequent mentions of the late James T. Roberts, Rob's grandfather, a big supporter of the business, who died recently at the grand age of 100. Now, the company has taken its homey writings and recipes to the web. In whatever form they communicate, Rob and Christine give the company a living, breathing personality.

"We concentrate on mail orders to individuals because that's what makes the business fun," says Rob. "Customers become friends. Our eldest son was married recently, and he even got gifts from customers. They felt that they'd watched him grow up!"

Rob, whose background is in advertising, had owned a chain of delicatessens before becoming an oatmeal expert. Christine had been a special-education teacher and had worked for a child-care chain. They have a mill make their products to their specifications and delivered to their renovated red barn, nicknamed "Oat Central."

Christine and Rob promote locally made fruit preserves, including marionberry, a cross between a Santiam and a Chehalem blackberry grown in the Willamette Valley. A box of three 12-ounce jars of preserves (marionberry, strawberry, and raspberry) is $17.95, shipping included. A Northwest Country Sampler gift pack combines all of the company's favorites: two 20-ounce boxes of oatmeal, a 20-ounce box of pancake and crepe mix, a 20-ounce box of biscuit mix, a 12-ounce jar of marionberry preserves, and a 12-ounce bottle of marionberry syrup. It is $34.95, delivered.

Oatmeal can be ordered by the case (twelve 20-ounce boxes) for $40.95 delivered, or three 2½-pound bags for $20.95, delivered. All prices include shipping charges to the continental U.S. only.

ORDERING ADDRESS
Christine & Rob's
41103 Stayton-Scio Road
Stayton, OR 97383
503/769-2993
FAX: 503/769-1291
www.christineandrobs.com
e-mail: bartell@wvi.com
Credit cards accepted

EDWARDS MILL GRITS AND FUNNEL CAKE MIX

Work-study has a deeper meaning at The College of the Ozarks than at most other four-year liberal arts colleges. All of the 1,500 students attending this southern Missouri school work for their room, board, and tuition at one of 65 campus jobs or industries. Each student is required to put in 560 hours per year at a campus job, as well as attend classes. They may toil at the printing presses, do landscaping, answer phones, or help operate the school's airport, public radio station, Holstein dairy farm, Ozark Museum, or water-powered flour mill.

The Edwards Mill is a replica of a late-19th century gristmill and contains support timbers that are nearly 200 years old. The timbers have stood in three mills prior to this one. The buhrs also are recycled and have celebrated more than 125 birthdays. The mill is named after the former chairman of Dixie-Portland Flour Mills, who provided the funds to build the project in the early 1970s. It is operated completely by students who work under a full-time miller. Upstairs in the mill is the school's weaving studio, where students sit at large floor looms, producing rugs, place mats, and scarves. (The original looms were installed at the school by the Works Progress Administration in the 1930s, after Eleanor Roosevelt saw handweaving as a way area women could earn money.) The woven goods are sold, along with student-baked fruitcakes, and student-made apple butter, jellies, and preserves, at the gift shop inside the Friendship House near the school's entrance. These items can also be ordered year-round from the same brochure that lists the mill products available by mail.

The mill produces yellow cornmeal, whole wheat flour, biscuit mix, and a popular pancake and waffle mix. Two more regional favorites are its yellow corn grits and its funnel cake mix. Funnel cakes, for those who never visit amusement parks, are sweet spirals of batter that are deep-fried, sprinkled with confectioners' sugar, and served hot. They are exceedingly bad for you, nutrition-wise, which makes them all the more alluring. They, of course, taste wonderful.

The only equipment needed to make the cakes is a funnel, a deep skillet (a cast-iron one is perfect), and one of your fingers. Sealing off the bottom of the funnel with your finger, you pour the batter into the funnel, then remove your finger and let the batter swirl into the hot oil. Explicit directions are printed on the back of the muslin bag that holds the mix.

All the mill's products come in muslin sacks, which adds to their charm. The bag for the grits has a very good recipe for a cheese casserole that is a more gradual way of introducing grits to the uninitiated than surprising them with a plain bowl for breakfast. Grits are notoriously easy to prepare and, in today's grain-conscious atmosphere, one of the nutrition squad's good guys—as long as you don't drown them in butter.

John Egerton, who writes about grits (and all other southern foods) in a well-researched but readable way, quoted the late Turner Catledge as calling grits "the first truly American food" because the Indians at Jamestown in 1607 gave English sailors hot softened maize seasoned with salt and animal fat. By reading an article on grits Egerton wrote in *Southern Magazine,* we learned the difference between supermarket grits and stoneground grits: supermarket grits are corn kernels that have been soaked to remove their hulls (sometimes called big hominy), and then are dried and ground up (sometimes called small hominy). The old-fashioned way to make grits, as the students do at Edwards Mill, is to grind the hard corn kernels and then sift out the hulls.

Prices at the mill are very low. A 2-pound sack of the yellow grits (or pancake or muffin mixes) is $8 postpaid. Two 2-pound sacks (your choice) are $16 postpaid. Two-pound bags of funnel mix or biscuit mix are $9 each, or two for $16. Whole wheat flour and yellow cornmeal are $7.50 per two-pound bag. Five-pound and 25-pound sacks of cornmeal, pancake, and biscuit mix are available.

ORDERING ADDRESS
Edwards Mill
The College of the Ozarks
P.O. Box 17
Point Lookout, MO 65726
417/334-6411, extension 3354
800/222-6525
www.cofo.edu
e-mail: admiss4@cofo.edu
No credit cards; checks OK

VISITS: The College of the Ozarks is in the southwest part of Missouri, not far from the Arkansas line. From Highway 65 at Branson, go south about 2 miles to the four-way stop, turn right at the school's entrance. The mill products are sold at the Friendship House just inside the entrance.
Monday–Saturday, 9 A.M.–4:50 P.M. Closed weekends during the winter.
Open on Saturday starting in early April.

FIDDLER'S GREEN FARM CEREALS AND MIXES

Why is it that baking mixes sacrifice nutrition for speed? Cake mixes, muffin mixes, and bread mixes are time-savers, but, oh, those ingredient encyclopedias on the sides of the boxes! For those who wouldn't be caught dead with a cake mix on the shelf, or for those who simply want some honestly prepared, toothsome baked goods, there is Fiddler's Green Farm.

The story behind the farm is as earnest and serendipitous as they come. There was eccentric sea captain David Kennedy, who led a dangerous life bringing oil tankers into port and flying his own plane to meet the ships. In 1985, Kennedy was killed when his plane went down in fog. His will specified that his 115-acre farm on the north-central coast of Maine be offered rent-free for one year to tenants that would farm organically. After that year, the tenants would be given an option to buy, with rent payments going toward the final purchase. Proceeds from the sale of the land would go to the Maine Coast Heritage Trust, which preserves endangered farmland.

Enter Nancy Galland and Richard Stander, who had spent a decade growing organic vegetables on a 10-acre plot in western Massachusetts that had been in her family for three generations. After pesticide drift from neighboring farms killed her mother's cat and contaminated their crops, the couple quit farming and began hunting for pesticide-free land. They heard about Fiddler's Farm in 1986, met with the farm's trustees one month, and moved to the farm the month following.

To keep money flowing into the operation, the couple began creating breakfast cereal and baked-good mixes for health-conscious eaters. They grew some grains and purchased others from other organic farms. All the grains are ground at Fiddler's Green.

In 1994, Nancy and Richard retired, moving about 15 miles up the coast. They sold the business to Allen Ginsberg and Judy Ottmann, a husband and wife, and Laine Alexander, a family friend. Ginsberg, a former carpenter, oversees production, and Alexander keeps the books and handles the creative part of the business. They don't farm the land, but have expanded the company's stoneground products. The company now offers enough variety to create healthful breakfasts for weeks on end.

For hearty hot cereals, there's Penobscot Porridge, named after the county in north-central Maine ("nutty, grainy, robust, rib-sticking" said the *New York Times*), and a finely textured Oat Bran & Brown Rice ("breakfast of tomorrow's champions," said *Cook's Magazine*). Islanders' Choice 7-Grain Hot Cereal combines wheat, oats, corn, rice, rye, millet, and barley in a creamy yet crunchy mix. The hot cereals cost between $4.35 and $4.65 for a 1½-pound bag.

The Bread & Biscuits mix takes but a few minutes to prepare and can be on the table in less than an hour. Rough-textured but not crumbly, it can be sliced and toasted the next day. If yeast breads intimidate you, or if you simply want a healthy, tasty alternative, the mix is perfect. It also is versatile. Use it as the topping for cobblers or as the base for quick fruit breads, spicy coffeecakes, or even vegetable muffins.

Other baking mixes are Buttermilk Spicecake & Cookie Mix and Bertha's Best Bran Muffin Mix, which is dairy free. The mixes range in price from $3.50 to $4.35 per bag.

There are three pancake mixes, including our favorite, Toasted Buckwheat, and two wheat-free varieties, Oats 'N Barley and Fiddle Cakes (made with corn and barley, rice and oats). The Toasted Buckwheat turns out nutty-flavored, even-textured, light pancakes. It also makes muffins that put the lie to the cliché that health-food pastries have to be dense and flat.

The newest products are Belleweather Scones, in three varieties. Each can be varied endlessly, by adding fresh or frozen fruit, chopped nuts, minced ginger, or citrus zest. An 11-ounce box that makes 8 scones is $3.50.

The farm's extensive catalog includes many gift packs, and other products made at the farm, such as blueberry jam, orange rhubarb butter, and organic dog biscuits. We especially like the breakfast gift packs—a perfect, healthy gift for breakfast lovers. The Maine Pancake Breakfast, for example, includes Fiddle Cake Mix, Toasted Buckwheat Pancake & Muffin Mix, blueberry syrup produced at the farm, and a tin of local maple syrup, for $24.95.

Prices listed do not include shipping costs. It's easiest to write, call, or fax Fiddler's Green and asked to be sent its complete catalog, or call up its website.

ORDERING ADDRESS
Fiddler's Green Farm
P.O. Box 254
Belfast, ME 04915
207/338-3872
800/729-7935 (phone and fax)
www.fiddlersgreenfarm.com
e-mail: fiddler@mint.net
Credit cards accepted

GIBBS WILD RICE

Early in the 1980s, a survey sponsored by the National Wild Rice Council found that only 15 percent of the public had ever heard of wild rice. Of those, only 10 percent had tried the grain, and only 4 percent used it regularly. Pretty depressing statistics, if you are a wild rice grower. Wild rice's high price is always given as a reason for low consumption, and it is true that hand-harvested lake-grown rice is expensive. It is also one of nature's great treats.

But the wild-rice picture changed dramatically in the 1980s. Mechanized harvesting of cultivated rice varieties on flooded paddies in California has made that state the leading producer of wild rice in the nation. The price of the paddy-grown rice, like most commodities, varies year to year, but it is usually several dollars per pound less than that of lake-grown rice.

The paddy-grown cultivated wild rice is smoother and darker than the hand-harvested rice, and usually takes longer to cook, since the seed coat of the rice is not scratched in processing.

It also yields about 25 percent less rice, which should be taken into consideration when comparing prices.

Gibbs Wild Rice, a producer and distributor in both California and Minnesota, handles a majority of the nation's paddy-grown wild rice. Currently, it sells a 1-pound box for $3.75, plus a $3 handling fee and shipping costs. It makes sense to order several pounds at a time. Call, fax, or write the company for its mail-order form.

We're optimistic that the big producers won't crowd the hand-harvested companies out of business. We get that optimism from the experience of the wine industry. Remember the fuss over inexpensive jug wines? As it turned out, they didn't sound the death knell for the smaller, high-quality wineries. They initiated millions of new wine drinkers, who then developed an appreciation for both levels of the market. It would be satisfying to see the same happen with wild rice.

ORDERING ADDRESS
G.E. Gibbs Wild Rice
P.O. Box 387
Live Oak, CA 95953
530/695-1612
800/824-4932
FAX: 530/695-1039
e-mail: gibbsrice@succeed.net
No credit cards; checks OK

VISITS
10400 Billings Road
Live Oak, California
Rice can be purchased directly at the plant. Live Oak is about 55 miles north of Sacramento. Take Highway 99 about 7 miles north of Yuba City to Pennington Road and turn left. Drive 2 miles to North Township Road, cross over it, and turn right into Billings Road, which dead-ends at the plant.
Monday–Friday, 8 A.M.–4:30 P.M.

GUILLORY'S LOUISIANA "POPCORN" RICE

With more and more companies claiming healthful qualities for their foods, the Food and Drug Administration is paying closer attention to food advertising these days. While some of the advertising smacks of latter-day snake oil pitches, there is no doubt that food can profoundly affect how you feel.

Which brings us to Guillory's "Popcorn" Rice. We first heard about it from someone caring for a cancer patient at home. This rice was one of the few foods the patient could tolerate. When we contacted Anne Guillory, who sells the rice that her husband Paul grows, she said the company has received several orders from purchasers who mentioned it was intended for sickly family members. "All rice is easy to digest," said Anne. "I'm not sure why ours is especially well tolerated, but we do hear that some people can eat our rice who wouldn't eat anything else."

The "popcorn" name refers to the popcorn-like aroma the rice gives off while cooking. The rice, which comes in brown or polished white-rice versions, has a delicate, nutlike flavor. The two versions come from the same rice, but the polished rice has some of the bran ground off. It is less healthful, but cooks faster. Both versions put the lie to bland rice. The brown rice is particularly flavorful and distinctive. "Here in Louisiana, we eat rice with every meal, like you eat potatoes," said Anne.

Paul Guillory has been growing rice in southwestern Louisiana for 28 years, ever since graduating from college. He was not from a farm background, "and everybody who knew him couldn't believe where he ended up," said his wife. She had grown up on a farm, however, and it was at the urging of her father that Paul tried farming. They have not regretted the decision. "It's been about the best place to raise a family there could be," said Anne. The couple has five children, all boys.

Paul has grown the popcorn variety for about 18 years. Although the variety isn't unique to the Guillorys, there are only a handful of growers in the country planting it. One reason is that its yields are lower than that of other rice. Another is the scarcity of seed. The Guillorys got their first batch from Louisiana State University's Rice Experiment Station and then grew their own seed rice.

Two-pound muslin bags of either unpolished brown or polished white rice are $3.50. (The brown rice is subject to availability.) Five-pound bags are $7, and 20-pound bags are $18. UPS shipping charges are added to these prices, and range from $3.95 for an order of $10 or less to $7.95 for an order of $50.

The Guillorys, who point out that gifts of rice have long been considered a symbol of good fortune and good heath the world over, particularly recommend giving their rice at Christmas and New Year's.

ORDERING ADDRESS
Louisiana Rice Company
P.O. Box 705
Welsh, LA 70591
337/734-4440
FAX: 337/734-4107
Credit cards accepted

VISITS
205 S. Adams Street
Welsh, LA
Welsh is east of Lake Charles in southwestern Louisiana. From I-10, take the Welsh exit and travel south into town. The shop is on your right. In the same building is an antique shop, Main Street Antiques, owned by Anne Guillory.
Tuesday–Friday, 10 A.M.–5 P.M. Saturday, 10 A.M.–4 P.M.

HUDSON CREAM FLOUR

Even if you never bake anything, you'd want to have a bag of Hudson Cream Flour on your kitchen counter. The label, circa 1904, is one of the prettiest in America. It features a Jersey cow standing in a green meadow beside a blue stream.

The question is often asked: What does a cow have to do with flour? The answer is that, at the turn of the last century, Jersey cows were considered to produce the richest milk and cream. The mill's founder, Gustav Krug, chose the cow to symbolize the white, rich quality of his mill's flour.

The company he founded, Stafford County Flour Mills Company, in Hudson, Kansas, has kept the logo. It is not a company that tampers with tradition. For example, it has only had four presidents in its nearly 100-year history. The current president, Alvin Brensing, 83, has worked from the same office for 63 years.

It is a company firmly anchored in its community. One of the last independent mills left in Kansas, the

Wheat State, Stafford buys hard red and white winter wheat from farmers in the area, supports baking contests at county fairs and the state fair, and has been a staunch supporter of various baking promotions sponsored by the Kansas Wheat Commission, Kansas Wheathearts, and the Kansas Department of Agriculture. The company's mail-order brochure notes that "all of us in the town of Hudson (all 150 of us!) want to say thank you and keep on baking!"

It is clear that there is pride in the mill and its products, as well there should be. Hudson Cream is a "short patent" flour, which means that it contains less of the wheat kernel than other flours. Most millers use 80 percent of the wheat berry; Stafford County Flour Mills uses 62 percent from the center of the berry. The result is a highly refined flour that resembles cake flour. Its high protein content translates into strong gluten strands and lighter breads.

We made plain white bread with the unbleached flour, and it rose so high and had such a fine crumb that we were tempted to look around for a county fair to show it off. Now the company has introduced a bread flour, with added gluten, and we are expecting to move one step closer to bread perfection.

The company's primary market is home bakers. Its flours are distributed in 25 states, but if you can't find them near you, the company will ship. The flour is a bargain ($1.95 each for 5 pounds of bleached, unbleached, self-rising, whole wheat flour, or cornmeal), and shipping costs exceed the cost of the product. (They aren't outrageous, however. It costs $5.50 to ship 5 pounds and $7 to ship 10 pounds. Twenty pounds of flour costs $13 to ship.) Judging from the fan mail, shipping costs don't seem to deter anyone who has baked with Hudson Cream. The company has a loyal, multigenerational following, and caters to that loyalty with products such as Hudson Cream Flour tins, aprons, muslin towels, tote bags, bread warmers, and dough scrapers.

New in its line are biscuit mix, cornbread mix, and country gravy mix. And, it has a dandy new cookbook. Alvin Brensing's daughter, Elaine Woolf, whom he proudly notes "was a double home ec major from K State," has just published a spiral-bound cookbook titled *Hudson Cream Flour Recipes, Volume One.* It has chapters on yeast breads, bread machines, specialty breads, quick breads, cakes, cookies, pies and desserts, and main dishes, and is chock-full of winning recipes from state and county fairs and from Hudson Cream Flour customers. Interesting fan letters the mill has received are reprinted between the chapters. It's a superior cookbook, well planned and edited, and can be ordered for $25, shipping included.

ORDERING ADDRESS
Stafford County Flour Mills Company
P.O. Box 7
Hudson, KS 67545
316/458-4121
800/530-5640
FAX: 316/458-5121

www.flour.com
e-mail: jeffw@flour.com

VISITS
Church Street
Hudson, Kansas
The mill dominates the town, located in central Kansas. From the intersection of Highways 50 and 281, go north 10 miles on 281, then drive east 5 miles on the county blacktop. You will see the grain elevator. The company has just built new offices, with a gift shop area.
Monday–Friday, 8 A.M.–5 P.M.

KENYON'S JOHNNYCAKE MEAL AND KAMUT FLOUR

Paul Drumm III has his customers figured out. "People don't come to the mill to buy johnnycake meal," he tells his employees. "They come to talk, and remember when their parents brought them to the mill."

The Kenyon Corn Meal Company is located in a historic red gristmill near the waterfall on the Queen's River in Usquepaugh, Rhode Island. Cornmeals and flours have been produced here since 1886. The Kenyon family, who owned it early in this century, gave the mill its name, which has been retained by its current owner, Paul Drumm, Jr., who has been running the mill for 28 years. His son, Paul Drumm III, works at his side. The Kenyon mill's granite wheels grind white corn kernels into a gritty, cream-colored meal. White cornmeal is the mill's best known product, the key ingredient for a nearly addictive crunchy, popcorn-tasting johnnycake.

Anyone who has not experienced the heavenly taste of a hot johnnycake—which is simply a mixture of cornmeal and water that is fried—is suffering from ignorance of one of our best culinary combinations.

It is believed to have originated with Native Americans, and there has sprung up a grand debate as to its composition. Whether milk or water is used, the johnnycake has become a staple of New England meals.

Johnnycakes are one of the fastest side dishes possible. New Englanders eat them plain, or spread them with butter, syrup, or jam. They deserve to travel outside the region, but for some inexplicable reason they have not. Because johnnycakes are so little known elsewhere, the mill packages the meal simply as "white cornmeal" for distribution outside New England. A handsome 3-pound blue and white box with a red drawing of the mill on the front is $6.55.

White cornmeal is but one of the many stoneground grains available at the red mill. Lately, it has been promoting Kamut flour, a brand name for an ancient variety of wheat grown exclusively by one company in Montana. This is an extremely high protein flour that grinds like hard wheat and is popular for those wanting added nutrition in a loaf of bread. A 1½-pound bag is $4.28.

If you are looking for blue cornmeal for Southwestern recipes, brown rice flour for persons with wheat allergies, spelt flour for added protein and nutrients, whole wheat berries for hot cereal, cracked wheat for bread, or whole quinoa for adding protein to a vegetarian diet, Kenyon's is your place. Ditto for hard-to-find Scotch oat flour, rye meal, and miller's bran.

The company's mail-order catalog is a treasure, with good descriptions of the products and good recipes for using them. We are fond of several of its baking mixes, such as Clam Cakes and Fritter Mix, Brown Bread Mix, and Hearty Oatmeal Bread Mix, but if we had to pick one, it would be the Buttermilk and Honey Pancake Mix. The ingredient list is brief—flour, graham flour, buttermilk, honey, baking powder, salt, and baking soda—and you add water, an egg, and shortening. The result is a sweet, light pancake with real flavor that doesn't require a bath in syrup.

A 1½-pound bag is $3.35. Shipping costs must be added to all the prices mentioned. For a more complete listing of Kenyon products, look at the mill's website or request a catalog.

ORDERING ADDRESS

Kenyon Corn Meal Company
P.O. Box 221
West Kingston, RI 02892
401/783-4054
800/753-6966 (800/7-KENYON)
FAX: 401/782-3564
www.kenyonsgristmill.com
e-mail: kmail@kenyonsgristmill.com
Credit cards accepted

VISITS

21 Glen Rock Road
West Kingston, RI
Although the mailing address is West Kingston, the mill and the gift shop across the street, located in the old miller's cottage, are in the village of Usquepaugh, about 10 minutes from the Rhode Island beaches. From U.S. 1 take Rhode Island Route 2 north to Route 138. Drive west for 2 miles. (If driving on I-95, take Rhode Island 138 east for 5 miles to Usquepaugh Village and follow the signs to Kenyon's.)

Shop Hours: June–September: Monday–Friday, 10 A.M.–5 P.M. Saturday–Sunday, Noon–5 P.M. Mill Hours (year-round): Monday–Friday, 9 A.M.–5 P.M. Saturday–Sunday, Noon–5 P.M.

MCFADDEN FARM WILD RICE, ORGANIC HERBS AND HERB BLENDS

Guiness McFadden's farm is diversified, but not with the sort of crops with which Old MacDonald was familiar. Near Potter Valley, in the Coast Range of northern California, the farm may just be the perfect example of agriculture for West Coast cuisine, with its crop mix of wine grapes, fat garlic braids, bay laurel wreaths, dried herbs, and California wild rice. The farm always has made its crops available directly to the consumer via mail order—another innovation that has set the farm apart.

But then again, Eugene Joseph McGuiness McFadden isn't your typical farmer. He came to farming 31 years ago, after Notre Dame, the Navy, and a year at the Stanford Business School. He and his late wife Fontaine started with wine grapes and added the other commodities as a means of keeping a relatively stable field crew employed year-round instead of relying on a new group of migrants each grape harvest. "Now it's the tail wagging the dog," McFadden observed, with the ancillary crops more important than the grapes.

Their organically grown herbs have been embraced by the health-food market and by the discriminating buyers for the Williams-Sonoma chain.

The 11 herbs grown or foraged on the farm are basil, oregano, rosemary, garlic, thyme, lemon thyme, tarragon, marjoram, summer savory, sage, and bay leaves. They come in 4-inch-high glass cylinders with wide-mouth green lids and are a far cry from the weak, pulverized herbs found at the grocery. These are pungent, recognizable herbs. A gift box of one of each of the herbs listed above, plus chile flakes, is $40, which includes shipping and handling.

More recently, the farm has begun selling herb blends. There are a dozen choices, including the best-selling Italian herb blend, herbes de Provence, grilling herbs, and salad herbs. Each blend is $4.25 a bottle, shipping included.

Wild rice has been grown in California for about 26 years, first in the traditional rice-growing areas of the Sacramento Valley and later in areas where night temperatures are cooler, such as the Sierra foothills and the Coast Range. McFadden Farm has grown its own rice in the past, and now selects and packages rice from others. Its handsome black and sienna box with a drawing of a quail on the front is popular as a gift item. The farm's most popular size is a 6-ounce box, which is $4, delivered. We like to buy them in multiples, to have on hand for food baskets and thank-you gifts.

Other popular items are hand-made garlic strands ($14 for 13 large bulbs to $20 for 16 jumbo bulbs) and bay laurel wreaths, available from November 1 through January. Many households display the glossy, aromatic wreaths for the holidays, let them dry, and then cannibalize them for the kitchen. They are $21, including shipping.

All McFadden Farm products can be purchased at the farm, or by writing or calling for a brochure.

ORDERING ADDRESS
McFadden Farm
Potter Valley, CA 95469
707/743-1122
800/544-8230
FAX: 707/743-1126
www.mcfaddenfarm.com
Credit cards accepted

VISITS: **Take Highway 101 north of Ukiah, and turn east on Highway 20. At the Potter Valley exit, turn left and drive through the valley about 5 miles until you see Eel River Road. Turn right and continue about 2 miles to Gibson Lane. Turn left and drive to Power House Road. Turn right and continue to the end of the road.**
Monday–Friday: Usually open 8 A.M. to 5 P.M., but it's best to call ahead.

MARIA AND SON TOASTED RAVIOLI

Toasted ravioli is as ubiquitous as the presence of the arch in St. Louis: old family restaurants serve it, trendy bars with neon sculptures serve it, and Italian counter joints serve it. It is a breaded, beef-filled ravioli that is quickly deep-fried until golden. Dipped in marinara sauce, it is a crunchy appetizer that often makes dinner unnecessary.

For home consumption, the city's best producer is Maria and Son, a 38-year-old firm run by the Cannovo family, who daily turn out superior ravioli, lasagna, gnocchi, cannelloni, manicotti, and tortellini. It is run by Ralph Cannovo, the son of Phillis and Louis Cannovo, who founded the firm. Phillis, who died in 1984, was a religious woman and gave the company not her name, but that of the Virgin Mary. The "Son," however, stands for Ralph.

Toasted ravioli is the firm's best-selling product. Like the other Cannovo products, it is made without colorings or preservatives. The filling has a hashlike consistency, with bits of spinach, carrots, and celery mixed in with the beef and egg. The small squares are dipped in evaporated milk and then in an egg and bread-crumb mixture to delicately coat the chewy pasta. They cook quickly, to become the perfect fast food. It's up to the diner to decide whether to sprinkle them with Parmesan cheese or to dip the pockets into marinara sauce.

The company has and will ship its products, frozen, but it must use overnight shipping services. FedEx charges vary from $30 to $100, depending on the weight of the package and distance it is traveling.

The products are available throughout St. Louis in grocery stores and at the company's plant. A 10-ounce bag of the ravioli—25 squares—is $2.20. A box of 100 squares is $7.20.

Maybe, if more restaurants nationwide start carrying toasted ravioli, other famous St. Louis foods, such as gooey butter cake and ice-cream custard "concrete" shakes, will follow.

ORDERING ADDRESS
Maria and Son Italian Products, Inc.
4201 Hereford Street
St. Louis, MO 63109
314/481–9009
800/513–9009
FAX: 314/481–9109
No credit cards; checks OK

VISITS: From downtown St. Louis, drive west on Highway 40. Exit at Kings Highway, driving south until Chippewa. Make a right on Chippewa. Maria and Son is at the corner of the first stoplight on Chippewa, which is Hereford. Watch for the red overhang on the shop. Visitors can purchase the company's products, but there are no plant tours.
Monday–Friday, 9 A.M.–4 P.M.

ROSSI PASTA

Ha, ha, ha, ha. Rossi Pasta has a real sense of humor. We like its labels, its recipes, its catalog, and its sensibilities. It certainly is the only food company we've encountered that sells Frank Sinatra, Mel Torme, and Miles Davis CDs on the side as dinner music selections. "I had to seriously test my CEO power to offer these," wrote co-founder John Rossi in an early catalog. "After all, we're a 'food' company."

Rossi Pasta

Yes, but a food company that includes pictures of Rossi's children in the catalog and prints well-edited lists of essential pantry items. Rossi Pasta started in the college town of Athens, Ohio, in 1981 and expanded 35 miles east five years later. It's a food company that hosts thousands of visitors every year.

We've been watching Rossi Pasta since an alert childhood friend, Dwight Woodward, who lives in Athens, sent us information about the company shortly after it opened. Now it has a website, and fancy department stores, food catalogs, and hotels have come calling. Yet it has remained an idiosyncratic company with personality.

Consider John Rossi's explanation of his last name. He wrote in one of his catalogs that the "i" in his family's name was dropped in the late twenties for political reasons, but was reprised in 1981 "because 'Ross Pasta' just didn't have it."

Entertaining reading and striking graphics are one thing, but the company manages to keep its emphasis squarely on its pastas, which come in arresting colors and combinations. They are made with unbleached spring wheat, not semolina, which cannot be used successfully in its hand-rolled method of manufacture. The pastas therefore are softer and take less time to cook than most commercial pastas—45 seconds for the angel hair pasta and about 3 minutes for the fettuccini.

The company is unique in its use of softer flour and hand-rolling, and in how it uses ingredients. Its website copy explains: "We daily acquire and prepare fresh peppers, onions, leeks, garlic, artichokes, spinach, horseradish (cough), basil, olives, wild mushrooms, red cabbage . . . pretty much everything. We are the only pasta maker we know who employs a dedicated kitchen staff to clean and chop vegetables. Exactly, a lot of work. But again, no shortcuts here."

Rossi's flavored pastas are original. Calamari fettuccini, tomato-basil-garlic fettuccini, red-cabbage-beet linguini, saffron linguini, and spinach-basil-garlic fettuccini are but a few brilliant examples. There are 25 varieties to choose from. All come in 12-ounce packages.

All of the pastas we sampled were assertive in their flavoring. No shy pinches of garlic or herbs here. A rainbow of various flavors makes these pastas worthy of gift giving. Five pastas in a box are $28.95. Seven boxed pastas are $38.95. Or, you can give pasta with red sauce.

The company offers 8 different red sauces in 16-ounce jars, including one with black olives and artichoke hearts, one with arugula and escarole greens with wild mushrooms, and one with clams, leeks, and dry vermouth. The House Red Sauce has basil, scallions, and porcini mushrooms. The catalog describes it as "tart, dry, medium body, slight mushroom nose." Two jars of sauce and 3 pastas in a box are $29.95. Shipping costs are added to all prices.

The company has expanded its offerings to include packages of "essential pantry" grain staples such as couscous, arborio rice, red and brown basmati rice blend, and cornmeal for polenta. It also sells original seasonings, such as spicy garlic sesame roast, Creole pepper, and Thai and veggie pepper.

We were charmed by the various unexpected tastes in the Rossi lineup and happy to discover that with a few basics in our cupboard, such as garlic, olive oil, white wine, and Parmesan cheese, and a few extras, such as sesame seeds, chopped pimientos, and olives and artichoke hearts, we could use Rossi pasta to create an infinite number of interesting meals. The company includes good recipes with its pastas, in case you need help. Even if you don't, they bring a smile. The message on one label instructs: "Okay. Settle down, regain composure, brace for hub-bub over seconds." Ends another: "Do not let sit in colander. Eat. Enjoy. Go on with life."

ORDERING ADDRESS

Rossi Pasta
P.O. Box 759
Marietta, OH 45750
614/373-5155
800/227-6774
FAX: 740/373-5310
www.rossipasta.com
e-mail: rossipasta@compuserve.com
Credit cards accepted

VISITS

114 Greene Street
Marietta, OH
Marietta is in southeastern Ohio on the West Virginia border, about 15 minutes from downtown Parkersburg. The plant is about 1¼ miles from I-77. From the Interstate, take exit 1 and go west on Route 7, which will turn into Greene Street.

Monday–Saturday: 9 A.M.–7 P.M. Sunday, Noon–5 P.M.

TUTHILLTOWN GRIST MILL FLOURS

We like the description George Smith gave of what it's like to scour a gristmill: "Imagine dumping a 100-pound sack of flour all over your living room," he told the *New York Times.* "That's what it's like around here after a milling. Then imagine cleaning every surface in that room without moving any furniture. That's what it's like to clean a mill, only worse. It's like trying to get a barn clean enough to do surgery in."

Every fall, Smith, 62, meticulously cleans the gristmill he and his wife, Elza, run in Gardiner, New York, and the process takes weeks. It must be absolutely spotless by October to pass the careful inspections of Hassidic rabbis from Brooklyn who oversee the mill's grinding of kosher flour for Passover matzoh. There are other mills that grind kosher flour, but Tuthilltown Grist Mill is the only water-driven mill to do so. Because the mill grinds flour the traditional way, the flour is prized by the rabbis and shipped all over the world, as well as trucked to matzoh bakeries in Brooklyn.

The Smith family, whose roots are Protestant, have been grinding kosher flour since the late 1940s, and the sideline has allowed the mill to survive the years when stoneground flours lost public favor to highly refined and bleached flours.

The mill is not a replica or restoration. Since 1788, it has been a working mill, with a man-made millrace that uses water from the Shawangunk River. Built by a politician named Selah Tuthill, it was purchased by George Smith's mother, Eleanor, and her late husband, also named George, in 1941.

Year-round, the mill grinds a variety of lovely flours and cereals under its Falling Waters label. A whole wheat pastry flour is particularly useful, and the all-purpose flour, blended from hard and soft wheats, makes a superior loaf of bread. The hard wheat flour with natural gluten—meant just for bread—is the most popular item. The mill has a pamphlet of Eleanor Smith's recipes, which includes white bread with honey, a moist, fragrant, cream-colored loaf.

Pumpernickel, cracked-wheat, bran, and rice flours; cornmeal; oatmeal; soy flour; wheat germ; rye flour; rice bran; and a self-rising pancake mix are offered at the mill, as well as honey from a local beekeeper, maple syrup, baking ingredients, seasonings, nut butters, cheese, wheat-free products, and dried-fruit mixes. Well-priced spices are a particular draw for customers.

Prices vary with the seasons but are quite reasonable. Elza Smith recommends that mail-order customers write for a current catalog. A $2 per order handling fee, along with shipping charges, is added. The mill's retail shop includes items found in a country store, such as jellies, baked goods, teas, baskets, and gifts.

The mill has a small museum devoted to milling and often conducts tours for students and tourists, if appointments are made in advance.

ORDERING ADDRESS
Tuthilltown Grist Mill and Country Store
20 Gristmill Lane
Gardiner, NY 12525
914/255-5695
Credit cards accepted

VISITS: Gardiner is west of Poughkeepsie, in the southern part of the state. From the New York Thruway, exit left on Highway 299 at New Paltz. Go down the hill through the town of New Paltz until you reach Highway 208. Turn left and continue several miles to the intersection with Highway 44-55. Turn right and go through the town of Gardiner. Cross the railroad tracks and continue to the intersection with Albany Post Road. Follow the signs to the grist mill.

Wednesday–Friday, 9:30 A.M.–5:30 P.M. Saturday, 9:30 A.M.–6 P.M. Sunday, 11 A.M.–4 P.M. For other times, call for an appointment.

WAR EAGLE MILL FISH FRY COATING MIX

We like how Zoe Medlin Caywood, proprietor and miller at the historic War Eagle Mill in northern Arkansas, ends her letters. "With my nose to the grindstone . . ." she signs off.

Caywood believes in whole grains and has made her mill a popular destination for travelers interested in good food, locally made. She also has a wide mail-order clientele, and has extended her reach by writing a series of cookbooks on whole grains.

She is the daughter of Jewell Medlin, who opened the mill in its picturesque setting on the War Eagle River in 1973. It was the fourth mill built on the site. The first mill, built in the 1830s, washed away less than a decade later. The second mill was burned by order of a Confederate general to prevent the Union army's capture and use of the facility. The third water-powered gristmill was constructed in 1873, and the current mill was built to resemble it.

The building, with its 18-foot Arkansas cypress waterwheel and old-fashioned "six over six" paned windows, operates like a country store, with an inventory of Ozark foodstuffs such as sorghum and preserves, and handcrafts. On the mill's third floor is a restaurant, "The Bean Palace," that serves the mill's whole grains in biscuits and cornbread for breakfast and lunch. The food is homestyle, served on graniteware dishes.

The mill's best known product is a fish coating developed by Harold Ensley, known as "The Sportsman's Friend" on radio and television throughout the Midwest. "One of the Most Famous Fishermen of North America" is his billing, and he has been on the air from Kansas City, Missouri, for decades.

Years ago, Ensley and a friend developed a fish-coating recipe, a concentrated blend of flour, white pepper, paprika, soda, onion, garlic, salt, and other spices. It was not produced commercially until Jewell Medlin, who was a friend of Ensley's, started producing Ensley's Fish Fry Coating Mix at the mill.

Ensley's advertising isn't shy about its charms. "The very finest, the tastiest, seasoned mix—all the people you serve will love it" is his endorsement on the label. The coating is very concentrated, and easily can be tempered a bit by adding cornmeal or flour. It sparks up fried chicken and vegetables in batter, such as mushrooms. It is designed to coat meats and vegetables that simply have been dipped in water first—no egg or milk bath required. A 2-pound bag is $3.95, plus shipping.

But the mill produces many other products. Its flours, meals, and cereals are ground daily from organically grown grains. This is the place to come for rye and buckwheat flour, whole wheat pastry flour, wheat bran, raw wheat germ, and corn grits, all packaged in charming calico cloth bags. There are many whole-grain mixes to choose from, including hush puppy mix, buckwheat pancake and waffle mix, a biscuit mix, and a honey-nut bread machine mix.

All the products and Zoe Caywood's cookbooks are available by mail or on its website. But if you find yourself in northern Arkansas, make time for a detour. It is a lovely drive from nearby Rogers down a heavily wooded hill to the mill. Every year in the mill yard, the mill hosts a well-attended antique show in May and a crafts show in October.

ORDERING ADDRESS
War Eagle Mill
11045 War Eagle Road
Rogers, AR 72756
501/789-5343
FAX: 501/789-2972
www.wareaglemill.com
e-mail: zoe@ipa.net
Credit cards accepted

VISITS: **Rogers is north of Fayetteville, in the northwest corner of Arkansas. The mill is 13 miles east of Rogers on Highway 12. At the intersection with War Eagle Road (Highway 98), go south 1½ miles.**
March–January: Every day, 8:30 A.M.–5 P.M.

WEISENBERGER HUSH PUPPY MIX AND STONE-GROUND GRITS

Philip Weisenberger doesn't use the language of Madison Avenue in describing his products and their appeal: "They're taking off like a scalded dog," he says of his 5-pound bags of hot roll mix and sweet muffin mix. Now that's a claim we understand. His mill elevates the status of the word "mix." Despite good intentions to make muffins, waffles, and pancakes from scratch, we find ourselves more likely to use Weisenberger mixes.

The Weisenberger grain mill, situated on South Elkhorn Creek, in the heart of the Kentucky bluegrass region, is the country's oldest water-powered commercial mill. It has been in operation since 1865, and is in its sixth generation of millers.

His great-grandfather used a waterwheel to power his grain mill and Philip Weisenberger uses electricity, but few other practices have changed in how flour and cornmeal are processed in this enterprise.

Most of the products are packed in 5½-ounce bags, which contain enough for most family's meals. The price is more than reasonable—50 cents per bag for many mixes, such as the biscuit mix (in both white flour and whole wheat versions), white cornbread mix, yellow corn muffin mix, pancake mix, and fish batter mix. In less than 5 minutes, the hush puppy mix yields crunchy cornmeal nuggets that have been slightly seasoned with onion and garlic.

The mill's fish batter is very good for coating vegetables for quick deep-frying and the spoonbread mix makes that incomparable dish easy to fix. Newer offerings include berry muffin mixes (raspberry and blueberry), and cream gravy mix.

Weisenberger white or yellow grits are true grits that take 20 minutes on the stove to cook, not the instant variety sold in supermarkets, but they are worth seeking out. As Sarah Fritschner of the *Louisville Courier Journal* explained, "coarse grinding allows the grits to give up lots of starch when they cook, so they make a creamy sauce while still holding onto essential grittiness." They are sold in 2-pound bags at $2.50 each, plus shipping.

The mill also is a good source for specialty flours (pumpernickel rye, rice, potato, soy, durum, buckwheat, and semolina), as well as every variety of flour (unbleached, self-rising, whole wheat pastry). The mill uses soft red winter wheat for biscuit making and hard wheat, grown organically in Colorado, for bread flours.

A case of 12 of the 5½-ounce hush puppy or fish batter mix is $4.15. The 5-pound bags of hot roll mix are $3.75, and a like size of sweet muffin mix is 25 cents less. Shipping costs are added to these prices. The mill's website lists its extensive offerings, and it's possible to order from the site.

ORDERING ADDRESS

Weisenberger Mills, Inc.
Box 215
Midway, KY 40347
606/254-5282
800/643-8678
www.weisenberger.com
e-mail: flourusa@gte.com
Credit cards accepted

VISITS

2545 Weisenberger Road
Midway, KY
Midway is halfway between Lexington and Frankfurt. From Lexington, drive out West Main Street, which becomes Route 421. After 10 miles, watch for the blue Weisenberger sign at an unmarked intersection road, known locally as Weisenberger Mill Road. Take a left and the mill is on the left.

Monday–Friday, 8 A.M.–4 P.M. Saturday, 9 A.M.–noon

WHITE LILY FLOURS

How different can one brand of flour really be from another?" we wondered. This was prior to trying self-rising flour from White Lily, a Tennessee miller that dates to 1850. Using a White Lily recipe for light biscuits, we were astounded to produce the single best batch of biscuits we had ever made. High and flaky, these looked like food magazine biscuits and tasted the part.

White Lily looks different from other flours. It is much, much whiter, for one. It seems that Southern cooks demand brilliant white cakes and biscuits. White Lily all-purpose and self-rising flours are made from 100 percent pure soft wheat, unlike most national brands of all-purpose flour, which are a blend of hard and soft wheat. Soft wheat is best for fine-textured cakes and biscuits, while hard wheat excels in yeast breads. (The company does sell an excellent bread flour, but its reputation rests on its soft wheat flours.)

White Lily flours also are ground finer than national-brand flours, going through extra sifting and milling to achieve an extremely light texture. The company uses only about half of the total wheat berry—the part best suited to pastries—for its flour.

Since the flour is less dense, it weighs less. In recipes, 1 cup plus 2 tablespoons of White Lily flour substitutes for 1 cup of other flours.

The company began in the middle of the 19 century as a steam-powered mill called Knoxville City Mills. It later became the J. Allen Smith Company, in honor of its president, a leader in the turn-of-the-century consumer protection battles in Congress who battled mills that were adulterating flour and selling contaminated feed. In 1972, after a series of corporate affiliations, the company took the name of its best-selling "Sunday Baking" flour, White Lily.

It celebrated its centennial in 1983, and a year later, began sending its flour by mail to individuals. The company made the decision after pleading letters from transplanted Southerners, and requests from others who read about White Lily in southern cookbooks, grew to a volume too great to ignore.

Recently, the company became a subsidiary of C.H. Guenther & Son, Inc., of San Antonio, Texas, another longtime miller known for its Pioneer brand flour and baking mixes. White Lily now has a web presence and sells products such as Goo Goo Supreme Brownie Mix, a happy marriage of White Lily and Goo Goo Clusters, another Tennessee tradition. Other appealing products are fruit muffin mixes in flavors such as morning glory, blackberry, and wild berry, and gravy mixes in four styles: biscuit, country, pepper, and brown. The website also offers promotional items such as White Lily biscuit cutters, a featured recipe of the week, and answers to baking questions.

The best-selling mail-order flour is the all-purpose, which is preferred for cakes, pastries, and cookies. It can successfully be substituted for an equivalent amount of cake flour.

The best-selling flour in White Lily's distribution area, however, remains the self-rising flour, which is designed for biscuits, muffins, and quick breads. It includes baking powder. Longtime Southern biscuit makers probably don't need a recipe, but we found White Lily's biscuit recipe brochure most helpful. It contains 10 biscuit recipes, including cream biscuits, yeast biscuits, buttermilk biscuits, and one biscuit that you shape by bouncing from hand to hand, instead of cutting with a cutter. Recipes for scones, shortcake, and cobbler also are included.

All of White Lily's recipes, in fact, are a definite notch above those found on most packages and are worth seeking out. Each recipe is tested at White Lily at least three times, and then it is subjected to home tests. To accomplish that, White Lily contacts local women's church groups, garden clubs, and the like, and gives members a chance to earn money for the organization by testing recipes.

In addition to the self-rising and all-purpose flours, the company makes bread flour, unbleached self-rising flour, self-rising cornmeal mix, and self-rising buttermilk cornmeal mix, as well as the brownie mixes, muffin mixes, and gravy mixes.

Five-pound bags of any flour or cornmeal mix are $2, plus shipping costs. It costs $5 to ship 5 pounds of flour, $8 to ship between 5 and 20 pounds of flour, and $12 to ship between 20 and 50 pounds of flour. So it definitely saves money to order more than a single bag. However, it should be noted that the company will send items only to the 48 contiguous states. If you live in Alaska, you are out of luck.

Upon request, the company will send its order form, or you may order from the website.

ORDERING ADDRESS
The White Lily Foods Company
P.O. Box 871
Knoxville, TN 37901
865/546-5511
FAX: 865/521-7725
www.whitelily.com
e-mail: bellis@chguenther.com
Credit cards accepted

Pretzels, Chips, & Popcorn

BLACK JEWELL POPCORN

Do your bit to promote genetic diversity! Try Black Jewell popcorn, a patented seed variety grown only by a family-owned company in St. Francisville, Illinois, a small town on the Indiana border. The Klein family has been in business for 15 years selling "the black popcorn that pops snow white."

The natural color of the kernels is black, and they do pop white, with a black center. It makes for a striking bowl of popcorn. They also have a new red popcorn named Crimson Jewell, which pops white with a deep red center. And, it isn't messy the way we discovered that commercially colored popcorn can be. (For a child's birthday party, we thought it would be fun to serve colored popcorn. However, the bits of artificially colored red, green, orange, and yellow hulls ended up everywhere. Too bad we didn't know about Black Jewell at the time.)

Black Jewell pops up smaller than other popcorn, but with a very thin hull. The result is a very tender popcorn with no hard center that is said to be easier than others to digest. We like it for its taste, which requires no butter and less salt than the large brands. Bigger is not always better when it comes to popcorn.

The company, bowing to the national mania for microwave popcorn, introduced two microwave packages, in natural and butter flavors. The butter flavor includes soybean or cottonseed oil, salt, natural butter flavor, and beta carotene for color. The natural flavor has just oil and salt. The black corn used in the microwave version is larger and is not completely hulless. It is a superior microwave popped corn.

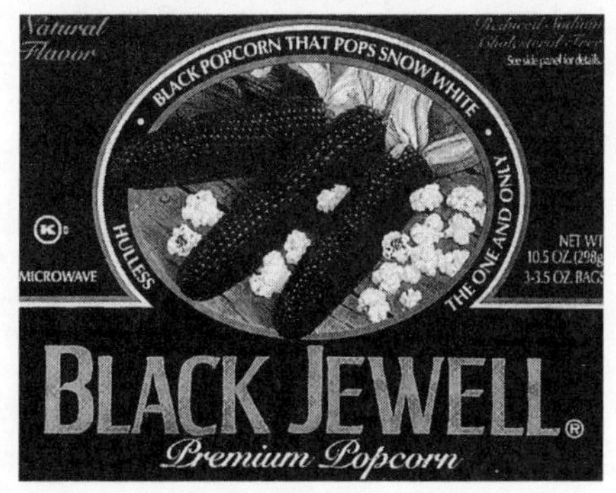

If Black Jewell is not available in your area, the company will ship it. The minimum order is a case of 12—either of 2-pound bags or of 3-packs of microwave popcorn.

ORDERING ADDRESS
Black Jewell Popcorn, Inc.
Route 1, Box 59
St. Francisville, IL 62460
800/948-2302
FAX: 618/948-2505
Credit cards accepted

BOB'S TEXAS STYLE POTATO CHIPS

There are dueling chipsters out there. As the homestyle potato chip market booms, the competition increases. Two companies with similar lines, Zapp's of Louisiana and Bob's Texas Style of Houston, both claim to produce the hottest chips. Bob's gets credit for being first. In 1984, owner Bob Rod came out with a jalapeño-seasoned chip. Zapp's followed a year later, and the major chip companies, playing catch up, followed in 1986.

We like Bob's cheese and jalapeño-seasoned variety better than the plain jalapeño version of either company. The cheeses involved are Cheddar and blue, and they temper the incendiary pepper taste.

If you have to test your internal organs, try Bob's new habanero potato chips. It is one burning chip.

Darker than the average chip, Bob's chips are worth seeking out. The company's distribution area includes Texas, Louisiana, and California, but its efficient mail-order operation sends chips worldwide. One of its contracts is with the U.S. Army, and Bob's red-and-white-striped packages can be found on bases here and abroad.

Individuals can call its toll-free number and order small snack bags or chips in tins that are decorated in various designs. You can get a 40-ounce tin filled with your choice of chips (jalapeño, Cajun, cheese and jalapeño, no salt, mesquite bar-b-que, dill pickle, steak and onion, Parmesan, sour cream and onion, or regular salted versions). Various gift packs also are available. Individual bags are $1.59 to $2.99.

ORDERING ADDRESS

Bob's Texas Style Potato Chips, Inc.
3500 S. La Cometa
Goodyear, AZ 85338
800/279-2250
www.poorebrothers.com
Credit cards accepted

DIEFFENBACH'S POTATO CHIPS

In the heart of Pennsylvania Dutch country, the Dieffenbach family makes a wonderful potato chip. Quite thick, nongreasy, and hearty, these are chips to savor and not stuff in mindlessly, as grocery chips seem to encourage us to do. These chips are fried in lard with only one ingredient—potatoes—and they make converts out of those who have been indifferent to potato chips. They make you dream of driving to Reading and swinging by Womelsdorf for a few bags. Once you've eaten them, you won't forget them.

To ensure freshness, the chips are sealed in thick bags that do not admit sunlight, which is declared "Potato Chip Freshness Enemy No. 1." The chips can be shipped in a 2-pound box for $11.25, postpaid, anywhere in the United States. Four pounds are $17.50; 6 pounds are $23.75, both including shipping. Subsequent orders will be priced according to your zipcode.

Mark Dieffenbach founded the company, which is now run by his sons, Elam and Nevin. Their small town is in eastern Pennsylvania, between Lebanon and Reading.

These are chips that are watched carefully in the cooking process. We've never seen an overly browned chip. These chips have such a strong potato taste that you don't think of them as chips, but as of slices.

The chips also are sold at the Womelsdorf IGA, the Dutchway Farm Store in Myerstown, and Martin's Farm Market in Lebanon.

ORDERING ADDRESS
Dieffenbach Potato Chips
60 Host Road
Womelsdorf, PA 19567
610/589-2385
No credit cards; checks OK

FISHER'S CARAMEL POPCORN

There are many sights and attractions along the boardwalk in Ocean City, Maryland, but none are as enduring as the Fisher Popcorn Company, which has been coating popcorn with its special caramel mixture since 1937. Donald Fisher was 7 years old when his father, Everett, devised the now-famous caramel, a combination of butter, corn syrup, brown sugar, and salt. Donald, his wife, Calvina, and two of their three children carry on the process unchanged at their boardwalk store. Their youngest daughter, Martha Hall, has brought the family's popcorn magic to Fenwick, Delaware, where she owns Fisher's Popcorn of Fenwick.

The Fisher method is to pour the hot caramel on the corn and mix the ingredients by hand, using wooden paddles made for the Fishers by a local carpenter. "We take special pride in not having white spots," Donald Fisher said. "It's more effort than if we used an automatic mixer, but we think there's a difference. It's hard work and it's tough finding the younger people who want to do it," he lamented.

Happy eaters can attest to the worth of their labors. The coating is very light, allowing the corn to keep its crunch. With one bite, you'll know that real butter, not a synthetic flavoring, is used. The popcorn is very good eaten out of the tubs the Fishers use for mail orders, but it is nearly irresistible when bought hot on the boardwalk. On summer weekends, the lines can stretch for half a block.

At its second, newer boardwalk location, at 7th Street, there is caramel popcorn with peanuts, along with fudge and assorted chocolates.

The corn is sold in boxes at 95¢, $1.50, and $3 on the boardwalk. Popcorn is shipped in white plastic tubs. Check the website for the price delivered to your address. In Maryland, for example, the 1½-gallon bucket is $14.85, delivered. There are 3½-gallon decorated tins and a large, 6½-gallon container.

The minimum mail order is a 1-gallon plastic tub, which ranges from $12.39 to $13.75 postpaid, depending on your location.

ORDERING ADDRESS
Fisher's Popcorn, Inc.
200 South Boardwalk
Ocean City, MD 21842
410/289-5638
888/395-0335
FAX: 410/289-1720
e-mail: fishers@dmv.com
www.fisherspopcorn.com
Credit cards accepted

VISITS: The original shop is located at Boardwalk and Talbot Street. There's a second location at 7th and Boardwalk.
Memorial Day–September 25: Every day 10 A.M.–midnight.
September 26–Memorial Day: Saturday–Sunday, 10 A.M.–5 P.M.

GARRETT CARAMELCRISP

What will make Chicagoans stand outside in freezing rain, stiff winds, or blowing snow? It looks like bread lines, but in Chicago it's the lines of fans waiting outside for Garrett's caramel popcorn. The storefronts—located throughout the downtown—are so tiny that only a handful of customers can be served inside. But the heavenly taste and buttery fragrance encourages consumption. We've rarely passed a Garrett shop without a line, no matter what the season.

We like the business practices of Garrett Popcorn Shops, which were founded in 1931. In the years since, the Garrett family presumably has had plenty of opportunity to add other flavors to its basic offerings. The fact that it has stuck with five basic flavors and done them very well speaks volumes about the company's restraint. Remember the flavored popcorn fad? Garrett ignored it.

Its short product list includes plain and plainer popcorn (with a light seasoning or without anything at all), cheese popcorn, cashew-caramel popcorn, a Macadamia CaramelCrisp, and its best-selling CaramelCrisp.

CaramelCrisp is Garrett's version of caramel corn, and it is outstanding. We tried it alongside another of the Midwest's favorite caramel corns that we were considering for this book, but CaramelCrisp had larger kernels, a much more even coating of caramel, and a richer, more buttery taste. No less a popcorn expert than food writer Michael Stern calls it "the best in the world."

Company president Karen Galaba took over when her mother retired. She agrees with many customers' description of CaramelCrisp as tasting like the crust of a crème brûlée.

The company has kept your choice of popcorn simple, but they've made up for it with 12 styles of decorated tins to choose from. Happily, at least half of them do not involve a goose or a teddy bear with a bow tied around its neck. We particularly like the Chicago at Night tin. A 1-gallon tin of CaramelCrisp is $18, plus shipping. A 2-gallon tin filled with cheese popcorn, CaramelCrisp, and plain popcorn is $30, plus shipping. Popcorn also is available in 3½- and 6½-gallon cans.

ORDERING ADDRESS
Garrett Popcorn Shops
P.O. Box 11342
Chicago, IL 60611

312/944-4730
888-4-POPCORN (476-7267)
FAX: 312/280-9611
www.garrettpopcorn.com
Credit cards accepted

TELEPHONE ORDERS
Monday–Thursday, 9 A.M.–4:30 P.M. Friday, 9 A.M.–1 P.M. November 27–December 23: Monday–Thursday, 8 A.M.–8 P.M. Friday, 8 A.M.–6 P.M. Saturday–Sunday, 10 A.M.–3 P.M. Credit cards accepted

VISITS: There are 5 Garrett stores in downtown Chicago, at 26 East Randolph, 2 West Jackson, 670 North Michigan Avenue, 4 East Madison, and 18 East Adams Street.

GOODS POTATO CHIPS

We promised ourselves to stop trying Pennsylvania potato chips, convinced that we had found the best that one area could offer. We're glad we didn't stop looking, because for three generations the Good family, in Pennsylvania Dutch country, has been turning out a fragile, tightly curled chip that is the ultimate in lightness and flavor.

Harold Good's son, Lewis, carries on the family tradition, selling their near-translucent amber chips on Thursdays and Fridays in the Shillington Farmer's Market, in Reading, Pennsylvania, and on all weekdays but Fridays from their home-based plant.

The lard-fried chip is now sold in a few local stores in the Reading area. When we first discovered the chips, we asked Harold's wife, Elva, why Pennsylvania had so many good chips. "The farmland isn't really good for big crops," she explained. "Most people just grow produce for the markets, and this was a sideline."

As is customary for so many of America's regional favorites, the prices are low. An attractive blue and white 2-pound box is $4.65 at their plant and $12.50 delivered by UPS. The Goods also sell a 6-ounce bag for $1.45, a 12-ounce bag for $2.55, and a 20-ounce bag for $3.85. They no longer are regularly using the wonderful metal tins that used to hold more than 8 pounds of chips. Customers used to give the Goods a $2 deposit and would reuse the tin. The Goods will refill the tins still owned by customers.

The loss of the tins is a good thing for our waistlines, though, because we often were tempted to finish the whole thing. The new sizes enforce a little bit of moderation.

VISITS
Goods Potato Chips
121 Jalyn Drive
New Holland, PA 17557
717/351-0084
FAX: 717/351-0086
No credit cards
Take Route 23 to New Holland. Turn onto South Custer Avenue, then a right on Orlon Road. Take a left onto Jalyn Drive.
Monday–Thursday, 7 A.M.–4:30 P.M.

THE HUMPHREY COMPANY'S EUCLID BEACH POPCORN BALLS

The continued existence of these superb, oversized popcorn balls is a testament to the persistence of the Humphrey family, whose name was synonymous with good food at Cleveland's grand old amusement park, Euclid Beach. When the park was demolished in 1969 to make way for a collection of mobile homes, the popcorn balls disappeared only briefly before Dudley Humphrey, Jr., great-grandson of their originator, began making them again.

Still made from the special hull-less, white hybrid popcorn grown on the family farm in Wakeman, Ohio, the popcorn is softly formed into large clear-syrup balls. If your only experience with popcorn balls has been the bullet-hard ones found in convenience stores or the amateur ones made at school fund-raisers, you are in for a delightful surprise. Their popularity has grown to the point that the company is making 8,000 balls daily.

Humphrey definitely enjoys carrying on the tradition of his ancestor, who first sold popcorn from a sidewalk stand in Cleveland's Public Square in the late 1890s. He also rescued the family's famous white pulled-taffy kisses from Euclid Beach. They are made with real cream, butter, sugar, and a hint of vinegar. These yellow-wrapped confections, packed in quarter-pound bags, are a bit sweet—something we never admit until the bag is empty.

Dudley and his wife, Betsy, have brought innovations to their venerable popcorn treats. A new confection—popcorn drizzled with white chocolate—is an addictive mix of savory and sweet. To support the Cleveland Indians, they've added a red-seamed baseball wrapper to their large popcorn balls. They've also introduced caramel popcorn balls and 3-inch balls, about half the size of the large. The smaller "snack" balls are sold in wrappers with a pumpkin face, Santa Claus, "Go Tribe," and the company's traditional park archway design.

The popcorn balls are a wonderful way to celebrate America's most popular snack food, and they can be bought at grocery stores in the Cleveland and Columbus areas. For nonlocals, the company will send its products, and now has developed several gift packs named after well-loved Euclid Beach attractions. The Photo and Ticket Canister, featuring photos of Laughing Sal, the park's entry arch, Over the Falls ride, and tickets, contains 10 large popcorn balls, two ¼-pound bags of kisses, and 30 ounces of its popping corn for $26.95. The Flying Turns Assortment, named for a white-knuckle ride, includes 50 large popcorn balls (perfect for Halloween or school parties), 4 bags of candy kisses, and two 30-ounce bottles of popping corn. It is $46.95.

The Euclid Beach sampler includes 4 caramel-flavored popcorn balls, 8 original popcorn balls, a bag of candy kisses, and a 30-ounce bottle of popcorn for $16.95. If you want to have your house remembered fondly at Halloween, order 100 of the smaller-size popcorn balls for $41.95. The chocolate drizzle popcorn is sold in four 5-ounce bags for $15.95.

For amusement park fans, the company also sells three books and videotapes, loaded with vintage photos about the park, and cassette tapes of the Gavioli, Artizan, and North Tonawanda band organs, all recorded at the park.

Those outside of Ohio should add $6 for shipping and handling on all orders. In-state customers add $5. Call or write for the company's illustrated brochure with all its prices.

ORDERING ADDRESS
The Humphrey Company
20810 Miles Parkway
Warrensville Heights, OH 44124
216/662-6629
800/486-3739
FAX: 216/662-6619
e-mail: humphreyco@ameritech.net
www.humphreycompany.com
Credit cards accepted

VISITS: *Please call ahead for hours.*

JOSIE'S BEST BLUE-CORN TORTILLA CHIPS

Blue corn is now an accepted part of the culinary landscape, but Morris Montoya was among the first we knew to introduce this meaty, healthy grain to consumers nearly two decades ago. At that time, the color was so unfamiliar that the family continually had to ward off the query, "Are these moldy?" when people looked at the tortilla chips.

This special corn, a staple in Mexican cooking, results in a tortilla that is dark blue-gray—a shock to the eyes, but not to the tongue. The rare corn, which is not as strong-stalked as yellow corn because it has not been toughened through hybrids, is too fragile to be picked by machine. Instead, it is harvested by hand by Pueblo Indians on reservations throughout New Mexico. The low-yield corn is not a popular crop, as it spoils faster than conventional grains. "But once you've tried a blue, you'll never go back," vows Morris Montoya, age 55, who has run the business since 1963.

The company's tortilla chips are made according to the recipe that his parents, Eppie and Josie Montoya, developed in the late 1940s as part of their restaurant business. The grain is cooked in lime, washed, ground, and then cooked into hand-cut rounds or triangles. They are thicker, and slightly sweeter, than customary chips.

The Montoyas also sell blue-corn flour, blue-corn pancake mix, blue cornmeal, blue-corn popcorn, a sopaipilla mix and Indian fry bread mix, corn husks and chicos, havas (a dark bean that's often roasted), red powdered chile, and other Southwestern specialties. They will be happy to send you a price list. Their salsas are particularly good and very reasonably priced. They're developing a line of Southwest heat-and-eat foods.

Shipping costs are additional. Sold at the plant are several items that can't be shipped, such as flour tortillas, blue-corn tortillas, taco and tostada shells, and whole-wheat tortillas.

ORDERING ADDRESS
Senor Pino's de Santa Fe
2600 Camino Entrada
Santa Fe, NM 87505
505/473-3437
e-mail: senorpinos@aol.com
www.senorpinos.com
Credit cards accepted

VISITS: *Monday–Friday, 9 A.M.–4 P.M.*

NIP'S CHIPS

When in Hawaii, look beyond the Maui potato chip. In particular, seek out Nip's Potato Chips, a small family-run firm that turns out shrimp chips, won tu pi chips, and excellent potato chips.

The company used to be known for its distinctive purple-veined tarot chips. It had to give up that product. As is true of so many small businesses, the reasons were personal, not economic. James Nip, who founded the company in 1929, died, and his wife, Y.L.T., suffered a stroke. Their children, Donna and Norman, could not keep up with the intensive hand labor required to make taro chips. The family had always painstakingly peeled the taro root by hand, unlike the large producers on the island, FritoLay and Granny Goose, who also make the indigenous Hawaiian snack.

We were terribly fond of Nip's taro chips, which were crisp, nongreasy, lightly salted, slightly sour, and addictive. The good news from Nip's is that the company continues to make its potato chips, shrimp chips, and won tun pi chips. The potato chips are light and nongreasy. Shrimp chips, puffed up slices that taste faintly of fish, have served as an early introduction to exotic food for children for years. The won tun pi chips are a sweet and salty fried wonton that are often crumbled on top of salads. A popular combination is with cold chicken salad.

Nip's products are available only in Oahu, and the company does not send by mail. Many visitors, after being introduced to Nip's on vacation, delay their inevitable withdrawal pangs by buying cases of the chips from the small factory.

If customers come to the factory, they can buy any of the Nip's chips for the wholesale price of $1.58 per bag. The potato chips and won tun pi chips come in 4-ounce bags, and the shrimp chips are in 2½-ounce bags.

VISITS
Nip's Potato Chips
806 Pohukaina Street
Honolulu, HI 96813
808/593-8549
e-mail: donnachang@hotmail.com
Nip's is located in a light industrial area known as Kakaako, about 5 minutes west of Waikiki Beach. From the Lulalilo Freeway, take the Kinau cutoff. The next intersection is Ward Avenue; turn right. Go 4 or 5 blocks to Halekawila and turn right. Take the first street to the left, go 2 blocks, and you will see the factory on the right-hand side. It's usually open weekday mornings, but call ahead to be sure.

OLE SALTY'S POTATO CHIPS

Honest. Before we started researching this book, we didn't even like potato chips. But that was before we knew the joys of America's small producers, people like Frank and Cindi Guasto, who turn out an excellent chip in one of the country's meccas for potato chips: Rockford, Illinois.

In this small city of 140,000 there are two small-scale potato chip companies. (The other is Mrs. Fisher's, with its always stylish 1930s-style yellow-and-red bags.) Ole Salty's uses an attractive brown, plastic-coated bag and its edges out the competition with a thicker chip that's sold homemade over the counter in their shop. "Our motto is to stay small and control the quality," says Frank Guasto. "We never intend to go to automatic cookers."

Until we tasted Ole Salty's, we thought we were loyal only to a lard-cooked chip. But the Guastos, who vary a mix of oils depending on the type of potato, have the knack of creating an almost meaty chip that manages the miracle of tasting exactly like what it is—a slice of fried potato.

Of their three varieties, regularly salted, lightly salted, and no salt, we prefer the compromise position. The chips are $2.25 per pound at the shop. The Guastos will ship the chips in its bags, which feature an old salt yelling the welcome words, "Your chip has come in, mate!" Two bags of 14½ ounces are $10.50, delivered. Four bags are $17 and 6 bags are $22, shipping included.

The potato chip is winning new converts in the elite food world. The American Institute of Food and Wine includes Ole Salty's in its exhibitions and the International Culinary Institute welcomed the chip in a recent confab with top chefs. Yes, even fine chefs aren't immune to the charms of a well-made potato chip.

OLE SALTY'S POTATO CHIPS™

ORDERING ADDRESS
Ole Salty's of Rockford, Inc.
3131 Summerdale Avenue
Rockford, IL 61101
815/963-3355
Credit cards accepted
www.olesaltys.com

VISITS: The shop is on the northwest side of Rockford, 6 blocks west of Rockford Memorial Hospital. From downtown Rockford, take Auburn Street (also known as Spring Creek Road) west. At Kilburn Avenue, take a right (north) and drive for 11 blocks until you reach Summerdale Avenue.

Monday–Friday, 9 A.M.–4:30 P.M. Saturday, 9 A.M.–noon

PHILADELPHIA SOFT PRETZELS

The soft-pretzel lover's vision of the world is that all other pretzel manufacturers made a mistake by overbaking. And while the Philadelphia tradition of slathering soft pretzels with mustard takes some getting used to, any first-time eater will understand the appeal of the Sidorick family's pretzels.

Dan and Jeanne Sidorick mortgaged their future, and that of their four children, 31 years ago to take over a small pretzel bakery in the Frankfurt section of Philadelphia that was owned by Fred Pappler, who was retiring. Dan Sidorick, who was an insurance agent, often bought pretzels there while endeavoring unsuccessfully to sell Pappler insurance. But he and his wife were nothing but successful with the bakery, much to the dismay of the city's seven other pretzel manufacturers. After building a thriving business, Dan left the business to his son, Joe. The "matriarch," as she laughingly calls herself, Jeanne, is secretary-treasurer and works at the plant every day.

Their pretzels, each about 3 ounces and studded with coarse salt, are cooked in a tunnel oven for a mere seven minutes, resulting in a chewy, doughy, slightly malt-flavored pretzel.

At the beginning, the Sidoricks and a single employee hand-twisted 3,000 pretzels each day. The oblong pretzels still are hand-twisted, but by 30 employees who turn out 45,000 daily. "The twisters do about twenty pretzels a minute," said Jeanne. "Automated machinery just does not give you the same texture or quality."

The biggest customers are parochial and public schools and local hospitals, where the pretzels are sold by vendors for 35¢ to 50¢. The Sidorick pretzels can be differentiated from rivals by vending cart signs that bear the slogan, "The Good Ones."

True fans know to stop by the bakery in the early morning, when a bag of just-baked pretzels is a bargain 5 for $1. Fifty pretzels at the shop are even less—$8. For large orders, customers may specify that no salt be added to the pretzels' exterior. There is no sugar or salt in the pretzel recipe, and the Sidoricks use soybean shortening and a high-protein flour. They are kosher pretzels. The Sidoricks also offer their favorite Philadelphia mustard, Keller's Bran Mustard, for dipping. Patrons may buy a gallon jug at the shop for the unbelieveably low price of $2.25.

For mail-order customers, the family will send you 50 pretzels for $55, including handling and overnight shipping.

"We eat them every day," remarked Jeanne, who takes home a small bag each day for her own noshing. "That's the best quality control."

ORDERING ADDRESS
Philadelphia Soft Pretzels, Inc.
4315 North Third Street
Philadelphia, PA 19140
215/324-4315
FAX: 215/324-7622
No credit cards; checks OK

VISITS: From downtown, drive north on Broad Street to the 4300 block. Turn right until Third.
Monday–Saturday, 5 A.M.–noon

ROUTE 11 SWEET POTATO CHIPS

Did you know that the sweet potato is not related to the ordinary potato? I didn't, until I got a copy of *The Oxford Companion to Food,* written by Alan Davidson. From our friendship with his daughter, Caroline, and their work with *Petits Propos Culinaires,* a food history journal, we knew this would be a surprising, comprehensive, and informative work. It is.

So, also for the record (and for all those clerks at Safeway who tell us we're wrong), a sweet potato is *not* the same thing as a yam. Virginia was one of the first places in America where sweet potatoes were cultivated. It makes sense that food enthusiast Sarah Cohen began experimenting in Virginia with sweet potato chips in 1991. Her family runs the venerable Tabard Inn in Washington, whose restaurant is known for invention—and its potato chips.

The Cohens bought an existing company, Chesapeake Chips, from chip maker Mike Miller and moved it from Waldorf, Maryland, to Middletown, Virginia, a decade ago. Now located in an old feed store, Miller's son, Chris, is production manager.

Sarah's venture into new chip varieties has been very successful. Although the regular potato chip, a thick, meaty round, is the most popular, we are very fond of the sweet potato chip. It's got just a hint of salt and is chewy, not mealy. There is a soft, roasted flavor to the chip and the color looks wonderful with a peasant or oatmeal bread sandwiches.

For other tastes, there are dill pickle chips, salt and vinegar, barbecue, and Death Rain, an extremely hot chip.

The company buys potatoes based on season—Florida for spring and summer potatoes and New York and Pennsylvania varieties for fall and winter. The dozen employees stand behind the cookers, sorting and watching each batch. The trade secrets involve slice thickness and the temperature when potatoes are added.

Route 11 is the oldest paved route in the United States, winding from northern New York to the Gulf of Mexico. It seemed appropriate to Sarah to name the chips after this farm to market road. Weekend travelers on Route 11 now load up at the plant. The chips also can be mail-ordered. A 1½-pound can of any variety is $14.50, plus shipping. Smaller bags are available in stores throughout Maryland, Washington, D.C., and Virginia.

ORDERING ADDRESS
Route 11 Potato Chips
U.S. Route 11, P.O. Box 351
Middletown, VA 22645
540/869-0104
800/294-7783
FAX: 540/869-0176
www.rt11.com
Credit cards accepted

VISITS: From Washington, D.C., travel west on Route 66. At I-81, go north. Take the first exit and take a left at the exit ramp. Drive ¾ mile to Route 11. Go left (south) for half a mile through Middletown's sole traffic light. The plant is on the right in a silver building.
Friday, 10 A.M.–6 P.M. Saturday, 9 A.M.–5 P.M.

STERZING POTATO CHIPS

The Sterzing Food Company rarely advertises, yet it sends hundreds of cartons of its all-natural potato chips each year to homesick Iowans across the country. The 66-year-old firm still makes only 8 pounds of chips per batch. Its boiling potatoes are stirred by hand, unlike the automatic fryers used by its mammoth competitors. The finished chips also are sorted by hand, a batch at a time, rather than by the quick-scan-by-conveyor-belt method used by larger firms.

All this hand labor and close attention pays off. The resulting chip is thicker, crunchier, and has not even a hint of oil. "Chemicals taint the flavor, so we don't use them," said Tom Blackwood, plant manager. "Our product sells fast enough we don't have to use preservatives."

The company also sells an unsalted chip and a ripple chip. We like them all, but like so many products, prefer the original.

If you buy the chips at the plant, or at one of the stores within a 70-mile radius of Burlington, Iowa, where they're made, you have a choice of five bag sizes for the original chip. The unsalted chip comes in a ½-pound size only. The ripple chip is sold in 1¼-ounce bags, and 12-ounce bags.

If you order by mail, the company can send 2 large (12-ounce) bags, 4 large bags, or 2 large bags with 2 cans of its sour cream and onion dip. The chips are reasonably priced, but the company prefers that customers contact it to get a current price, including shipping costs.

Current owners Dutch and Billie Duttweiler bought the company in 1959 from Dutch's cousin, Barney Sterzing, who founded the business. The chip making is now overseen by the third generation.

ORDERING ADDRESS
The Sterzing Food Company
1819 Charles Street
Burlington, IA 52601
319/754-8467
800/754-8467
FAX: 319/752-7195
Sterzing@lisco.com
www.sterzingchips.com
Credit cards accepted

VISITS: The plant is on the north side of town, one block west of Roosevelt Avenue. *Monday–Friday, 8 A.M.–4:30 P.M.*

STURGIS PRETZELS

Pretzels have found new favor as a diet snack food. This hints at its medieval origin, where the pretzel symbolized long life.

If you are serious about going to the source, the lineage of Sturgis pretzels should suffice. Anointing any location as the birthplace of a food is bound to get you in trouble. Food lovers enjoy arguing about food origins almost as much as they like eating, and many claims of "the original" this or that need to be taken with a grain of salt.

But there is no disputing the pedigree of the Julius Sturgis Pretzel House in the Pennsylvania Dutch town of Lititz. Begun in 1861 as America's first commercial pretzel bakery, it continues today in a building that predates the company by seven years. Its owners, Clyde and Barbara Tshudy, are

Sturgis descendants, and Clyde was taught to twist pretzels by one of Julius Sturgis's sons. He, in turn, has taught his son, Michael, who now works for the company.

Since he took over the bakery in 1970, Clyde has become America's best-known pretzel twister, captivating preschoolers on the *Mr. Rogers* television show, appearing on *Jeopardy!*, having his technique immortalized in four stop-action photos in the *New York Times,* and so on. His hand-twisted soft pretzels can be purchased warm at the bakery (with or without mustard), but they are not sent by mail. However, the bakery will ship its excellent hard pretzels, which are machine-formed in various sizes, shapes, and flavors.

"Pretzels Your Way" states the Sturgis brochure, and that's no empty promise. There are regular pretzels, oat-bran pretzels, jalapeño, garlic and herb, honey mustard and onion, and terrific cheese pretzels tangy with sharp blue cheese. Any flavor can be ordered unsalted, if you prefer. The versions can be purchased in the traditional knot, in a "mini" size (about the size of a quarter) or a "penny" size (3 inches long), or shaped like an Amish horse and buggy. Clyde Tshudy says that the horse-and-buggy shape is the most popular, with the oat-bran flavor coming on strong.

The penny and horse-and-buggy pretzels are individually wrapped in cellophane, which means they grow old gracefully. We ordered several 3-pound boxes of various pretzels and munched happily on them for months. As snacks go, the unsalted oat-bran version can almost be considered health food, since it contains no shortening.

The bakery offers a variety of decorated tins for the pretzels (Pennsylvania Dutch, a wildlife scene, and the like) in 2-, 3-, and 6-pound sizes, but it is also possible to order unadorned boxes of pretzels. A 3-pound can of pretzels, for example, is $15.49, plus shipping via UPS. Without the can, it is $7.98, plus shipping. You receive approximately 120 pretzels in a large plastic bag inside a shipping box. Tie a bow around the bag and you have an unbeatable gift for $8. If that isn't thrifty enough for you, a 4-pound box of broken pretzels (not individually wrapped) is a mere $7, plus shipping.

Sturgis pretzels are meaty, with real flavor. Supermarket pretzels, in comparison, are anemic, brittle, and taste mainly of salt. America's first pretzel bakery clearly isn't coasting on its illustrious past.

ORDERING ADDRESS

The Julius Sturgis Pretzel House
219 East Main Street
Lititz, PA 17543
717/626-4354
FAX: 717/627-2682
Info@sturgispretzel.com
www.sturgispretzel.com
Credit cards accepted

VISITS

The brick bakery, built in 1784 and on the National Register of Historic Places, is directly on Main Street (Route 772) east of Lititz Square. Lititz is about 6 miles north of Lancaster, in southeastern Pennsylvania, at the intersections of routes 501 and 772.

Monday–Saturday, 9 A.M.–5 P.M.

TOURS: There is a $2 per person fee for tours. (Children two and under are free.) The last tour is at 4:30 P.M.

UNIQUE PRETZEL SPLITS

A German pretzel maker, in the midst of many other German pretzel makers in Reading, Pennsylvania, the Pretzel Capital of the World, needs an advantage. Bill Spannuth's father found his by accident. His esteemed split pretzel was an error in baking. By overbaking it to the point where crevices develop, Spannuth has made a chewier and more flavorful twisted pretzel. It's thicker than most pretzels and isn't as hard on the teeth.

What we like most is that there is very little salt used in comparison to most other pretzels. With Unique pretzels, we don't spend time chipping off the exterior salt. This is a company that cares about its customers with concerns about sodium—it makes all of its pretzels in unsalted versions. Besides the original split, there are also the following varieties: cheese, extra dark, oat bran, fat free, extra salt, jalpeño Cheddar, and butter flavor (which contains vegetable oils, not butter, but is one of our favorites nonetheless because it is softer). The splits also come coated in milk, white, and dark chocolate—either plain pretzels or pretzels turned in peanut butter first.

The company still is owned by the Spannuth family, although Bill's name has come off the packages and "Unique Pretzels" used instead. The firm will send a 4-pound box of one flavor of splits (no chocolate) for $19.40, including shipping. A 6-pound box is $24.40 and you may choose up to 6 different flavors, excluding chocolate. There is an attractive assortment of painted tins for the pretzels, and the company will send a colored brochure with prices and ordering information upon request.

The employees are happy to sell to customers who happen to be in the Reading area and want to see where the pretzels are made. At the plant's store, you can buy a 1-pound bag for $2.35 and a 4-pound box for a bargain $8.40.

ORDERING ADDRESS
Unique Pretzel Bakery
215 E. Bellevue Avenue
Reading, PA 19605
610/929-3172
888-4-SPLITS (477-5487)
FAX: 610/929-3444
e-mail: uniquesplits@fast.net
www.uniquesplits.com
Credit cards accepted

VISITS: The plant is on the north side of Reading, adjacent to Fairgrounds Square Mall. Bellevue is two blocks off of State Route 61.
Monday, Tuesday, Wednesday, Saturday, 8:30 A.M.–5 P.M. Thursday, Friday, 8:30 A.M.–6 P.M.

VELVET CREME POPCORN

Those people fortunate enough to live in Kansas City enjoy a wealth of special hometown foods, from Wolferman's English muffins to Stroud's fried chicken. If you're a local, you know that you can stop by the Velvet Creme store right by the Shawnee Mission plant and get refills of Velvet Creme Popcorn in any container and in nearly any amount.

It may seem like the height of laziness, or decadence, to buy your popcorn already popped. But the family of co-founder Dona White, 96, produce such a memorable, fresh corn at such a reasonable price that these objections fade.

Although many upstart firms got into the popcorn shipping business a decade ago, adding such foolishness as cherry and lemon flavors, most of them have faded from sight. Velvet Creme, however, continues, as it has for the last 63 years, to be owned and operated by the White family. The name is taken from the company's motto, "Smooth as velvet, rich as cream."

Our favorite of this Shawnee Mission, Kansas, firm is the cheese variety, as it imparts its mild Cheddar flavor without leaving lurid orange powder on your hands, which appears to be standard industry practice. But you don't have to choose, as Velvet Creme sells its buttered, cheese, and caramel popcorn in a three-way can.

The operation began against Dona's wishes in 1937. Her late husband, Howard, was on strike from Ford Motor Company, needed money, and decided to sell popcorn to tavern owners, who offered it free to customers.

Dona was reluctant to sell to taverns, as she didn't want her family making deliveries to them. But after buying each of their three children a pair of shoes with Howard's last Ford paycheck, the Whites used the remaining $10 to start the business. It consisted of hanging a kettle over a gas flame in their basement and using corn borrowed from a movie theater to begin popping nickel bags. The couple filled waxed-paper bags and sealed them with Dona's iron.

It's truly a family business. Daughter-in-law Patricia White hand-painted many of the 6½-gallon tins, which are now lithographed because of the number required. Daughter-in-law Mary Lou suggested the cardboard dividers that allowed the firm to begin shipping three-way cans 40 years ago.

All corn is popped for exactly 2 minutes and 10 seconds in one of 16 round poppers. Rotating screens sift out the hard kernels. The Velvet Creme Kernel is a denser than most, with a strong hull. A three-way tin is $17.50, plus shipping. Decorator tins are $3.50 extra. The buttered popcorn may be ordered unsalted. Christmas orders must be received by November 24.

The corn arrives with remarkably few crumbled kernels. Velvet Creme workers start the process right by filling the cans by hand. The company's motto for employees, "Fill every bag as if you are filling it for yourself," is helping to speed the Velvet Creme Company on to another century of vigilant popping.

ORDERING ADDRESS
Velvet Creme Popcorn
4710 Bellinder Avenue
Shawnee Mission, KS 66205
913/236-7742
800/552-6708 or 888/551-6708
FAX: 913/236-9631
e-mail: vcpop@swbellnet
Credit cards accepted

VISITS: **Belinder Avenue is in the Westwood section, 6 blocks west of State Line Road, the actual line between Kansas and Missouri. From downtown Kansas City, take I-35 south. Exit at Mission Road (Exit 233A) and follow it south to 47th Street. Turn left and take the first right onto Belinder and look for the Velvet Creme plant.**

Monday–Saturday, 9 A.M.–5:30 P.M.

WIDMAN'S CHIPPERS

Potato chips bathed in chocolate are not a new idea—the Widman family, which has been making candy since 1885, has been selling such chips for decades in North Dakota.

In fact, the Widmans are single-handedly keeping the Red River Valley sweet by covering prairie foods in chocolate. Three stores, owned by Widmans, carry the unusual recipes for chocolate-covered potatoes, wheat nuts, soybeans, and sunflower seeds at low prices. The Widmans have experimented by taking almost anything the prairie grounds will grow and sweetening it with chocolate. They also sell a peanut-butter candy molded in the shape of North Dakota and "cow pies" of marshmallow, pecans, and caramel.

Betty Widman and her husband, George, a third-generation candy maker, and their youngest son, Dan, run the store in Grand Forks. Their oldest son, George, Jr., his wife, Lois, and George Sr.'s sister, Margaret, run the original store, in Crookston, Minnesota, which is about 20 minutes southeast of Grand Forks. Betty and George's daughter Carol Widman Kennedy and her husband, Dave, run a Widman's shop in downtown Fargo, North Dakota.

All three feature the "chipper"—a ruffled fried chip of Red River Valley potato bathed in fine chocolate. This confection is a testament to a simple idea done well. The uninitiated might blanch, but it's a delicious and addicting combination that joins two of America's favorite tastes.

The Widmans laugh when they read glossy catalogs from New York and California that feature similar chocolate-covered potato chips for $18 a pound. "We can't imagine why they charge so much," said Betty Widman.

"Someone brought us back some chocolate covered chips from Maui," Betty Widman related. "They were $6 for a tiny 4-ounce bag!" Their chippers are $9 per pound at the stores. For chippers that are shipped, add $4.50 for the first pound, and 50¢ for each additional pound.

Ordering by mail is one sure way to get the chippers (except in summer, when it's too hot to send chocolate). At Christmas, crowds stand outside in two lines waiting for chippers and several of the Widman's other treats.

ORDERING ADDRESS
Widman's Candy Shop
106 South 3rd Street
Grand Forks, ND 58201
701/775-3480
800/688-8351
Credit cards accepted

VISITS: The store is in downtown Grand Forks, next to the railroad tracks. *Monday–Friday, 9:30 A.M.–5:30 P.M. Saturday, 9:30 A.M.–5:00 P.M.*

ZAPP'S POTATO CHIPS

Someday soon, a restaurant is going to open a potato chip bar, with menus listing the varieties, by region and temperature.

The latest species to win favor are known variously as "hard-bite," "home-style," or "kettle-cooked." They differ from the thin traditional chip (known as "continuous-cooked") in that they are cut thicker and fried in batches in kettles of hot oil instead of being cooked on a conveyor belt.

The batch-fried chips hold more seasoning—perfect for spicy varieties. For a battalion of peppy varieties, look no further than Zapp's Potato Chips, located in an old Chevrolet showroom in Gramercy, Louisiana. There, the company's best-selling Cajun Craw-Tators (with a crawdad clamped on to a chip in its logo) are made, as well as a truly incendiary jalapeño-seasoned chip, Cajun Dill Gator-Tators (they taste like dill pickles), Mesquite Smoked Bar-B-Que Flavored Chips, and other more mundane varieties, like no-salt and regular chips.

To our taste buds, the jalapeño chips are for diehard fire-eaters, but the Cajun Craw-Tators are another story. Cooked in peanut oil, as are all Zapp's chips, the Cajun chips have a whole paragraph of ingredients, most of them not especially terrific for you. But the whole point of potato chips is that they aren't especially terrific for you. They aren't the sort of food where you study the labels. (But for students, Zapp's chips have 8 grams of fat per serving versus 9 to10 grams of fat for most national brand chips).

The reddish Cajun chips are unusually tasty, not too oniony and not too salty. In other words, you can still tell there's a slice of potato under there. The Dill Gator-Tators are a unique taste sensation, well seasoned and balanced.

Ron Zappe (rhymes with "happy") began his business in 1985, after tasting a thick chip in Houston and learning the rudiments of the chip business from a company there. He was familiar with Louisiana from having sold oil-field equipment there, and picked Gramercy, halfway between New Orleans and Baton Rouge, a petrochemical area where unemployment was high. Initially, preference was given in hiring to people who had been out of work at least six months, and that still holds true for new hires. Currently, the firm employs more than 100 people.

One of his smart moves was in hiring a top-notch graphic artist who designs seasonal bags. Zapp's had a Zappy Holiday bag at Christmas and a

Zappy Mardi Gras design for Fat Tuesday. There's a terrific purple New Orleans T-shirt and limited edition chips, in flavors such as steak.

One of the company's most popular mail-order shipment sizes is the sample box containing eight 6-ounce bags of your choice of flavors. The cost is $18, including shipping. Another popular item is a $30 Cajun survival kit, with 4 six-ounce bags, 2 Zapp's dips, 1 Zatarain's jambalaya mix, 1 bag of red beans, 1 jar Creole mustard, 1 bottle Tabasco sauce, 1 container of seasoning, and a CD of Zydeco and Cajun music. Shipping is included.

ORDERING ADDRESS
Zapp's Potato Chips
P.O. Box 1533
Gramercy, LA 70052
800/HOT-CHIP (468-2447)
FAX: 888/FAX-CHIP (329-2447)
www.zapps.com
Credit cards accepted

TELEPHONE ORDERS: *Every day, 8 A.M.–5 P.M.*

Savory Sauces

COUNTRY BOB EDSON'S ALL PURPOSE SAUCE

We encountered Country Bob's sauce in a small eatery in the Missouri bootheel, not far from the Tennessee border. It served chopped-meat sandwiches, with coleslaw inside the bun and a bottle of Country Bob's sauce on the side. The place was grimy, the lighting dim, but the sandwiches were sensational.

Bob Edson of the southern Illinois town of Mt. Vernon started his sauce business in 1977 in a small shed behind his house. Three years later, he moved it to an empty storeroom of a local grocery. Three years after that, it grew to a tin building of its own. Five years passed, and in 1988, Country Bob Edson's All Purpose Sauce had its own "semi-modern building," in the words of Al Malekovic, one of the company's four owners.

The sauce has a lot of ingredients, the result of Bob's initial experiment when he "went over to a little neighborhood grocery store and bought a lot of different items that I thought might give me the flavor I liked." It must have been a well-stocked store, because his list includes anchovies, tamarind, red peppers, and soy sauce, as well as the more expected ketchup, Worcestershire sauce, vinegar, tomatoes, molasses, and garlic.

As Bob explained, "Before I got the taste I wanted, I had made six gallons. O.K. I had six gallons of sauce that I wanted to use, so I started cooking up all different kinds of meat—hamburger, Polish sausage, beef steaks, rabbits, pheasant, deer, and many other kinds. They were all perfect as far as we were concerned." That confidence continued to the point where Bob sold his other business (an oil distributorship) in 1980 to concentrate on sauce making.

It is not a fiery sauce, nor is it especially sweet. It doesn't have too much of a tomato or vinegar taste, either. What does it taste like? The Worcestershire taste is fairly pronounced, and it has a definite tang. It is very good warmed with thin slices of leftover roast beef or pork, or poured on meat sandwiches.

The company now makes a seasoning salt and a canned "Sloppy Bob" sandwich sauce with regular or Cajun-style seasoning. There is no meat in the can (you mix the contents with a pound of cooked ground beef), and we were distracted by the dehydrated onions and green peppers. Better to buy the All Purpose Sauce, add fresh onions and tomato sauce, and make your own. The sauce comes in 12½-ounce bottles, and is sold by the case of 12 only, at $24.60, plus shipping.

When you contact the company, you'll know it's a family-run operation. Eileen Malekovic, Al's wife, works in the office, and their son, Reed, is one of the owners. The other two owners are Bob Edson and his son, Terry. To confuse matters further, Terry Edson and Reed Malekovic are brothers-in-law.

Country Bob's is always looking for recipes using its products. Customers are invited to send their favorites to the company for consideration in its brochures. If yours is used, it's worth a free case of sauce.

ORDERING ADDRESS
Country Bob Inc.
211 South Lincoln
Centralia, IL 62801
618/533-2375
800/373-2140
FAX: 618/533-7828
e-mail: cntrybob@accessus.net
www.countrybobs.com
Credit cards accepted

EL PASO CHILE COMPANY SALSAS

Consumption of Southwestern foods has skyrocketed in this country, and the competition for shelf space is getting fierce. Everybody has a salsa, it seems.

Salsa is simply the Spanish word for "sauce," and it most commonly has come to mean a tomato, green chile, onion, and vinegar mixture to spoon on tacos or serve with tortilla chips. But there are cooked salsas, uncooked salsas, green salsas, red salsas, avocado salsas, jicama salsas, and on and on, as we discovered reading—and cooking with—Jacqueline Higuera McMahan's excellent cookbook *The Salsa Book* (available for $9.95, plus shipping, from The Chile Shop, 109 East Water Street, Santa Fe, NM 87501; tel 505/983-6080). The shop, which mail-orders a wide variety of Southwest foods and crafts, is the last word on chile-motif items, from strands of chile Christmas lights to children's chile-shaped sleeping bags to chile wrapping paper and chile ristras, or garlands.

One of the fastest growing of the fiery food entrepreneurships is El Paso Chile Company, a mother-and-son venture begun in 1981. It actually began on a street corner, where young Park Kerr sold chile ristras. His mother, Norma, joined him a year later, using her recipe for chili powder as their first manufactured product. Now the third generation is participating, as Park's son, Greyson, and his sister Monica's, daughter, Emery Anne, are involved.

We have not yet met Park Kerr, but we know he's a kindred soul. He shares our enthusiasm for collecting junk, including tombstone art, old cowboy jewelry, Americana, and Mexican folk sculpture. Thus far, there isn't a lot of overlap between his food and collecting passions, except that he's looking for finds wherever his food business takes him.

Lately, that's been a lot of places, because the business has exploded thanks to our mania with Tex-Mex foods. El Paso Chile has a tasty, no-preservative chile con queso, which greenhorns know as the melted cheese that goes on nachos; spicy chile beans; a very smoky meat marinade designed for fajitas and briskets; and three excellent salsas.

The company's mildest salsa is called Salsa Primera. It is the classic tomato, cilantro, onion, green chiles, vinegar, and spices sauce, and is delicious straight from the jar. It's a straightforward, chunky salsa with no weird canned flavors. A much, much hotter version goes by the catchy name of Snakebite Salsa. "Not for the light-hearted" stated El Paso's brochure, and the Kerrs aren't kidding.

A green salsa, called Cactus Salsa in honor of the diced leaves of the prickly pear cactus, or nopatillos, rounds out the trio. The green salsa also contains tomatillos, the green tomato-like vegetable with the papery husk and lemony taste that has become a staple in produce sections in the past few years. This salsa has a bit of a kick, too. We liked it better as an ingredient in burritos and fajitas than straight from the jar. Park says the two hotter salsas are the bestsellers. "People love hot things."

Chile heat levels are rated by Scoville units, named after Wilbur Scoville, who devised a test in 1912 to measure the level of capsaicin in plants. Today, labs use liquid chromatography to measure a food's heat, but use the Scoville units as a measure of respect. The scale runs from 0 for bell peppers to 80,000 to 300,000 Scoville units for habanero and Scotch bonnet peppers.

To keep things not only hot but also fresh, all of the products carry "born on dates" so that employees can trace back to the raw ingredient stage.

The three salsas come in 16-ounce jars and sell by mail for $5.95 each, plus shipping. A 12-ounce bottle of meat marinade is $5.95, and will flavor about 12 pounds of ribs, roasts, or chicken. Bean dips, cowboy catsup, jalapeño jelly, trail mix, and spiced peanuts also are available.

The company has a number of gift packages, chile wreaths, and ristras it will send along with its foods.

ORDERING ADDRESS
The El Paso Chile Company
909 Texas Avenue
El Paso, TX 79901
915/544-3434
800/274-7468
FAX: 915/544-7552
www.elpasochile.com
Credit cards accepted

VISITS: From I-10 going west, take the downtown exit. Drive left onto Kansas Street and continue until Texas Street, then take a right. The plant and store are 4 blocks farther on the left.
Monday–Friday, 10 A.M.–5 P.M. Saturday, 10 A.M.–2 P.M.

JOHNNY HARRIS FAMOUS BARBECUE SAUCE

When Johnny Harris moved to Savannah, Georgia and bought a restaurant that he named after himself in 1924, the place came with a longtime cook who made a legendary barbecue sauce. Customers used to buy the sauce over the counter, poured into empty Coca–Cola bottles or whatever other bottles they brought from home.

Phil Donaldson explains why this tangy sauce is different from most sauces that are mixed, heated, and bottled. "Ours is cooked down like a French sauce. We make our own ketchup, so the resulting sauce is like a heavy concentrate." The sauce resides in its own category—neither mustard-based or a pure ketchup style.

The sauce is bottled 3–4 days each week, for an output of between 6,500 and 8,000 bottles. It is primarily sold in Georgia, the Carolinas and Florida, but can be sent anywhere else in the country by mail. Six 12-ounce bottles of the barbecue sauce in a gift carton costs $21.50, including shipping costs. If you are in Savannah, it is worth buying the sauce at its source and enjoying a meal at Johnny Harris restaurant, where the ceiling looks like sparkling stars.

ORDERING ADDRESS
Johnny Harris Famous Barbecue Sauce Co.
2801 Wicklow Street
Savannah, GA 31404
912/354-8828
888-JHSAUCE (547-2823)
FAX: 912/354-6567
www.johnnyharris.com
Credit cards accepted

VISITING ADDRESS:
The Johnny Harris Restaurant is at
1651 E. Victory Drive,
Savannah, GA 31404.
Restaurant hours:
Monday–Thursday, 11:30 A.M.–10 P.M.
Friday–Saturday, 11:30 A.M.–midnight

ROB SALAMIDA'S STATE FAIR SPIEDIE SAUCE

"Spiedie" is a slightly Anglicized version of spiedi, which is Italian for "stick" and refers to fragrant meat chunks that are broiled and served shish-kebab style. Long popular among the immigrant communities in upstate New York's Triple Cities (Binghamton, Johnson City, and Endicott), they are made of lamb, pork, or beef that's been marinated in a mixture of red wine vinegar, oil, mint, garlic, thyme, parsley, and other spices. The Slovak, Italian, and Greek immigrants often make a sandwich of the meat, pulling the chunks off the skewer onto a slice of bread.

Native son Rob Salamida got his first experience selling spiedies as an eighth grader, hawking them on the street outside an Endicott delicatessen. Later, at age 16, he cooked spiedie sandwiches on a charcoal grill in front of a local tavern.

When he realized there was no bottled version of the spiedie marinade, he decided to produce one as a moneymaking venture to put himself through college. He started in 1971, writing letters for a year to New York State Fair officials, asking to rent a booth to sell his home-produced blend. This determined entrepreneur, in time-honored fashion, began by selling the sauce from the trunk of his car while on lunch hour from his day job. The company soon outgrew his parents' home and is now made in a small factory in nearby Johnson City.

The marinade, which is available in grocery stores throughout New York and in other parts of the Eastern Seaboard, the South, and Arkansas, tenderizes meat and gives it the aroma of mint and vinegar. The seasoning does not overwhelm the meat, but gives it just enough bite to be interesting.

The sauce now is joined by a chicken barbecue and lemon garlic sauce.

To explain his hometown treat to outsiders, Salamida has gone as far as printing a "What is a Spiedie?" T-shirt. He also has devised a "Spiedie Survival Kit," containing both a 16- and an 8-ounce bottle of spiedie sauce and an 8-ounce bottle of chicken barbecue sauce, as well as chrome skewers and two containers of Pinch, an Italian gourmet spice blend the company has devised. The kit is $22.95, including shipping. A case of 12 of the 16-ounce bottles of spiedie sauce is $41.95, including shipping. A 4-pack of any sauce combination is $15.95, including shipping. Five 4-ounce jars of Pinch seasoning and spice rubs are $14.95.

ORDERING ADDRESS
The Rob Salamida Company
71 Pratt Avenue
Endicott, NY 13790
607/729-4888
800/545-5072
FAX: 607/797-4721
e-mail: info@spiedie.com
www.spiedie.com
Credit cards accepted

VISITS: **From NY Route 17 westbound, take exit 71 south and turn south onto Airport Road. Then turn right onto CFJ Boulevard, drive to the end of the boulevard, and take a right onto Lester Avenue, then a quick left onto Pratt Avenue. The company is 2 blocks down Pratt Avenue, on the right.**

Monday–Friday, 8:30 A.M.–3:30 P.M.

SCHIAVONE'S SPAGHETTI SAUCE

We don't believe the TV commercials showing happy Italian families gathered around a pot of assembly-line spaghetti sauce. If a bubbling pot of Schiavone's sauce was placed off-camera, we bet the Central Casting actors would move out of the klieg lights and make a beeline for it.

Developed by Yolanda and Frank Schiavone for their family's Schiavone's Casa Mia restaurant, in Middletown, Ohio, three versions of the sauce have been canned for 25 years, and a hot, spicy sauce has been added. (We love that the new label features a green Fiestaware sauceboat and a 1950s-style Technicolor dinner scene. There also is a Schiavone Quality Pledge on all labels, signed by the Schiavone Family, vowing never to use artificial additives or preservatives.)

We prefer the best-seller, the original marinara spaghetti sauce with basil. The masterful thing about the sauce is its use of fresh garlic—enough, but not so it lingers for hours. There's also a practiced hand adding the basil. This sauce is not a gloppy coating that sticks to every strand, but the lighter, more traditional spaghetti sauce.

The family has been selling the sauce for a mere $1.33 per 19.5-ounce can, or $15.95 for a case of 12. Area stores tack on an extra 30¢ to 40¢ per can.

The Schiavones will ship their special sauces (original, all-purpose, sausage, and hot & spicy). The price is $15.95 per case, plus shipping. Customers can call and use a credit card or send a check and the Schiavones will spend the sauce C.O.D. for the freight only.

ORDERING ADDRESS
Schiavone's Foods
1907 Tytus Avenue
Middletown, OH 45042
513/422-8650
Credit cards accepted

VISITS: **Sauce can be bought at Schiavone's Casa Mia restaurant. From I-75, follow Route 122 into Middletown. Once you are downtown, turn right on Reinartz Boulevard. At the first light take a right on Charles Street. Follow Charles Street to its end. The restaurant is across the street.**
Wednesday–Saturday, 6 A.M.–10 P.M.

SHOW-ME BAR-B-Q SAUCE

Harry Berrier, professor emeritus at the University of Missouri's College of Veterinary Medicine, probably has the only basement in Missouri that is approved by the state public health department. What it is approved for is the mixing of Show-Me Bar-B-Q Sauce, a sweet-sour, smoky sauce that since 1974 has found its way to all 50 states and many foreign countries, all by word-of-mouth. The closest Berrier came to advertising was 14 years ago, when the owner of a barber shop in Columbia, where Berrier lives, kept a case of a sauce near the witch hazel. The barber would run the cap under patron's noses after they got their hair cut, stimulating interest.

Today, it is all that Berrier, his wife, and four part-time employees can do to keep up with the business, run entirely in the basement of the Berriers' home in a residential neighborhood. Requests have become so numerous, in fact, that Berrier asks prospective customers to send a self-address stamped envelope when they request a price list.

True to his scientific background, Berrier is very precise about what is—and is not—in his sauce. There is no water or other extenders, which makes it weigh 1 pound more per gallon than supermarket brands. That means you won't find various oils, soybean flour, cornstarch, pectin, gum arabic, tapioca, and modified proteins in the sauce. "Extenders add no flavor to a recipe, only bulk and volume," Berrier says in his fact sheet. "They cheapen the product while giving the illusion of more sauce and/or a thicker sauce." There also are no preservatives, artificial colors, or flavorings. There is Heinz ketchup, brown sugar, Worcestershire sauce, Liquid Smoke, salt, and spices.

Berrier makes it clear that his is not a hot sauce. If you want it hotter, he advises adding a few drops of Tabasco. He uses a distilled Liquid Smoke to ensure that there are no carcinogens present. Show-Me Sauce does not require refrigeration even after opening—a real plus to those who refrigerators are choking with half-used bottles of condiments. The reason? It has a pH of 3, and bacteria, including the kind that causes botulism, will not grow in a medium of pH 4.6 or below, Berrier assures buyers.

The taste is best described as smoky-sour-sweet, and it is a valued addition to meat loaf and baked beans, as well as grilled meats. Berrier's recipe for meat loaf is found in teeny type on the label. The recipe works equally well with low-fat ground turkey and fish.

Show-Me Sauce fans, like many barbecue lovers, tend to be fanatics. An Air Force pilot at Chanute Field, in Illinois, made three trips to Columbia to pick up bottles of the sauce. He had to log a required number of flying hours, so he figured he might as well go to Columbia since he was crazy about the sauce. A few years ago the president of the University of Tulsa shipped 65 cases of the sauce across the nation as holiday gifts. And a Missouri youth gave it the ultimate challenge at his mess hall table on a ship in the Adriatic. The youth wrote Berrier: "Your sauce can even make Navy steak taste good."

One buyer from Texas summed up the feelings of many when she wrote: "Though I come from North Carolina, where barbecue is the best, and now reside in Texas, where they think it's the best, I must tell you that your sauce is the best I have ever had."

Berrier has one price list. "I sell wholesale to anyone!" The sauce can be ordered in cases of twelve 21-ounce bottles, cases of six ½-gallon jugs, cases of four 1-gallon jugs, or in single bottles, ½-gallon, or 1-gallon jugs. A single pint bottle is $2.25, and a case of bottles is $22, plus shipping. A single gallon jug is $11, plus shipping. With the sauce, Berrier sends an invoice, figuring in the proper UPS charge. You send a check upon receipt of the sauce in good condition.

This method of doing business is very much in keeping with the spirit of the name of the sauce, by the way. "The Show-Me State" is Missouri's nickname, and it is traced to a speech by Missouri Congressman Willard Duncan Vandiver, made in Philadelphia in 1899. Said Vandiver: "Frothy eloquence neither convinces nor satisfies me. I am from Missouri. You have got to show me." Berrier does.

ORDERING ADDRESS
Dr. Harry Berrier
1250 Cedar Grove Boulevard, South
R.D. #2
Columbia, MO 65201
314/442-5309
No credit cards; checks OK

TEXAS PETE HOT SAUCE

America's professional curmudgeon, Andy Rooney, once groused about the fact that Texas Pete Hot Sauce is made in North Carolina. Honest, Andy, founder Thad Garner was just trying to be patriotic. In his quest for a name for a hotter barbecue sauce, the winner had been "Mexican Joe." But Garner's father, who had lost his own taxi business during the Depression, objected on patriotic grounds and wanted the sauce affiliated with the United States. Thad used his younger brother's nickname, Pete, and the rest is culinary history. So don't get too picky about the state, Mr. Rooney, because this company should be applauded just for jumping the high hurdles to get started.

Garner began the business in the year of disaster, 1929. With $300 he had saved for college by carrying newspapers, trapping rabbits, selling white cloverine salve, and driving a school bus, he bought the Dixie Pig pork barbecue stand in Winston-Salem. He was all of 15 years of age. He started selling barbecue to other stands and then directed his attention to the sauce side of the business.

In addition to its barbecue sauce, there is Texas Pete Hot Sauce, a spicy pepper sauce that has become a staple on restaurant tables throughout the South and is especially good on turnip greens. The Garners also make a thick hot dog chili sauce (with or without beans) and piquant seafood cocktail sauce, and pack whole green Tabasco peppers in vinegar. The company, which now employs about 60 workers, also produces jellies and jams.

TEXAS PETE®
SAUCES

"We get letters from all over the country," said Thad Garner, who continues to battle for shelf space with the bland offerings from manufacturing conglomerates. "People almost make you cry. They're like gold to me."

All members of the Garner family have devoted their work lives to the business. Now the second generation is active, which is encouraging news for those who want Texas Pete to keep on roping those hot peppers.

The hot sauce is bottled in 5 sizes, beginning at 3 ounces. A case of a dozen 12-ounce bottles is $17.25, including shipping. A case of the green Tabasco peppers, with twelve 4½-ounce bottles, is also $17.25, including shipping. A case of 24 cans of the 10-ounce hot dog chili sauce is $19.10, including shipping.

The company has several gift boxes, including one that contains four of its savory sauces: the hot sauce, seafood cocktail sauce, honey mustard sauce, and Buffalo-style chicken wing barbecue sauce. It is $15. 50, including shipping.

ORDERING ADDRESS

T. W. Garner Food Company
Box 4329
Winston-Salem, NC 27115-4329
336/661-1550
800/476-7383
FAX: 336/661-1901
www.texaspete.com
Credit cards accepted

VISITS

4045 Indiana Avenue
Winston-Salem, NC 27105
Take I-40 to Winston-Salem. Take the U.S. 52 North exit, staying on U.S. 52 for 2 miles to the Akron Drive exit. At the top of the ramp, make a left onto Akron Drive. Drive 1 mile and turn right onto Indiana Avenue.
Monday–Friday, 8:30 A.M.–5 P.M.

WICKER'S BARBECUE COOKING SAUCE

Letters to the Wicker Company tend to be desperate: "We have recently moved from Tennessee and find that we are now in Wicker Sauce Withdrawal," wrote a couple in Lemoore, California. "We are using the last bottle of two cases purchased before we left." "Help!" pleaded a Reno, Nevada, woman. "I can't stand the thought of an entire summer with an anemic-looking chicken on the grill." A Pennsylvania man declared: "The prospect of another summer without Wicker's is driving me stark, raving mad."

When the company replies with the good news that the firm's cooking sauce, barbecue baste, seasoning, au jus, marinade, gravy, tenderizer (it doesn't want to overlook any sales possibilities) can be shipped anywhere in the country for the undeniably low price of $21.13 for six 28-ounce bottles, plus shipping and handling, return letters have a decidedly more cheerful tone. Wrote one happy customer: "Every time we sit down at the table to a Wicker's feast my husband says, 'Teresa, was there life before Wicker's? And I reply, 'Not civilized life!'"

The object of his adulation is a very thin liquid that is vinegar-based. It has no sugar (the entire bottle contains but 45 calories), no preservatives, and no tomatoes, despite its reddish color. The sauce takes its name from one Peck Wicker, a barbecue legend around Hornersville, Missouri, a town of 740 in the Missouri bootheel. Owner of an enclosed barbecue pit with a dirt floor, he made a popular barbecue and an even more popular barbecue sauce. He began bottling the sauce in the 1940s and, 20 years ago, sold his recipe to a Hornersville couple, L. E. and Ruth Christain. L. E. supervised the sauce making until August of 1983 when he died unexpectedly, but his daughter-in-law, Becky, who had worked at the plant, and other employees stepped in to continue.

Now the company is owned by a group of five Hornersville natives. Its products are available in grocery stores in Tennessee, Arkansas, Mississippi, and Missouri.

Since being introduced to Wicker's we've used it with great success in baked beans, boiled shrimp, baked chicken, and as an enhancer with other, thicker barbecue sauces to give them more punch. To capture those who prefer a heavier sauce, Wicker's now sells a version it calls, simply, "thicker barbecue sauce." It sells for slightly more, at $27.13 for six 28-ounce bottles, including shipping and handling. Wicker's does pack a wallop but is not so fiery that it burns.

As a satisfied Indiana customer put it, "Send me more bottles of the barbecue gold."

ORDERING ADDRESS
Wicker Company
Box 129
Hornersville, MO 63855
573/737-2416
800/847-0032
FAX: 573/737-2113
e-mail: wickers@vip1.net
Credit cards accepted

VISITS
501 Main Street
Hornersville, MO 63855
Hornersville is nearly in Arkansas and not far west of Tennessee. From I-55, take the Highway 164 exit west to Hornersville. The factory is downtown and can't be missed.
Monday–Friday, 9 A.M.–4 P.M.

ZARDA'S BARBECUE SAUCE

Baseball players tend to indulge in rituals—for luck or to ward off jinxes, like batting slumps. A springtime ritual for the Kansas City Royals involves importing their hometown barbecue for a feast at their annual training camp in River Falls, Wisconsin.

The honored barbecue sauce and meat is Zarda's, a 24-year-old company that has gone to the head of the class in the most competitive barbecue city in America. In blind taste tests we conducted for dozens of lifelong barbecue fans, Zarda's beat such heady competition as Hayward's, Gates and Son, and Arthur Bryant's, all of Kansas City.

It's a Bohemian recipe—a tangy tomato and vinegar mixture, with molasses as an extinguishing agent. There are 24 ingredients, and the recipe was crafted by Michael Zarda after cross-country eating trips with his late brother, Jerry, a co-founder, and brother, Steve, now a joint owner. Recently, the brothers added a mild version.

Zarda's operates two always-busy restaurants in Kansas City, turning out barbecued pork, beef, chicken, and turkey lunches and dinners. Business is so good that both Mike and Steve join their 230 full- and part-time workers on the sandwich line, making sure orders reach cus-

tomers in less than seven minutes. The brothers also are known throughout the Kansas City area for catering large crowds, including wedding receptions.

Their special sauce is inexpensive: At the restaurants it's sold for $1.95 for a 19-ounce bottle, or $24 per case. Area stores charge about $2.09 per bottle. For mail-order customers, the company will send a case of 12 bottles of original or mild (or a mixed case) for $40, including shipping.

As far as barbecue sauces go, America still is the land of opportunity. Whenever we get discouraged about the sameness of our country's franchised eateries, we're heartened by the abundance of good local barbecue sauces in nearly every region of America. Zarda's is a prime example of a truly superlative sauce.

ORDERING ADDRESS
Zarda's Barbecue Sauce
214 North Seven Highway
Blue Springs, MO 64104
816/229-3670
800/776-RIBS (7427)
FAX: 816/224-3171
e-mail: terry@zarda.com
Credit cards accepted

VISITS: **One restaurant is at the above address, the other in Lenexa, a suburb of Kansas City, Kansas, near Shawnee Mission. The street address is 11931 West 87th Street (tel: 913/492-2330). To get to the Blue Springs restaurant from downtown Kansas City, take Route 43 East to I-70 East. Take the Blue Springs exit south onto Seven Highway. Travel 5 blocks south and Zarda's is on the left side of Seven Highway.**
Labor Day–Memorial Day: Sunday–Thursday, 11 A.M.–9 P.M.
Friday–Saturday, 11 A.M.–10 P.M. (Summer hours are one hour later in the evening.)

SOUPS & CHILIS

ANDERSEN'S SPLIT PEA SOUP

It seems unlikely that an entire town of more than 2,000 people could exist largely on the drawing power of the green pea, but anyone driving along Highway 101 in Santa Barbara County, California, will verify that such a town does exist. It is Buellton, just north of Santa Barbara, and its presence is announced in numerous billboards for miles in either direction. Actually it is not the town itself the billboards are promoting, but Pea Soup Andersen's Restaurant, where nearly 60 million bowls of steaming split pea soup have been dished up since it opened its doors in 1924.

Then it was known as Andersen's Electrical Cafe (to honor its new electric stove) and it boasted but six stools and three booths. But owner Anton Andersen's wife, Juliette, had a wonderful pea soup recipe, and soon customers were clamoring for it. These days, 61 tons of green peas, trucked in from Idaho weekly in 100-pound sacks, are consumed at the restaurant each year. The restaurant itself is sprawling, with eight dining rooms, a gift shop, and a motel, as well as numerous service stations and motels to either side that feed off its customers.

In 1977, the company sold the rights to can the soup to Real Fresh, Inc., a Visalia, California, food processor, and it has been available at grocery stores in western states.

The canned soup can't duplicate the taste of the rich soup served at the restaurant or the experience of gorging yourself on the "all-you-can-eat" pea soup special. But as canned soups go, it comes close to homemade. The mixture tastes faintly of carrots and celery, and the puree is properly thick. It is not a concentrate, and no water needs to be added.

The soup can be found at grocery stores in Arizona, Washington, Oregon, California, and Colorado. Or it can be ordered by the can or case from the restaurant's gift shop. A case of twelve 15-ounce cans of the original pea, or pea with bacon, or tomato soup is $18, plus shipping costs. Individual cans cost $1.50.

VISITS AND ORDERING ADDRESS

Pea Soup Andersen's Restaurant
376 Avenue of the Flags
Buellton, CA 93427
805/688-5581
FAX: 805/686-5670
www.silcom.com/~splitpea
e-mail: splitpea@silcom.com
Credit cards accepted
Buellton is at the intersection of Highway 101 and Highway 246 in southern California, north of Santa Barbara. Watch for the billboards.
Every day, 7 A.M.–10 P.M.

GRANDMA PAT'S SOUP MIXES

"The West was Won on Beans," is the slogan of this family-run Wyoming company, and this particular family ought to know. The Palms live on the ranch near the Nebraska border and grow wheat and oats and raise cattle, but for the past nine years they have grown pinto and sometimes Great Northern beans. They also custom-clean beans grown by other farmers in the area and grow sunflowers, millet, sugar beets, and alfalfa.

These are tough times for farmers in their region, and in 1986 the Palms were looking for a way to diversify their business and promote local products. After seeing a 16-bean soup mix for sale in Pat Palm's home state of Arkansas, her husband, Chuck, went into town one day and came back with 50-pound bags of 16 different kinds of beans. Pat was properly astonished, but recovered and put her home economics training to good use by experimenting until she found a recipe the family liked.

They have graduated from mixing beans in a wheelbarrow and sealing bags with a Seal-a-Meal to buying used factory equipment. A cement mixer is used to mix the beans.

The 16-bean soup mix is a staple at many church bazaars and fundraisers, and it does have several attractive qualities. Like all bean dishes, the percentage of calories from fats is very low (the Wyoming Department of Agriculture estimated 4 percent for the Palms' mix), with most of the calories coming from carbohydrates. It is inexpensive. It can be easily added to and adapted, and tastes even better as a leftover than it does freshly made.

The unique Grandma Pat's product is the Lentil Soup Mix, a blend of yellow and green split peas, barley, rice, and lentils. Following the recipe on the package results in a thick, mild bean soup that has an appealing texture and a crunch of barley. It's a pretty, light-colored soup and can win over those who say they don't like beans.

The Palm family has a chili-bean mix, and sells excellent yellow popcorn. If you desire 12-ounce bags of winter wheat, which is grown on their farm, they'll send that, too. ("We haven't had too much call for that," Chuck reports, "but if you put it in the blender, it makes a good whole wheat breakfast cereal. You can make flour with it, too.")

If you'd like bags of a single bean in their soup mixes, the Palms will ship you those. Some of the harder-to-find beans they carry include pinks, small reds, small limas, yellow peas, and yellow split peas. Sixteen-ounce bags of the soup mix are a reasonable $1.50 each, plus shipping.

The Palms' ranch has been in the family since it was homesteaded by Chuck's immigrant Swedish ancestors in 1896. The family welcomes visitors to see them cleaning, sacking, and shipping.

ORDERING ADDRESS
Grandma Pat's Products
Box 158
Albin, WY 82050
308/246-3351
No credit cards

VISITS: The Palm Farm is east of Albin, Wyoming, in the southeast corner of the state. Take the road east out of Albin to a dead-end (at a cemetery, appropriately) and go ¼ mile north. Then drive 1 mile east and ¼ mile north. There is a 5-foot steel palm tree at the farm's mailbox. There is someone at the farm most any time, the Palms say, but call ahead to be sure.

GREEN TURTLE CANNERY SOUPS

Employees of the Green Turtle Cannery are quick to tell you that the company doesn't use green turtles from the endangered species list for its turtle soup and consommé. North Florida river turtles are used.

Good regional canned soups are an endangered species, and it is a joy to report that this 39-year-old Florida Keys cannery produces six excellent fish soups and chowders, plus Key lime pie filling.

Its most popular soup is conch chowder. Like the other soups from Green Turtle, the ingredients list is short: conch meat, potatoes, tomatoes, bell peppers, celery, onions, cornstarch, salt, and spices. Conch, a mollusk found in southern waters, has a tendency to be tough. To be truthful, most of the times we've had it, the sensation has been not unlike chewing bits of old tires. It is best stewed or braised to tenderize it, and Green Turtle's conch chowder keeps the bits of conch small. The flavor is excellent and is improved by adding a dash of sherry, as recommended on the label.

We also liked the turtle chowder, which is similarly dark and thick. The soups have a clean taste, without being overly salty and without the unpleasant aftertastes of dehydrated vegetables and additives.

Turtle soup consommé can be served cold and jellied, or warmed with sherry. It is lighter in color and flavor than beef consommé.

A New England–style clam chowder is very good. The clams and potatoes are in very fine dice, resulting in a smooth, not chunky, mixture. Ditto for the fish chowder, which also is a milk-based soup. There also is a Manhattan-style clam chowder.

All of the soups are served at the Green Turtle Inn, which began as a fishing camp in 1947 in the Florida Keys. It's no longer an inn, as the guest cottages have been incorporated into the restaurant. It's known for local seafood, Florida lobsters, stone crabs, conch steak, and shrimp. The restaurant does its own canning, using the Sid & Roxie's label, in honor of the restaurant's original owners. The current owners, Henry and Bette Rosenthal, now advertise their canned items nationwide, to good response.

Another of the restaurant's specialties is Key lime pie, and the Green Turtle sells canned pie filling. The filling is a mixture of Key lime puree, sugar, milk, egg yolks, and margarine. Key limes are in short supply, a victim of housing and commercial development that wiped out many of the citrus trees, and only a few places offer the real thing. (If you want an authentic Key lime pie and made by a lime grower, try another Islamorada landmark restaurant, Manny and Isa's, at mile marker 81.6 on Highway 1. Manny Ortiz grows and squeezes his own Key limes for pie.) We thought the Green Turtle filling had an uncooked, floury taste (even though the label said it did not require further cooking), but were glad to see it wasn't colored lime green.

All the cannery items come in 16-ounce cans. The soups are not concentrated, so no water should be added. There are about two servings per can for a main course, four as an appetizer. A 6-pack of Green Turtle products, with the customer selecting the items, is $17.95, shipping included. A 12-pack is $30.95 delivered. All packs may be mixed and matched with any of the cannery's products.

ORDERING ADDRESS
Green Turtle Inn
Oceanside at MM 81
Islamorada, FL 33036
305/664-9031
FAX: 305/664-9564
www.greenturtleinn.com
e-mail: gtcannery@aol.com
Credit cards accepted

VISITS: **Islamorada is about an hour and a half south of Miami on Highway 1 in the Florida Keys. Telephone orders are taken 8 A.M.–1 P.M. After those hours, an answering machine is used.**
Tuesday–Sunday, Noon–10 P.M.

MO'S CLAM CHOWDER

It's hard to say which is the better-known legend in Newport, Oregon—the clam chowder at Mo's, the tiny restaurant that has been a bayside fixture for 44 years, or Mo herself, the colorful, raspy voiced, woman who built a successful food-processing and restaurant chain around her chowder. Her New England–style clam chowder is soup that turncoat New Englanders had raved to us about.

Mo (her full name was Mohava, after the Mohave Desert, where she was born) came to Newport when she was in her late twenties. She was divorced, with two young boys, and started a restaurant and tavern. She later became a local radio personality, announcing new births and best food buys, and hosting a number of shows. Later, she was the co-owner of a tavern, and then she and a girlfriend started yet another restaurant— Freddie and Mo's—in what, since 1947, has been simply Mo's.

In the early days, Mo's was open 24 hours a day and was more known for the ham and eggs it served than for the fish or chowder. "The joint," as the family fondly refers to it, went through the longshoremen's-union organizing period, the hippie era, the numerous business upheavals on Bay Boulevard, to endure as a major magnet for tourists who are lured by its reputation for excellent, reasonably priced seafood.

The chowder slowly gained in popularity and evolved into a consistent best-seller in the early sixties. "The recipe came from the dear old ladies, the good home cooks, who worked here for years," said Mo's granddaughter, Cindy McEntee. "Each one would have her special way of preparing it, though. One would add nutmeg or something and the others wouldn't."

The recipe Mo's stuck with, which has been available frozen in grocery stores for 10 years, starts with a flour roux and includes potatoes, ground clams, clam nectar, onions, bacon, and spices. It is uncommonly rich and thick, although the restaurant uses only whole milk, not cream, and suggests that cooks heating it up at home do the same. It may be the bacon, but the chowder has a fuller flavor than others we've tried. Miraculously, when we bought a frozen tub at a grocery store and tried it at home, the result was identical to the bowlful we were served at the restaurant.

Mo's dishes out the chowder into bowls that have a mixture of butter and margarine in the bottom. "That's how we tell if the chowder is hot enough," said Cindy. "If it comes to the top, it's ready.

Mo died in 1992. Thankfully, her granddaughter continues to run things. Cindy, a deep-voiced, no-nonsense woman, literally has lived her life in the restaurant. She spent summers working there since she was 7, and met her husband there when he was washing dishes. Their daughter, Gabrielle, works there, as did Cindy's father, who was called out of retirement to help with the growing enterprise. Mo's expanded to an annex across the street more than 25 years ago, and has added four other restaurants, all on the Oregon coast, in recent years.

So Mo's continues, seven days a week, each morning churning out an incredible 500,000 pounds of chowder upstairs, all from one enormous pot. It is available frozen at grocery stores in Oregon and in some locations in Idaho and Montana, as well as at the restaurant. It is cheaper at the restaurant, where a 1-pound tub, which makes about 3 cups of chowder, is $3.25. Mo's curly-haired, bespectacled likeness still graces the label on the tubs of frozen chowder base.

VISITS
657 Southwest Bay Boulevard
Newport, OR 97365
541/265-7512
e-mail: mos@newportnet.com
Newport is on the coast, due west of Corvallis. From 101 in Newport, turn east at City Hall and drive down the hill to Bay Boulevard, a crowded street of fish processors and restaurants. The original Mo's is on the east side of the street and the annex is on the bay. The annex takes credit cards; Mo's does not.

Mo's: Every day, except Thanksgiving and Christmas, 11 A.M.–9 P.M.
Annex: Monday–Friday, 11 A.M.–3 P.M. Saturday, 11 A.M.–9 P.M. Sunday, 11 A.M.–6 P.M.
Annex Summer Hours: Monday–Friday, 11 A.M.–9 P.M.

MRS. FEARNOW'S BRUNSWICK STEW

Like all Brunswick stew that's sold across state lines, Mrs. Fearnow's stays in the good graces of the federal meat inspectors by using chicken instead of the authentic squirrel. This stew has been a favorite of Virginians and North Carolinians since the Fearnow family opened a cannery in Mechanicsville, Virginia, in 1946. It just may be the best canned stew in America, with huge chicken chunks, crispy white corn, and other plentiful vegetables. Until the last decade, the chicken was added by hand. Because of demand for the stew, a machine now places the meat in the can before any other ingredients are added.

The stew was developed during the Depression by Lily Pearl Fearnow as a means of supplementing her farm income. She used the prize-winning vegetables from the family's Hope Farm, these ingredients being another departure from traditional Brunswick stew. As Raymond Sokolov noted in his important book *Fading Feast,* purists do not add vegetables to this backwoods concoction.

Lily Pearl sold the stew locally since 1930, with the help of her two daughters-in-law, Finnella and Norma, and their pressure cookers. The first shop to take the stew was the Women's Exchange in Richmond, Virginia, "a place where farm wives could bring in some money from the good things they put up," said Lily's grandson, Raymond Fearnow. Richmond's two department stores, Thalhimer's and Miller & Rhoades, were the next customers.

The women were doing all the canning in their home kitchens, trying to keep up during pregnancies and the normal farming duties. "My aunt had twins and my mom was pregnant with me," said George Fearnow, another grandson. "And they kept standing on their feet, canning."

Demand grew to the point where the Fearnows bought a nearby farm and opened the cannery. Although the 154-acre farm can no longer supply the volume of vegetables needed for the stew, the tomatoes, potatoes, lima beans, and onions used do not resemble their pallid counterparts in the nation's big-time canning operations. The stew also uses white Shoe Peg corn from Iowa and Wisconsin, a variety that retains all its sweetness and crunch.

A hearty, delicious stew with its various flavors intact, Mrs. Fearnow's stew is now put up by Bunker Hill Foods in Bedford, Virginia. George Fearnow and his son Patrick still are involved with the business, running frequent taste tests and checking on suppliers.

It's sold in two sizes: 20 ounces and 29 ounces, costing about $2 and $3, respectively, plus shipping costs. Mail orders are sent in boxes of 6, 12, or 24 cans of the smaller size and 12 of the larger size. Stew also may be bought at the cannery.

ORDERING ADDRESS
Bunker Hill Foods
P.O. Box 1048
3678 Moneta Road
Bedford, VA 24523
540/586-8274
800/222-7839
FAX: 540/586-6106
Credit cards accepted

VISITS: **Bedford is between Lynchburg and Roanoke, Virginia, on Route 460.**
Monday–Friday, 8 A.M.–5 P.M.

RAY'S CHILLI

There is a longstanding rivalry among members of the top chili making family in Illinois. Ray's Chilli (note the two l's) has been canned in Illinois for more than 70 years. For the first six decades, it was canned by the family of Ray De Frates. Distributed primarily within the state, Ray's Chilli has loyal fans who seek out the tender, peppery chili in the homey blue-and-orange cans with the drawing of a smiling chef.

In 1951, Ray had a falling-out with his nephew, Joe, moved to Litchfield, Illinois, and began canning a rival chili, also using two l's (he named his "Chilli Man") but made from his own recipe.

It may be that we're fond of Ray's label. Maybe it's because Ray's is still a regional product, while Chilli Man has gone big-time. At any rate, we prefer the smooth taste of Ray's chili, and plan to remain loyal for life.

A former manager of the Ray's brand, Jay Nicole, along with two partners, now owns the company. Operations are based in Decatur.

Ray's makes chili with beans in a 15-ounce can and the Coney sauce in a 7.25-ounce can. Six cans of the 15-ounce chili with beans are $18, including shipping. Six cans of the 7.25 Coney sauce packed with the same number and size can of chili with beans is $34, postage included. Write for a one-page listing of Ray's products and prices.

ORDERING ADDRESS
Ray's Brand Products, Inc.
P.O. Box 793
Decatur, IL 62525
217/422-6153
www.rayschilli.com
e-mail: raysbrand@aol.com
Credit cards accepted

TAYLOR'S MEXICAN CHILI

Oops. That's our heartfelt response to clumsily missing central Illinois' other famous canned chili. In the 1984 *Food Finds,* we detailed the culinary controversy between Illinois' Chilli Man and Ray's Chilli and somehow missed the long-established Taylor's Mexican Chili, made since 1904 in nearby Carlinville.

To make matters worse, we had even spent an entire day in Carlinville (population 6,000) and neglected to notice either the chili factory or the Taylor restaurant. To be fair, we were there on assignment writing about coal mining, but our food radar was definitely out of order.

A reader, Rich Minster of Lake Zurich, Illinois, wrote to register his dismay at the omission in our book. He wrote: "Taylor's is a connoisseur's delight, in terms of (1) spicy hotness, (2) method of production, (3) texture, (4) medicinal effects on the sinuses, (5) legend and lore, and (6) history. Many people who are lucky enough to have sampled Taylor's give cans of the chili as Christmas gifts and include it on their gift lists."

Rich was absolutely correct. Taylor's is as colorful a product as they come. Ed Taylor and his brother, Tom, ran the chili parlor and cannery using the recipe their great-grandfather was given by a Mexican man 96 years ago. "Carlinville was a wide-open place with about twenty-five taverns then," Ed related, "and the story goes that a Mexican man had gotten in some minor trouble with the law and was put in jail. He was hollering out the window to my great-grandfather that if he'd pay his $3 fine, he would work for him to pay it off." The man worked for 50¢ a week to pay off his indenture, helping Mr. Taylor sell tamales from tavern to tavern. In the process, he showed his benefactor, who disliked chili, how to make a chili that would agree with him. (The recipe for the finger-sized tamales was lost over the years, much to the family's dismay.)

A friend of ours and Litchfield, Illinois, native, Harlan Hofeling, brought us a case of the chili to correct our ignorance. When we first sampled it, we thought it was too spicy. Now, a few years later, after jalapeños and chili powder have become everyday ingredients, it seems just right. If this is what folks were eating at the turn of the century, maybe we haven't come as far in our pyrotechnic abilities as recent publicity would suggest.

Taylor's Chili is an orangish-brown mixture of shredded beef, red beans, chili peppers, salt, onion, garlic, and oleo oils, which are made from selected beef fat. It has a distinctive flavor and a very soft "mouth feel," as the food industry calls it. You can spoon the chili straight into a blender, pulverize it, and then heat to serve as a dip with unsalted crackers.

The chili was canned for 53 years in an old-fashioned cannery a block away from the restaurant. The operation closed for two years in the early nineties, when the Taylors could not modernize their old equipment. The company was sold to Joe Gugger, a Carlinville native, who kept the recipes, upgraded the packaging, and re-opened a chili parlor on the Carlinville Square. The chili sauce is now canned separately from the red beans, and the two components are packaged together with the firm's distinctive red-green-and-white label. The label has founder C.O. Taylor's signature on the front. "Not Authentic Without This Signature," the label states.

The meat sauce, which is rich, can be used to flavor spaghetti sauce, or it can be extended by adding a second can of beans to your chili. The firm also sells a habanero chili, and spices to create hot wing sauce, salsa, and steak sauce. There's also a butterbean soup kit, a nod to the company's first chili parlor, which introduced a butterbean soup in the 1930s.

The cans are 21.5 ounces and cost about $4 each, or $25 for a 6-pack. Shipping is additional. The company ships 6, 12, or 24 cans. For a case of 24, the price is reduced to $86. Either call the chili parlor first to get the exact shipping charges to your location, or click on a helpful map on its website.

TAYLOR'S MEXICAN CHILI CO. ®
EST. 1904

ORDERING ADDRESS
Taylor's Mexican Chili
116 South West Street
Carlinville, IL 62626
217/854-8713
800/382-4454
FAX: 618/692-1606
www.taylorschili.com
e-mail: dave@taylorschili.com
Credit cards accepted

VISITS: The chili parlor is at 219 West Main Street in Carlinville, adjacent to The Anchor Inn. Canned chili can be purchased there or at the plant one block away. The phone number above is for the restaurant.
Chili parlor: Tuesday–Saturday, 11 A.M.–7:30 P.M. Sunday, Noon–7: 30 P.M.

VEGETABLES

BELLE OF MAINE CANNED FIDDLEHEADS, AND DANDELIONS

Popeye would be in a dilemma if he had access to the greens packed by W. S. Wells & Son of Wilton, Maine. Next to them, his beloved canned spinach seems awfully pedestrian.

This small, family-run business is the only cannery in the world packing dandelion greens and the only firm in the United States canning fiddlehead ferns. The dandelion canning dates back to 1896, when the grandfather of the present owner, Adrian "Butch" Wells, founded the company. A variety of vegetables were canned until the 1950s, but by 1961, the firm's market had declined to its original product—dandelion greens. Twenty years ago, W. S. Wells & Son added fiddleheads. It cans under its own Belle of Maine label and also for the Vermont Country Store "It's a small forgotten part of the canning market," Wells told *Country Journal* magazine, "but it's all mine."

Strangely enough, dandelions, which proliferate effortlessly in lawns where they are not wanted, are temperamental when grown as a crop. They are susceptible to blight and mildew, and weeds cannot be excised chemically, since all weed killers regard dandelions as foe, not friend. For years, the Wells family clawed out the weeds with putty knives, but now a small tractor does the cultivating in the family's three-acre dandelion plot. The greens are dark olive colored, with a spinach-like smell about them, and have a characteristically bitter taste. The traditional way to serve them is heated with salt pork or bacon.

Fiddleheads require no cultivation, since they grow wild in shady, wet areas. But their season is short—a few weeks in April. Over the years, the Wells family has built up a network of fiddlehead pickers stretching hundreds of miles across New England—from Bangor, Maine, to Montpelier, Vermont. Fiddleheads have a mild flavor and a distinctive curled shape that brings a fiddle top to mind.

All of the greens have no fat and are low in calories, high in protein, and abundant in vitamin A and iron. They are packed without preservatives or salt. Only water is added. If you lack ideas for serving, the company has a recipe brochure with possibilities such as cream of fiddlehead soup, dandelion spoon bread, and fiddlehead shrimp salad. The company also pickles fiddleheads, freeze-dries them in three soup mix blends, and packs a Maine version of baked beans (no pork) and cans dilly beans—green beans with vinegar and spices.

The company will send its canned greens by the case, with twenty-four 15-ounce cans in each, and will send mixed cases, if you desire. The price is $48, shipping included. There also are combination gift packs. A three-can pack is $7.50, 6-can pack $13.50, and 12-can pack $25, all plus shipping.

ORDERING ADDRESS
W. S. Wells & Sons
P.O. Box 109
Wilton, ME 04294
207/645-3393
FAX: 207/645-3393
No credit cards; checks OK

VISITS: Wilton is in western Maine, north of Lewiston at the junction of Highways 2 and 4. From Main Street, turn north on High Street. The cannery is on High Street, across from the state bank.
May–September: Monday–Friday, 5:30 A.M.–6 P.M.

BLAND FARMS VIDALIA ONIONS

The temperature, with the wind-chill factor, was 40 degrees below zero when the Federal Express truck pulled up with a sturdy cardboard crate from Bland Farms. There, in the midst of a raw January blizzard, was a bouquet of fresh young Vidalia onions, with green tops still attached. They were so fresh that the greens squeaked when rustled—an excellent sign, we had learned from an Asian greengrocer. Onion tops and snow peas should "sing" to you, he said, then you can be sure they are absolutely fresh.

Bland Farms, a family-run business located in Tattnail County in southeast Georgia, has built its reputation on mature Vidalia onions and relishes. The mature onions are available only in May and June, but customer demand knows no season. So in 1988, the Blands began shipping Vidalia onions before they reached maturity, in February and April. These "baby" Vidalias always are shipped overnight.

The tops can be used as scallions are, in salads, and the bulbs can be used by following the recipe booklet the Blands provide. The easiest recipe, and the one that shows off best the sweet taste of Vidalias, is simply to bake them in foil, with salt, pepper, and butter. (With mature onions, you should core them first and then add the condiments.) The onions also are shipped chopped, in a bottle.

The Blands sell a large variety of onion relishes, and pickled onions and vegetables. If you can't find something in their catalog with which to perk up a sandwich, it's hopeless. They've also added a full line of baked goods, using family recipes, including casseroles, quiches, chocolate cake, a five-layer lemon cake, red velvet cake, and pecan pie. All can be shipped. A real treat from mid-November to mid-April would be fresh tomatoes, which are shipped in quantities of six to two dozen.

The family has been farming for 50 years, and has been growing onions successfully since 1975. Their first crop, in 1974, was a disaster. But they decided to try again, just to prove they could grow onions. They have been in the mail-order business for 17 years, and have adopted many conveniences: credit card orders, a toll-free number, a four-color catalog, and gift packaging. All the accouterments rest on the quality of the onions, and the onions are as fresh and beautiful and mild as they come.

A bunch of 15 to 18 baby Vidalia onions, sent overnight, is $24.95, including shipping and handling. Ten pounds of medium mature onions, shipped in the spring, are $24.95. Twenty pounds of jumbo onions are $33.95; the mediums are $34.95, both including shipping. Three 12-ounce bottles of chopped onions are $29.95, including shipping. The fresh tomatoes are $41.95 per dozen and $59.95 for two dozen, delivered.

ORDERING ADDRESS
Bland Farms
P.O. Box 506
Glennville, GA 30427
912/654-1426
800/VIDALIA (843-2542) and 800/671-7901
FAX: 912/654-2742
www.blandfarms.com
Credit cards accepted

VISITS
Bland Farms
Route 4, Highway 169
Glennville, GA 30427
Glennville is about 60 miles west of Savannah. The farm is between Highways 169 and 121. There is a sign on Highway 169.
Monday–Friday, 9 A.M.–5 P.M.

GRANDMA BROWN'S HOME-BAKED BEANS

A realistic picture of Grandma Brown appears on each can of her beans and soups, and there is little chance that Grandma Brown's Beans, Inc., is going to update her hairdo and wardrobe every few years. For unlike Ann Page, Jane Parker, and Betty Crocker, Grandma Brown really existed, and today her granddaughter runs the Mexico, New York, company that bears her name.

The late Lulu Brown, a lifelong resident of the Mexico area, was a remarkable woman, and her story, told in a recipe booklet the company has printed, is one of perseverance and ingenuity. "During the Great Depression of the thirties, at the age of 63, when many people of Grandma's age were looking to welfare programs for assistance, Grandma Brown searched for other means," the history states. Her baked beans had been popular at church suppers and family picnics, and she asked local grocers if she could display pans of her baked beans to be weighed and sold by the pound in their stores. They agreed, and demand soon overtaxed her kitchen stove. "With commercial equipment out of the question due to limited means, the solution was simply to buy another used four-burner oil stove," continues the history.

Grandma Brown began selling to nearby communities as well, delivering pans of beans in an old car with the back seat replaced by wooden shelf racks. Her method of expansion in the kitchen stayed the same—she simply visited more auctions and bought more used ovens. At one time she had 18 four-burner oil stoves! She outgrew her home kitchen and established her bean kitchen on the second floor of a local grocery store. By 1943, more modern ovens were purchased and the beans were delivered—still in open pans by a small fleet of trucks to grocery stores in a 75-mile radius.

When she was nearly 70, Grandma Brown embarked on a campaign to can her beans, overcoming the skepticism of people who reminded her that home-baked beans of her type had never been canned successfully. Her small-scale experiments were a success, and so the company built a small plant "whose design and unorthodox application of equipment were so unusual that until the plant was put in actual operation, no one was really sure it would function as planned," notes the history. Luckily, the equipment worked, and now the plant has enlarged to more than 10 times the capacity of the original.

The home-baked beans are light-colored pea beans, and they are a sweet and smooth bean mixture, unlike any we've had. The beans are a solid mass in the can, not loose beans swimming in sauce, and tomato is not an ingredient. Grandma Brown's favorite method of fixing them was to sprinkle the top with sugar, garnish with bacon strips, and then broil in a hot oven until the beans were a golden brown.

Other Grandma Brown's products are a very good, light pea-bean soup with bacon, green split-pea soup with bacon, and saucepan beans with bacon, which is a more traditional tomato-bean sauce.

The beans are considered an upstate New York food, although they are distributed in parts of Pennsylvania, Massachusetts, New Hampshire, Vermont, New Jersey, and Florida (to supply former New York residents). A healthy mail-order business sends Grandma Brown's products around the country. "People get desperate when they are down to their last can," says Sandra Brown, executive vice-president of the company and granddaughter of Lulu Brown.

The beans and soups are available by mail in 12-packs or a case of 24, and the prices are a bargain, even including UPS charges. The beans are in 16-ounce cans, the soups 15-ounce cans. There is a variety pack of 2 cans of beans, 2 cans of bean soup, 1 can of saucepan beans with bacon, and 1 can of split-pea soup. Please call, as all prices are quoted including shipping.

ORDERING ADDRESS
Grandma Brown's Beans, Inc.
P.O. Box 230
Mexico, NY 13114-0230
315/963-7221
FAX: 315/963-4072
No credit cards; checks OK

THE GIANT ARTICHOKE

The drive along Highway 1 on the California coast is spectacular, no question about it. Landmarks like Big Sur and San Simeon are internationally known. We have a lesser-known, but sentimental, favorite that we'd like to see even more tourists discover. It is the Giant Artichoke fruit stand and restaurant, smack dab on Highway 1 in Castroville. You can't miss it, thanks to the 20-foot green stucco artichoke out front. Inside, larger-than-life orange and apple bins beckon you to the fruit aisles.

Roadside sculptures such as the giant artichoke are disappearing monuments to American eccentricity. We mourn their passing, and encourage all attempts to preserve their quirky beauty. Hats off to the Society of Commercial Archeology, The Kansas Grassroots Art Association, and books such as *The Colossus of Roads* by Karal Ann Marling and *The Well-Built Elephant* by J. J. C. Andrews. All celebrate the triumph of spirit over formal architecture.

The Giant Artichoke has been in business for 35 years, and an oversized artichoke has been a symbol of the company since its founding. A huge artichoke decorated the roof of the original building, and when owner Raymond Bei built the present building 25 years ago, he decided to put an even larger artichoke out front. Why? "That's a good question," chuckled the 67-year-old Bei. "I just thought 'Why not have a real large one outside?' Advertise artichokes a little bit, you know."

It makes sense because Castroville bills itself as the Artichoke Capital of America. Indeed, it is surrounded by fields of the thistle like plant. (It is one of Mother Nature's practical jokes that a member of the thistle family can produce such succulent food.) Bei, who was born and raised around artichokes—his father grew them—has seen his larger-than-life artichoke sculpture succeed wildly. "People are out here every day taking pictures of it, so it's been a good thing for us."

Artichokes are available nearly all year, but supply is at its peak from March through May. Fall and winter artichokes may be "frost-kissed" with a whitish, blistery look to the outer leaves, or dark discolored leaves. These artichokes are still good to eat, because the inner leaves and heart are not affected. Just make sure the dark outer leaves were caused by frost and not age. Young artichokes, frost-burned or not, will be compact and will not have started to open. Fresh artichokes rubbed against each other will "sing" or squeak.

If you've never had a really fresh artichoke, reward yourself with a box from Castroville. A bonus is the ability to select the size you'd like. You can order extra-small artichokes for hor d'oeuvres; small, medium, medium-large; or extra large-perfect for stuffing. The Giant Artichoke ships large boxes (your choice of 24 large artichokes, 30 medium large, 48 medium, 60 small, or about 180 extra small) for $62 east of the Mississippi and $60 west, or $45 within California. Smaller boxes (choice of 10 large, 12 medium-large, 16 medium, 24 small, or 80 extra-small) are $36 east of the river, $34 west, and $30 in California. Shipments to Alaska and Hawaii are extra.

The company also will ship jars of its marinated artichoke hearts, crowns, Brussels sprouts, and mushrooms.

Good artichokes make a thoughtful gift. They're also a creative alternative to chocolates or cookies for someone concerned about diet. The boxes come with a well-designed recipe and preparation guide. The recipes, for an artichoke-zucchini sauté, artichoke lasagna, several dips, and warm and cold salads, include a complete nutritional analysis of calories, carbohydrates, fat, sodium, and cholesterol.

ORDERING ADDRESS
Giant Artichoke
11241 Merritt Street
Castroville, CA 95012
408/633-2778
Credit cards accepted

VISITS: Castroville is on Monterey Bay, between Monterey and Santa Cruz. The Giant Artichoke fruit stand and restaurant is located at the intersection of Highways 1 and 156.
Every day, 8 A.M.–7 P.M.

MAINE SEAWEED COMPANY

Larch Hanson engages in one of the more unusual Maine harvests—the rough physical toil of gathering seaweeds from the rocky coastline. Hanson is a sea vegetable harvester, selling dulse, kelp, alaria, digitata, and nori for use in soups, beans, grains, snack foods, herbal supplements, and vitamins. Ecological soundness is a way of life for Hanson. He has observed the same sea-plant beds for 25 years, and has learned to harvest them so they regenerate every year. He takes apprentices, and one five-year apprentice is now building his first boat and preparing to work two peninsulas away from Larch.

What sets Larch's operation apart is that he builds his own wooden container boats, coating them only with vegetable oil. He unties the container boats from the power boat and rows each one through the surf to the plant beds, eliminating all possibility of petrol contaminants. "One drop of gas on the water near a harvest boat is an oil slick, as far as I'm concerned," he said. "A lot of so-called organic seaweed is harvested too close to the outboard motor for my tastes!"

Clothed in a wetsuit, he harvests off the Sally Islands, a cluster of tiny rock ledges at the mouth of Gouldsboro Bay. On an ideal day, he harvests at the low tide at sunrise. By 11 A.M., he and his crew will have 2,000 pounds of seaweed hung up to dry on long clotheslines at the edge of a beautiful cove. The load shrinks throughout the day as it dries. The final yield is 200 dry pounds of dry seaweed within 48 hours of harvest. Larch uses a solar and wood-fired building for final drying, keeping temperatures below 100 degrees. Plants harvested and dried this way will keep in cool, dark, and dry storage for at least two years.

May and June are prime harvest months for kelp and alaria. The dulse and nori harvest is July and August. Larch's son, Jay, 10, is following in his dad's footsteps. He now has his own business, harvesting rockweed fertilizer for gardeners. Larch's daughter, Sarah, 17, is an apprentice to her dad and very much at home in the surf. Larch's youngest son, David, 8, will be your tour guide if you phone ahead in the summer to get directions. He'll show you the greenhouses, gardens, and woodworking shop. If you time it right, Larch will take you to the islands and show you the seals.

Those familiar with sushi may have seen processed nori–the silvery-green sheets in which rice and fish are rolled and sliced. The whole nori that the Hansons package looks quite different. It resembles crumpled, dried paper, but can quickly be soaked into thin, nearly translucent sheets. Though irregular in shape, it is more pliable and flavorful than that formed by machine.

Kelp can be fried in oil as a crunchy snack, or used in bean and vegetable dishes to create a delicious creamy broth. Dulse can be eaten as is, as is a popular source of minerals for people who like to eat raw foods. Whole leaf nori can be roasted and crumbled over grains, fish, or vegetables. It tastes good plain, as well.

Larch ships his seaweeds year-round via mail and UPS. If you call his message machine, his partner, Candace, will call you back. Their most popular item is a "family pack" that includes more than 3 pounds of assorted seaweeds, plus a forager's handbook with recipes and stories. It is $55, shipping included. You may specify the types of seaweed you want included in the pack.

ORDERING ADDRESS
Maine Seaweed Company
P.O. Box 57
Steuben, ME 04680
207/546-2875
No credit cards; checks OK

VISITS: Steuben is halfway between Ellsworth and Machias on Highway 1. Please call first and Larch will give you directions to his home, which is east of Steuben, located on Gouldsboro Bay. Tenters are welcome to stay overnight.

MISTER SPEAR ASPARAGUS

Are you laboring under the misimpression that only thin asparagus stalks are tender? Thin stalks can be young asparagus, but they can also be the last gasps of a worn-out plant. Thick spears are usually associated with the tough cookies left too long in the ground. But they can also be premium-quality spears that are bred to be extremely tender. These plump specimens are stunning on a plate, and, being uniform, are easier to cook to a tender-crisp state.

Mister Spear, located in California's San Joaquin River delta area, has been shipping thick, fresh asparagus nationwide for the past 12 years. The spears, which are hand-picked in the morning, washed, cooled, packed, and shipped out the same afternoon, arrive by overnight or second-day delivery in a heavy green cardboard case.

The green spears are simplicity itself to prepare. They make an indelible Mother's Day present, Easter showpiece, or first day of spring celebration. Seven and a half pounds, delivered, is $46.90. This translates to between 50

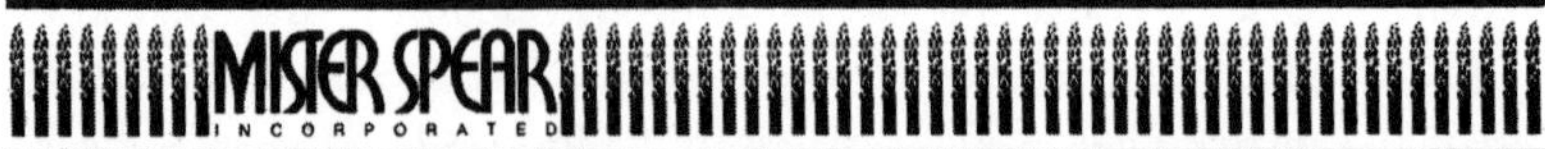

and 60 perfect, fat spears—enough to serve 12 or more generously. We shared ours with two other households, and had enough for two dinners and soup. The spears are so large that two or three per person are plenty. Three-pound boxes are available for $28.90.

The spears stay fresh 7 to 10 days after delivery, and can be frozen. The recipe booklet that arrives with the spears makes it unlikely that you'll lack for asparagus ideas, however.

Mister Spear will take advance orders for the fresh asparagus. Those living or traveling near Stockton can call ahead and pick up fresh asparagus during the season at the packing facility (1004 Navy Drive), thus saving the overnight air-freight expense.

Company president Chip Arnett, who sees a growing demand for healthy food gifts, also offers other fruits and vegetables. Currently, he ships shitake mushrooms, artichokes, Fuji apples, tomatoes, avocados, sugar snap peas, Bing cherries, corn, jumbo strawberries, and organic lettuce. He's thinking of establishing a "vegetable of the month business." It's a great idea. Using his contacts with the area's top growers and his commitment to good packaging, we think he's uniquely suited to launch it.

ORDERING ADDRESS
Mister Spear
P.O. Box 1768
Stockton, CA 95201
209/464-5365
800/677-7327
FAX: 209/464-5365
www.misterspear.com
e-mail: misterspear@misterspear.com
Credit cards accepted

MORSE'S SAUERKRAUT

Of the hundreds of items we received through the mail, none was as surprising as the bucket of Morse's Sauerkraut that arrived from North Waldoboro, Maine. It arrived without ado, and without a box—just an 8-pound bucket of sauerkraut sitting in our mailbox. There was no other packing, no padding, simply a white plastic bucket with a lid. Inside was slightly sweet sauerkraut with character, made from firm white winter cabbage with a just-short-of-crisp texture.

For nearly 70 years, the Morse family made superlative sauerkraut, growing the cabbage on their farm and hand-mixing each barrel according to old German recipes. Upon the retirement in 1988 of Ethelyn Morse, the daughter-in-law of the founder, Virgil Morse, the business was bought by

Commander Thomas D. Cockcroft, of Presque Isle, Maine, and his wife, Rebecca, following Cockcroft's retirement from the U.S. Navy.

Commander Cockcroft is following the time-honored process, storing the weighty cabbage heads in cellars and then taking them to the small cinderblock building on the Morse farm where they are chopped and allowed to ferment in a brine of cabbage juice, salt, and sugar for about two weeks. As always, visitors are invited to observe the harvesting and production of the 70 tons of fresh sauerkraut that are made yearly.

The company also still produces Aunt Lydia's Beet Relish, named after Virgil Morse's wife, who developed the recipe. The scarlet relish is a heady mix of finely diced beets, shredded cabbage, horseradish, sugar, and vinegar, and it is a delicious, tangy, old-fashioned side dish that reminds you of family picnics.

The products are still shipped in buckets, and those wishing to pay extra may specify barrels or buckets made of wood. New products include sauerkraut with wine, pickled beets, barbecued beans, mustard in salt-free or regular styles, honey, spicy chutneys, low and no-sugar jams, and five varieties of dried beans (yellow eye, Jacob's cattle, red kidney, soldier, and pea beans). There's also a Black Dog Salsa, which can be bought fresh at the farm or processed via mail order.

The sauerkraut and other products are shipped year-round. A 7-pound bucket of sauerkraut is $21.50, plus shipping. It also is sold in 3-, 5-, 10-, and 15-pound buckets. A 12-ounce jar of beet relish is $3.95, plus shipping; 16-ounces is $4.25, plus shipping.

Two samplers, shipped in wooden crates, are available. The Kraut House sampler contains sauerkraut, beans, blueberry jam, 1 pound soup mix, pickled beets, and beet relish. The Waldoboro Supper Sampler includes sauerkraut, beans, beet relish, beets, bread and biscuit mix, and a chocolate chip cookie mix. Both samplers are $29.95, plus shipping.

ORDERING ADDRESS
Morses's Sauerkraut
Route 220, 3856 Washington Road
North Waldoboro, ME 04572
207/832-5569
FAX: 207/832-2297
e-mail: morse's@midcoast.com
Credit cards accepted

VISITS: North Waldoboro is east of Augusta, in central Maine. The Morse farm is directly on Route 220 and is 8 miles north of Route 1 and 2½ miles south of Route 17.
September–May: Monday–Friday, 8 A.M.–3 P.M. Saturday, 10 A.M.–4 P.M.

STATE OF MAINE BEANS

About five miles east of the Kennebec River, in Maine, there sits the town of North Vassalboro, whose downtown is pretty well defined by a grocery store, post office, garage, and the Kennebec Bean Company, located in a former woolen mill. This 50-year-old company, started by one Wilmer Hussey in his North Vassalboro garage, specializes in Maine grown beans: yellow eye, soldier, Jacob's cattle, and red kidney.

It's a small, informal place. Its president is Ronald Loubier. The dozen year-round employees include Bob Briggs, who has been foreman since the company began, and five women who hand sort the beans. The beans are packed under the brand name of State of Maine, and some of them are raised by on farms in nearby Milo. But the company also packs other varieties of beans grown elsewhere under the A-1 label: pinto, lima, garbanzo, Great Northern, black-eyed, and pink beans, as well as green and yellow split peas, lentils, and pearl barley.

Because of the great benefits of beans (high protein, high fiber, low fat), the company's 16-bean soup mix has become a success.

The soldier beans are sweet and plump, large, reddish brown beans with brown markings. Yellow-eye beans get their name from the dark spots or "eyes" on their light flesh. Jacob's cattle beans get their name from the Bible: they resemble the "spotted and speckled" cattle raised by Jacob. They are sweet, fat, and fine-grained. The red kidneys are showy, with uniform, glossy skins.

Kennebec packs the dried beans and contracts with a cannery in East Machias, Maine, to steam and can the Maine-grown varieties, adding pork, molasses, sugars, salt, and spices. Both dried and canned beans are available from the company via UPS in reasonably priced assortments. Three 28-ounce cans of each of the Maine specialties—the yellow-eye, soldier, Jacob's cattle, and red kidney beans (12 cans in all)—are $36, including shipping. The company will ship six 1-pound bags of the 16-bean soup mix for $12.50, including delivery charges. Dried beans are 6 pounds for $17 and 12 pounds for $39.95, including shipping.

ORDERING ADDRESS
Kennebec Bean Company
Main Street, P.O. Box 218
North Vassalboro, ME 04962
207/873-3473
FAX: 207/877-9280
Credit cards accepted

VISITS: North Vassalboro is just south of Waterville, in central Maine, on Highway 32, which runs directly through town.
Monday–Friday, 8 A.M.–noon, 2:30 P.M.–4:30 P.M.

TALK O'TEXAS PICKLED OKRA

Okra is a vegetable a stand-up comedian would pick on. It's misunderstood and has a funny name. Most people blanch when we tell them how delicious these green morsels are. Their only recall of okra is that of gummy slices in vegetable soup. But a San Angelo, Texas, firm is single-handedly bringing new prestige to the plant known as "ladies fingers." In fact, demand is so great for this mild, crunchy appetizer that the firm had to cease its well-received red bell pepper relish in order to keep up.

The pickling recipe was developed by a San Angelo couple who began packing the okra in their garage. Albert C. Ricci, now chairman of Talk O'Texas, bought their secret 37 years ago. His firm now employs 75 people who still pickle, cook, and pack the okra by hand. Although slightly resembling a pickled pepper in appearance, these have only a slight tartness, and a little hotness to them. They have been used in martinis instead of olives, an "okratini," as it's called. The okra comes in two forms, the original (mild) and hot.

The company packs a 16-ounce jar, which can be found in select groceries across the country. A 6-jar gift box can be ordered by mail for about $14.95, plus shipping. Please call for shipping charges. The gift pack can be a mix of hot and mild varieties.

Visitors may tour the plant between May 15 and October 15 and see the pickling process. The company also produces a bottled variety of Liquid Smoke, to add to marinades for meat and fish and for use in fajitas, dips, and salads.

ORDERING ADDRESS
Talk O'Texas
1610 Roosevelt Street
San Angelo, TX 76905
915/655-6077
800/749-6572
e-mail: tot@wcc.net
Credit cards accepted

VISITS: **San Angelo is northwest of San Antonio, at the intersection of Routes 87 and 67.**
Monday–Friday, 9 A.M.–5 P.M.

WICKLUND'S SPICED GREEN BEANS

When you order a Bloody Mary in a bar in the Northwest, chances are you won't find a celery stick resting in the glass. In its place will be a tall, thin green bean. When you bite into the bean, you will discover that it is no escapee from a steam table. It is a Wicklund's Spiced Green Bean, and it is both crispy and spicy. In a word, it has character.

The beans are the long, slender Blue Lake variety that grow on poles, and the Wicklund family has been growing them commericially since 1953 on their picturesque 100-acre farm just east of Eugene. Down a gravel road adjacent to the McKenzie River, whose water irrigates the beans, the farm is nestled in a clearing of tall old maples. Dorcas and Eric Wicklund live in one house on the farm and their youngest son, Larry, and his wife, Lorie, live in the other. Behind the houses is a small blue building where the beans are processed daily throughout the year.

It was, indirectly, a shortage of farm laborers that caused the Wicklunds to get into the pickling business 23 years ago. Gradually, bean growers in their area had been switching from pole beans, which must be picked by hand, to low-bush beans, which could be harvested mechanically, because they had problems finding enough workers willing to pick beans. The Wicklunds wanted to stay with the Blue Lake pole bean, believing it has a superior taste and texture, and began to look for other outlets for their crop. Two years before the cannery they dealt with stopped accepting pole beans, Larry Wicklund began pickling beans in the basement of his parents' house, using a recipe from a family friend, Eve Horn. "When it's correctly made," said Dorcas Wicklund, a direct, gray-haired woman with a youthful face, "you can taste each one of the ingredients one after another. First the vinegar, then the garlic, dill, bay leaf, and so on."

Although the Wicklunds' first success was placing the beans in bars as unique swizzle sticks, they now are used as hors d'oeuvres, on relish trays, in omelets, and in tuna salad instead of pickles. The beans are eaten cold (they should be refrigerated after opening) and are an absolutely one-of-a-kind treat. The Wicklunds believe theirs is the only company in the world pickling green beans. The closest competitor would be dilly beans, a favorite in New England kitchens, but the Wicklund bean is not as strongly flavored with dill and has more of a hot bite, thanks to the red pepper floating in the bottom of each jar. Their beans also are low in salt for a pickled product, with a salt content of 3.5 percent, instead of the normal 9 to 11 percent. (They cannot be labeled low salt, however, as the federal standards save that notation for products under 1 percent salt.)

The beans are hand-picked, then blanched, and hand-packed so they all stand vertically in the jars. A brine is added and the beans are processed in a hot water bath. The Wicklunds have developed a process with the help of Oregon State University that allows them to hold their entire harvest in 11,000-gallon tanks, allowing them to pack cases on demand. Theirs also is an environmentally sound operation that reuses the brine. A new spiced bean relish, used as a barbecue sauce for turkey and fish, is made, utilizing the shorter beans. The family also introduced South Louisiana–style spicy beans, flavored with McIlhenny Company Tabasco.

Wicklund's is the epitome of a family business, with Lorie handling the office, Larry and his parents overseeing the farming and pickling, and his brother acting as business manager. Two gigantic dogs and several cats greet visitors. The company will ship a case of 12 of its 16-ounce jars of any of its beans for $21.85, plus shipping and handling. A case of 12 of its 32-ounce jars of beans is $38.75, plus shipping and handling. There are distributors in select stores throughout the United States and some parts of Canada.

ORDERING ADDRESS
Wicklund Farms
3959 Maple Island Farm Road
Springfield, OR 97477
541/747-5998
FAX: 541/747-7299
www.wicklundfarms.com
e-mail: spicedgreenbeans@wicklundfarms.com
No credit cards; checks OK

VISITS: **Springfield is to the east of Eugene, on Route 126.**
Monday–Friday, 9 A.M.–5 P.M.

INDEXES

BY PRODUCT

BY STATE

WYOMING